Medals and Decorations of
Independent India

Medals and Decorations of Independent India

EDWARD S. HAYNES
RANA T. S. CHHINA

MANOHAR
2008

First published 2008

© Edward S. Haynes and Rana T.S. Chhina, 2008

ISBN 978-81-7304-719-0

Published by
Ajay Kumar Jain for
Manohar Publishers & Distributors
4753/23 Ansari Road, Daryaganj
New Delhi 110 002

Printed at
Salasar Imaging Systems
Delhi 110 035

Contents

CONTENTS

Preface

This volume started its existence well over twenty years ago, as undisciplined heaps of notes, ideas, scribblings, and ideas began to congeal into two massive piles of disaggregated information on South Asian medals, decorations, and orders. The original intent had been to survey the development and myriad manifestations of a distinctively 'South Asian' sense of represented honour from the earliest (Vedic?) phases of South Asian history and to follow this aspect of state, society, and culture through the intervening years, past the external influences of Huns, Turks, Persians, and even from the English, Scots, Welsh, and Irish to the present day and to the contemporary systems of publicly recognized honour by independent India. As this dream evolved, it became increasingly obvious that this agenda would produce a truly massive piece of research, which would simultaneously be both unfocused and verbose. For South Asia before the European invasion, the sources were too thin to permit much detail and the 'base-line' would, therefore, be weak. The sources for 'British India' are, of course, rich and in many ways this period has already been covered in adequate detail. There are some major exceptions (the [Indian] Order of Merit or the Indian Title Badges, to cite but two examples), but most of this period has been so well covered in other volumes that to recapitulate that work here would, at best, only contribute to global deforestation in a modest way. The recent impressive work by Tony McClenaghan on the awards of the Indian 'Princely' States has made this aspect of our work, as originally imagined, less important. We therefore planned to pare back the initial expectations for this work into a more focused and manageable volume, one that concentrated on the post-Independence awards of the various States of South Asia. Yet even this has proved un-manageable for this stage in our work given the lack of sources on some of the nations of the subcontinent. Thus, this initial volume covers only Indian awards since independence. The exception to this is a brief survey of the awards of the Provisional Government of Free India, established in 1943. Not only are these awards generally unknown but they arguably represent the first phaleristic manifestations of Indian freedom. It is our hope that a future, 'revised and expanded', edition or even subsequent volumes of this work will take up the wider South Asian subject area.

Portions of this work have appeared previously in the *Medal Collector*, the journal of Orders and Medals Society of America, in 1971. That material is adapted here with the kind permission of the OMSA.

For a large number of awards, the location of complete and fully reliable information has been incredibly difficult and, in a number of cases, has proved to be simply impossible. Rather than postpone the publication of this book and spend another decade or so chasing a few elusive scraps of data, we have gone ahead with a less than complete book. We feel, emulating others, that it is more important to disseminate what information we have rather than hold back awaiting elusive data. Obviously, all corrections and additional information would be appreciated. We view this volume, despite its size, as essentially the first phase in the ongoing process of disentangling awards and decorations in India since 1947.

An aspect of this project has been the examination of the underlying honours policy of the Republic of India. While any such examination runs the risk of leading us down corridors of political commentary, we feel that, to an appropriate degree, this facet of our study is important. Nevertheless, we have attempted to keep such commentary out of the main text and have relegated our most direct comments to a focused appendix. While it is in no way our intention to criticize or offend, we do feel that our focused study of independent India's honours system—perhaps the first such study ever conducted—raises some important questions for national leaders to consider. Having conducted this study, we have the duty to draw appropriate conclusions.

Throughout, we have attempted to treat with respect the proper (Hindi) naming of medals and clasps. This has required the rendering of a range of names in Hindi, but for the foreign and non-Hindi-speaking readers, we have rendered the names into transliteration and, when possible or appropriate, into an English translation. These English translations are at best approximate, but in many cases seem incredibly clumsy when compared with the more elegant Hindi originals.

Throughout, we have used a numerical outline system to identify and cross-reference the awards we discuss. While this may seem pretentious and perhaps overly pseudo-scientific, we have found this system useful for reference and organizational purposes and hope others share our feeling. So, when referencing the 'New York' clasp to the Videsh Seva Medal, one may be directed to 1052.242.

In the decades that this project has been gestating, we have received help and advice from a wide range of individuals, and it would be the height of ingratitude not to acknowledge their assistance. We are honoured to thank Lieutenant-Colonel Aadesh Chopra, Lieutenant-Colonel Gaurav Karki, Major P.C. Choubay (Assistant Military and Naval Attaché, Embassy of India, Washington, DC, 1970), Leopold de Coutère, Major-General C.N. Das O.B.E., Mrs. R. Dhanedhar, Shri Om Shankar and staff of the MoD History Division, Shri S.K. Datta, Shri J.S. Gill, DIG, CRPF, Brigadier Clive R. Elderton O.B.E., Paulo Estrela, Goga Jain, Rajesh Jain, Major B.N. Kumar (Assistant Military and Naval Attaché, Embassy of India, Washington, DC, 1970), Avinash Maheshwary (South Asia Collections, Perkins Library, Duke University), Tony McClenaghan, the director and staff of the National Archives of India, Colonel Kaushik and Mr Om Prakash Bhagat of the Directorate General Civil Defence, Dave Parsons, Jagan Pillarisetti, Mark Sellar, Balbir Singh, and the director and staff at the United Service Institution of India for their assistance in the completion of this work. Special thanks are also due to Sushil Talwar and Ashok Nath for their unstinting friendship, cheerful assistance, and their seemingly bottomless pool of new questions that we have needed to ponder (and, on occasion, even to resolve). Others who have assisted have preferred anonymity and we shall respect their request.

We also owe a tremendous debt of thanks to the director, editors, and staff at Manohar Publishing. Without their help and amazing tolerance this book probably would never have appeared and certainly not in the form it now has.

This volume will, by its very nature, be incomplete. Obtaining reliable and timely information, has been a task ranging between the difficult and the impossible. In some cases, the illustrative examples we hoped to provide have simply proved unavailable. We have been impressed—and not positively so—at the chasms of knowledge that exist among some of those whose responsibility it is—or ought to be—to coordinate these awards. If, in the incompleteness of our work, we are able to coax into the light additional information, then we shall have accomplished our goal.

In some unfortunate cases, the illustrations are either absent or of lower quality than we might desire. We have obtained great assistance in this regard, but this has not always led to the high quality and standard format that we might have desired. We have, nevertheless, worked with the assumption that an illustration, even an imperfect one, is better than no illustration at all.

Even with such assistance, it is important to stress that the interpretations expressed in this volume are those of the authors alone, especially when they stray, as they sometimes must, into the realm of political and historical analysis. Had anyone or any nation wanted a spokesperson, it would certainly not be either one of us. When we seem to make controversial statements, we speak for ourselves alone, though only rarely is any sort of political commentary intended. This is supposed to be a work of historical and phaleristic scholarship, and neither a polemic nor a hagiography.

Additional assistance, of a more personal nature, has come from those in our lives who have suffered with what at times has certainly seemed to them to be an odd field of inquiry, a task that demanded so much, sometimes too much, of our lives over too many years. They know who they are, and listing their names here would not serve further to highlight the ongoing debt of honour and gratitude that we owe to them.

Rock Hill, SC, USA   EDWARD S HAYNES
New Delhi, India   RANA TS CHHINA
August 2007

1

भारत—Bharat (India)
(Dominion 1947-50, Republic 1950-)

India achieved independence on 15 August 1947 after a long, difficult, and painful struggle for freedom from British colonial rule. Yet that independence represented only a partial break with the colonial past. India built upon the inherited traditions of democracy and strong central government to create a state which in shedding parts of its past, would move into a future of independence and prosperity.

Independence was, however, not entirely happy. India, as it had existed prior to 1947, was partitioned between the newly created nations of India and Pakistan. The two siblings were divided along religious lines and the divide was further reinforced in blood as the fears that had developed between the religious communities of pre-Partition India erupted in killings and bloodshed which coloured the views of more than the first post-Independence generation of both nations. In matters of State policy, this heritage and major inter-State rivalries gave birth to a tension between the new nations of India and Pakistan that has erupted into full-scale international violence on a number of occasions; this process is marked in the medals that represent those campaigns.

What was for most people of South Asia a time of freedom was, for those who lived in the Indian 'Princely' states, a political transformation of a very different kind, an eclipse of sovereignty, and an integration into one of the new dominions that emerged from the colonial system. In a number of cases, most importantly in Jammu and Kashmir and in Hyderabad, this integration was a painful process. In the case of Kashmir, it is a problem which haunts the region until the present day. Yet these states represented, even in Independent India, an alternative ethic of rule and a parallel system of honour that has often been ignored.

India's vanguard role in the international anti-colonial struggle has given her natural moral leadership of the Third World in its quest for international peace, equality, and justice. Refusing to be drawn into the dangerous confrontationalist politics of superpower rivalries, India was a moving force behind the formation of the non-aligned movement in 1961. The international prestige enjoyed by the country has enabled India to take a leading role in multilateral initiatives towards finding solutions to some of the critical issues of the day, such as nuclear disarmament, apartheid, the rights of the Palestinian people, protection of the environment, and the evolution of a more just international economic order. Mutual respect and cooperation have also been the basis of India's relationship with her neighbours. This has led India to take, from almost the moment of its birth, a major role in international peacekeeping efforts and these important activities are reflected in these pages.

Another central value of the early nation was a commitment to secular, socialist, and egalitarian principles and policies. As will be discussed, all the old feudal trappings of both British imperialism and the princes who were the Crown's allies in India were to be swept aside in a new spirit of a new India, one in which the ancient divisions of caste, class, and religion were to be de-emphasized. Creating a system of honours under this revolutionary ideology would, predictably, pose problems.

The Indian military had no direct role in the relinquishment of control by the British and the division of India into two parts—India and Pakistan. By and large, the freedom struggle was not an armed struggle. Under their British commanders, the armed forces had resisted or ignored the rising tide of nationalism, and then, when London changed its course, Indian military personnel obediently shifted their sundered allegiance to a new flag. After Partition and Independence, the relationship between the military and the new nationalist government in India was at first problematic. India's first prime minister, Jawaharlal Nehru, deliberately limited the expansion and modernization of his country's armed forces, fearing that an excessive emphasis on the military would lead to the militarization of society and undermine the nation's fledgling democratic institutions. Indeed, it was the general attitude of both India's political leaders and military planners that armed conflict and confrontation of the sort that had dominated India's pre-1947 history was unlikely to take place after Independence, that a new world with new international relationships had in fact dawned. The number of campaign awards depicted in this volume speaks to the accuracy of their prediction.

The iconography of the new state is also important, both as it reflects national values and as it provides an artistic vocabulary for the awards on which we shall focus. The tricolour flag of India will, for example, provide a palate for early ribbons for awards. Throughout, when reference is made to the Indian state emblem, it refers to the lion capital from the pillar of the Mauryan ruler Ashoka (*r.* 269-232 BCE), originally erected at Sarnath. In fact, there are four lions, standing back to back, mounted on an abacus with a frieze carrying sculptures in high relief of an elephant, a galloping horse, a bull, and a lion separated by intervening wheels (the Ashoka Chakra, see Fig. 1) over a bell-shaped lotus. Carved out of a single block of polished sandstone, the capital is crowned by the Wheel of the Law (Dharma Chakra). This was adopted on 26 January 1950 (Republic Day) as the official Indian state emblem, though only three lions are visible.

सत्यमेव जयते

1. India's State Emblem

Beneath the lions is the state motto, 'सत्यमेव जयते', 'Satyameva Jayate' or 'Truth Alone Triumphs' (from the *Mundaka Upanishad*). In addition, there will be reference to Ashoka's chakra, or wheel. This is the spoked wheel seen at the base of the capital. It, too, is a recurring pattern in state iconography, including in the centre of the Indian flag, where it also recalls the spinning wheel of Mahatma Gandhi. The example shown comes from the reverse of the Wound Medal (1034).

2. Ashoka's Chakra

It is important to recall a central constitutional fact: while India became independent in 1947, she remained a dominion, under limited royal authority, and was administered through a Governor-General, until the proclamation of the constitution and the Republic in 1950. This dominion period posed severe complexities in the honours system and some of these issues will be addressed below.

As of the date of Independence, 15 August 1947, the official order of wearing of orders, decorations, and medals (India Army Order 752/1947) was as follows:

1. Victoria Cross
2. George Cross

BRITISH ORDERS OF KNIGHTHOOD, ETC.

3. Order of the Garter
4. Order of the Thistle
5. Order of St. Patrick
6. Order of Bath
7. Order of Merit (immediately after Knights Grand Cross of the Order of the Bath)
8. Order of the Star of India
9. Order of St. Michael and St. George
10. Order of the Indian Empire
11. Order of the Crown of India
12. Royal Victorian Order (Classes 1, 2, and 3)
13. Order of the British Empire (Classes 1, 2, and 3)
14. Order of the Companions of Honour (immediately after Knights and Dames Grand Cross of the Order of the British Empire)
15. Distinguished Service Order
16. Royal Victorian Order (Class 4)
17. Order of the British Empire (Class 4, OBE)
18. Imperial Service Order
19. Royal Victorian Order (Class 5)
20. Order of British Empire (Class 5, MBE)
21. Baronet's Badge
22. Knights Bachelor's Badge
23. Indian Order of Merit (military)
24. Order of Burma (for gallantry)

DECORATIONS

25. Royal Red Cross (Class 1)
26. Distinguished Service Cross

27. Military Cross
28. Distinguished Flying Cross
29. Air Force Cross
30. Royal Red Cross (Class 2)
31. Order of British India
32. Kaisar-i-Hind Medal
33. Order of Burma (for good service)
34. Order of St. John
35. Albert Medal

MEDALS FOR GALLANTRY AND DISTINGUISHED CONDUCT

36. Union of South Africa King's Medal for Bravery (in gold)
37. Distinguished Conduct Medal
38. Conspicuous Gallantry Medal
39. George Medal
40. King's Police and Fire Services Medal for Gallantry
41. Edward Medal
42. Royal West African Frontier Force Distinguished Conduct Medal
43. King's African Rifles Distinguished Conduct Medal
44. Indian Distinguished Service Medal
45. Burma Gallantry Medal
46. Union of South Africa King's Medal for Bravery (in silver)
47. Distinguished Service Medal
48. Military Medal
49. Distinguished Flying Medal
50. Air Force Medal
51. Constabulary Medal (Ireland)
52. Medal for Saving Life at Sea
53. Indian Order of Merit (civil)
54. Indian Police Medal for Gallantry
55. Burma Police Medal for Gallantry
56. Colonial Police Medal for Gallantry
57. British Empire Medal
58. Canada Medal
59. Life Saving Medal of the Order of St. John

WAR MEDALS (in order of the date of campaign for which awarded

POLAR MEDALS (in order of date)

60. Royal Victorian Medal (gold, silver and bronze)
61. Imperial Service Medal

POLICE MEDALS FOR VALUABLE SERVICES

62. King's Police and Fire Service Medal for Distinguished Service
63. Indian Police Medal for Meritorious Service
64. Burma Police Medal for Meritorious Service
65. Colonial Police Medal for Meritorious Service

JUBILEE, CORONATION AND DURBAR MEDALS

66. Queen Victoria's Jubilee Medal, 1887 (gold, silver, and bronze)
67. Queen Victoria's Police Jubilee Medal, 1887
68. Queen Victoria's Jubilee Medal, 1897 (gold, silver, and bronze)
69. Queen Victoria's Police Jubilee Medal, 1897
70. Queen Victoria's Commemoration Medal, 1900 (Ireland)
71. King Edward VII's Coronation Medal, 1902
72. King Edward VII's Police Coronation Medal, 1902
73. King Edward VII's Durbar Medal, 1903 (gold, silver, and bronze[1])
74. King Edward VII's Police Medal, 1903 (Scotland)
75. King's Visit Commemoration Medal, 1903 (Ireland)
76. King George V's Coronation Medal, 1911
77. King George V's Police Coronation Medal, 1911
78. King Visit Police Commemoration Medal, 1911 (Ireland)
79. King George V's Durbar Medal, 1911 (gold, silver, and bronze[2])
80. King George V's Silver Jubilee Medal, 1935
81. King George VI's Coronation Medal, 1937
82. King George V's Long and Faithful Service Medal
83. King George VI's Long and Faithful Service Medal

EFFICIENCY AND LONG SERVICE DECORATIONS AND MEDALS

84. Long Service and Good Conduct Medal
85. Naval Long Service and Good Conduct Medal
86. Medal for Meritorious Service
87. Indian Long Service and Good Conduct Medal (for Europeans of Indian Army)
88. Indian Meritorious Service Medal (for Europeans of Indian Army)
89. Royal Marine Meritorious Service Medal
90. Royal Air Force Meritorious Service Medal
91. Royal Air Force Long Service and Good Conduct Medal
92. Indian Long Service and Good Conduct Medal (for Indian Army)
93. Royal West African Frontier Force Long Service and Good Conduct Medal
94. King's African Rifles Long Service and Good Conduct Medal
95. Indian Meritorious Service Medal (for Indian Army)
96. Trans-Jordan Frontier Force Long Service and Good Conduct Medal
97. African Police Medal For Meritorious Service
98. Royal Canadian Mounted Police Long Service Medal
99. Colonial Police and Fire Brigades' Long Service Medal
100. Volunteer Officers' Decoration
101. Volunteer Long Service Medal

[1] The bronze, of course, never existed, and this unfortunate error has lodged in published places whence it should have been banished long since.

[2] Here, too, there was never a bronze medal.

102. Volunteer Officer's Decoration (for India and the colonies)
103. Colonial Auxiliary Force Officers' Decoration
104. Colonial Auxiliary Forces Long Service Medal
105. Medal for Good Shooting (naval)
106. Militia Long Service Medal
107. Imperial Yeomanry Long Service Medal
108. Territorial Decoration
109. Efficiency Decoration
110. Territorial Efficiency Medal
111. Efficiency Medal
112. Special Reserve Long Service and Good Conduct Medal
113. Decoration for Officers of the Royal Naval Reserve
114. Decoration for Officers of the Royal Naval Volunteer Reserve
115. Royal Naval Reserve Long Service and Good Conduct Medal
116. Royal Naval Volunteer Reserve Long Service and Good Conduct Medal
117. Royal Naval Auxiliary Sick Berth Reserve Long Service and Good Conduct Medal
118. Royal Fleet Reserve Long Service and Good Conduct Medal
119. Royal Naval Wireless Auxiliary Reserve Long Service and Good Conduct Medal
120. Air Efficiency Award
121. King's Medal (for Champion Shots in the Military Forces)
122. Rocket Apparatus Volunteer Long Service Medal
123. Special Constabulary Medal
124. Union of South Africa Commemoration Medal
125. Service Medal of the Order of St. John
126. Badge of the Order of the League of Mercy
127. Voluntary Medical Service Medal
128. South African Medal for War Services

FOREIGN ORDERS (in order of date of award)

FOREIGN DECORATIONS (in order of date of award)

FOREIGN MEDALS (in order of date of award)

While not all of these had, of course, been awarded to Indians, this list reflects India's place in the wider Imperial network of honour. Conspicuously absent from this list, however, are the Indian Title Badges (in great complexity of classes and degrees). These, in effect, fell as 34a, following the Order of St. John of Jerusalem. Nevertheless, this is a useful benchmark for what is to follow.

Until independence, India's honours system, like that of Pakistan and Bangladesh, was fully integrated into that of Great Britain, the colonial ruler, as can be seen from the order of wearing listed above. In addition to the regular imperial awards which were, over time, progressively opened up to both Europeans in India and to Asians, the (Indian) Order of Merit (in both military and civil divisions) and the Indian Distinguished Service Medal were available for bravery, the Order of British India was awarded for military merit, the Kaisar-i-Hind medal and the various title badges were available for general merit, while the more general Kings' Police Medal and India-specific police medals for gallantry and meritorious service were used to reward personnel of the police and fire services. From the date of Independence, almost all these awards (plus the Indian orders of knighthood: The Most Excellent Order of the Star of India, The Most Eminent Order of the Indian Empire, and The Imperial Order of the Crown of India) lapsed into immediate obsolescence for India (and, for most of the above, for the empire as a whole). Only the four police medals survived into India's independent honours toolbox. This left newly independent India with a virtual awards vacuum. While a good case might have been made for a redesign and continuance of some of these awards—the Indian Order of Merit, for example—the simple issue of custody of this award—would India or Pakistan inherit the unique right to award it?—made such a logical and historically sensitive step a political and practical impossibility.[3] New systems of rewarding honour would need to be invented.

With independence, India became a dominion, a somewhat ambiguous constitutional status. While India was independent, it did not enjoy full Independence prior to the drafting of a constitution. The king, though no longer king-emperor, still played some rather vague legal role in the nation's life and such matters as honours still required reference to him. The medal awarded to commemorate the attainment of India's independence (1070) enjoyed an establishing warrant jointly signed by the political 'odd couple' of Prime Minister Jawaharlal Nehru and King George VI. For another example, early in 1948, discussions were opened with London regarding the possible award of the older military decorations (presumably selectively redesigned) to Indian troops for bravery in the Kashmir conflict with Pakistan. The logical conundrum of the same pre-Independence decorations possibly being awarded for combat bravery against the other successor state to pre-1947 India posed obvious difficulties and the scheme was dropped. Instead, explorations began for the creation of India's own set of awards.

While provisions of law and constitution made the award of honours in independent India the preserve of the president of the Republic, the role of political leaders in the honours system (especially the prime minister) has been significant since 1950 and adds additional complexity to the tale. The president became, constitutionally, both the 'fount of all honour' and the commander-in-chief of the armed forces. While in theory, all awards should, therefore, emanate from presidential authority and be coordinated through a presidency which exercises 'quality control' over the system, this has rarely if ever been the case. Yet all awards, unless otherwise noted, will normally be established by presidential authority and presidential notification as published in the *Gazette of India*. Awards from government bodies, from the office of the prime

[3] Many of the issues raised in this section will be addressed in greater detail in Edward S. Haynes, *From Izzat to Honour: Changing Modes of Representing Honor in Nineteenth- and Twentieth-Century India* (forthcoming).

minister, from provinces and union territories, and from private bodies have muddied the waters of the 'fount of honour'. While such awards have, by and large, been excluded from our study, some do appear, more as cautionary examples than anything else (see Chapter 2).

By June 1948, a special Prime Minister's Committee on Honours and Awards in India had been convened and had proposed names and preliminary designs for the new bravery decorations (the Param Vir Chakra, Maha Vir Chakra, and Vir Chakra).[4] Yet mammoth constitutional difficulties remained. If the decorations were to have precedence throughout the Commonwealth, they would require royal sanction (and would, presumably, have had to include the king's image or the royal cypher). In October 1948, a draft was prepared for a royal warrant establishing these new decorations and was forwarded to London for the king's approval. They could have been created unilaterally by India, but then the decorations would have enjoyed no wider formal standing within the Commonwealth (similar to the massive constitutional problems that the New Zealand Cross presented when it was established in 1869).[5] The proposed order of precedence[6] (much abbreviated here, but including, for comparative purposes, relevant pre-1947 Indian and British awards) would have been:

1. Victoria Cross
2. Param Vir Chakra
3. George Cross
4. Knight of the Most Noble Order of the Garter

. . .

29. Officer of the Most Excellent Order of the British Empire
30. Companion of the Distinguished Service Order
31. Maha Vir Chakra
32. Member of the Fifth Class of the Royal Victorian Order
33. Member of the Most Excellent Order of the British Empire
34. Indian Order of Merit (military)
35. Order of Burma (for gallantry)
36. Member of the Royal Red Cross
37. Distinguished Service Cross
38. Military Cross
39. Vir Chakra
40. Distinguished Flying Cross
41. Air Force Cross

. . .

A similar draft warrant was prepared for a new Indian general service medal in January 1949 and it was also sent to London for approval. In retrospect these proposals involved too many compromises in authority—on the part of both parties—and were eventually not carried to fruition. While it would have been preferable to present awards for gallantry close to the date of the act of bravery, the constitutional difficulties led to a postponement of any action on the new awards until the promulgation of the new Indian constitution.

Yet, as far as the Indian police were concerned, no such

[4] Private Secretary to the Viceroy (National Archives of India), F.44(1)-H/48.

[5] For information on the New Zealand Cross, see Abbott and Tamplin, *British Gallantry Awards*, pp. 227-37. Yet the New Zealand Cross has now been reborn as the highest New Zealand award for non-combat gallantry.

[6] This is based in part on the 11 February 1947 order of wearing, *London Gazette*, cited in Tuson, *Medals Will be Worn*, pp. 97-102. See also the draft royal warrant for these awards, 4 October 1948, Office of the Private Secretary to the Viceroy (National Archives of India), file 25-H/1948, pp. 95-110.

problems seem to have existed, for on 1 May 1948, the pre-Independence medals for gallantry (1017 and 1028) and meritorious service (1054 and 1062) by Indian police were simply extended for award under the Dominion. While some modest redrafting of warrants was required, there seemed—perhaps oddly—to have been no problem with the ex-king-emperor, titles intact (the only place in the empire where he was still styled 'Ind Imp' or 'Emperor of India') gracing medals awarded to police personnel in independent India. These were, in fact, the same medals that had been created for and awarded to those police personnel who had beaten and jailed Indian freedom fighters. The irony of this seems to have been unrecognized and unappreciated. While some of the king's police medals issued to Indians during the Dominion period may have borne the new royal titles, the preponderance of the evidence suggests that the vast majority carried the pre-1947 titles.

As debate on India's new constitution proceeded, the draft clause 7 focused the discussion on awards.[7] This draft clause, reading simply, 'No heritable title shall be conferred by the Union' was debated by the Constituent Assembly on 30 April 1947. The crux of the debate turned around the issue of a title that would allow the appending to one's name of any sort of title or honorific. As discussed in debate by M.R. Masani, this issue was more important than the heritability of any such title:

... the Free Indian State will not confer any titles of any kind, whether heritable or otherwise, that is, for the life of the incumbent. It may be possible for the Union to honour some of its citizens who distinguish themselves in several walks of life like sciences and the arts, with other kinds of honours not amounting to titles; but the idea of a man putting something before or after his name as a reward for service rendered will not be possible in a Free India. I think, Sir, the House will support this principle, because it has been found not only in subject countries, that titles become dangerous and a source of corruption to those who bestow them and to those who accept them. Therefore relying on patriotism, self-respect and the motive of service, we shall do without titles of any kind.

It was also decided to exempt academic degrees in so far as they bestowed titles, to account for honorific titles (e.g. *Mahatma*) that might be bestowed spontaneously by the people, and to leave open the possibility of military decorations. Yet when, in the course of the debate, one of the members made a verbal slip in making reference to another member, the nature of the debate was focused by the irony expressed by Sri Prakasa:

Sir, I was horrified at the last session when you yourself referred to a member from your province as 'Rai Bahadur Sahib'. I felt that the parents of the poor dear had forgotten to given him a name, and he had to wait for long years for the State to step in and give him one and ensure his being called 'Rai Bahadur' for ever. While one title embarasses the receiver, the other makes him feel vain and proper. I think it is necessary in the name of freedom to ask for freedom from the imposition of such titles from the State and freedom from having to curry favour with the authorities to get a distinction from them.

Sir, I would like to make it plain that this clause does not prohibit

[7] Most of the discussion of the Constituent Assembly that follows is drawn from their debates of 30 April 1947 and is based upon the on-line version of these debates (see the Indian Parliament web site's links to these debates at http://parliamentof india.nic.in/ls/debates/debates.htm).

even the State from bestowing proper honours. We are distinguishing between titles and honours.

The issue, put simply, was an ingrained opposition to what had come to be seen as a 'Rai Sahib Mentality', which was seen linked with colonialism, subservience, and fawning obedience to authority. While free India reserved the right to honour achievement, the old régime of titles, orders, and honours was to be consigned to the dustbin of the feudal past. In practice, this high commitment would prove difficult to maintain.

The final constitutional text on this issue, included as Article 18 under fundamental rights, right to equality, reads:

18. Abolition of titles.

(1) No title, not being a military or academic distinction, shall be conferred by the State.
(2) No citizen of India shall accept any title from any foreign State.
(3) No person who is not a citizen of India shall, while he holds any office of profit or trust under the State, accept without the consent of the President any title from any foreign State.
(4) No person holding any office of profit or trust under the State shall, without the consent of the President, accept any present, emoluments, or office of any kind from or under any foreign State.

The first properly Indian decorations (the Param Vir Chakra [1002], Maha Vir Chakra [1008], and Vir Chakra [1014]) were created, simultaneously with the promulgation of the Constitution, on 26 January 1950. On 5 June, these were followed by the first general service medal (1035). On 7 February 1950, the first general order of precedence was announced in a circular letter sent to all local administrations in India. In the overall history of Indian awards, this constitutes a document of immense historical importance and is worth citing here.[8] The order of wearing—stated only in general terms as many awards were yet under development—was:

1. Indian military gallantry awards (Param Vir Chakra, Maha Vir Chakra, and Vir Chakra).
2. Indian civilian gallantry awards (the Ashoka Chakra, though it was then still hypothetical).
3. Indian campaign medals after 26 January 1950 (i.e. The Indian General Service Medal, 1947, though it had yet to be notified).
4. Commemorative medals (i.e. The Indian Independence Medal, 1947).
5. Medals conferred by the Indian ruling princes.
6. Commonwealth medals (including all pre-1947 awards).
7. Other awards.

Thus, by this new scheme, the Silver Jubilee Medal, 1947, of Maharaja Man Singh of Jaipur, would rank ahead of a Victoria Cross. While later published orders of wearing ignored the awards of the States—reflecting, perhaps, their waning from independent India's political consciousness—it is significant that the first order of wearing provided a place for their awards.

On 10 March 1951, new police medals were established for India, removing any ambiguity about the ongoing standing of

[8] Circular letter, Ministry of States to all local administrations, 7 February 1950, Records of the Central India Agency (National Archives of India), Political Department, 40-A/1950.

the royal police medals and replacing the odd continuance of the pre-Independence awards. On that date, the new President's Police and Fire Services Medal for Gallantry (1018), the Police Medal for Gallantry (1029), the President's Police and Fire Services Medal for Distinguished Service (1055), and the Police Medal for Meritorious Service (1063) were created. On 4 January 1952, the Ashoka Chakra was created in three classes (1003, 1009, and 1015) to recognize non-combat bravery. On 1 February of the same year, the Territorial Army Decoration (1068) and the Territorial Army Medal (1069) were added to India's awards. However, there was no formal order of wearing yet established.

On 15 March 1952 (by No. 27-Pres./52), the first published order of precedence for Indian awards was announced as follows:

1. Param Vir Chakra
2. Ashoka Chakra, Class I
3. Maha Vir Chakra
4. Ashoka Chakra, Class II
5. Vir Chakra
6. Ashoka Chakra, Class III
7. General Service Medal, 1947
8. Territorial Army Decoration
9. Territorial Army Medal
10. Indian Independence Medal, 1947
11. Commonwealth awards (including pre-1947 awards)
12. Other awards

On 3 May 1952 (by No. 35-Pres./52) a separate and parallel precedence for police and fire services medals was established:

1. President's Police and Fire Services Medal for Gallantry
2. Police Medal for Gallantry
3. President's Police and Fire Services Medal for Distinguished Service
4. Police Medal for Meritorious Service
5. Independence Medal 1950 for Police
6. All decorations awarded prior to 26 January 1950
7. Other awards.

This set the stage for the largely uncoordinated and independent development of civil and military awards within the Republic in the years to come. These separate orders of wearing would not coalesce until 2 January 1959.

In 1954 (2 January), India's general awards for meritorious national service—the Bharat Ratna (1001), Padma Vibhushan (1004), Padma Bhushan (1005), and Padma Shri (1010) (although it would take some time for the awards to achieve this precise nomenclature)—were put into place after what seems to have been an animated debate. On 26 February 1957, almost ten years after Independence, India's own Meritorious Service Medal (1060) and Long Service and Good Conduct Medal (1061) were established, reviving the pre-1947 awards of the same names. In 1958, the Prime Minister established an extra-constitutional life saving medal (1086) for award to Indian police personnel.

To account for these new awards, the order of precedence was revised on 2 January 1959 (by No. 2-Pres./59):

1. Bharat Ratna
2. Param Vir Chakra
3. Ashoka Chakra, Class I
4. Padma Vibhushan
5. Padma Bhushan
6. Maha Vir Chakra
7. Ashoka Chakra, Class II
8. Padma Shri
9. Vir Chakra
10. Ashoka Chakra, Class III
11. President's Police and Fire Services Medal for Gallantry
12. Police Medal for Gallantry
13. General Service Medal, 1947
14. President's Police and Fire Services Medal for Distinguished Service
15. Meritorious Service Medal
16. Long Service and Good Conduct Medal
17. Police Medal for Meritorious Service
18. Territorial Army Decoration
19. Territorial Army Medal
20. Indian Independence Medal, 1947
21. Independence Medal, 1950
22. Commonwealth awards (including pre-1947 awards)
23. Other awards.

In 1960, a number of new awards were created in the first systematic expansion of the earlier, lean, honours system. On 26 January, the Vishisht Seva Medal was created in three classes (1007, 1013, and 1027) for distinguished service by military personnel and the Sainya Seva (1048) and Videsh Seva (1052) medals were established for service in harsh climatic conditions and overseas service, respectively. On 17 June, the Sena Medal (1023), Nao Sena Medal (1024), and Vayu Sena Medal (1025) were established to recognize both gallantry and meritorious accomplishments in the three services. The next year, lifesaving medals (the Jeevan Raksha Padak series in three classes, 1011, 1033, and 1067) were established on 30 September 1961. On 23 February 1962, the Police (Special Duty) Medal (1050) was established to recognize police services under harsh conditions.

With the creation of these new awards, the order of wearing had to be again revised on 13 November 1961 (No. 49-Pres./61):

1. Bharat Ratna
2. Param Vir Chakra
3. Ashoka Chakra, Class I
4. Padma Vibhushan
5. Padma Bhushan
6. Vishisht Seva Medal, Class I
7. Maha Vir Chakra

8. Ashoka Chakra, Class II
9. Padma Shri
10. Vishisht Seva Medal, Class II
11. Vir Chakra
12. Ashoka Chakra, Class III
13. President's Police and Fire Services Medal for Gallantry
14. Sena/Nao Sena/Vayu Sena Medal
15. Vishisht Seva Medal, Class III
16. Police Medal for Gallantry
17. General Service Medal, 1947
18. Sainya Seva Medal
19. Videsh Seva Medal
20. President's Police and Fire Services Medal for Distinguished Service
21. Meritorious Service Medal
22. Long Service and Good Conduct Medal
23. Police Medal for Meritorious Service
24. Territorial Army Decoration
25. Territorial Army Medal
26. Indian Independence Medal, 1947
27. Independence Medal 1950
28. Commonwealth awards (including pre-1947 awards)
29. Other awards

It is noteworthy that neither the Jeevan Raksha Padak series nor the Police Special Duty Medal appeared in this order of wearing.

On 10 July 1964, the Defence Security (Raksha Suraksha) Corps Medal was established in two classes (1078 and 1079). To commemorate the 1965 war with Pakistan, the Raksha Medal (1044) was established on 26 January 1967 and the Samar Seva Star 1965 (1038) for combat service was added on 11 February. Both apparently enjoyed for some time an ambiguous place in the official order of wearing.

In 1967, the nominal 'class system' that existed in the Indian awards system was addressed. The egalitarian values of the Republic had come to be seen as inconsistent with awards which were denominated as 'Class I, Class II, Class III' and new, separate, distinct names were created for the Ashoka Chakra series, the Vishisht Seva Medal series, the Jeevan Raksha Padak Series, and, subsequently, the Defence Security Corps medals. In the case of the 'Padma' series of awards for distinguished service at the national level instituted in three classes in January 1954, as the Padma Vibhushan, Pahela Varg, Dusra Varg, and Tisra Varg (first, second, and third class, respectively), this anomaly had been addressed relatively early by removing the offending 'class' structure in January 1955 and renaming the decorations as the Padma Vibhushan, Padma Bhushan, and Padma Shri, respectively.

On 3 July 1970 (by No. 35-Pres./70) a new order of wearing was announced:

1. Bharat Ratna
2. Param Vir Chakra
3. Ashoka Chakra

4. Padma Vibhushan
5. Padma Bhushan
6. Param Vishisht Seva Medal
7. Maha Vir Chakra
8. Kirti Chakra
9. Padma Shri
10. Sarvottam Jeevan Raksha Padak
11. Ati Vishisht Seva Medal
12. Vir Chakra
13. Shaurya Chakra
14. President's Police and Fire Services Medal for Gallantry
15. Sena / Nao Sena / Vayu Sena Medal
16. Vishisht Seva Medal
17. Police Medal for Gallantry
18. Uttam Jeevan Raksha Padak
19. General Service Medal, 1947
20. Samar Seva Star, 1965
21. Raksha Medal
22. Sainya Seva Medal
23. Police (Special Duty) Medal
24. Videsh Seva Medal
25. President's Police and Fire Services Medal for Distinguished Service
26. Meritorious Service Medal
27. Long Service and Good Conduct Medal
28. Police Medal for Meritorious Service
29. Jeevan Raksha Padak
30. Territorial Army Decoration
31. Territorial Army Medal
32. Indian Independence Medal, 1947
33. Independence Medal, 1950
34. Commonwealth awards (including pre-1947 awards)
35. Other awards

On 19 April 1971, medals were created for twenty years (1076) and nine years (1077) of service in the military. Further, as a result of the 1971 war with Pakistan, the Wound Medal (1034) and the campaign medals (Poorvi Star [1039], Paschimi Star [1040], and Sangram Medal [1045]) were created on 17 January 1973. A medal was also established to commemorate the silver jubilee of Independence on the same date (1072).

A new order of wearing appeared on 27 January 1973 (No. 9-Pres./73) with many additions:

1. Bharat Ratna
2. Param Vir Chakra
3. Ashoka Chakra
4. Padma Vibhushan
5. Padma Bhushan
6. Param Vishisht Seva Medal
7. Maha Vir Chakra
8. Kirti Chakra
9. Padma Shri
10. Sarvottam Jeevan Raksha Padak
11. Ati Vishisht Seva Medal

12. Vir Chakra
13. Shaurya Chakra
14. President's Police and Fire Services Medal for Gallantry
15. Sena / Nao Sena / Vayu Sena Medal
16. Vishisht Seva Medal
17. Police Medal for Gallantry
18. Uttam Jeevan Raksha Padak
19. Wound Medal
20. General Service Medal, 1947
21. Samar Seva Star, 1965
22. Poorvi Star
23. Paschimi Star
24. Raksha Medal
25. Sangram Medal
26. Sainya Seva Medal
27. Police (Special Duty) Medal
28. Videsh Seva Medal
29. President's Police and Fire Services Medal for Distinguished Service
30. Meritorious Service Medal
31. Long Service and Good Conduct Medal
32. Police Medal for Meritorious Service
33. Jeevan Raksha Padak
34. Territorial Army Decoration
35. Territorial Army Medal
36. Indian Independence Medal, 1947
37. Independence Medal, 1950
38. 25th Independence Anniversary Medal
39. 20 Years Long Service Medal
40. 9 Years Long Service Medal
41. Commonwealth awards (including pre-1947 awards)
42. Other awards

Note that the Jeevan Raksha Padak series (as renamed on 26 August 1967) and the Police (Special Duty) Medal now joined the order of wearing.

On 7 October 1974, a series of medals paralleling those for the police and fire services were added to reward services by the home guards and civil defence personnel: the President's Home Guards and Civil Defence Medal for Gallantry (1022), the Home Guards and Civil Defence Medal for Gallantry (1032), the President's Home Guards and Civil Defence Medal for Distinguished Service (1059), and the Home Guards and Civil Defence Medal for Meritorious Service (1066). On 8 May 1975, a new general service medal, the Samanya Seva Medal, 1965 (1036), was created to replace the 1947 medal. By this time a pattern seemed to be emerging in the manner in which the Republic chose to recognize operational military service. Full-blown conflicts were marked by the award of the 'star-and-medal' WW II-style combinations such as which emerged in the wake of the 1965 and 1971 India–Pakistan wars. Smaller scale operations, including counter-insurgency operations were marked by the award of a 'clasp' to the General Service, and later Samanya Seva Medal. The multiple-clasp 'general service medal' was the Indian Army's unique contibution to the world dating back, as it did, to the first Anglo-Sikh War of 1845/46 and to the later backdated Army of India Medal, 1799. Institution of the new Samanya Seva Medal indicated a desire to keep the older model in tandem with the 'WWII'-style system employed for the 1965 and 1971 conflicts.

On 16 June 1976 (No. 41-Pres./76) another order of precedence appeared:

1. Bharat Ratna
2. Param Vir Chakra
3. Ashoka Chakra
4. Padma Vibhushan
5. Padma Bhushan
6. Param Vishisht Seva Medal
7. Maha Vir Chakra
8. Kirti Chakra
9. Padma Shri
10. Sarvottam Jeevan Raksha Padak
11. Ati Vishisht Seva Medal
12. Vir Chakra
13. Shaurya Chakra
14. President's Police and Fire Services Medal for Gallantry
15. President's Police Medal for Gallantry
16. President's Fire Services Medal for Gallantry
17. President's Home Guards and Civil Defence Medal for Gallantry
18. Sena / Nao Sena / Vayu Sena Medal
19. Vishisht Seva Medal
20. Police Medal for Gallantry
21. Fire Services Medal for Gallantry
22. Home Guards and Civil Defence Medal for Gallantry
23. Uttam Jeevan Raksha Padak
24. Wound Medal
25. General Service Medal, 1947
26. Samanya Seva Medal, 1965
27. Samar Seva Star, 1965
28. Poorvi Star
29. Paschimi Star
30. Raksha Medal
31. Sangram Medal
32. Sainya Seva Medal
33. Police (Special Duty) Medal
34. Videsh Seva Medal
35. President's Police and Fire Services Medal for Distinguished Service
36. President's Police Medal for Distinguished Service
37. President's Fire Services Medal for Distinguished Service
38. President's Home Guards and Civil Defence Medal for Distinguished Service
39. Meritorious Service Medal
40. Long Service and Good Conduct Medal
41. Police Medal for Meritorious Service
42. Fire Services Medal for Meritorious Service

43. Home Guards and Civil Defence Medal for Meritorious Service
44. Jeevan Raksha Padak
45. Territorial Army Decoration
46. Territorial Army Medal
47. Indian Independence Medal, 1947
48. Independence Medal, 1950
49. 25th Independence Anniversary Medal
50. 20 Years Long Service Medal
51. 9 Years Long Service Medal
52. Commonwealth awards (including pre-1947 awards)
53. Other awards

A new order of precedence was announced in December 1998 (No. 104-Pres./98, dated 11 November 1998):

1. Bharat Ratna
2. Param Vir Chakra
3. Ashoka Chakra
4. Padma Vibhushan
5. Padma Bhushan
6. Sarvottam Yuddh Seva Medal
7. Param Vishisht Seva Medal
8. Maha Vir Chakra
9. Kirti Chakra
10. Padma Shri
11. Sarvottam Jeevan Raksha Padak
12. Uttam Yuddh Seva Medal
13. Ati Vishisht Seva Medal
14. Vir Chakra
15. Shaurya Chakra
16. President's Police and Fire Services Medal for Gallantry
17. President's Police Medal for Gallantry
18. President's Fire Services Medal for Gallantry
19. President's Home Guards and Civil Defence Medal for Gallantry
20. Yuddh Seva Medal
21. Sena Medal / Nao Sena Medal / Vayu Sena Medal
22. Vishisht Seva Medal
23. Police Medal for Gallantry
24. Fire Services Medal for Gallantry
25. Home Guards and Civil Defence Medal for Gallantry
26. Uttam Jeevan Raksha Padak
27. Wound Medal
28. General Service Medal, 1947
29. Samanya Seva Medal, 1965
30. Special Service Medal
31. Samar Seva Star, 1965
32. Poorvi Star
33. Paschimi Star
34. Siachen Glacier Medal
35. Raksha Medal, 1965
36. Sangram Medal
37. Sainya Seva Medal
38. High Altitude Service Medal

39. Police (Special Duty) Medal, 1962
40. Videsh Seva Medal
41. President's Police and Fire Services Medal for Distinguished Service
42. President's Police Medal for Distinguished Service
43. President's Fire Services Medal for Distinguished Service
44. President's Home Guards and Civil Defence Medal for Distinguished Service
45. Meritorious Service Medal
46. Long Service and Good Conduct Medal
47. Police Medal for Meritorious Service
48. Fire Services Medal for Meritorious Service
49. Home Guards and Civil Defence Medal for Meritorious Service
50. Jeevan Raksha Padak
51. Territorial Army Decoration
52. Territorial Army Medal
53. Indian Independence Medal, 1947
54. Independence Medal 1950
55. 25th Independence Anniversary Medal
56. 30 Years Long Service Medal
57. 20 Years Long Service Medal
58. 9 Years Long Service Medal
59. Commonwealth awards (including pre-1947 awards)
60. Other awards

Later additions, such as the 50th Anniversary of Independence Medal (1073), had yet to be fully integrated into the order of precedence.

A 26 April 2001 revision in the order of precedence (No. 75-Pres./01, published 26 May 2001) resolved some problems, but also added new confusions.

1. Bharat Ratna
2. Param Vir Chakra
3. Ashoka Chakra
4. Padma Vibhushan
5. Padma Bhushan
6. Sarvottam Yuddh Seva Medal
7. Param Vishisht Seva Medal
8. Maha Vir Chakra
9. Kirti Chakra
10. Padma Shri
11. Sarvottam Jeevan Raksha Padak
12. Uttam Yuddh Seva Medal
13. Ati Vishisht Seva Medal
14. Vir Chakra
15. Shaurya Chakra
16. President's Police and Fire Services Medal for Gallantry
17. President's Police Medal for Gallantry
18. President's Fire Services Medal for Gallantry
19. President's Correctional Service Medal for Gallantry
20. President's Home Guards and Civil Defence Medal for Gallantry
21. Yuddh Seva Medal

22. Sena Medal / Nao Sena Medal / Vayu Sena Medal
23. Vishisht Seva Medal
24. Police Medal for Gallantry
25. Fire Services Medal for Gallantry
26. Correctional Service Medal for Gallantry
27. Home Guards and Civil Defence Medal for Gallantry
28. Uttam Jeevan Raksha Padak
29. Parakram Padak
30. General Service Medal, 1947
31. Samanya Seva Medal, 1965
32. Special Service Medal
33. Samar Seva Star, 1965
34. Poorvi Star
35. Paschimi Star
36. Siachen Glacier Medal
37. Raksha Medal, 1965
38. Sangram Medal
39. Sainya Seva Medal
40. High Altitude Service Medal
41. Police (Special Duty) Medal, 1962
42. Videsh Seva Medal
43. President's Police and Fire Services Medal for Distinguished Service
44. President's Police Medal for Distinguished Service
45. President's Fire Services Medal for Distinguished Service
46. President's Correctional Service Medal for Distinguished Service
47. President's Home Guards and Civil Defence Medal for Distinguished Service
48. Meritorious Service Medal
49. Long Service and Good Conduct Medal
50. Police Medal for Meritorious Service
51. Fire Services Medal for Meritorious Service
52. Correctional Service Medal for Meritorious Service
53. Home Guards and Civil Defence Medal for Meritorious Service
54. Jeevan Raksha Padak
55. Territorial Army Decoration
56. Territorial Army Medal
57. Indian Independence Medal, 1947
58. Independence Medal 1950
59. 50th Anniversary of Independence Medal
60. 25th Independence Anniversary Medal
61. 30 Years Long Service Medal
62. 20 Years Long Service Medal
63. 9 Years Long Service Medal
64. Commonwealth awards (including pre-1947 awards)
65. Other awards

The Wound Medal (1034), inexplicably renamed in August 2000, appears in this list in its new *avatar* (incarnation), as the Parakram Padak.[9] Some awards remained unintegrated into the order of precedence: the President's Coast Guard Medal (1026), the Coast Guard Medal (1053), and the medals for long service (12 and 7 years) in the National Cadet Corps (1080

[9] Not to be confused with the 'Op Parakram Medal' (1047).

and 1081). More recent creations—the Police (Internal Security) Medal (1051), the Coast Guard Silver Jubilee Medal (1074), and the 9 and 20 Years Coast Guard Service Medals (1083 and 1082)—remain, as of the time of writing, un-represented in any order of wearing. The most recent Op Parakram Medal (1047) has, of course, not yet appeared in any formal order of wearing, though its place immediately following the Op Vijay Medal (1046) is certain and secure.

To the date of writing, no new orders of wearing notifications have appeared although, inevitably, such undertakings are a constant 'work in progress.'

While miniature awards have been mentioned in the instituting *Gazette of India* notifications, this has not been the case with all awards. In 1971, the Ministry of Defence permitted service officers to wear miniatures of all medals and decorations to which they were entitled, even if no clear provision was contained in the notification instituting the awards.[10]

The official procedure for dealing with matters relating to honours and awards is laid down in the Government of India's *Manual of Rules and Orders for Army, Naval and Air Headquarters, Inter Services Organisations.* All recommendations for gallantry decorations, viz., P.V.C., M.V.C., Vr.C., A.C., K.C., S.C., as well as certain other selected awards such as the Vishisht and Yudh Seva Medal series, Sena, Nao Sena, Vayu Sena Medals, are submitted to the Central Honours and Awards Committee for consideration. The committee was set-up in the Ministry of Defence in March 1962, and is composed of the defence minister, the defence secretary, and the chiefs of staff of the army, navy, and air force. Recommendations for award of the Ashoka Chakra to civilians, received from the Ministry of Home Affairs, are also placed before this committee. The home secretary is co-opted as a member of the committee when such recommendations are considered. Similarly, when recommendations in respect of Assam Rifles personnel and Naga Hills Village Guards Organisation were considered, the foreign secretary, Ministry of External Affairs, was co-opted on the committee. The recommendations of the committee are forwarded by the Ministry of Defence to the prime minister for approval. Approved recommendations are in turn sent to the president's secretariat for notification in the *Gazette of India*, part 1, section 1.

A question is frequently raised regarding the equivalencies of Indian awards to those of other countries, most especially those of the United Kingdom and the Commonwealth. While, on one level, this may be the wrong question to be asking, it is also a normal and, perhaps, inevitable question. We should offer an answer.

There has recently been an official attempt to establish a degree of parity or equivalence between pre- and post-Independence honours and awards bestowed upon the Indian Armed Forces, largely during the period immediately preceding independence in 1947. The following tables accordingly list the relative position of various decorations awarded to personnel

___

[10] MoD letter F.3/36/70/D(Ceremonials) dated 17 March 1971.

of the Indian armed forces in the period immediately before Independence and attempt to offer an approximate equation of these awards within the honours system as it has evolved since then.

At the very outset, it must be understood and borne in mind that the earlier system of honours and awards, with the exception of the Victoria Cross, was rank-based, i.e. personnel received a certain category of award based on their rank and/ or social position in the hierarchy. This differs completely from the theoretically egalitarian basis of honours and awards constituted by the Republic of India after independence.

The following table lists the military gallantry medals for each service. These are the entitlements that applied during WW II. As these awardees differed by rank, they also differed by service. For the Royal Indian Navy (the senior service before 1947, following British practice):

Officers	Other Ranks
V.C.	V.C.
D.S.O.	I.O.M./I.D.S.M.
D.S.C.	D.S.M./I.D.S.M./C.G.M.
MiD	MiD

For the Indian Army:

Officers	Other Ranks
V.C.	V.C.
D.S.O.	I.O.M./I.D.S.M.
M.C.	M.M.
MiD	MiD

For the Royal Indian Air Force:

Operational		Non-Operational	
Officers	Other Ranks	Officers	Other Ranks
V.C.	V.C.	–	–
D.S.O.	I.O.M./I.D.S.M.	–	–
D.F.C.	D.F.M.	A.F.C.	A.F.M.
MiD	MiD	–	–

The term 'officer' includes VCOs and Warrant Officers, though they did not always fit comfortably within this category.

As new India-specific awards were proposed early in the Dominion period, the intent—as has been discussed above—was to create them under royal warrant and, thereby, to grant them a place within the wider (pre-1947) 'Commonwealth' system of decorations. As originally proposed (see above), the Param Vir Chakra was to follow the Victoria Cross in the order of wearing, the Maha Vir Chakra was to follow the Distinguished Service Order, and the Vir Chakra was to come immediately after the Military Cross.[11] It is important to note that these new Indian awards were seen as representing only three successive levels of gallantry and they were not intended to be analogized to the pre-1947 awards which they were allotted to follow in the proposed order of precedence. This

[11] It is interesting to note that in so positioning the Vr.C. immediately after the M.C., but before the D.F.C., the drafing authority saw it as primarily an army award.

linkage of the P.V.C. to the V.C., of the M.V.C. to the D.S.O., and of the Vr.C. to the M.C. has, however, and regrettably, sprung up, perhaps reflecting their proposed places within the order of wearing.

If it is—as it may yet be—necessary to address equivalences, The following table lists the equivalent military gallantry awards for each service pre- and post-Independence. This is only approximate and inexact and, as has been discussed, such comparisons probably ought not to be made, even though they are probably inevitable and unavoidable. There is no service-wise distinction, except for the S.M./N.M./V.M. series:

Post-Independence Award	Pre-Independence Award
P.V.C.	V.C.
A.C. (military and civil)	G.C. (military and civil)
M.V.C.	D.S.O./I.O.M./I.D.S.M.
K.C. (military and civil)	No direct equivalent.
Vr.C.	D.S.C./M.C./D.F.C. (for officers) & D.S.M./ M.M./D.F.M. (for ORs); and I.D.S.M. (ORs) if awarded before 15 February 1944
S.C. (military and civil)	G.M./A.F.C./A.F.M. No direct equivalent for other services. May be equated depending on circumstances of award.
S.M./N.M./V.M.	Very roughly may be equated to G.M./ A.F.C./A.F.M. (Peacetime). No direct equivalent for other services in wartime or peacetime. May be considered a closer equivalent to a King's Commendation for Gallant Conduct (War/Peace).

In India, for many years, the armed forces have served as the *de facto* custodians of 'the system' and 'the tradition' of honours and awards. This has, however, resulted in granting a free hand to other arms of government, especially the Ministry of Home Affairs. As we discuss in Appendix 3, before 1947 the Private Secretary to the Viceroy would have exercised general supervision and 'quality control' over honours matters, but since Independence, and especially since the proclamation of the Republic of India in 1950, that role has been exercised by no one, neither by the president nor by the prime minister. Today, however, with the creation of a plethora of new medals without much sense of their place in history and tradition and the recent decision to augment ribbon bars with miniature clasps— even miniature clasps for ribbons that do not have clasps authorized!—can be taken as a sign of the early twenty-first-century sacrifice of both system and tradition on the altar of maximizing superfluous ornate touches to the uniform.

3. Ribbon bar with miniature clasps

1001 भारत रत्न / BHARAT RATNA[12]

The Bharat Ratna is India's supreme decoration and honour, awarded for the highest degrees of national service.

Established: Established by No. 1-Pres./54 of 2 January 1954. The regulations were revised by No. 1-Pres./55 of 8 January 1955 (to alter the design) and amended by No. 10-Pres./56 of 20 February 1956 (to establish the ribbon width), by

[12]*Encyclopedia of Soldiers with Highest Gallantry Awards*, pp. 8-9; *India's Highest Gallantry Awards*, pp. 7-11; Haynes, 'Medals and Decorations of the Republic of India', pp. 3-5; Das, *Traditions and Customs*, p. 270; Dorling, *Ribbons & Medals*, p. 293; Scandaluzzi, *Medal Ribbons of the World*, vol. 3: *India*.

No. 27-Pres./56 of 10 September 1956 (to provide for a miniature) and by No. 6-Pres./57 of 26 January 1957 (to alter the depiction of the devices on the obverse and reverse). From 13 July 1977 to 26 January 1980, awards of the Bharat Ratna were suspended.

General Appearance: A toned bronze *pipal* (*Ficus religiosa*) leaf design, 60 mm ($2^5/_{16}$ inches) by 47 mm ($1^7/_8$ inches), 'stem' downwards. (Note, however, comments on the original design, in background.)

Obverse: In the centre, a platinum sunburst with the name of the decoration in silver gilt in Sanskrit/Hindi 'भारत रत्न', 'Bharat Ratna' below. In 1957, the legend was changed to burnished bronze.

Reverse: In the centre, the state emblem in platinum and the motto in silver gilt. In 1957, the motto was altered to burnished bronze.

Ribbon: Originally established as 50 mm (2 inches), white moiré *khadi* silk. In 1956, the width was altered at the express request of Prime Minister Nehru to 38 mm (1½ inches).[13]

Suspension: Worn around the neck from an oval fixed suspender.

Naming: Issued unnamed.

Miniature: In 1956, a miniature was established at half the size of the decoration.

Background: The services for which the Bharat Ratna is awarded include artistic, literary, and scientific achievement, as well as 'recognition of public service of the highest order'. Throughout the history of the decoration, it has been very carefully stressed that the award of the Bharat Ratna carries with it no title, no 'knighthood', and no particular status.

The original statutes of January 1954 did not make allowance for posthumous awards (and this perhaps explains one reason why the decoration was never awarded to Mahatma Mohandas Karamchand Gandhi), though this provision was added in the January 1955 statute (and there have, subsequently, been a number of posthumous awards, some rather controversial). While there was no formal provision that recipients of the Bharat Ratna should be Indian citizens, this seems to have been the general assumption. The relevant paragraph in the statutes reads '6. Any person without distinction of race, occupation, position or sex shall be eligible for the award.' There has been one award to a naturalized Indian citizen (to Agnes Gonxha Bojaxhiu, 'Mother Theresa', in 1980) and two to non-Indians (to Khan Abdul Ghaffar Khan, the 'Frontier Gandhi,' in 1987 and to the South African freedom fighter Nelson Mandela in 1990).[14]

The original specifications for the award called for a circular gold medal, 34 mm ($1^3/_8$ inches) in diameter, with the sun and the legend 'भारत रत्न' or 'Bharat Ratna' above and a floral wreath below. The reverse was to carry the state emblem and motto. It was to be worn round the neck suspended from a white ribbon. There is no indication that any specimens of this design (except, perhaps, prototypes?) were ever produced and one year later the design was altered as is detailed below.

1001.220 Bharat Ratna

[13]See correspondence in Home Ministry (National Archives of India), file 1/6/Public II (1957)

[14] The award of the Bharat Ratna to Khan Abdul Ghaffar Khan prompted the response from Pakistan in which the Nishan-i-Pakistan was awarded to the ex-Prime Minister of India, Morarji Desai.

(Though the special medal awarded for the first successful Mt. Everest expedition hints at this design, see 1090.)

The political history of the Bharat Ratna (as well as that of the Padma Vibhushan [1004], Padma Bhushan [1005], and Padma Shri [1010]) has been controversial. As has been mentioned above, no title, royalty, knighthood or other special status is conferred with the decoration. This legal philosophy is central to any understanding of the idealism and psychology underlying all Indian awards. It has been stated clearly in an official government publication:

The Government of India have instituted several civilian awards to honour individual acts of outstanding merit in the sphere of social service or art, science, literature, industry, sports, etc., or for conspicuous bravery and self sacrifice otherwise than in the face of the enemy including acts of conscientious devotion to duty in general. The cardinal thinking behind the institution of these awards all along has been that apart from serving to be tangible tokens of recognition by the Government of the outstanding services rendered by individuals in particular areas or fields of specialisation, such distinctions could act as powerful motivators to greater efforts by others to reach peaks of excellence in the several spheres of public activity.

The above considerations notwithstanding, it may be noted that these decorations are not titles. They cannot be prefixed or suffixed to the names of the recipients in official documents. In the words of Pandit Jawaharlal Nehru, these are 'merely honours conferred for distinguished service of a high order'.[15]

Nevertheless, the constitutional validity of this award (as well as the Padma Vibhushan, Padma Bhushan, and Padma Shri) has always been, at best, vague. From 13 July 1977 (No. 65-Pres./77) until 26 January 1980 (No. 25-Pres./80), the award of this decoration were suspended. In January 1993, the entire issue was referred to the Supreme Court and awards were suspended pending an opinion from the court. On 15 December 1995, the court upheld the validity of these awards.[16] The government convened a High Level Review Committee, chaired by Vice-President K.R. Narayanan and, in November 1996, put forward recommendations for the Bharat Ratna and Padma series of awards. The recommendations called for a more systematic method of submitting recommendations for national awards and for an independent body to review these recommendations. In the aftermath of these decisions, the award of these national decorations has continued.

The ban on the use of 'Bharat Ratna' and the names of the other national awards as a title has been a source of ongoing trouble and many recipients, many supporters of those recipients, and, on occasion, even national bodies such as the Indian Parliament have employed the names of these awards as part of the augmented name of the awardee (for example, as in 'Bharat Ratna Baba Saheb Dr B.R. Ambedkar'). Despite dire warnings from the Ministry of Home Affairs that the use of these decorations as titles could result in the revocation of these awards, there is no sense of an early abatement of such misuse of these national honours.[17]

---

[15] *A Compilation of the Recipients of Bharat Ratna and Padma Awards*, 1: iii.

[16] See http://judis.nic.in/supremecourt/qrydisp.asp?tfnm=10166.

[17] See, for example, http://ambedkarfoundation.nic.in/html/bharat.htm or http://www.parliamentofindia.nic.in/ls/bulletin2/03/310703/html.

Awards: To date, there have been thirty-eight recipients of the Bharat Ratna, and many other names have been raised in public discussion:

Dr Sarvepalli Radhakrishnan, 1954—philosopher, President of India, 1962-1967—No. 40-Pres./54 of 15 August 1954

Chakravarti Rajagopalachari, 1954—Governor-General of India, 1948-1952—No. 40-Pres./54 of 15 August 1954

Dr Chandrasekhar Venkat Raman, 1954—physicist—No. 40-Pres./54 of 15 August 1954

Dr Bhagwan Das, 1955—philosopher and scholar—No. 7-Pres./55 of 26 January 1955

Dr Mokshagundam Visvesvaraya, 1955—engineer and social reformer—No. 7-Pres./55 of 26 January 1955

Pandit Jawaharlal Nehru, 1955—freedom fighter, Prime Minister of India, 1947-1964—No. 21-Pres./55 of 15 July 1955

Govind Ballabh Pant, 1957—freedom fighter and politician—No. 10-Pres./57 of 26 January 1957

Dr Dhondo Keshave Karve, 1958—social reformer—No. 4-Pres./58 of 26 January 1958

Dr Bidhan Chandra Roy, 1961—freedom fighter—No. 3-Pres./61 of 26 January 1961

Purushottam Das Tandon, 1961—freedom fighter—No. 3-Pres./61 of 26 January 1961

Dr Rajendra Prasad, 1962—President of India, 1950-1962—No. 38-Pres./62 of 13 May 1962

Dr Zakir Husain, 1963—President of India, 1967-1969—No. 11-Pres./63 of 26 January 1963

Dr Pandurang Vaman Kane, 1963—historian and philosopher—No. 11-Pres./63 of 26 January 1963

Lal Bahadur Shastri, 1966 (posthumous)—Prime Minister of India, 1964-1966—No. 1-Pres./66 of 11 January 1966

Indira Gandhi, 1971—Prime Minister of India, 1966-1977, 1980-1984—No. 84-Pres./71 of 18 December 1971

Varahagiri Venkata Giri, 1975—President of India, 1969-1974—No. 6-Pres./75 of 26 January 1975

Kumaraswami Kamraj, 1976 (posthumous)—freedom fighter and politician—No. 6-Pres./76 of 26 January 1976

Mother Mary Teresa Bojaxhiu ['Mother Teresa', Agnes Gonxha Bojaxhiu], 1980—social rights activist—No. 32-Pres./80 of 26 January 1980

Acharya Vinobha Bhave, 1983 (posthumous)—activist for social and economic rights—No. 27-Pres./83 of 26 January 1983

Khan Abdul Ghaffar Khan, 1987—freedom fighter—No. 59-Pres./87 of 10 August 1987

Manidur Gopalan Ramachandran, 1988 (posthumous)—politician—No. 18-Pres./88 of 26 January 1988

Dr Bhim Rao Ramji Ambedkar, 1990 (posthumous)—fighter for rights for India's *dalits* ('untouchables')—No. 36-Pres./90 of 14 April 1990

Dr Nelson Rolihlahla Mandela, 1990—fighter for South African freedom—No. 90-Pres./90 of 16 October 1990.

Morarji Ranchhodji Desai, 1991—freedom fighter and Prime Minister of India 1977-1979—No. 52-Pres./91 of 26 January 1991

Rajiv Gandhi, 1991 (posthumous)—Prime Minister of India 1984-1989—No. 76-Pres./91 of 6 July 1991

Sardar Vallabhbhai Patel, 1991 (posthumous)—freedom fighter and politician—No. 77-Pres./91 of 12 July 1991

Maulana Abul Kalam Azad, 1992 (posthumous)—freedom fighter and politician—No. 31-Pres./92 of 23 January 1992

Jehangir Ratanji Dadabhai Tata, 1992—industrialist—No. 32-Pres./92 of 26 January 1992

Satyajit Ray, 1998 (posthumous)—film director—No. 28-Pres./98 of 1 March 1998

Gulzarilal Nanda, 1998 (posthumous)—freedom fighter and Prime Minister of India, 1964 and 1966—No. 28-Pres./98 of 1 March 1998

Aruna Asaf Ali, 1998 (posthumous)—freedom fighter—No. 28-Pres./98 of 1 March 1998

Dr Avul Pakir Jainulabdeen Abdul Kalam, 1998—pioneer in missile technology (later Presidednt of India)—No. 28-Pres./98 of 1 March 1998

Madurai Shanmukhavadivu Subbulakshmi, 1998—classical singer in Carnatic vocal style—No. 28-Pres./98 of 1 March 1998

Chidambaram Subramaniam, 1998—veteran politician and guiding force behind India's 'Green Revolution'—No. 69-Pres./98 of 18 February 1998

Jayaprakash Narayan, 1999 (posthumous)—politician—No. 45-Pres./99 of 16 February 1999

Prof. Amartya Sen, 1999—economist—No. 45-Pres./99 of 16 February 1999

Gopinath Bardoloi, 1999 (posthumous)—freedom fighter—No. 45-Pres./99 of 16 February 1999

Pandit Ravi Shankar, 1999—internationally famous classical musician of the sitar—No. 45-Pres./99 of 16 February 1999

Lata Dinanath Mangeshkar, 2001—internationally famous singer—No. 50-Pres./2001 of 26 January 2001

Ustad Bismillah Khan, 2001—internationally famous classical musician of the shehnai—No. 76-Pres./2001 of 26 January 2001

Awards are normally published in the *Gazette of India Extra-ordinary*, part 1, section 1, although no citations are given. These notifications are notoriously difficult to trace.

In 1992, the award was mooted for *Netaji* Subhas Chandra Bose, the freedom fighter and leader of the Indian National Army in Europe and South-East Asia during WW II. The original citation was specified as a 'posthumous' award, though the circumstances of his disappearance in an air crash in 1945 are still hotly debated. Accordingly, the Supreme Court reviewed the award and, in 1997, ordered its cancellation.

Outline

1001.100 original circular design and with 50 mm ribbon (1954-55)—Never awarded (the award to Dr S. Radhakrishnan was of the leaf-shaped variety).

1001.200 peepal-leaf design and with 38 mm ribbon.

1001.210 devices in platinum and silver gilt (1955-57)—This was, apparently, awarded only seven times (through the G.B. Pant award in 1957?).

1001.220 inscriptions changed to burnished bronze (1957-77 and post-1980)—all awards since that to Dr D.K. Karve have, apparently, been of this variety.

1002 परम वीर चक्र / PARAM VIR CHAKRA[18]

Awarded for the highest degree of valour or self-sacrifice in the presence of the enemy.

Established: A draft royal warrant was prepared in October 1948 for the possible institution of this award in the name of the British sovereign as, during the dominion period, such a step would have been necessary to give the award status within the Commonwealth. On consideration, this course was abandoned and the medal was created by No. 1-Pres./50 of 26 January 1950, by the President of India, with awards effective from 15 August 1947; the statues were amended by No. 2-Pres./52 of 4 January 1952, by No. 54-Pres./69 of 18 September 1969, by No. 61-Pres./69 of 14 October 1969, when it was moved to second place in the order of wearing, behind the Bharat Ratna.

General Appearance: 35 mm circular dark bronze medal.

Obverse: In the centre, the state emblem is depicted on a raised circle. Surrounding this are four replicas of Indra's *Vajra* (the all-powerful mythic weapon on the ancient Vedic god of war). Great mythology surrounds this mysterious weapon of Vedic origin. It was the *amogha astra* (unfailing weapon) used by Indra to kill Vritra, the demon of drought, to release life-giving waters for the benefit of mankind. In Puranic literature it is said that this Vajra was made out of the *asthis* (bones) of Dadhici, a sage of high attainments, for the benefit of the world.

Reverse: Around a plain centre, two legends separated by lotus flowers: above 'परम वीर चक्र' and below 'PARAM VIR CHAKRA'.

Ribbon: 32 mm, medium purple. Some sources suggest a chronological progression of ribbons: 1950-71, 32 mm deep reddish violet; 1971-81, 36 mm magenta; and post-1981, 32 mm deep claret. There seems, however, to be no basis for this and these reported ribbon variants reflect no changes in policy or design, and are merely differences in manufacture.

Suspension: The decoration is suspended from a straight swivelling suspension bar.

Naming: It is named on the edge. Observed specimens have been named on the edge in either English or Hindi and the date of action is usually included. Recently awarded PVCs are coarsely named in Hindi with name, followed by number, rank, and regiment; this is an unusual naming pattern not otherwise encountered.

Miniature: Miniatures have been issued.

Background: Awarded to officers and enlisted personnel of all military branches for the highest degree of valour or self-sacrifice in the presence of the enemy, it may also be awarded posthumously and, indeed, most of the awards have been posthumous. In many ways, the Param Vir Chakra can be seen as a post-Independence equivalent of the Victoria Cross. Award of the decoration carries with it the right to use P.V.C. as a post-nominal abbreviation.

Provision was made for the award of a bar for second (or subsequent) awards of the Param Vir Chakra. To date, there have been no such awards (and, indeed, there have been only

1002.100 Param Vir Chakra

[18] Cardozo, *Param Vir; Encyclopedia of Soldiers with Highest Gallantry Awards*, pp. 1-3, 197-205; *India's Highest Gallantry Awards*, pp. 1-2, 195-206; Haynes, 'Medals and Decorations of the Republic of India', pp. 5-6, 13-26; Das, *Traditions and Customs*, p. 271; Dorling, *Ribbons & Medals*, pp. 144; Scandaluzzi, *Medal Ribbons of the World*, vol. 3: *India*.

1002A Param Vir Chakra
'Vajra' ribbon device

1002B Bar to Param Vir Chakra

seven non-posthumous awards). When the ribbon alone is worn, a *vajra* device is supposed to be employed.

Subsequent bars to the awards (which have never occurred) would be represented by an additional device. Although provided for in the gazette notification, the Vajra emblem has not been issued for wear with recent awards.

The award also carries a cash allowance for those under the rank of second lieutenant (or the appropriate service equivalent) and, in some cases, a lump sum cash award. On the death of the recipient, the pension is transferred to the widow until her death or remarriage. This pension has been a rather controversial issue throughout the life of the decoration. When first created, the monthly stipend was Rs. 50 (Rs. 70 for those who had been awarded the British Distinguished Service Order or Indian Order of Merit) with an additional Rs. 20 for the award of a bar to the decoration. For Gorkhas of Nepalese domicile, the award was a lump sum payment of Rs. 4,000. Over time, these stipends have been increased although they are, in the opinion of many public commentators, still too low. By March 1999, the stipend stood at Rs. 1,500 per month with an additional Rs. 40 authorized for the award of a bar (which in any case has never taken place). In addition, many states have established individual pension rewards for the recipients of the decoration. These are summarized in Appendix 2.

Mrs Savithribai Khanolkar (born Eva Yuonne Linda Maday-de-Maros) designed the medal. By coincidence, the first recipient was her son-in-law, Major Som Nath Sharma.

The President may cancel and annul the award of the decoration at his discretion. The offences for which his discretion may be invoked are: treason, sedition, mutiny, cowardice, desertion during hostilities, murder, dacoity, rape, and unnatural offences. The same criteria are to be applied for cancellation of awards of the Maha Vir Chakra and Vir Chakra, as well as the Ashoka Chakra, Kirti Chakra, and Shaurya Chakra.

Awards:

IC-521 Major Som Nath Sharma, 4th Battalion, Kumaon Regiment—3 November 1947—Badgam, Jammu and Kashmir (posthumous)—No. 2-Pres./50 of 26 January 1950

27373 Naik Jadunath Singh, 1st Battalion, Rajput Regiment—6 February 1948—Naushera, Jammu and Kashmir (posthumous)—No. 16-Pres./50 of 11 December 1950

SS-14246 2/Lieutenant Rama Raghoba Rane, Corps of Engineers—8 April 1948—Naushera/Rajauri, Jammu and Kashmir—No. 5-Pres./50 of 21 January 1950

2831592 Company Havildar Major Piru Singh, 6th Battalion, Rajputana Rifles—17/18 July 1948—Tithwal, Jammu and Kashmir (posthumous)—No. 8-Pres./52 of 26 January 1952

22356 Lance-Naik Karam Singh, M.M., 1st Battalion, Sikh Regiment—13 October 1948—Tithwal, Jammu and Kashmir—No. 2-Pres./50 of 26 January 1950

IC-8497 Captain Gurbachan Singh Salaria, 3rd Battalion, 1st Gorkha Rifles—5 December 1961—Elizabethville, Katanga, Congo (posthumous)—No. 8-Pres./62 of 24 January 1962

IC-7990 Major Dhan Singh Thapa, 1st Battalion, 8th Gorkha Rifles—

20 October 1962—Ladakh, Jammu and Kashmir—No. 68-Pres./ 62 of 12 November 1962

JC-4547 Subadar Joginder Singh, 1st Battalion, Sikh Regiment— 23 October 1962—Tongpen La, North East Frontier Agency (posthumous)—No. 68-Pres./62 of 12 November 1962

IC-6400 Major Shaitan Singh, 13th Battalion, Kumaon Regiment— 18 November 1962—Rezang La, Ladakh, Jammu and Kashmir (posthumous)—No. 14-Pres./63 of 26 January 1963

2639885 Company Havildar Major Abdul Hamid, 4th Battalion, Grenadiers—10 September 1965—Chima, Khem Karan Sector (posthumous)—No. 111-Pres./65 of 17 September 1965

IC-5565 Lieutenant-Colonel Ardeshir Burzorji Tarapore, Poona Horse—15 October 1965—Phillora, Sialkot Sector, Pakistan (posthumous)—No. 112-Pres./65 of 15 October 1965

4239746 Lance-Naik Albert Ekka, 14th Battalion, Brigade of Guards— 3 December 1971—Gangasagar, Bangladesh (posthumous)— No. 7-Pres./72 of 20 January 1972

10877 F (P) Flying Officer Nirmal Jit Singh Sekhon, Indian Air Force—14 December 1971—Srinagar, Jammu and Kashmir (posthumous)—No. 7-Pres./72 of 20 January 1972

IC-25067 2/Lieutenant Arun Khetarpal, Poona Horse—16 December 1971—Jarpal, Shakargarh Sector (posthumous)—No. 7-Pres./72 of 20 January 1972

IC-14608 Major Hoshiar Singh, 3rd Battalion, Grenadiers—17 December 1971—Basantar River, Shakargarh Sector—No. 7-Pres./ 72 of 20 January 1972

JC-155825 Naib Subedar Bana Singh, 8th Battalion, Jammu and Kashmir Light Infantry—23 June 1987—Siachen Glacier, Ladakh, Jammu and Kashmir—No. 9-Pres./88 of 22 January 1988

IC-32907F Major Ramaswamy Parmeswaran, 8th Battalion, Mahar Regiment—25 November 1987—Sri Lanka (posthumous)— No. 9-Pres./88 of 22 January 1988

IC-57556 Captain Vikram Batra, 13th Battalion, Jammu and Kashmir Rifles—20 June 1999—Point 5140, Dras/Kargil area, Jammu and Kashmir (posthumous)—No. 16-Pres./2000 of 15 August 1999 [sic]

IC-56959 Lieutenant Manoj Kumar Pandey, 1st Battalion, 11th Gorkha Rifles—23 June 1999—Khaluber/Juver Top, Batalik sector, Kargil area Jammu and Kashmir (posthumous)—No. 16-Pres./ 2000 of 15 August 1999 [sic]

2690572 Grenadier Yogendra Singh Yadav, 18th Battalion, Grenadiers—4 July 1999—Tiger Hill, Kargil area, Jammu and Kashmir—No. 16-Pres./2000 of 15 August 1999 [sic]

13760533 Rifleman Sanjay Kumar, 13th Battalion, Jammu and Kashmir Rifles—4 July 1999—Flat Top, Kargil area, Jammu and Kashmir—No. 16-Pres./2000 of 15 August 1999 [sic]

Citations are published in the *Gazette of India*, part 1, section 1.

Outline

1002.100 medal.

1003 अशोक चक्र / ASHOKA CHAKRA[19]

Awarded for the highest degree of bravery other than in the face of the enemy.

Established: Established as the 'Ashoka Chakra, Class I' in No. 1-Pres./52 of 4 January 1952 (with effect from 15 August

[19]*Encyclopedia of Soldiers with Highest Gallantry Awards*, pp. 10-12; *India's Highest Gallantry Awards*, pp. 12-14; Haynes, 'Medals and Decorations of the Republic of India', pp. 10-12; Das, *Traditions and Customs*, p. 272; Dorling, *Ribbons & Medals*, p. 293; Scandaluzzi, *Medal Ribbons of the World*, vol. 3: *India*.

1003.200 Ashoka Chakra

1003A Bar to Ashoka Chakra

1947). The statutes were revised and the decoration renamed in No. 30-Pres./67 of 27 January 1967. A further amendment was incorporated in No. 52-Pres./84 of 10 April 1984, making non-Indian citizens eligible for the award.

General Appearance: The medal is described as a circular 'gold gilt' medal, but presumably the base metal is silver. The medal is 35 mm in diameter.

Obverse: In the centre, the *chakra* (wheel) of Ashoka, surrounded by a lotus wreath and with an ornate edge of lotus leaves, flowers, and buds.

Reverse: Blank in the centre, with 'अशोक चक्र' along the upper edge on the medal and the same name in English along the lower rim, 'ASHOKA CHAKRA' the two inscriptions being separated by two lotus flowers. There is no indication of the class on the pre-1967 awards in the first class, and, in fact, there is no difference between these medals and the post-1967 'Ashoka Chakra' awards.

Ribbon: 32 mm, dark green divided into two halves by a 2 mm central orange stripe. The green colour is intended to denote auspiciousness while the orange-saffron denotes renunciation and sacrifice. Some sources suggest that the ribbon went through changes over time: 1952-67, 32 mm with a 2 mm orange central stripe; 1967-81, 38 mm with a 1.5 mm white central stripe; and after 1981, 32 mm with a 1.5 mm orange central stripe. There is, however, no evidence to support this assertion, and these are mere manufacturing varieties. A bar, were it to be awarded, would be indicated on the ribbon when worn alone by the addition of a miniature chakra.

Suspension: Suspended by a non-swivelling straight-bar suspender.

Naming: The medal was initially both named and dated on the edge. However, since about 1970, the date is no longer inscribed on the rim.

Miniature: Miniatures have been issued.

Background: Awarded for the 'most conspicuous bravery or some act of daring or pre-eminent valour or self-sacrifice' other than in the face of the enemy. The decoration may be awarded either to military personnel or to civilians and may be awarded posthumously. Recently, for the military, this has come to encompass a range of awards for counter-insurgency operations; the distinction between 'combat' and 'non-combat' gallantry has become increasingly vague as new types of deployments have been added to the traditional mission of the Indian armed forces. Personnel of police forces and recognized fire services were expressly excluded from the award in the gazette notification instituting the three classes of the Ashoka Chakra. Over the years this clause appears to have been overlooked and there have been several police recipients of the award. Notification of awards is published in the *Gazette of India*, part 1, section 1.

Subsequent awards of the Ashoka Chakra are recognized by a bar to the medal ribbon (to date, none have been awarded). It is possible for a recipient to be awarded the Kirti Chakra (1009) or Shaurya Chakra (1015) in addition for separate acts of gallantry, yet this has taken place but once, in the case of Colonel N.J. Nair, K.C., 16th Battalion, Maratha Light Infantry. In many ways, the Ashoka Chakra can be seen as a post-Independence equivalent of the George Cross.

The medal was originally established in 1952 as the 'Ashoka Chakra, Class I' as the highest of a three-class sequence of non-combat bravery decorations. In 1967, these decorations were removed from the three-tiered 'class-based' system and renamed as the Ashoka Chakra, Kirti Chakra (1009), and Shaurya Chakra (1015). This is an important point in understanding the independent Indian view of decorations: the desire to reduce or eliminate any inegalitarian class structure to Indian awards, while apparently contradictory to the very idea of granting any awards at all, has been an ongoing policy theme. It would also lead to changes in the Padma Vibhushan series (1004, 1005, 1010), the Vishisht Seva (distinguished service) medal series (1007, 1013, and 1027), the Jeevan Raksha (life-saving) medal series (1011, 1033, and 1067), and the Defence Security (Raksha Suraksha) Corps medal series (1078 and 1079).

While most Indian awards were created without the provision or apparently the intent that they would ever be awarded to non-Indian citizens, the rules of the series were modified in 1984 (No. 52-Pres./84 and No. 53-Pres./84) to allow for the awards of the Ashoka Chakra (No. 57-Pres./84) and Kirti Chakra (No. 58-Pres./84) to Soviet cosmonauts as a part of the reciprocal exchange of awards that traditionally accompanied the participation of foreign nationals (Squadron Leader Rakesh Sharma, Indian Air Force, and his back-up crew) in the Soviet space programme (SOYUZ T-11).

When the decoration was established no provision was made for any monetary stipend from the central government. It was, however, decided that for recipients whose families were in 'indigent' circumstances (defined as having an annual income under Rs. 3,000), a monthly allowance of Rs. 40 was appropriate. Over time, these stipends have been increased although they are still considered by many to be too low. From 1 February 1999, the stipend stood at Rs. 1,400 per month with an additional Rs. 35 authorized for the award of a bar (which, in any case, has never taken place). Provincial stipends are detailed in Appendix 2.

In 1956, the ability of the President to cancel this medal was extended, along the same lines as the potential cancellation of the P.V.C./M.V.C./Vr.C., as mentioned earlier.

Award of the decoration carries with it the right to use A.C. as a postnominal abbreviation.

Awards: To date, the Ashoka Chakra has been awarded to:

13730 Havildar Bachittar Singh, 2nd Battalion, Sikh Regiment (posthumous)—13 September 1948—Naldrug, Hyderabad, Andhra Pradesh—No. 12-Pres./52 of 26 January 1952

10341 Naik Nar Bahadur Thapa, 5th Battalion, 5th Gorkha Rifles (F.F.)—13 September 1948—Tamsir, Hyderabad, Andhra Pradesh—No. 12-Pres./52 of 26 January 1952

2883 Flight Lieutenant Subhas Biswas, Indian Air Force GD (P)—3 February 1952—Lucknow/Delhi, Uttar Pradesh — No. 35-Pres./52 of 12 February 1952

15103 A/L/Naik Sunder Singh, 4th Battalion, Jammu and Kashmir Rifles—18/19 March 1956—Hussainiwala, Punjab — No. 29-Pres./56 of 26 September 1956

Captain Damodar Kashinath Jatar, Air India (posthumous)—11 April 1955—South China Sea– No. 11-Pres./55 of 18 June 1955

18576 PA/Havildar Joginder Singh, 2nd Battalion, Sikh Regiment (posthumous)—24 April 1956—Phake, Naga Hills, Nagaland—No. 36-Pres./57 of 31 August 1957

IC-7415 2/Lieutenant Polur Muthuswamy Raman, 3rd Battalion, Sikh Light Infantry (posthumous)—3 June 1956—Chephema, Naga Hills, Nagaland—No. 36-Pres./57 of 31 August 1957

IC-3472 Lieutenant-Colonel Jagan Nath Raoji Chitnis, 1st Battalion, 3rd Gorkha Rifles—14 June 1956—Mokokchung/Zunheboto, Naga Hills, Nagaland (posthumous)—No. 36-Pres./57 of 31 August 1957

IC-5034 Captain Eric James Tucker, 2nd Battalion, Maratha Light Infantry (posthumous)—2 August 1957—Chakabama/Phok, Naga Hills, Nagaland—No. 21-Pres./58 of 15 September 1958

30385 Subdadar-Major Kharaka Bahadur Limbu, M.C., 8th Battalion, Assam Rifles (posthumous)—26 April 1961—Naga Hills, Nagaland—No. 9-Pres./62 of 24 January 1962

IC-5261 Captain Man Bahadur Rai, M.C., I.D.S.M., 1st Battalion, 11th Gorkha Rifles—April/May 1961—Nagaland—No. 9-Pres./62 of 24 January 1962

Shri Tej Singh (posthumous)—12 September 1964—Morena District, Madhya Pradesh—No. 1-Pres./65 of 1 January 1965

Shri Lajjaram (posthumous)—12 September 1964—Morena District, Madhya Pradesh—No. 1-Pres./65 of 1 January 1965

Shri Purushottam (posthumous)—12 September 1964—Morena District, Madhya Pradesh– No. 1-Pres./65 of 1 January 1965

Shri Chaman Lal (posthumous)—13 September 1965—Gurdaspur, Punjab—No. 135-Pres./65 of 20 December 1965

Shri Govind Singh—4 January 1966—Chattarpur District, Madhya Pradesh—No. 2-Pres./68 of 8 January 1968

Shri Hukum Singh—4 January 1966—Chattarpur District, Madhya Pradesh—No. 2-Pres./68 of 8 January 1968

Shri Lakhan Singh—4 January 1966—Chattarpur District, Madhya Pradesh—No. 2-Pres./68 of 8 January 1968

Shri Takhat Singh—4 January 1966—Chattarpur District, Madhya Pradesh—No. 2-Pres./68 of 8 January 1968

Shri Shankar Lal[20]—10 August 1966—Mudheri, Madhya Pradesh (posthumous)—No. 82-Pres./67 of 2 September 1967

Shri Dhanpat Singh—27 February 1967—Jabalpur District, Madhya Pradesh—No. 2-Pres./68 of 8 January 1968

EC-53763 Captain Jasram Singh, 16th Battalion, Rajput Regiment—30 October 1968—Mizo Hills, Mizoram—No. 63-Pres./69 of 18 November 1969

Shri Baijnath Singh (posthumous)—22 October 1969—Bhind District, Madhya Pradesh—No. 2-Pres./71 of 14 January 1971

Shri Bhure Lal—14/15 July 1970—Guna, Madhya Pradesh—No. 3-Pres./72 of 19 January 1972

IC-17696 Captain Ummed Singh Mahra, 19th Battalion, Rajputana Rifles (posthumous)—6 July 1971—Nagaland—No. 3-Pres./72 of 19 January 1972

Shri Munilal, (posthumous)—12 April 1972—Sagar District, Madhya Pradesh—No. 25-Pres./74 of 20 January 1974

[20] Shankar Lal was a retired head constable.

JC-47692 Naib Subedar Gurnam Singh, Bombay Sappers (posthumous)—23 September 1973—Kirkee, Maharashtra—No. 25-Pres./74 of 20 January 1974

SS-30122 2/Lieutenant Cyrus Addie Pithawalla, 17th Battalion, Jammu and Kashmir Rifles—6 July 1981—Tekcham area, Manipur—No. 76-Pres./81 of 28 December 1981

Colonel Yurie Vasielevich Malyshev, Soviet Air Force and cosmonaut—3 April 1984—SOYUZ T-11—No. 57-Pres./84 of 7 May 1984

12396 Squadron Leader Rakesh Sharma, F (P), Indian Air Force and cosmonaut—3 April 1984—SOYUZ T-11—No. 57-Pres./84 of 7 May 1984

Gennady Mikhailovich Strekalov, Soviet cosmonaut—3 April 1984—SOYUZ T-11—No. 57-Pres./84 of 7 May 1984

IC-37068 Captain Jasbir Singh Raina, 10th Battalion, Brigade of Guards—3-6 June 1984—Amritsar, Punjab—No. 17-Pres./85 of 26 January 1985

IC-39994 Lieutenant Ram Praksah Roperia, 26th Battalion, Madras Regiment (posthumous)—5/6 June 1984—Amritsar, Punjab—No. 17-Pres./85 of 26 January 1985

4050561 Naik Bhawani Datt Joshi, 5th Battalion, Garhwal Rifles (posthumous)—5/6 June 1984—Amritsar, Punjab—No. 17-Pres./85 of 26 January 1985

4167546 Naik Nirbhay Singh, 15th Battalion, Kumaon Regiment (posthumous)—5/6 June 1984—Amritsar, Punjab—No. 17-Pres./85 of 26 January 1985

IC-22479 Major Bhukant Misra, 15th Battalion, Kumaon Regiment (posthumous)—5/6 June 1984—Amritsar, Punjab—No. 17-Pres./85 of 26 January 1985

Shri Vijay Jagirdar (posthumous)—1 November 1984—Indore District, Madhya Pradesh—No. 7-Pres./86 of 21 January 1986

9920311 L/Havildar Chhering Mutup, Ladakh Scouts—21 February 1985—Jammu and Kashmir—No. 103-Pres./85 of 7 October 1985

Shrimati Neerja Mishra, Pan American World Airways (posthumous)—5 September 1986—Karachi, Pakistan—No. 4-Pres./87 of 16 January 1987

Shri Randhir Prasad Verma, IPS, SP Dhanbad (posthumous)—3 January 1991—Dhanbad, Bihar—No. 11-Pres. 91 of 26 Jan 1991

IC-43956 Captain Sandeep Shankla, 18th Battalion, Dogra Regiment (posthumous)—8 August 1991—Zafarkhani, Jammu and Kashmir—No. 5-Pres./92 of 14 January 1992

IC-51242 2/Lieutenant Rakesh Singh, 22nd Battalion, Grenadiers—5 December 1992—Padarpur village, Pulwama district, Jammu and Kashmir—No. 8-Pres./93 of 26 January 1993

IC-25070 Colonel Neelakantan Jayachandran Nair, K.C., 16th Battalion, Maratha Light Infantry (posthumous)—20 December 1993—Mokochung-Mariani road, Nagaland—No. 11-Pres./94 of 25 January 1994

IC-50443 Major Rajiv Kumar Joon, 22nd Battalion, Grenadiers (posthumous)—16 September 1994—Arijan Deosar village, Anantnag district, Jammu and Kashmir—No. 178-Pres./95 of 15 August 1995

JC-216611 Subedar Sujjan Singh, 13th Battalion, Kumaon Regiment (posthumous)—26 September 1994—Zalurah village, Kupwara district, Jammu and Kashmir—No. 80-Pres./95 of 25 January 1995

IC-36177 Lieutenant Colonel Harsh Uday Singh Gaur, 10th Battalion, Bihar Regiment (posthumous)—29 November 1994—Bazipura village, Baramullah district, Jammu and Kashmir—No. 80-Pres./95 of 25 January 1995

IC 48171 Captain Arun Singh Jasrotia, SM, 9th Battalion, Parachute Regiment (Special Forces) (posthumous)—15 September 1995—Lolab valley, Jammu and Kashmir—No. 9-Pres./96 of 25 January 1996

IC-34425 Lieutenant Colonel Shanti Swaroop Rana, 3rd Battalion, Bihar Regiment/13th Rashtriya Rifles (posthumous)—2 November 1996—Haphurda forest, Kupwara District, Jammu and Kashmir—No. 10-Pres./97 of 25 January 1997

IC-53987 2/Lieutenant Puneet Nath Datt, 1st Battalion, 11th Gorkha Rifles (posthumous)—July 1997—Srinagar, Jammu and Kashmir—No. 81-Pres./97 of 15 August 1997

IC-47623 Major Sudhir Kumar, S.M.*, 9th Para Commando (Special Forces) (posthumous)—August 1999—Kupwara District, Jammu and Kashmir—No. 15-Pres./2000 of 26 January 2000

4183850 Naik Rambeer Singh Tomar, Kumaon/26th Rashtriya Rifles (posthumous)—18 October 2001—Doda District, Jammu and Kashmir—No. 29-Pres./02 of 25 January 2002

943040199 Constable (Mahila) Kamlesh Kumari, Central Reserve Police Force (posthumous)—13 December 2001, Parliament House, New Delhi—No. 20-Pres./02 of 25 January 2002

Shri Jagdish Prasad Yadav, Security Assistant, Parliament House (posthumous)—13 December 2001, Parliament House, New Delhi—No. 20-Pres./02 of 25 January 2002

Shri Matbar Singh Negi, Security Assistant, Parliament House (posthumous)—13 December 2001, Parliament House, New Delhi—No. 20-Pres./02 of 25 January 2002

JC-498232 Subedar Surinder Singh, 3rd Battalion, Sikh Regiment (posthumous)—3 March 2002—Rajouri sector, Jammu and Kashmir—No. 213-Pres./2002 of 15 August 2002

Subedar Suresh Chand Yadav, National Security Guard (NSG) (posthumous)—24 September 2002, Akshardham temple, Gujarat—No. 29-Pres/2003 of 25 January 2003

9423984 Paratrooper Sanjog Chhetri, 9th Para Commando (Special Forces) (posthumous)—22 April 2003—Hill Kaka, Jammu and Kashmir—No. 251-Pres./2003 of 21 November 2003

IC-61417 Lieutenant Triveni Singh, 5th Battalion, Jammu and Kashmir Light Infantry (posthumous)—Jammu, Jammu and Kashmir—No. 17-Pres./2004 of 25 January 2004

Outline

1003.100 Ashoka Chakra, Class I (1952-67)—there is no difference between this medal and the one that follows, only the records would reveal the distinction.

1003.200 Ashoka Chakra (1967-   )—there is no difference between this medal and the one which precedes, only the records would reveal the distinction.

1004 पद्म विभूषण / PADMA VIBHUSHAN[21]

Awarded to recognize exceptional and distinguished service to the nation.

Established: Established by notification No. 2-Pres./54 of 2 January 1954. The statutes were revised by No. 2-Pres./55 of 8 January 1955 (to redesign the badge and remove the class structure) and further amended by No. 26-Pres./55 of 30 August 1955 (to make provision for a miniature badge of the award) and No. 7-Pres./57 of 26 January 1957 (when the award was

[21]*Encyclopedia of Soldiers with Highest Gallantry Awards*, pp. 13-15; *India's Highest Gallantry Awards*, pp. 15-17; Haynes, 'Medals and Decorations of the Republic of India', pp. 26-28; Das, *Traditions and Customs*, p. 270; Dorling, *Ribbons & Medals*, p. 293; Scandaluzzi, *Medal Ribbons of the World*, vol. 3: *India*.

further redesigned, as detailed below). Award of the decoration was suspended from 13 July 1977 to 26 January 1980 (No. 65-Pres./77 and No. 25-Pres./80).

General Appearance: The decoration is a large circular geometrical badge, 30 mm in diameter.

Obverse: The badge specified in January 1955 was to be a 'mainly circular' 30 mm toned bronze badge with geometrical patterns and, in the centre, a lotus flower with four major petals embossed in white gold. Above and below this flower, the name of the decoration 'पद्म विभूषण' or 'Padma Vibhushan' was to be embossed in silver gilt. In 1957, the badge itself was altered to be of burnished bronze, with all embossing in white gold.

Reverse: In the centre, the national emblem with motto below, in white gold.

Ribbon: 32 mm, lotus pink. Female recipients are authorized to wear the badge from a bow fashioned from this ribbon. Some sources suggest that the initial ribbon for the Padma Vibhushan, Pahela Varg, was to have been a light pink with a single narrow white central stripe; ribbons in such design exist in some collections. Since 1981, a darker pink has been used for the Padma Vibhushan ribbon and the ribbon has had corded edges. While no documentation for these ribbon alterations has been found, the shifts in ribbon colour are supported by observation of specimens. All badges are awarded with a silver floriated brooch bar.

Suspension: The badge is suspended by a fixed, non-swivelling ring.

Naming: Issued unnamed.

Miniature: A miniature with brooch bar was provided for in 1957.

Background: The Padma Vibhushan is awarded to recognize exceptional and distinguished service to the nation, in any field, including services rendered by government servants. The decoration may be awarded posthumously.

The Padma Vibhushan was originally established, in January 1954, as the 'Pahela Varg' or 'First Class' of a three-class 'Padma Vibhushan' award. This was originally described as a circular gold gilt medal, 34 mm ($1^3/_8$ inches) in diameter, with an embossed lotus flower in the centre with the legend 'पद्म विभूषण' ('Padma Vibhushan') above and a floral wreath below. The reverse was to depict the state emblem with the legend 'देश सेवा' ('Desh Seva' or 'National Service') above and a lotus wreath below. This medal was to be worn from the ribbon described earlier. The first award of the Padma Vibhushan, Pahela Varg, was to H.H. Maharaja Jigme Dorji Wangchuk of Bhutan on 13 January 1954 (No. 7-Pres./54) and it seems likely that this award was of the first design. This design was altered within a year, on 8 January 1955, to that described above.

The original (1954) statutes of the decoration provided for bars to represent subsequent awards of the medal; no record of any such awards has been located. This provision has been dropped since the 1955 modifications and, in practice, most initial appointments have been to Padma Shri (1010), with subsequent promotions to Padma Bhushan (1005) and Padma

1004.220 Padma Vibhushan

Vibhushan representing continued national service of an increasingly high order. Direct appointments to higher levels of the award have also been noted.

As is discussed in the entry for the Bharat Ratna (1001), the constitutional status of these national awards has always been vague. From 13 July 1977 until 26 January 1980, awards of this decoration were suspended. In January 1993, the government requested the opinion of the Supreme Court, which upheld their award in a decision in 1995. The Venkataraman Committee in 1996 recommended their continuation, but with modifications in the process by which recommendations were reviewed.

Representative Citation: To understand the award better, a sample recipient would be Air Chief Marshal Om Prakash Mehra, Indian Air Force, awarded 26 January 1977:

Former Chief of the Air Staff, Air Chief Marshal Om Prakash Mehra, served the Indian Air Force with distinction. Born on 19-1-1919, he joined the IAFVR on 30th November 1940 as a Commissioned Officer. He served in the North West Frontier and in Burma-Arakan Coast with No. 3 Squadron. In 1946 he served as representative of the Indian Air Force with the Indian defence contingent of the Joint Chiefs of Staff in Australia, an organization representing Britain, Australia, New Zealand and India which was responsible for the control of elements/formations of the defence services of these countries in Japan.

In 1947 he took over command of the Flying Training School at Jodhpur. In the Air Force, he held various posts, including Director of Training, Senior Air Staff Officer of Operational Group, Commander Armament Training Wing and Air Officer-in-Charge Policy and Plans at Air HQ. He served as Dean of the Institute of Armament Technology for 3 years. He was appointed Deputy Chief of the Air Staff in 1969. In January 1971 he was selected as Chairman, Hindustan Aeronautics Limited, Bangalore. He took over as Chief of the Air Staff on 15th January, 1973 and relinquished the appointment on 31st January, 1976, on retirement.

Air Chief Marshal Mehra was awarded the Param Vishisht Seva Medal in 1968. Being deeply interested in sports and physical education, he is currently the President of the National Indian Olympic Association and is a member of the Board of Governors of the Society for the National Institutes of Physical Education and Sports.[22]

Awards are notified in the *Gazette of India Extraordinary*, part 1, section 1. Although citations are not given, they do appear in the brochures distributed at the investiture ceremonies.

Outline

1004.100 Padma Vibhushan, Pahela Varg (1954-55).

1004.200 Padma Vibhushan, geometrical badge.

    1004.210 badge in toned bronze and embossing in white gold and silver gilt (1955-57).

    1004.220 badge in burnished bronze and embossing in white gold (1957-).

[22] India, Ministry of Home Affairs, *Compilaton of the Recipients of Bharat Ratna and Padma Awards*, 3: 54.

1005 पद्म भूषण / PADMA BHUSHAN[23]

Awarded to recognize distinguished service to the nation of a high order.

Established: Established in notification No. 2-Pres./54 of 2 January 1954. The statutes were revised by No. 3-Pres./55 of 8 January 1955 to alter the design and to remove the class structure and further amended by No. 27-Pres./55 of 30 August 1955 (to make provision for a miniature badge of the award) and by No. 8-Pres./57 of 26 January 1957 (when the award was further redesigned, as detailed below). Award of the decoration was suspended from 13 July 1977 to 26 January 1980.

General Appearance: A large circular geometrical badge, 30 mm in diameter.

Obverse: The badge specified in January 1955 was to be a 'mainly circular' 30 mm toned bronze badge with geometrical patterns and, in the centre, a lotus flower with three major petals embossed in silver gilt. Above and below this flower, the name of the decoration 'पद्म भूषण' or 'Padma Bhushan' was to be embossed in silver gilt. In 1957, the badge itself was altered to be of burnished bronze, with all embossing in silver gilt.

Reverse: In the centre, the national emblem, with motto below, in silver gilt.

Ribbon: 32 mm, medium pink (officially, 'lotus-coloured') with a 6 mm central white stripe (medium pink 13 mm, white 6 mm, medium pink 13 mm). Female recipients are authorized to wear the badge from a bow fashioned from this ribbon. Some sources suggest that the initial ribbon for the Padma Vibhushan, Dusra Varg, was to have been a light pink with two narrow white central stripes; ribbons in such design exist in some collections. Since 1981, a darker pink has been used for the Padma Bhushan ribbon and the ribbon has had corded edges. While no documentation for these ribbon alterations has been found, the shifts in ribbon colour are supported by observation of specimens. All badges are awarded with a silver gilt floriated brooch bar.

Suspension: The badge is suspended by a fixed, non-swivelling ring.

Naming: Issued unnamed.

Miniature: A miniature with brooch bar was provided for in 1957.

Background: The Padma Bhushan is awarded to recognize distinguished service of a high order to the nation, in any field, including services rendered by government servants. The decoration may be awarded posthumously.

The Padma Bhushan was originally established, in January 1954, as the 'Dusra Varg' or 'Second Class' of a three-class 'Padma Vibhushan' award. This medal was originally described as circular silver medal, 34 mm (1³/₈ inches) in diameter, with an embossed lotus flower in the centre with the legend 'पद्म विभूषण' ('Padma Vibhushan') above and a floral wreath below. The reverse was to depict the state emblem with the legend 'देश सेवा' ('Desh Seva' or 'National Service') above and a lotus wreath below. This medal was to be worn from the ribbon described above. The first award of the Padma Vibhushan, Dusra Varg,

1005.220 Padma Bhushan

[23]*Encyclopedia of Soldiers with Highest Gallantry Awards*, pp. 16-17; *India's Highest Gallantry Awards*, pp. 18-20; Haynes, 'Medals and Decorations of the Republic of India', pp. 27-28; Das, *Traditions and Customs*, p. 270; Dorling, *Ribbons & Medals*, p. 293; Scandaluzzi, *Medal Ribbons of the World*, vol. 3: *India*.

was to Lieutenant Colonel Maharaj Kumar Palden Thondup Namgyal of Sikkim on 22 February 1954 (No. 14-Pres./54) and it is probable that this award was of the first pattern. This design was altered within a year, on 8 January 1955, to that described above.

The original (1954) statutes of the decoration provided for bars to represent subsequent awards of the medal; no record of any such awards has been located. This provision has been dropped since the 1955 modifications and, in practice, most initial appointments have been to Padma Shri (1010), with subsequent promotions to Padma Bhushan and Padma Vibhushan (1004) representing continued national service of an increasingly high order, although direct appointments to higher levels of the award have been also noted.

As is discussed in the entry for the Bharat Ratna (1001), the constitutional status of these national awards has always been vague. From 13 July 1977 until 26 January 1980, awards of this decoration were suspended. In January 1993, the government requested the opinion of the Supreme Court, which upheld their award in a decision in 1995. The Venkataraman Committee in 1996 receommended their continuation, but with modifications in the process by which recommendations were reviewed.

Representative Citation: To understand the award better, a sample recipient would be the 26 January 1971 award to Shri Jainendra Kumar Jain:

Born at Kaundiaganj (Aligarh) in 1905, Shri Jainendra Kumar Jain received his early education in Risyam Brahmachary-ashram, Hastinapur. His college education was interrupted by his participation in the freedom movement.

Shri Jain took to writing and his first collection of stories 'Phansi' was published in 1929. His novel 'Parakh' and his first book on his thoughts 'Jainendra Ke Vichar' was published in 1930. His writings soon established him as a distinguished author sensitive to the socio-political changes with a degree of compassion and perspicacity worthy of a social reformer. He has set a new trend in Hindi fiction after Prem Chand. One of his novels 'Tyaga Patra' has been translated in several Indian and foreign languages. His works mark him out as an able exponent of Gandhian thought and philosophy.

Sri Jain has made significant contribution to the development of Hindi literature, and literary organizations. He has received a number of awards including the Sahitya Academy Award for his book 'Muktibodh'. He has attended several international literary seminars, conferences and conventions.

He has to his credit several novels, collections of stories, thought-books, translations (novel, drama and collection of stories) and travelogues.[24]

(No. 8-Pres./71 of 26 January 1971)

Awards are notified in the *Gazette of India Extraordinary*. Although citations are not given, they do appear in the brochures distributed at the investiture ceremonies.

[24] India, Ministry of Home Affairs, *Compilaton of the Recipients of Bharat Ratna and Padma Awards*, 2: 208.

Outline

1005.100 Padma Vibhushan, Dusra Varg (1954-55).

1005.200 Padma Bhushan, geometrical badge.

1005.210 badge in toned bronze and embossing in white gold and silver gilt (1955-57).

1005.220 badge in burnished bronze and embossing in silver gilt (1957-).

1006 सर्वोत्तम युद्ध सेवा मैडल / SARVOTTAM YUDDH SEVA MEDAL[25]

Awarded to members of the armed forces for distinguished services of a most exceptional order during war/conflict/hostilities.

Established: No. 40-Pres./80 of 26 June 1980.

General Appearance: Circular 35 mm 'gold-gilt' medal. Some specimens observed have very light gilding.

Obverse: The state emblem with the name of the decoration in Hindi and English above, सर्वोत्तम युद्ध सेवा मैडल / Sarvottam Yuddh Seva Medal'. In some cases, including official investiture brochures and even officially distributed specimen medals, this seems to have been shown as the reverse, but this description is based on the gazette notification, which has not been altered. In fact, the depiction of the state emblem on the obverse follows a policy decision taken in 1970, whereby all future medals, commencing with the 9 and 20 Years Long Service and 25th Independence Anniversary medals, were to be 35 mm in diameter with the state emblem (Ashoka Lion with motto) and the name of the medal in Hindi depicted on the obverse.[26]

Reverse: A five-pointed star. The five-pointed star occupies a central space in Indian medal design, occurring as a motif in the distinguished service (Yuddh and Vishisht Seva) series, as well in the second and third tier of gallantry awards (Maha Vir and Vir Chakra). The official explanation of its symbolic intent states: 'The star, a heavenly body known for its firm, steady and fixed position, symbolises everlasting glory.'[27] This was confirmed by the officer who was responsible for finalising the design of the Vishisht Seva medals at Army headquarters in 1960, Brigadier A.K. Sahukar, A.V.S.M.[28]

Ribbon: 32 mm, golden, with a central 2 mm red stripe. Award of a second award bar is indicated on the ribbon when worn alone by the addition of a circular gold-gilt rosette.

Suspension: Suspended from a fixed straight-bar suspender.

Naming: The medal is named on the edge. Unlike the earlier issues of other Presidential awards (both Chakra and Vishisht Seva series), the Yudh Seva series of medals were never dated on the rim.

Miniature: Miniatures have been issued.

Background: This is an operational version of the Param Vishisht Seva Medal (1007) and, following its creation, the P.V.S.M. has been restricted to peacetime awards. The award carries with it the right to use 'S.Y.S.M.' as postnominal letters. Provision has been made for the award of a bar for subsequent awards. Though no such bars have been awarded; such a bar

1006.100 Sarvottam Yuddh Seva Medal

[25] *India's Highest Gallantry Awards*, pp. 21-22; Das, *Traditions and Customs*, pp. 272-73.

[26] MoD History Division Heraldic Section. Army HQ AG's Branch letter dated 9 January 1970 'Design of New Medals'.

[27] B.C. Chakravorty, *Stories of Heroism*, ed. U.P. Thapliyal, History Division, Ministry of Defence, Government of India (New Delhi: Allied Publishers, 1995), p. 39.

[28] Interview with the authors. Brigadier Adi Sahukar was commissioned into the RIASC in 1941 and served with the RIASC GPT convoys carrying supplies from Iran to Russia during the Second World War. Posted to the AG's Branch at Army HQ, Delhi, in 1959, he was tasked with finalising the design of the new set of medals then being instituted. Apart from the VSM series, he also was instrumental in designing the Sainya Seva and Videsh Seva Medals and their ribbons.

would be designated on dress ribbons by the addition of a gilt rosette. The decoration may also be awarded posthumously. Provincial stipends awarded for this decoration are detailed in Appendix 2.

Awards: Through 26 January 2003, the S.Y.S.M. has been awarded only three times. The first award, in 1989, was to Lieutenant General A.S. Kalkat for leading the IPKF operations in Sri Lanka. On 15 August 1999, the medal was awarded to Air Marshal Vinod Patney, P.V.S.M., A.V.S.M., Vr.C., Air Officer Commanding-in-Chief Western Air Command, Indian Air Force, who led the highly successful Indian air operations in 'Safed Sagar/Operation Vijay' in the Kargil area of Jammu and Kashmir in May/July 1999. In January 2000, Lieutenant General Hari Mohan Khanna, P.V.S.M., A.V.S.M., was awarded the decoration, also for Operation Vijay.

Representative Citation: In order to understand the award better, a sample recipient would be IC-12315 Lieutenant General Hari Mohan Khanna, P.V.S.M., A.V.S.M., Infantry:

Lieutenant General Hari Mohan Khanna, P.V.S.M., A.V.S.M., was appointed to the command of the operationally strategic Northern Command in January 1999.

A seasoned soldier with a vast and varied experience in operational commands, Lieutenant General Hari Mohan Khanna, P.V.S.M., A.V.S.M., provided inspiring generalship, and strategic direction of the highest order during the conduct of OP VIJAY which were decisive in repelling the Pak-inspired aggression in Jammu and Kashmir in May 1999.

OP VIJAY was a conflict like no other, fought in extremely inhospitable terrain, under severe operational constraints (to prevent it from spilling into an all-out-war), against an enemy which held unassailable commanding heights in a neo-nuclear scenario, under constnt international scrutiny and media attention—an extremely delicate operational tight-rope for senior military commanders. It was against this extraordinary backdrop that Lieutenant General Hari Mohan Khanna, P.V.S.M., A.V.S.M. conducted a surgically precise and finely orchestrated military campaign in the Mushkoh, Drass, Batalik and Turtuk sectors of Jammu and Kashmir which involved extensive mobilisation aganist time, rapid deployment of operational forces in consonance with well-conceived plans and judicious application of scarce logistic resources to meet the threat of Pakistani aggression. In his single minded pursuit of the campaign, he constantly revised and recast plans to meet new and rapidly evolving operational situations and seized virtually non-existent opportunities to snatch the initiative, finally unhinging and throwing back the enemy from his occupied positions to restore the sanctity of the line of control. His refreshingly unorthodox ideas in the use of artillery and air power, and inclination to seek less than obvious solutions in the employment of ground forces, both of which were evident in the campaign in abundant measure were chiefly responsible for the accelerated conduct of operations and an early victory well before winter.

During the campaign, he synergised and rallied his army moving tirelessly from military formation to formation, often at great personal risk, to counsel, guide and exhort his subordiante commanders in achieving time bound operational goals. His frequent presence on the front served as a source of inspiration for men and officers alike. Motivated by his inspiring generalship and consummate operational direction, officers and jawans under his command rose to the occasion in the face of great odds and performed rare feats of bravery and sacrifice in combat to decisively annihiliate the Pakistani Army intruders in Kargil.

As the principal architect of our triumphs in OP VIJAY, Lieutenant General Hari Mohan Khanna, P.V.S.M., A.V.S.M., General Officer Commanding-in-Chief, Northern Command demonstrated in ample measure, inspiring generalship, rare operational vision, profound commitment in attainment of goals, thus rendering to the country, war-time military service of the highest distinction and national significance.

(No. 64-Pres./2000 of 26 January 2000)

Outline

1006.100 medal.

1007 परम विशिष्ट सेवा मैडल / PARAM VISHISHT SEVA MEDAL[29]

Awarded for the highest levels of distinguished service by members of the armed forces.

Established: By No. 19-Pres./60 of 26 January 1960 and by No. 32-Pres./60 of 2 June 1960, as the 'Vishisht Seva Medal, Class I'. The statutes were revised by No. 34-Pres./62 of 30 April 1962 to clarify the fact that awards were conferred by the President of India by a *sanad* (parchment) under his hand and seal. The award was further revised, redesigned, and renamed by No. 31-Pres./67 of 27 January 1967. It was later further modified by No. 25-Pres./91 of 14 February 1991 to include members of the General Reserve Engineer Force among the eligible personnel.

General Appearance: A 35 mm circular gold-gilt medal. The gilt is very thin, and frequently is virtually invisible.

Obverse: A five-pointed star in the centre.

Reverse: The state emblem with the name of the decoration in Hindi above. Until 1967, this would have been 'विशिष्ट सेवा मैडल' ('Vishisht Seva Medal'), the class being implied by the metal in which the decoration was produced. After 1967, the legend was altered, predictably, to 'परम विशिष्ट सेवा मैडल' ('Param Vishisht Seva Medal').

Ribbon: 32 mm, yellow, described as 'gold' in the instituting notification, with a 2 mm central stripe of dark blue. Some sources suggest two varieties of ribbon: 1960-81, 32 mm with a 2 mm central stripe; and after 1981, changed to a darker yellow and the central stripe narrowed to 1 mm. But this seems to merely reflect widely variant manufacturing of the ribbon and not official change in design or policy.

Suspension: Suspended from a fixed straight-bar suspender.

Naming: Named and dated (for early awards) on the edge.

Miniature: Miniatures have been issued.

Background: The Param Vishisht Seva Medal is awarded to recognize 'distinguished service of the most exceptional order' by all ranks of the armed forces. In practice, however, the award tends to be granted only to the most senior officers of the various branches of the Indian military. Today, the medal has

1007.100 Vishisht Seva Medal, Class I

1007.200 Param Vishisht Seva Medal

[29]*Encyclopedia of Soldiers with Highest Gallantry Awards*, pp. 18-19; *India's Highest Gallantry Awards*, pp. 23-24; Haynes, 'Medals and Decorations of the Republic of India', pp. 29-39; Das, *Traditions and Customs*, p. 273; Scandaluzzi, *Medal Ribbons of the World*, vol. 3: *India*.

1007A Bar to P.V.S.M.

become virtually a subsidiary badge of rank for Lieutenant-Generals and their equivalents in the other services; the days when the P.V.S.M. was open to other ranks and enlisted personnel have seemingly long passed. The award may be granted posthumously and subsequent awards are represented by a bar worn on the ribbon.

When such a bar is awarded, it is indicated by the addition of a gilt rosette to the ribbon bar when worn alone. At least two bars to the P.V.S.M. have been awarded (Rear Admiral Bansh Raj Singh, P.V.S.M., I.N., 17-Pres/72 of 20 January 1972, and Major General Naresh Kumar, P.V.S.M., Artillery, 27-Pres./89 of 26 January 1989). The award carries with it the right to use 'P.V.S.M.' as postnominal letters.

The Param Vishisht Seva Medal was originally established as the 'Vishisht Seva Medal, Class I' and only on 27 January 1967 was it renamed and the badge redesigned as detailed above.

Until 1980, the P.V.S.M. could be awarded for distinguished service in both war and peace. However, in 1980, the Sarvottam Yuddh Seva Medal (1006) was created to recognize distinguished services in an operational environment. Since that date, awards of the P.V.S.M. have been restricted to peacetime service. Provincial stipends accompanying this award are detailed in Appendix 2.

Through 26 January 2003, the award has been bestowed 762 times, of these, there were thirty-one awards of the VSM, class I.

Representative Citation: To understand the award better, a sample recipient would be IC-1641, Major General Inderjit Singh Gill, M.C., Infantry:

Major General Inderjit Singh Gill was commissioned in the Corps of Engineers in 1942 and later on transferred to the Infantry. He saw active service during World War II in the Middle East and was awarded [the] Military Cross. He was also mentioned in Despatches. He served as a member of the Security Force in Korea in 1953-54. He graduated from the Defence Services Staff College in 1956 and successfully completed the Command and General Staff Course in the USA in 1962. He has credibly [*sic*] held several staff and command appointments including those of Officer Commanding a Battalion of the PARA Regiment, Instructor Class 'A' at the Defence Services Staff College, Commandant, Army Headquarters Training Team, Commander of a Mountain Brigade and an Infantry Brigade. He is holding the appointment of General Officer Commanding a Mountain Division since April, 1968. During 2nd to 4th October, 1968, when there were heavy floods and land slides in Sikkim due to torrential rain, and the road and signal communications were completely disrupted, Major General Gill, on his own initiative, organized the re-establishment of communications in his entire sector speedily and efficiently. He walked on all the roads through land slides and nullahs to carry out proper assessment of the task. He also assisted the civil population.

(No. 11-Pres./69 of 26 January 1969)

Outline

1007.100 Vishisht Seva Medal, Class I (1952-67).
1007.200 Param Vishisht Seva Medal (1967-).

1008 महावीर चक्र / MAHA VIR CHAKRA[30]

Awarded for acts of valour in the presence of the enemy.

Established: A draft royal warrant was prepared in October 1948 for the possible institution of this award in the name of the British sovereign as, during the Dominion period, such a step would have been necessary to give the award status within the Commonwealth. On consideration, this course was abandoned and the medal was created by No. 1-Pres./50 of 26 January 1950, by the President of India (with effect from 15 August 1947). The statutes were amended by No. 2-Pres./52 of 4 January 1952, by No. 54-Pres./69 of 18 September 1969, and by No. 61-Pres./69 of 14 October 1969.

General Appearance: A 34 mm (1-3/8 inch) circular silver medal.

Obverse: A five-pointed star. On the centre of this star, a domed gilded state emblem.

Reverse: Around a plain centre, two legends separated by lotus flowers: above 'महावीर चक्र' and below 'MAHA VIR CHAKRA'.

Ribbon: 32 mm, half white, half orange-saffron. The orange is worn towards the left shoulder.

Suspension: The medal is suspended from a swivelling straight-bar suspender.

Naming: The medal was almost always seen named and dated on the edge until about 1970, after which the date no longer seems to have been inscribed on the rim.

Miniature: Miniatures have been issued.

Background: Awarded for acts of valour in the presence of the enemy. It may be awarded posthumously.

Provision was made for the award of a bar for a second award of the Maha Vir Chakra, the first two being awarded in 1965. To date, there are six known awards of a first bar: Squadron Leader (later Wing Commander) Jag Mohan Nath (1962 and 1 September 1965), Major General Rajindar Singh (19 March 1948 and 6 September 1965), Brigadier (later General) Arun Shridar Vaidya (16 September 1965 and 5 December 1971), Wing Commander Padmanabha Gautam (6 September 1965 and 5 December 1971), Major Chewang Rinchen (July 1948 and 8 December 1971), and Brigadier Sant Singh (2 November 1965 and January 1972). To date, no second bars have been awarded. When such bars are awarded, an 11 mm silver chakra is added to the ribbon when worn alone.

Award of the decoration carries with it the right to use M.V.C. as a postnominal abbreviation.

The award originally carried a cash allowance for those under the rank of second lieutenant (or the appropriate service equivalent) and, in some cases, a lump sum cash award; over the years these benefits have been expanded across the ranks and increased as discussed elsewhere. On the death of the recipient, the pension was transferred to the widow until her death or remarriage. This pension has been a rather controversial issue throughout the life of the decoration. When the decoration was created, the monthly stipend was Rs. 30 (Rs. 50 in the case of those who had previously been awarded

1008.100 Maha Vir Chakra

1008A Undress ribbon 'chakra' device used to indicate award of a second award bar to a medal.

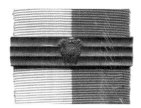

1008B Bar to Maha Vir Chakra

[30] *Encyclopedia of Soldiers with Highest Gallantry Awards*, pp. 4-5, 207-70, 592, 594; *India's Highest Gallantry Awards*, pp. 3-4, 207-303; Haynes, 'Medals and Decorations of the Republic of India', pp. 7-8; Das, *Traditions and Customs*, p. 271; Dorling, *Ribbons & Medals*, p. 144; Scandaluzzi, *Medal Ribbons of the World*, vol. 3: *India*.

the British Military Cross or Military Medal) with a provision for an additional Rs. 10 per month for each bar to the M.V.C. For Gorkhas of Nepalese domicile, the award was a lump sum payment of Rs. 2,000. Over time, these stipends have been increased although they are, in the opinion of many public commentators, still too low. By March 1999, the stipend stood at Rs. 1,200 per month with an additional Rs. 25 authorized for the award of a bar. In addition, many states have established individual pension rewards for the recipients of the decoration. These stipends are detailed in Appendix 2.

Through 2003, the award has been bestowed 212 times.

Representative Citation: To understand the award better, a sample recipient would be IC-9015 Lieutenant Colonel Sawai Bhawani Singh, Parachute Regiment:

On the night of 5 December 1971, Lt. Col. Sawai Bhawani Singh, who was commanding a battalion of the Parachute Regiment (Commandos), led his men deep into the enemy territory and for four days and nights, with complete disregard for his personal comfort and safety, made skillful and relentless raids on the strongly held enemy posts at Chachro and Virawah.

His inspired leadership and personal courage led to the capture of large areas of the enemy territory and created panic and confusion among the enemy, forcing him to retreat leaving behind large number of prisoners and equipment.

In this operation, Lt. Col. Sawai Bhawani Singh set an example of personal courage, exceptional qualities of leadership and devotion to duty in the highest traditions of the Indian Army.

(No. 18-Pres/72 of 20 January 1972)

Outline

1008.100 medal.

1009 कीर्ति चक्र / KIRTI CHAKRA[31]

Awarded for conspicuous gallantry other than in the face of the enemy.

Established: Established as the 'Ashoka Chakra, Class II' by No. 1-Pres./52 of 4 January 1952 (with effect from 15 August 1947). The statutes were revised and the decoration renamed by No. 30-Pres./67 of 27 January 1967. A further amendment was incorporated in No. 53-Pres./84 of 10 April 1984, making non-Indian citizens eligible for the award.

General Appearance: Circular silver medal, 35 mm in diameter.

Obverse: In the centre, the *chakra* (wheel) of Ashoka, surrounded by a lotus wreath and with an ornate edge of lotus leaves, flowers and buds.

Reverse: For pre-1967 awards, the medal is blank in the centre, with 'अशोक चक्र' along the upper edge on the medal and the same name in English along the lower rim, 'ASHOKA CHAKRA', the two inscriptions being separated by two lotus flowers. The centre is blank. There is no indication of the class on the pre-1967 awards and it is implied by the metal and

[31]*Encyclopedia of Soldiers with Highest Gallantry Awards,* pp. 20-21; *India's Highest Gallantry Awards,* pp. 25-26; Haynes, 'Medals and Decorations of the Republic of India', pp. 11-12; Das, *Traditions and Customs,* p. 272; Dorling, *Ribbons & Medals,* p. 293; Scandaluzzi, *Medal Ribbons of the World,* vol. 3: *India.*

ribbon design. For the post-1967 awards, the inscriptions were changed to 'कीर्ति चक्र' above and 'KIRTI CHAKRA' below.

Ribbon: 32 mm, dark green divided into three equal segments by two equally spaced 2 mm orange stripes. The green colour is intended to denote auspiciousness and the orange represents renunciation and sacrifice. While some variation has been observed in the ribbon over time, officially there has been no change in the ribbon design. The variations seen in ribbon design over time are: 1952-67, 32 mm with two equally spaced 2 mm orange stripes; 1967-81, 38 mm with two 1.5 mm white stripes in the centre, 1.5 mm apart; and after 1981, 32 mm with two equally spaced 1.5 mm orange stripes. There is no evidence to support these assertions of change over time and, as usual, much is being made of simple variations in manufacture.

Suspension: Suspended by a non-swivelling straight-bar suspender.

Naming: The medal is named and dated on the edge. However, it is not clear if the practise of dating still continues or has been discontinued along with the combat gallantry series of awards since about 1970.

Miniature: Miniatures have been issued.

Background: Awarded for 'conspicuous gallantry' in situations other than in the face of the enemy. Many of the awards, especially recently, have been made to military and paramilitary personnel for counter-insurgency and anti-terrorist operations. The Kirti Chakra can be awarded to military personnel as well as to civilians. Police personnel and members of recognized fire services are, however, explicitly excluded from the award in the notified statutes. The medal may be awarded posthumously. Notification of awards is published in the *Gazette of India*, part 1, section 1.

Subsequent awards of the Kirti Chakra are recognized by a bar to the medal ribbon (but to date none have been awarded). When such a bar is awarded, it is indicated on the ribbon when worn alone by the addition of a silver miniature of the chakra. It is possible for a recipient to be awarded the Ashoka Chakra (1003) or Shaurya Chakra (1015) in addition for separate acts of gallantry.

In 1984, non-Indian citizens were also made eligible for the award of the medal 'in exceptional circumstances'. While a high standard of gallantry has been maintained for the award of this decoration, a somewhat incongruous 'political' award was that made to the officer who was the 'standby' to India's first cosmonaut, Squadron Leader Rakesh Sharma, who was awarded the Ashoka Chakra for his mission into space. Similarly, the exceptional award to Shri A.K. Doval, IPS, for exhibiting 'remarkable resourcefulness, dedication and devotion to duty'[32] was not only in violation of the instituting statutes, but also served to degrade the accepted standard of gallantry apparently to suit a temporary expedient.

When the decoration was created, no provision was made for any monetary stipend from the central government. It was, however, decided that for recipients whose families were in

1009.100 Ashoka Chakra Class II

1009.200 Kirti Chakra

[32] Chakravorty, *Stories of Heroism*, vol. II *(Ashok Chakra & Kirti Chakra Winners)*, ed. U.P. Thapliyal, History Division, Ministry of Defence, Govt. of India, 1997, p. 109.

'indigent' circumstances (defined as having an annual income under Rs. 3,000), a monthly allowance of Rs. 25 was appropriate. Over time, these stipends have been increased although they are, in the opinion of many public commentators, still too low. By 1 February 1999, the stipend stood at Rs. 1,050 per month with an additional Rs. 20 authorized for the award of a bar. Provincial stipends are detailed in Appendix 2.

The decoration carries with it the right to use 'K.C.' as a postnominal abbreviation.

Through 2003, the award has been bestowed 563 times.

Representative Citation: To understand the award better, a sample recipient would be No. 90919 Lance-Naik Amar Singh Rana, 9th Battalion, Assam Rifles:

On the 14th Aug. 1957 at about 1800 hours two sections of Assam Rifles while escorting some porters and stores from Lukhyekhe to Seyochang ran into a hostile ambush. Due to poor visibility the troops got separated from the porters and there was much confusion. L-Nk Amar Singh Rana and another Rfn found themselves cut off from the rest by a group of hostiles. The first volley of hostile fire badly wounded his comrade in the stomach. L-Nk Rana dashed forward to rescue the wounded Rfn. In doing so he was wounded in the left arm. Despite this injury he engaged the enemy group of about 10 men singlehanded for some time and carried the wounded Rfn to safety. As the return of fire from him was intermittent, the hostile party took courage and charged the cover behind which L-Nk Rana and his companion were sheltered. L-Nk Rana then pulled out a grenade and removing the pin with his teeth threw it at the charging hostiles. The first grenade killed the leader of the hostile party. He then quickly threw a second grenade removed from the wounded Rfn and inflicted wounds on two more of the hostiles causing them to retreat.

L-Nk Amar Singh Rana's courageous action prevented the wounded soldier and his weapons and ammunition from falling into the hands of the hostiles. His gallant action was in the highest traditions of the Assam Rifles.

(No. 27-Pres./59, of 23 April 1959)

Outline

1009.100 Ashoka Chakra, Class II (1952-67).
1009.200 Kirti Chakra (1967-).

1010 पद्म श्री / PADMA SHRI[33]

Awarded to recognize distinguished service in any field.

Established: Established by No. 2-Pres./54 of 2 January 1954. The statutes were revised by No. 4-Pres./55 of 8 January 1955 to alter the design remove the class structure and further amended by No. 28-Pres./55 of 30 August 1955 (to make provision for a miniature badge of the award) and by No. 9-Pres./57 of 26 January 1957 (when the award was further redesigned, as detailed below). Award of the decoration was suspended from 13 July 1977 to 26 January 1980.

General Appearance: The medal is a large circular geometrical badge, 30 mm in diameter.

Obverse: The badge as specified in January 1955 was to be a 'mainly circular' 30 mm toned bronze badge with geometrical

[33] *Encyclopedia of Soldiers with Highest Gallantry Awards,* pp. 22-23; *India's Highest Gallantry Awards,* pp. 27-29; Haynes, 'Medals and Decorations of the Republic of India', pp. 27-28; Das, *Traditions and Customs,* p. 270; Dorling, *Ribbons & Medals,* p. 293; Scandaluzzi, *Medal Ribbons of the World,* vol. 3: *India.*

patterns and, in the centre, a lotus flower with five major petals embossed in white gold. Above and below this flower, the name of the decoration 'पद्म श्री' or 'Padma Shri' was to be embossed in silver gilt. In 1957, the badge itself was altered to be of burnished bronze, with all embossing in silver.

Reverse: In the centre, the state emblem, with motto below in silver.

Ribbon: 32 mm, medium pink ('lotus-coloured') with two 6 mm white stripes. Female recipients are authorized to wear the badge from a bow fashioned from this ribbon. Some sources suggest that the initial ribbon for the Padma Vibhushan, Tisra Varg, was to have been a light pink with three narrow white central stripes; ribbons in such design exist in some collections. Since 1981, a darker pink has been used for the Padma Shri ribbon and the ribbon has had corded edges. While no documentation for these ribbon alterations has been found, the shifts in ribbon colour are supported by observation of specimens.

Suspension: The badge is suspended by a ring.

Naming: The award is unnamed.

Miniature: A miniature was provided for in 1957.

Background: The Padma Shri is awarded to recognize distinguished service to the nation in any field, including services rendered by government servants. The decoration may be awarded posthumously.

The Padma Shri was originally established in January 1954 as the 'Tisra Varg' or 'Third Class' of a three-class 'Padma Vibhushan' award. This medal was originally described as circular bronze medal, 34 mm ($1^3/_8$ inches) in diameter, with an embossed lotus flower in the centre with the legend 'पद्म विभूषण' or 'Padma Vibhushan' above and a floral wreath below. The reverse was to depict the state emblem with the legend 'देश सेवा' ('Desh Seva' or 'National Service') above and a lotus wreath below. This medal was to be worn from the ribbon described below. The first awards were gazetted on 27 April 1954 (No. 27-Pres./54) and may well have been of this first pattern. This design was altered within a year, on 8 January 1955, to that described above.

The original (1954) statutes of the decoration provided for bars to represent subsequent awards of the medal; no such awards were made. This provision has been dropped since the 1955 modifications and in practice most initial appointments have been to Padma Shri, with subsequent promotions to Padma Bhushan (1005) and Padma Vibhushan (1004) representing continued national service of an increasingly high order, although direct appointments to higher levels of the award have also been noted.

As is discussed in the entry for the Bharat Ratna (1001), the constitutional status of these national awards has always been vague. From 13 July 1977 until 26 January 1980, awards of this decoration were suspended. In January 1993, the government requested the opinion of the Supreme Court, which upheld their award in a decision in 1995. The Venkataraman Committee in 1996 recommended their continuation, but with

1010.220 Padma Shri

modifications in the process by which recommendations were reviewed.

Representative Citation: To understand the award better, a sample recipient would be the award of 26 January 1971 to Dr Harbhajan Singh, Head of the Plant Introduction Division, Indian Agricultural Research Institute, New Delhi:

Dr Harbhajan Singh (55) has conducted intensive research in Plant Breeding, Plant Genetics and Taxonomy and evolved a number of high yielding varieties of vegetables. He has arranged the systematic collection and dissemination of richly diverse germ plasm from exotic and indigenous sources for a wide variety of agri-horti-sylvicultural plants under phytosanitary conditions. Plant Breeders the world over, and those of India in particular have benefited from this activity. In the field of plant exploration he has carried out one-man trips and has also led teams of agricultural plant explorers, to different parts of India and neighbouring countries. This has helped in the collection of wide germ plasm comprising primitive and obsolete cultivation of many crop plants as well as of their wild relatives, which is a major contribution to the important task of stemming genetic erosion.

He played a leading role in the breeding and selection of nearly 40 varieties of field crops and vegetables several of which are of all-India importance. As Head of the Division of Plant Introduction, Indian Agricultural Research Institute, he has played an active part in the establishment and organization of the National Plant Introduction Service. He has published 120 scientific, technical and popular articles including monographs, bulletins, research reviews and others relating to agri-horticultural plants.

(No. 8-Pres./71 of 26 January 1971)[34]

Outline

1010.100 Padma Vibhushan, Tisra Varg.
1010.200 Padma Shri, geometrical badge.

1010.210 badge in toned bronze and embossing in white gold and silver gilt (1955-57).

1010.220 badge in burnished bronze and embossing in silver (1957-).

1011 सर्वोत्तम जीवन रक्षा पदक / SARVOTTAM JEEVAN RAKSHA PADAK / SUPREME LIFESAVING MEDAL[35]

Awarded to recognize conspicuous courage in acts of lifesaving.

Established: By No. 45-Pres./61 of 30 September 1961, as the 'Jeevan Raksha Padak, Class I'. The instituting gazette notification was unique in that apart from the Bharat Ratna and Padma awards, it is the only notification to carry an illustratitive sketch of the award, possibly because of its rather awkward design. The illustration shown in the original notification was amended in No. 7-Pres./62 of 18 January 1962. The statutes were revised and the decoration renamed by No. 79-Pres./67 of 26 August 1967.

General Appearance: A 58 mm essentially circular gold medal with a rectangular projection 22.5 × 12.5 mm at the top, and at the bottom, a 42.5 × 10 mm projection. This incredibly large

[34] India, Ministry of Home Affairs, *Compilaton of the Recipients of Bharat Ratna and Padma Awards*, 2: 230.

[35] *Encyclopedia of Soldiers with Highest Gallantry Awards*, pp. 24-25; *India's Highest Gallantry Awards*, pp. 30-31; Das, *Traditions and Customs*, p. 274; Scandaluzzi, *Medal Ribbons of the World*, vol. 3: *India*.

award seems more appropriate for table-top display than for wearing, and it is believed that most recipients who wear the award actually wear the half-sized miniature, which would be almost the same size as a normal medal.

Obverse: In the centre, a hand in the *Abhai Mudra* and, above 'मा भैः' and below 'जीवन रक्षा' ('Jeevan Raksha') (1961-67). The second variety uses the new name, 'सर्वोत्तम जीवन रक्षा' ('Sarvottam Jeevan Raksha') (after 1967).

Reverse: The state emblem with the motto 'Satyameva Jayate' (Truth Triumphs) in Devanagari in the lower projection.

Ribbon: 32 mm red with 4 mm light blue edge stripes and a 1 mm green centre stripe. These colours are said to symbolize fire (red), water (blue), and life (green).

Suspension: By a ring suspension.

Naming: Issued unnamed.

Miniature: Miniatures have been issued.

Background: Awarded to civilians to recognize acts of life-saving, including cases of drowning, fire, or mine accidents, 'for conspicuous courage under circumstances of very great danger to the life of the rescuer'. The only cases in which members of the armed forces, police, or fire services can be awarded the medal is when such acts take place outside the course of their duty. The medal may be awarded posthumously and subsequent awards are recognized by the addition of a bar to the medal ribbon. When the ribbon alone is worn, a bar is indicated by the addition of a gold miniature of the medal to that ribbon. Through 26 January 2004, no bar had yet been awarded; in that same period, the Sarvottam Jeevan Raksha Padak had been awarded only 67 times.

Recipients receive a cash award of Rs. 75,000.

Like many other Indian awards, the Sarvottam Jeevan Raksha Padak was originally established as a part of a three-class decoration, the Jeevan Raksha Padak in 1961. The first class of this award was renamed the Sarvottam Jeevan Raksha Padak in 1967.

Representative Citation: To understand the award better, a sample recipient would be the 1987 award to Smt. Ilaben Nayankumar Patel of Ahmedabad, Gujarat:

On the 4th February, 1984 at about 6:00 a.m., a panther, $7^1/_2$ feet long and $2^1/_2$ feet in height, apparently wandered off from a forest, entered the city of Ahmedabad, injured five persons, and thereafter entered the house of Mrs. Ilaben Nayankumar Patel where it attacked her $3^1/_2$ years old child. Smt. Ilaben showed remarkable courage. She not only snatched the child from the jaws of the panther but also managed to bolt the panther inside a room of her house. By this the area was saved from the wild animal; the panther was later captured and removed by the Zoo authorities. Smt. Patel was presented with a scroll of honour, a gold medal, and a reward of Rs. 2,001.00 by the Ahmedabad Municipal Corporation.

Smt. Ilaben Nayankumar Patel displayed exemplary courage and promptitude in saving the child from the clutches of the panther as well as in the capturing of the beast in her house.

(No. 13-Pres./87 of 5 February 1987)

1011.200 Sarvottam Jeevan Raksha Padak

1012.100 Uttam Yuddh Seva Medal

Outline

1012 उत्तम युद्ध सेवा मैडल / UTTAM YUDDH SEVA MEDAL[36]

Awarded to members of the armed forces for distinguished services of an exceptional order in war/conflict/hostilities.

Established: No. 40-Pres./80 of 26 June 1980.

General Appearance: Circular 35 mm gilt medal.

Obverse: The state emblem with the name of the decoration in Hindi and English above, 'उत्तम युद्ध सेवा मैडल / Uttam Yuddh Seva Medal'.

Reverse: A five-pointed star.

Ribbon: 32 mm, golden with two equally spaced 2 mm red stripes.

Suspension: Suspended from a fixed straight-bar suspender.

Naming: The medal is named on the edge. Unlike the earlier issues of other Presidential awards (both Chakra and Vishisht Seva series), the Yuddh Seva series of medals were never dated on the rim.

Miniature: Miniatures have been issued.

Background: Awarded for a high degree of distinguished service during war/conflict/hostilities. In many ways, this is an operational version of the Ati Vishisht Seva Medal (1013) which, since 1980, has been restricted to non-operational awards. The award carries with it the right to use 'U.Y.S.M.' as postnominal letters. The first awards of this medal were made in 1989, to five senior army, navy and air force officers for services rendered during Op Pawan in Sri Lanka.

Bars may be awarded for second or subsequent awards and when service ribbons are worn alone such a bar is indicated by the addition of a gilt rosette to that ribbon.

Provincial stipends for this award are detailed in Appendix 2.

Through 26 January 2003, the U.Y.S.M. has been awarded only thirty-seven times and no bars have been awarded.

Representative Citation: To understand the award better, a sample recipient would be Air Vice Marshal Jagnandan Kumar Pathania, A.V.S.M., V.S.M., Indian Air Force:

Air Vice Marshal JK Pathania (8053) Adm was commissioned on 11 Dec 1963 in Administrative branch. During his service career of 36 years he has held important field and staff assignments. He is a graduate of DSSC and is a recipient of Vishisht Seva Medal and Ati Vishisht Seva Medal.

During Op 'Safed Sagar', he was Senior Officer in-charge Administration at HQ WAC IAF. Immediately on declaration of operations, he initiated essential and vital measures at forward operational bases in J&K Sector, Punjab and Haryana to support sustained air operation. Augmented manpower was properly received, distributed and requisite admin facilities were set up in record time. Security arrangements at bases particularly at Srinagar and Awantipur were promptly beefed up through effective ground defence system and camouflaging to provide safe working environment. Emergency works services were planned and initiated most efficiently. Admin

[36] *India's Highest Gallantry Awards*, pp. 32-33; Das, *Traditions and Customs*, p. 273.

support services like uninterrupted stabilised electric and power supply were monitored and maintained to ensure that air operations are not hampered at bases due to these factors. Runway rehabilitation schemes were formulated, practiced and kept at a high state of preparedness to meet any contingency. The administrative requirements of the forward bases were closely monitored through personal visits and constant dialogue with commanders to ensure optimum admin efficiency and high state of morale of the personnel in the field.

(No. 23-Pres./00 of 15 August 1999 [*sic*])

Outline

1012.100 medal.

1013 अति विशिष्ट सेवा मैडल / ATI VISHISHT SEVA MEDAL[37]

Awarded to members of the armed forces to recognize distinguished service of an exceptional order.

Established: By No. 19-Pres./60 of 26 January 1960 and by No. 32-Pres./60 of 2 June 1960 as the 'Vishisht Seva Medal, Class II'. The statutes were revised by No. 34-Pres./62 of 30 April 1962 to clarify the fact that awards were conferred by the President of India by a *sanad* (parchment) under his hand and seal. The award was further revised, redesigned, and renamed by No. 31-Pres./67 of 27 January 1967. It was later further modified by No. 25-Pres./91 of 14 February 1991 to include members of the General Reserve Engineer Force among the eligible personnel.

General Appearance: A 35 mm circular silver medal.

Obverse: A five-pointed star in the centre.

Reverse: The state emblem with the name of the decoration in Hindi above. Until 1967, this would have been 'विशिष्ट सेवा मैडल' ('Vishisht Seva Medal'), the class being implied by the metal in which the decoration was produced and the ribbon. After 1967, the legend was altered, predictably, to 'अति विशिष्ट सेवा मैडल' ('Ati Vishisht Seva Medal').

Ribbon: 32 mm, yellow, described as 'gold' in the instituting notification, with two 2 mm dark blue stripes. Some sources suggest an alteration in ribbons over time: 1960-81, 32 mm with two equally spaced 2 mm dark blue stripes; and after 1981, a darker yellow colour and the blue stripes reduced to 1 mm. There is no official sanction to these although the actual ribbon produced may have varied in practice.

Suspension: Suspended from a fixed straight-bar suspender.

Naming: Named and dated (early awards) on the edge.

Miniature: Miniatures have been issued.

Background: The Ati Vishisht Seva Medal is awarded to recognize 'distinguished service of an exceptional order' to all ranks of the armed forces. The award may be granted posthumously and subsequent awards are represented by a bar worn on the ribbon. Twenty-nine second award bars are known to have been awarded.

The award carries with it the right to use 'A.V.S.M.' as postnominal letters.

1013.100 Vishisht Seva Medal Class II

1013.200 Ati Vishisht Seva Medal

[37]*Encyclopedia of Soldiers with Highest Gallantry Awards*, pp. 26-27; *India's Highest Gallantry Awards*, pp. 34-35; Haynes, 'Medals and Decorations of the Republic of India', p. 30; Das, *Traditions and Customs*, p. 273; Scandaluzzi, *Medal Ribbons of the World*, vol. 3: *India*.

1013A Bar to Ati Vishisht Seva Medal

The Ati Vishisht Seva Medal was originally established as the 'Vishisht Seva Medal, Class II', and only on 27 January 1967 was it renamed and the badge redesigned as detailed above.

Until 1980, the A.V.S.M. could be awarded for distinguished services in both war and peace. However, in 1980, the Uttam Yuddh Seva Medal (1012) was created to recognize distinguished services in an operational environment. Since that date, awards of the A.V.S.M. have been restricted to non-operational service. Over the years the medal has become almost the prerogative of senior officers, although in the initial years following its institution, it was awarded to deserving JCOs and junior officers as well, in keeping with the true spirit of the award.

Provincial stipends for this award are detailed in Appendix 2.

Through 26 January 2003, the A.V.S.M. has been bestowed 1,612 times, of these, there were fifty-nine awards of the V.S.M., class II. Twenty-nine bars to the A.V.S.M. have been awarded.

Representative Citation: An example citation for the A.V.S.M. would be the 1969 award to IC-1081 Brigadier Adi Kaikhusaroo Sahukar, Army Service Corps:

Brigadier Adi Kaikhusaroo Sahukar was commissioned in the Army Service Corps in 1941. He saw active service during World War II and was mentioned in Despatches. He graduated from the Defence Services Staff College, Wellington, in 1951. After holding various Corps appointments, he was posted on the Staff at Army Headquarters as Assistant Adjutant General in 1959 which appointment he held with distinction. In 1960 he was appointed General Staff Officer 1 in the Military Adviser's Department in the High Commission of India in the United Kingdom, where he displayed initiative, resourcefulness and leadership of a high order. After serving in the Punjab and Himachal Pradesh Area, he was posted at Headquarters, Southern Command, in 1966. Later on, he was posted as Brigadier in Charge Administration at Headquarters, Eastern Command, in 1967, in which his intelli-gence, imagination, perseverance and planning for the future have been remarkable.

(No. 12-Pres./69 of 26 January 1969)

Outline

1013.100 Vishisht Seva Medal, Class II (1952-67).
1013.200 Ati Vishisht Seva Medal (1967-).

1014 वीर चक्र / VIR CHAKRA[38]

Awarded for acts of gallantry in the presence of the enemy.

Established: A draft royal warrant was prepared in October 1948 for the possible institution of this award in the name of the British sovereign as, during the Dominion period, such a step would have been necessary to give the award status within the Commonwealth. On consideration, this course was abandoned and the medal was created by the President of India in No. 1-Pres./50 of 26 January 1950 (with effect from 15 August 1947). The statutes were amended by No. 2-Pres./52 of 4 January 1952, by No. 54-Pres./69 of 18 September 1969, and by No. 61-Pres./69 of 14 October 1969.

[38] *Encyclopedia of Soldiers with Highest Gallantry Awards*, pp. 6-7, 271-574, 591-94; *India's Highest Gallantry Awards*, pp. 5-6, 305-816; Haynes, 'Medals and Decorations of the Republic of India', pp. 8-10; Das, *Traditions and Customs*, p. 271; Dorling, *Ribbons & Medals*, p. 144; Scandaluzzi, *Medal Ribbons of the World*, vol. 3: *India*.

General Appearance: 36 mm circular silver medal.

Obverse: A five-pointed star, with the chakra in the centre, and, on this, the domed gilt state emblem; although due to polishing this thin gilding is often found worn away. Likewise, the background area behind the star is darkened, but this darkening is often lost.

Reverse: Around a plain centre, two legends separated by lotus flowers: above 'वीर चक्र' and below 'VIR CHAKRA'.

Ribbon: 32 mm, half dark blue and half orange-saffron. The orange is worn toward the left shoulder.

Suspension: The decoration is suspended from a swivelling straight-bar suspender.

Naming: The decoration is named on the edge. Until approximately 1971, the medal was also usually dated on the edge with the date of the action for which it was awarded.

Miniature: Miniatures have been issued.

Background: Awarded for acts of gallantry in the presence of the enemy. The medal may be awarded posthumously. Provision was made for the award of a bar for a second award of the Vir Chakra, with the first three awards of such a bar coming in 1948. The ten known awards of bars are: Subadar Har Singh (10 December 1947 and 4 March 1948), Risaldar Kartar Singh (8 February 1948 and 1 November 1948), Subadar Major Bhim Chand (23 August 1948 and 27 December 1948), Major General Venkatapathy Rangaswami (20 May 1948 and 29 March 1951), Air Commodore Anthony Ignatius Kenneth Suares (26 January 1950 and 6 December 1961), Group Captain Purshotam Lal Dhawan (26 January 1950 and October 1962), Lieutenant Colonel Satish Chandra Joshi (14 June 1948 and 10 September 1965 [posthumous]), Wing Commander Vinod Kumar Bhatia (8 September 1965 and December 1971), Squadron Leader Vinod Kumar Neb (6 September 1965 and 4 December 1971), and Wing Commander Bhupendra Kumar Bishnoi (7 September 1965 and 14 December 1971). When such a bar is awarded, a miniature silver chakra is added to the medal ribbon when worn alone.

Award of the decoration carried with it the right to use Vr.C. as a postnominal abbreviation (note the care to distinguish this abbreviation from that for the Victoria Cross [V.C.]).

The award originally carried a cash allowance for those under the rank of second lieutenant (or the appropriate service equivalent) and a lump sum cash award; over the years these benefits have been expanded across the ranks and increased as discussed elsewhere. On the death of the recipient, the pension was transferred to the widow until her death or remarriage. This pension has been a rather controversial issue throughout the life of the decoration. When the decoration was created, the monthly stipend was Rs. 20 with provision for an additional Rs. 8 for any additional bar. For Gorkhas of Nepalese domicile, the award was a lump sum payment of Rs. 1,000. Over time, these stipends have been increased although they are, in the opinion of many public commentators, still too low. From 1 February 1999, the stipend stood at Rs. 850 per month with an additional Rs. 20 authorized for the award of a bar. In

1014.100 Vir Chakra

addition, many states have established individual pension rewards for the recipients of the decoration. These provincial stipends are detailed in Appendix 2.

Through 2003, the award has been bestowed 1,315 times.

Representative Citation: To understand the award better, a sample recipient would be the 1948 award to 3234 Havildar Mokand Singh, 1st Patiala (R.S.) Infantry:

On 4 November 1948 at ZOJILA PASS. Havildar MOKAND SINGH was the Platoon Havildar of the leading platoon of a company detailed to destroy an enemy resistance pocket. The advance lay over 5 or 6 feet of snow in full view of the enemy. On reaching a position about 500 yards from the enemy the platoon came under heavy fire. Havildar MOKAND SINGH was detailed with one section to manoeuvre round to the enemy position, while the rest of his platoon gave covering fire. For a distance of about 200 yards from the enemy position every inch was covered by heavy enemy automatic fire. This brave NCO was the leading man of the section and by his dauntless action persuaded every man to follow him fearlessly over the area heavily swept by enemy fire. When he was about 50 yards from the enemy position two of his men were seriously wounded but this did not in any way damp his determination to destroy the enemy. Leading five of his men, he blitzed the enemy position with grenades, killing five of the enemy and capturing two. In addition he captured a Bren Gun, a collection of arms and a large amount of ammunition, equipment and documents.

Throughout this operation, Havildar MOKAND SINGH showed leadership, courage and determination of a very high order.

(No. 35-Pres./55 of 30 November 1955)

Outline

1014.100 medal.

1015 शौर्य चक्र / SHAURYA CHAKRA[39]

Awarded for gallantry other than in the face of the enemy.

Established: Established as the 'Ashoka Chakra, Class III' by No. 1-Pres./52 of 4 January 1952 (with effect from 15 August 1947). The statutes were revised and the decoration renamed in No. 30-Pres./67 of 27 January 1967.

General Appearance: Circular bronze medal, 35 mm in diameter. (At first glance, there may be some difficulty in distinguishing recent specimens of this award from the Ashoka Chakra [1003], as the bronze used now is very bright.)

Obverse: In the centre, the chakra (wheel) of Ashoka, surrounded by a lotus wreath and with an ornate edge.

Reverse: For pre-1967 awards, the medal is blank in the centre, with 'अशोक चक्र' along the upper edge of the medal and the same name in English along the lower rim, 'ASHOKA CHAKRA'. On either side is a lotus design. The centre is blank. There is no indication of the class on the pre-1967 awards and it is implied by the metal and ribbon design. For the post-1967 awards, the names are changed to 'शौर्य चक्र' above and 'SHAURYA CHAKRA' below.

Ribbon: 30 mm, dark green with equally spaced three 2 mm orange stripes. Some sources suggest variations in ribbon design over time: 1952-67, 32 mm with three equally spaced 2 mm

1015.100 Ashoka Chakra Class III

[39]*Encyclopedia of Soldiers with Highest Gallantry Awards*, pp. 28-29; *India's Highest Gallantry Awards*, pp. 36-37; Haynes, 'Medals and Decorations of the Republic of India', pp. 11-13; Das, *Traditions and Customs*, p. 272; Dorling, *Ribbons & Medals*, p. 293; Scandaluzzi, *Medal Ribbons of the World*, vol. 3: *India*.

orange stripes; 1967-81, 38 mm with three 1.5 mm white stripes in the centre, 1.5 mm apart; and after 1981, 32 mm with three equally spaced 1.5 mm orange stripes. There is no indication that these variants represent anything other than variability in ribbon manufacture.

Suspension: Suspended by a non-swivelling straight-bar suspender.

Naming: The medal is named and dated on the edge. However, it is not clear if the practice of dating still continues or has been discontinued along with the combat gallantry series of awards since about 1970.

Miniature: Miniatures have been issued.

Background: Awarded for gallantry other than in the face of the enemy. This award may be granted to civilians or to military personnel and may be awarded posthumously. Subsequent awards of the Shaurya Chakra are recognized by a bar to the medal ribbon. To date, at least four bars are known to have been awarded: 267944 Junior Warrant Officer Venkata Phani Raju Kala, Air Field Safety Operator, Indian Air Force (No. 67-Pres/93 of 26 January 1993), 2676892 Naik Jardish Ahmed, Grenadiers (No. 181-Pres/95 of 15 August 1995), IC 49510 Major Hitesh Bhalla, S.M., 11th Battalion, Maratha Light Infantry (No. 106-Pres/2002 of 26 January 2002), and IC 46889 Major Sukhmeet Singh, Artillery/HQ 23 Sector Assam Rifles (No. 47-Pres/2003 of 26 January 2003). When ribbons are worn alone, the award of a bar is indicated by the addition of a miniature bronze chakra to the ribbon. It is possible for a recipient to be awarded the Ashoka Chakra (1003) or Kirti Chakra (1009) in addition for separate acts of gallantry.

When the decoration was created, no provision was made for any monetary stipend from the central government. It was, however, decided that for recipients whose families were in 'indigent' circumstances (defined as having an annual income under Rs. 3,000), a monthly allowance of Rs. 15 was appropriate. From 1 February 1999, the central government set a monthly stipend of Rs. 750 for recipients of the award. Provincial stipends are detailed in Appendix 2.

Award of the decoration carries with it the right to use 'S.C.' as a postnominal abbreviation.

Through 2003, the award has been bestowed 1,326 times.

Representative Citation: To understand the award better, a sample recipient would be the 1957 award of the Ashoka Chakra, Class III, to No. 12049 Havildar Murli Ram, 7th Battalion, Grenadiers:

On 19th February [1956] a strong patrol led by Capt. Rane whilst patroling the Indo-Pakistan border suddenly came under heavy small arms fire from area Chhad Bet. Before the men could dismount from their camels, Sep. Pema Ram and two other men of No. 12049 Hav. Murli Ram's section were hit. A few minutes later the attackers' fire became heavy and sustained, and it became impossible for the point section to move without drawing accurate fire from a range of 150 yards. Completely scornful of the danger Hav. Murli Ram encouraged his men to return fire, as a result of which the attackers were hit by our fire. With scant regard for his personal safety he then crawled forward to evacuate his wounded comrade Sep. Pema Ram. As he

1015.200 Shaurya Chakra

approached near him he was hit on the chest near the left shoulder. He paid no heed and kept on dragging the wounded soldier until he was brought to safety.

This heroic action showed boldness, self-sacrifice and courage in the best traditions of our Army.

(No. 5-Pres./57 of 26 January 1957)

Outline

1015.100 Ashoka Chakra, Class III (1952-67).
1015.200 Shaurya Chakra (1967-).

1016 युद्ध सेवा मैडल / YUDDH SEVA MEDAL[40]

Awarded for distinguished services of a high order in war/hostilities/conflicts.

Established: No. 40-Pres./80 of 28 June 1980.

General Appearance: Circular 35 mm gilt medal.

Obverse: The state emblem with the name of the decoration in Hindi and English above, 'युद्ध सेवा मैडल / Yuddh Seva Medal'. This is the obverse indicated in the statute, though the decoration is often depicted reversed, and is even shown thus in some official publications.

Reverse: A five-pointed star.

Ribbon: 32 mm, golden with three equally spaced 2 mm red stripes.

Suspension: Suspended from a fixed straight-bar suspender.

Naming: The medal is named on the edge. Unlike the earlier issues of other Presidential awards (both Chakra and Vishisht Seva series), the Yuddh Seva medals were never dated on the rim.

Miniature: Miniatures have been issued.

Background: Awarded for a high degree of distinguished service during war, conflicts, or hostilities. In many ways, this is an operational version of the Vishisht Seva Medal (1027) which, since 1980, has been restricted to non-operational awards. The award carries with it the right to use 'Y.S.M.' as postnominal letters.

Bars may be awarded for subsequent services. In cases where a bar is awarded for a second or subsequent award, this is indicated on the ribbon bar when worn alone by the addition of a gilt chakra. To date, no awards of bars have been traced.

Provincial stipends for this award are detailed in Appendix 2.

Through 26 January 2003, the Y.S.M. has been bestowed 129 times, and no bars have been awarded.

Representative Citation: To understand the award better, a sample recipient would be Flight Lieutenant Sanjay Mittal (16773) Flying (Pilot), Indian Air Force:

Flight Lieutenant Sanjay Mittal has been on the posted strength of one of the Helicopter units since 22 Dec. 86.

He was first among the few pilots from the unit to join the Indian Peace Keeping Force in Oct. 87. During the hostilities in Jaffna, the officer flew 211 missions, both day and night. The unit moved to its new location in February and ever since, the officer continuously participated in various operations like troop induction/deinduction,

1016.100 Yuddh Seva Medal

[40] *India's Highest Gallantry Awards*, pp. 38-39; Das, *Traditions and Customs*, p. 273.

casualty evacuation, logistic support, etc., under extremely hostile conditions and unfamiliar terrain. While carrying out operations in areas vulnerable to enemy fire, his professional handling instilled confidence amongst other crew.

For his flying effort, dedication and devotion to duty, the President is pleased to award the Yuddh Seva Medal to Flt Lt Sanjay Mittal.

(No. 40-Pres/90 dated 26 January 1990)

Outline

1016.100 medal.

1017 KING'S POLICE AND FIRE SERVICES MEDAL FOR GALLANTRY[41]

Awarded to police and fire services to recognize acts of exceptional courage. While this medal was awarded in British-ruled India from 1909 until their departure in 1947, this entry deals only with the medal as it was awarded in independent India, during the Dominion and early Republic period.

Established: Originally instituted as the King's Police Medal by King Edward VII by Royal Warrant on 7 July 1909. The design was subsequently modified for succeeding monarchs and the design and structure of the award was changed in 1933 to establish separate distinguished service and gallantry distinctions in what had previously been a single-division award. The medal continued to be awarded in India, without a distinct notification allowing this, from India's Independence on 15 August 1947 until the creation of the President's Police and Fire Services Medal for Gallantry (1018) on 1 March 1951.

General Appearance: Circular silver medal, 35 mm in diameter.

Obverse: The crowned bust of King George VI, facing left and surrounded by the royal titles 'GEORGIVS VI D: G: BR: OMN: REX ET INDIAE IMP:'. These are, of course, the king's titles prior to the Indian Independence Act. While a strong case might have been made for a redesign of the medal to reflect the new constitutional status, there is no indication that this ever took place. In 1949, the legend surrounding the bust of the King was changed to 'GEORGIVS VI DEI: GRA: BRITT: OMN: REX FID: DEF:', reflecting the changed titular status of the British monarch. As least some of the awards in India during the Dominion period may have borne the second type obverse legend.

Reverse: A standing robed figure, with sword and shield. The shield carries the legend 'TO GUARD / MY / PEOPLE' and in the exergue below the figure the legend 'FOR GALLANTRY' appears. Behind this figure there is a monumental construction with other guarding figures (representing the police) and behind them an urban skyline.

Ribbon: 36 mm, white with two broad dark blue stripes. There are thin red stripes on each of the three white stripes.

Suspension: A ring.

Naming: Named and dated on the edge.

Miniature: Miniatures have been issued.

1017.100 King's Police and Fire Services Medal for Gallantry

[41] Abbott and Tamplin, *British Gallantry Awards*, pp. 286-98.

Background: In the ambiguous constitutional circumstances of the Dominion period, this medal was continued from the period of British rule into the early years of Independence. This medal, which had been awarded widely throughout the empire, thus constituted an anachronistic continuation of royal authority into post-Independence India.

Awards: From 1947 to 1950, the medal with gallantry reverse was awarded twenty-eight times, including one bar, although some of these were almost certainly pre-Independence awards which were only gazetted after 15 August 1947. These included one fire services award. Medals for distinguished service also continued to be awarded during the Dominion period until January 1950.

Representative Citation: To understand the award better, sample recipients would be the awards to Shri Takhatsing Kalyansing, Unarmed Head Constable (officiating), Ahmedabad City, and Janab Lalkhan Dadumia (Deceased), Unarmed Head Constable (officiating), Ahmedabad City:

On the morning of 26th May 1949, a very daring robbery and murder took place on Richey Road in Ahmedabad City. Three notorious Sindhi dacoits carrying revolvers and pistols waylaid a van belonging to the Central Bank of India. After shooting dead the driver and wounding another employee of the Bank, they fired two more shots at the retreating cashier and then got into the van and drove it away through the crowded street.

Hearing the report of the revolver shots, Head Constable Takhatsing Kalyansing, who was proceeding towards the Fernandiz Bridge Police Chowkey guessed that something serious had happened and although unarmed immediately mounted his cycle and pursued the van. The robbers were firing at random in order to scare away the public, but the Head Constable continued the chase undaunted. He could not, however, keep pace with the motor van and lagged a certain distance behind it. After about three-quarters of a mile, the van developed carburetor trouble and came to a stop on the Relief Road. The robbers jumped out of the van and made a dash down Cheekantha Road. They then seized cycles belonging to pedestrians and rode off. As they reached Mirzapur Road, one of the robbers lost his balance and fell off his cycle, and his revolver was thrown on the road. This attracted the attention of Head Constable Lalkhan Dadumia who happened himself to be passing by and he immediately threw himself on the robber. The latter, quickly recovering his revolver fired three shots at Head Constable Lalkhan Dadumia, one of which wounded him. Another member of the gang then came to the rescue of his accomplice and fired a shot at the Head Constable. A struggle ensued.

In the meantime Head Constable Takhatsing Kalyansing surmising that the robbers had gone towards the Post Office rode in that direction and came upon them on the Mirzapur Road struggling with Head Constable Lalkhan Dadumia. Takhatsing immediately threw aside his cycle and, taking a stick from the hand of a passerby, struck one of the robbers a powerful blow on the head. The robber turned on him and shot him in the neck—the bullet entering from the right side of Takhatsing's neck, and coming out on the left side of his back. Still undaunted, Takhatsing grappled with him aided by Head Constable Lalkhan. The robber shot at Lalkhan also, but he and Takhatsing did not let go, nor did they relax their grip when the first robber fired three shots into the struggling group mortally wounding Head

Constable Lalkhan and injuring the second robber. Abandoning his accomplice, the first robber made off on his cycle and is still at large. The third member of the gang was also arrested by the Police aided by members of the public.

Head Constable Lalkhan succumbed to his wounds two days after the incident. He had been shot through the head and the abdomen as well as through the left forearm.

Throughout this encounter Head Constable Takhatsing Kalyansing and Head Constable Lalkhan Dadumia displayed great resolution and exemplary devotion to duty. Though themselves unarmed they did not hesitate to tackle two armed desperadoes and despite grievous wounds they continued the struggle with conspicuous and sustained gallantry.

(No. 2-Hons. of 10 January 1950)

Outline

1017.100 first legend.
1017.200 second legend.

1018 राष्ट्रपति का पुलिस और अग्नि शमन सेवा पदक वीरता के लिये/ RASHTRAPATI KA POLICE AUR AGNI SHAMAN SEVA PADAK VIRTA KE LIYE / PRESIDENT'S POLICE AND FIRE SERVICES MEDAL FOR GALLANTRY[42]

Awarded to police, fire services, and central security organizations to recognize acts of exceptional courage.

Established: By No. 3-Pres/51 and No. 4-Pres./51 of 1 March 1951, replacing the King's Police and Fire Services Medal for Gallantry (1017). This was later modified by notifications No. 27-Pres./51 of 12 June 1951 (amendment of the rules), No. 18-Pres./52 of 31 January 1952 (specifying that the silver medal and rose would be gold gilt), No. 28-Pres./52 of 17 March 1952 (amendment of the rules), No. 59-Pres./52 of 22 September 1952 (amendment of the rules), No. 18-Pres./53 of 7 July 1953 (amendment of the rules), No. 11-Pres./56 of 8 March 1956 (amendment of the rules), No. 65-Pres./62 of 10 October 1962 (to include members of the Central Intelligence Bureau among the eligible categories) and No. 66-Pres./62 of 10 October 1962 (amendment of the rules), No. 78-Pres./63 (to include members of the Railway Protection Force among the eligible categories) and No. 79-Pres./63 of 17 October 1963 (amendment of the rules), No. 43-Pres./71 (to amend the eligible categories by replacing the added 'members of the Central Intelligence Bureau and Railway Protection Force with 'Central Police/ Security Organisations) and No. 44-Pres./71 of 5 August 1971 (amendment of the rules), 118-Pres./74 of 1 December 1974 (amendment of the rules). The rates of monthly allowance for the award were altered by notification No. 59-Pres./52 of 22 September 1952, No. 50-Pres./54 of 14 December 1954, and No. 25-Pres./57 of 1 June 1957. In 1975 (No. 34-Pres./75 of 19 May 1975), the medal was split into separate police (1019) and fire services (1020) medals.

General Appearance: Circular silver gilt medal, 35 mm in diameter. The first description called for a silver medal (and

1018.200 President's Police and Fire Services Medal for Gallantry

[42]*Encyclopedia of Soldiers with Highest Gallantry Awards*, p. 30; *India's Highest Gallantry Awards*, p. 40; Dorling, *Ribbons & Medals*, p. 144; Scandaluzzi, *Medal Ribbons of the World*, vol. 3: *India*.

some may have been awarded thus), but this was altered eleven months later to gilt to achieve a visual similarity to the Ashoka Chakra Class I, to which there was a desire to equate this award, as the police had been specifically excluded from eligibility for the Ashoka Chakra series of awards. In many cases, such as the specimen shown below, the gilt is especially thin and may seem to be absent entirely.

Obverse: In the centre, the coat of arms of the President of India on a shield and the legend 'PRESIDENT'S POLICE AND FIRE SERVICES MEDAL' above and 'INDIA' below. Five-pointed stars separate these two legends.

Reverse: The state emblem in the centre with 'FOR GALLANTRY' above and a wreath below.

Ribbon: 32 mm, half dark blue, half white, with a 2 mm red central stripe.

Suspension: A fixed non-swivelling straight-bar suspender.

Naming: Named on the edge in running script.

Miniature: Miniatures have been issued.

Background: Awarded to those in the organized police, Central Intelligence Bureau, Railway Protection Force, or organized fire services who have performed acts of conspicuous gallantry in the course of their duty. This may include the saving of live and property, preventing crime, or arresting criminals. Bars may be awarded for subsequent acts of gallantry. These bars are silver slip-on bars and have the details of the awardee engraved on the reverse. When ribbons are worn alone, the possession of a bar is indicated by the addition of a silver rosette to the ribbon. Under normal circumstances, no more than forty-five Presidential police medals for gallantry are to be awarded in any single year.

The first award was to 283 Mounted Head Constable Mukna Ram, Punjab Police, Ferozepore District, Punjab, on 7 May 1951 (No. 10-Pres./51). The last awards were to DSP M. P. Natanael, Constables Guman Singh and Om Prakash of the 10th Battalion Central Reserve Police Force (No. 82-Pres./75 of 18 July 1975).

As mentioned earlier, in 1975, this medal was split into the President's Police Medal for Gallantry (1019) and the President's Fire Services Medal for Gallantry (1020).

Representative Citation: To understand the award better, a sample recipient would be Manphool Singh, Constable No. 714, Civil Police, District Agra, Uttar Pradesh.

By the morning of the 13th August 1956, flood waters from Bharatpur had reached the neighborhood of Fatehpur Sikri in Agra District and the surrounding area was a vast sheet of water spread over several miles. The water level at Tera Mori Bandh near Fatehpur Sikri had already over-shot the danger mark by a foot and was still rising rapidly. It was quite apparent that unless the sluice gates of the Bandh [dam] were opened immediately, the rising waters would endanger the safety of the dam itself and the devastation of the adjoining villages would result if the dam was breached.

This Tera Mori Bandh had been constructed in the days of Emperor Akbar [1556-1605 CE] and it had been in disuse for a considerable length of time. No mechanical devices were available for opening the sluice gates and the employees of the Canal Department were themselves unable to open them. At this crucial stage Constable

Manphool Singh volunteered to enter the swift current and bodily remove the planks of the sluice gates. With a rope tied round his waist he entered the water and with considerable difficulty and at great personal risk succeeded in removing 14 wooden planks at the gates. Thereafter the current became so swift that he was carried away and had to be pulled out of the water.

Two days later more flood water came into the area and would undoubtedly have caused great damage had not the sluice gates been partially dismantled.

Constable Manphool Singh displayed great courage and devotion to public service outside the line of his official duty.

(No. 15-Pres./57 of 9 February 1957)

Outline

1018.100 silver medal (issued?).
1018.200 gilt medal.

1019 राष्ट्रपति का पुलिस पदक वीरता के लिये / RASHTRAPATI KA POLICE PADAK VIRTA KE LIYE / PRESIDENT'S POLICE MEDAL FOR GALLANTRY[43]

Awarded to police personnel to recognize acts of exceptional courage.

Established: By No. 42 and 43-Pres./75 of 19 May 1975. This was modified by No. 125-Pres./75 of 24 December 1975 (amendment of the rules), No. 64-Pres./79 of 4 December 1979 (increase of monetary allowance), No. 42-Pres./82 of 24 September 1982 (amendment of the rules), No. 77-Pres./87 of 4 November 1987 (increase of monetary allowance), No. 81-Pres./88 of 29 July 1988, and No. 101-Pres./98 of 18 August 1998 (increase of monetary allowance). Redesigned by No. 88-Pres./98 of 20 July 1998.

General Appearance: Circular 35 mm silver gilt medal. In some specimens, the gilt is extremely thin. The second variety:

Obverse: First variety: A silver gilt medal; in the centre the coat of arms of the President of India on a shield and the legend 'PRESIDENT'S POLICE MEDAL' above and 'INDIA' below. These two legends are separated by five-pointed stars. *Second variety:* A silver gilt medal with a five-pointed star with the inscription 'राष्ट्रपति का पुलिस पदक–भारत' above, and 'President's Police Medal-INDIA' below.

Reverse: First variety: The state emblem in the centre with 'FOR GALLANTRY' above and a wreath below. *Second variety:* Within a wreath, the state emblem, surrounded by the legends, 'वीरता के लिए' and 'FOR GALLANTRY', above and below, respectively.

Ribbon: 32 mm, half dark blue, half white, with a 2 mm red central stripe.

Suspension: Both are suspended by a non-swivelling fixed straight-bar suspender.

Naming: Named on the edge.

Miniature: Miniatures have been issued of both varieties.

Background: In 1975, the previous President's Police and Fire Services Medal for Gallantry (1018) was divided into separate police and fire service (1020) equivalents.

1019.200 President's Police Medal for Gallantry, second variety[44]

[43] Scandaluzzi, *Medal Ribbons of the World*, vol. 3: *India*.
[44] This image, though not of high quality, is from the Ministry of Home Affairs website, http://mha.nic.in/medal.htm.

This medal is awarded for conspicuous gallantry in saving life and property, or in preventing crime or arresting criminals. All police personnel of the country irrespective of rank and length of service are eligible for this award. The recipients of this medal are granted an allowance of Rs. 200 per month which continues to be paid to them at the same rate even after retirement. After the death of the recipient of the medal, this allowance continues to be paid to his widow at the same rate. The recipients of this award are also eligible to travel free by train in the 2nd Class AC II tier or in the first class with an attendant.

The first award, 7 August 1975, was to Shri Chittaranjan Mukharji, Inspector of Police, Hoogly, West Bengal (No. 88-Pres./75).

Two varieties of the medal have appeared, the first was instituted when the change of name took place in 1975 and is, for the most part, simply a renaming and legend-alteration of the earlier medal (1018). The second variety (introduced in 1998) is a totally redesigned medal.

Over the years, excessive use of this medal appears to have devalued it in the eyes of the police forces, leading to the tendency to inappropriately award police personnel with the 'Chakra' series of awards for exceptional acts of bravery.

Representative Citation: To understand the award better, a sample recipient would be the 1987 award to Shri Nagendra Nath Mishra, Deputy Commandant, 29th Battalion, Central Reserve Police Force:

On the 15th February, 1980, an information was received that a gang of insurgents as camping in the interior jungle of Kaunu hill in Manipur. A police party including Shri Nagendra Nath Mishra, Deputy Commandant, left Imphal in vehicles up to village Kanglatongbi and from there they covered the rest of the distance on foot. The raiding party was divided into three groups, one led by Shri Nagendra Nath Mishra, Dy. Commandant, another by Additional S.P. and the third by two Inspectors of Police.

It was intimated that the insurgents had strong sympathisers in village Makhan. One platoon under the command of an inspector was deputed to encircle the village. The Inspector searched the suspected houses early in the morning of 16th February, 1980 and found two persons who were handed over to the Civil Police. The second group of the raiding party reached near the camp of the insurgents early in the morning on 16th February, 1980. When the raiding party was at a distance of about 50 yards from the camp, the leading Scout Constable was fired upon and was wounded by the bullet on the leg. He immediately took up the position and returned fire. One insurgent, who was hiding nearby, charged at the Constable. Immediately the other Constable fired on the insurgent and killed him on the spot. On hearing the sound of firing other insurgents started firing on the raiding party and threw one hand grenade on the Police party, but that did not explode. One of the insurgents tried to shoot the Constable who was manning the LMG, but the insurgent was shot dead. In the meantime the other party headed by Shri Nagendra Nath Mishra, Dy. Commandant charged on the camp of the insurgents to capture them alive. Seeing the courage of the raiding party led by Shri Mishra [the insurgents] were so demoralized that they ran helter-skelter in panic, leaving behind huge quantities of arms, ammunition and other equipment. As the visibility was very poor in the thick forest, some of the insurgents managed to escape. Two insurgents were killed and a large quantity of arms and ammunition was recovered.

In this encounter Shri Nagendra Nath Mishra, Dy. Commandant, displayed conspicuous ballantry [*sic*], courage and devotion to duty of a high order.

(No. 45-Pres./87 of 6 June 1987)

Outline

1019.100 first variety (1973-98).
1019.200 second variety (1998-).

1020 राष्ट्रपति का अग्नि शमन सेवा पदक वीरता के लिये / RASHTRAPATI KA AGNI SHAMAN SEVA PADAK VIRTA KE LIYE / PRESIDENT'S FIRE SERVICES MEDAL FOR GALLANTRY

Awarded to fire service personnel to recognize acts of exceptional courage.

Established: By No. 40-Pres./75 and No. 41-Pres./75 of 19 May 1975. It was further modified by No. 76-Pres./76 of 31 August 1976 (amendment of the rules), No. 103-Pres./84 of 26 September 1984 (to alter the rates of monthly allowance), and No. 15-Pres./88 of 22 February 1988.

General Appearance: A 35 mm circular silver gilt medal.

Obverse: The State Emblem and motto with the legend 'राष्ट्रपति का अग्नि शमन सेवा पदक' 'PRESIDENT'S FIRE SERVICES MEDAL'[44a] on either side, separated by two five-pointed stars.

Reverse: Ashoka's chakra in the centre, with a wreath above and 'वीरता के लिये' 'FOR GALLANTRY' below.

Ribbon: 32 mm, half brown, half yellow, with a 3 mm black stripe down the centre.

Suspension: Although the statutes specify a ring suspension, the medal is suspended by a non-swivelling straight-bar suspender.

Naming: Named on the edge.

Miniature: Miniatures have been issued.

Background: In 1975, the previous President's Police and Fire Services Medal for Gallantry (1018) was divided into separate police (1019) and fire service equivalents.

The medal is awarded for conspicuous gallantry in saving life and property by members of the fire services. From 2002, the medal has carried a monthly allowance of Rs. 750. The medal may be awarded posthumously and bars may be awarded for additional acts of gallantry.

Representative Citation: To understand the award better, a sample recipient would be the posthumous award to Shri Kishori Singh, Station Officer, Delhi Fire Station:

On the 6th June, 1983, at 11.47 hrs., a devastating fire occurred in Gopala Towers, a multi-story building at 25, Rajendra Place, New Delhi. Being a serious fire, all senior officers of the Delhi Fire Service responded to the scene of the fire. The main staircase and the fire escape were rendered unserviceable due to smoke and heat and almost 500 people were stranded on the terrace as well as on the top floors.

1020.100 President's Fire Services Medal for Gallantry

[44a] The actual inscription on the medal reads 'PRESIDENT'S FIRE SERVICE MEDAL'.

About 30 persons, who were trapped on the upper floor, were rescued by fire service personnel, using tall ladders. However, a large number of people were still stranded on the terrace of the building. On instructions from the Chief Fire Officer, a party of officers and men from the Fire Service were sent upto [*sic*]the roof of the building to rescue the persons on the roof-top. Shri Kishori Singh, Station Officer, was guiding the evacuation operations on the staircase of the 12th floor, assisting the people who were making use of the staircase for going down. Simultaneously, persons on the roof-top were being rescued through an improvised bridge also. Soon after the helicopter rescue from the roof-top was done, there was a flash over and there was a sudden shooting up of flames and clouds of thick smoke from the upper floors. No one was aware of the fate of Shri Kishori Singh who stucked [*sic*] to his post on the 12th floor in his mission of assisting the evacuation of the trapped persons, quite unmindful of his own personal safety. In this action, Station Officer Shri Kishori Singh was overcome by the sudden flare-up of flames and smoke and sacrificed his life in the discharge of his duties.

Shri Kishori Singh, thus, exhibited exemplary courage and devotion to duty of a very high order.

(No. 2-Pres./84 of 4 February 1984)

Outline

1020.100 medal.

1021 PRESIDENT'S CORRECTIONAL SERVICE MEDAL FOR GALLANTRY

Awarded to personnel engaged in prison administration for acts of exceptional gallantry performed within India.

Established: By No. 62-Pres/1999 of 5 April 1999, with effect from 1 July 1999. The rules governing the award were notified by No. 63-Pres/1999 of 5 April 1999.

Eligible Categories: Awarded to the officers and staff of state governments or union territories administrations engaged in prison administration.

General Appearance: A 34 mm (1³/₈ inches) diameter circular silver gilt medal.

Obverse: The obverse is described in the notification as four elevated pairs of trapezium design along the rim. In the centre of the middle circle, the state emblem and motto, and the Devnagari inscriptions 'PRESIDENT'S CORRECTIONAL SERVICE MEDAL FOR GALLANTRY' and 'INDIA', separated by flowers on either side. As we have not seen this award, we are unable to reconcile this description to the tangible reality of a medal.

Reverse: The notification described four elevated pairs of trapezium designs along the rim and a circle with vertical lines inside surrounded by the inscription 'PRESIDENT'S CORRECTIONAL SERVICE MEDAL FOR GALLANTRY' in English.

Ribbon: 34 mm wide, half green and half saffron, the two colours being separated by a 3 mm yellow line. There is no distinction in the ribbon of the medal whether awarded for gallantry or for distinguished service.

Suspension: Suspended by a non-swivelling straight-bar suspender.

Naming: The medal is presumably named on the edge.

Miniature: Miniatures have not apparently been issued.

Background: Awarded to members of the correctional service for performing acts of exceptional courage within India. The rules governing the award qualify such acts as those of conspicuous gallantry in apprehending or preventing the escape of prisoners, the risk incurred being estimated with regard to the obligations and duties of the concerned officer. Subsequent awards of the medal are recognized by the addition of a bar to the medal ribbon, each bar being denoted by a gold-gilt silver lotus emblem on the ribbon of the medal when worn alone. The medal may be awarded posthumously, although there is no specific annotation in the instituting gazette to this effect but the rules governing the award make provision of posthumous grant. Names of personnel awarded the medal are notified in the *Gazette of India* and a register of such names is maintained by the Ministry of Home Affairs. Grant of the medal and each subsequent bar carries with it an allowance of Rs. 100 per month. All recipients, irrespective of rank, are entitled to the allowance at a uniform rate. Recipients who may already have been awarded the President's Police Medal for Gallantry are eligible to the full allowance, in addition to the earlier allowance attached to the earlier award. There is no limit on the number of President's Correctional Service Medals for gallantry that can be awarded in a year. The medal may be forfeited if the holder is held to be guilty of 'disloyalty, cowardice in action or such conduct as in the opinion of the President, brings the force into disrepute.'

Representative Citation: To understand the award better, a sample recipient would be the posthumous award to Shri Shobha Lal Nishad, Warder, Central Prison, Naini, Allahabad, Uttar Pradesh, in 2000:

Shri Shobha Lal Nishad was put on guard duty over an undertrial prisoner, Sanjay Srivastav, who was admitted in Swarup Rani Nehru Hospital, Allahabad on 26-6-1997. On 27-6-1997, at about 6:00 a.m., some people knocked on the door. Despite being asked by Shri Nishad, they did not disclose their identity. The moment Shri Nishad opened the door, the persons standing outside fired at him. Even after sustaining bullet injuries in the chest, Shri Nishad grappled with the assailants. In the meanwhile a bomb exploded in the hand of one of the assailants resulting in one of his hands being blown off. According to eye-witnesses, Shri Nishad managed to entangle the assailant with his legs and this led to the arrest of the latter. Shri Nishad was admitted to the emergency ward of the aforesaid hospital where he succumbed to his injuries on 28-6-1997.

In this encounter, Shri Shobha Lal Nishad, Warder displayed exemplary gallantry, courage and devotion to duty.

(No. 13-Pres./00 of 26 January 2000)

Outline

1021.100 medal.

1022 राष्ट्रपति का गृह रक्षा व नागरिक सुरक्षा पदक वीरता के लिये / RASHTRAPATI KA GRIH RAKSHA WA NAGARIK SURAKSHA PADAK VIRTA KE LIYE / PRESIDENT'S HOME GUARDS AND CIVIL DEFENCE MEDAL FOR GALLANTRY[45]

Awarded to members of the home guards and civil defence organizations to recognize acts of exceptional courage.

Established: By No. 100-Pres./74 of 7 October 1974, by the President of India (with effect from 15 August 1974). The rules governing the award were published in No. 101-Pres./74 of 7 October 1974 and modified by No. 17-Pres./90 of 27 February 1990.

General Appearance: A circular 35 mm silver gilt medal.

Obverse: The state emblem and motto and, below it in the centre, the emblem of the Home Guards, surrounding it the legends 'राष्ट्रपति का गृह रक्षा व नागरिक सुरक्षा पदक' ('Rashtrapati ka Grih Raksha wa Nagarik Suraksha Padak' or 'President's Home Guards and Civil Defence Medal') and 'PRESIDENT'S HOME GUARDS AND CIVIL DEFENCE MEDAL'.

Reverse: The chakra of Ashoka in the centre, surrounded by the legend 'वीरता' ('Virta' or 'Gallantry') and 'GALLANTRY'.

Ribbon: 32 mm, black with an 8 mm white centre, these stripes are separated by 4 mm saffron-orange stripes. The same ribbon is used for both gallantry and distinguished service (*cf.* 1058).

Suspension: Suspended by a fixed straight bar suspender.

Naming: The medal is named on the rim.

Miniature: Miniatures have possibly been issued, though they were not provided for in the statute.

Background: Awarded to those members of the home guards, civil defence, and mobile civil emergency forces who have performed acts of exceptional courage and skill within the territory of India. The acts for which the medal shall be awarded are stipulated as conspicuous gallantry in saving life and property, or in preventing crime or arresting criminals, the risks incurred being estimated with due regard to the obligations and duties of the members of these organizations. The award of the gallantry medal was limited to fifty awards in any single year until 1977, when the statutes were amended and no limit was placed on the number of medals to be awarded for gallantry (No. 48-Pres./77 of 11 May 1977). The award of the medal carries with it a lump sum financial reward. The amount so granted was Rs. 1,000 for the medal and Rs. 500 for each bar. In 1990, this was revised to allow for a lump sum monetary grant of Rs. 3,000 for the medal, and a similar amount of Rs. 3,000 for each subsequent bar. The medal may be awarded posthumously and bars may be awarded to the medal for additional brave acts. The bar is oblong with a laurel-leaf design and is engraved on the reverse with the recipient's details. When ribbon bars are worn alone, the receipt of a bar is indicated by the addition of a miniature silver gilt rosette to the ribbon.

The Home Guards were raised in 1946 and are recruited from a broad cross section of the population who give their spare time to the organization for betterment of the com-

[45]*Encyclopedia of Soldiers with Highest Gallantry Awards,* pp. 31-32; *India's Highest Gallantry Awards,* pp. 41-42.

munity. All citizens of India who are in the age group of 18 to 50 are eligible to become members of the Home Guard. The normal tenure of membership in the Home Guards is three to five years. The Home Guards serves as an auxiliary to the police in maintenance of law, order, and internal security. It assists the community in any kind of emergency, helps in the maintenance of essential services, promotes communal harmony, assists the civil administration in protecting weaker sections of society, participates in socio-economic and welfare activities, and performs civil defence duties.

The civil defence establishment was set-up in December 1962 as an office attached to the Ministry of Home Affairs for organizing civil defence measures in the country and advising the state governments. In April 1963 the Directorate General of Civil Defence came into being under the Ministry of Home Affairs. Its scope and functions were later enlarged to include fire services as well. In India, civil defence aims at saving lives, minimizing damage to property, and maintaining continuity of industrial production in the event of a hostile attack. Civil defence is primarily organized on a voluntary basis except for a small nucleus of paid staff and establishment which is augmented during emergencies.

The first award of this medal took place on 15 August 1975, to Volunteer Jarnail Singh, Border Wing, Home Guards, Punjab (No. 102-Pres./75).

Representative Citation: To understand the award better, a sample recipient would be the 1975 award to Volunteer Uttam Chand, Border Wing, Home Guards, Punjab:

Volunteer BY-6928 Uttam Chand son of Shri Guru Ditta was of 6th Border Wing Home Guards, Fazilka. His Bn was attached to the 22 Bn Border Security Force and was under the operational control of Army Brigade at Fazilka and was posted at Khokar Post on the Fazilka Border. This post came under heavy shelling on the night of 3rd and 4th December, 1971. During the firing, another volunteer, Shri Magh Singh received serious injuries. Notwithstanding the fact that his own ammunition had been exhausted, Volunteer Uttam Chand unmindful of his own personal safety carried his wounded comrade on his shoulders back to the base picket and saved the life of his comrade. Volunteer Uttam Chand showed a comaraderie [*sic*] in action and under enemy pressure, carried his wounded comrade for over a mile to the base Picket of Border Security Force. Thus for this act of bravery and valour, Volunteer Uttam Chand deserved to be rewarded.

(No. 102-Pres./75 of 15 August 1975)

Outline

1022.100 medal.

1023 सेना मैडल / SENA MEDAL / ARMY MEDAL[46]

Awarded to army personnel for acts of courage or exceptional achievement. In special circumstances, it can also be awarded to non-military personnel if they are borne on the rolls of an army formation.

Established: By No. 16-Pres./60 of 26 January 1960. Amended by No. 32-Pres./60 of 17 June 1960 (publishing details of the

[46]*Encyclopedia of Soldiers with Highest Gallantry Awards*, p. 33; *India's Highest Gallantry Awards*, p. 43; Haynes, 'Medals and Decorations of the Republic of India', pp. 32-33; Das, *Traditions and Customs*, p. 275; Scandaluzzi, *Medal Ribbons of the World*, vol. 3: *India*.

1023.100 Sena Medal

1023A Bar to Sena Medal

design of the medal and its ribbon); and No. 85-Pres./83 of 22 November 1983 (to specify that names of awardees will be published in the *Gazette of India*).

General Appearance: A 35 mm circular silver medal.

Obverse: A bayonet, point upward.

Reverse: A standing soldier with the Devanagri legend 'सेना मैडल' ('Sena Medal') above.

Ribbon: 32 mm, red, with a 2 mm silver-grey central stripe. Some sources suggest that this ribbon altered over time: 1960-81, 32 mm with a 2 mm silver-grey central stripe; and after 1981, a deeper red with a 1 mm central stripe. There is no indication that these variations in ribbon have any basis in policy and that they are anything other than manufacturing variations.

Suspension: A fixed ring attached to a 3 mm-wide straight-bar suspender ornamented with Ashoka leaves suspends the medal. The design of the suspension bar makes the task of changing the ribbon a nearly impossible one.

Naming: The medal is usually seen named on the edge in engraved capitals (naming has been observed in both English and Hindi). Until about 1970 the medal was issued with the year of award also on the edge; thereafter, this dating seems to have been discontinued.

Miniature: Miniatures have been issued.

Background: Awarded to all ranks of the army, 'for such individual acts of exceptional devotion to duty or courage as have special significance for the Army'. Awards may be made posthumously and a bar is authorized for subsequent awards of the Sena Medal.

When a bar has been awarded, it is indicated on service ribbons when worn alone by a silver rosette. A number of bars have been awarded, but a unique second bar was awarded in 1988 to IC-40348 Captain Pankaj Awasti, S.M.* Parachute Regiment (No. 76-Pres./88).

In effect, the Sena Medal—in common with the Nao Sena Medal (Navy, see 1024) and Vayu Sena Medal (Air Force, see 1025)—serves a dual purpose for the Indian Army as a medal for distinguished service and as an award for bravery. There is, however, no distinguishing emblem to differentiate between these two categories of award. This is similar to the confusion that exists in the awards practices of the United States, where the commendation medals of the various services function both as low level gallantry and as distinguished service decorations. Award of the decoration carries with it the right to use 'S.M.' as a postnominal abbreviation.

From 1 February 1999, the central government set a monthly stipend of Rs. 250 for recipients of the awards for bravery. Provincial stipends for this award are given in Appendix 2.

Through January 2003, the award has been bestowed 4,780 times (including 674 posthumous awards). The notification in the *Gazette of India* has distinguished between the two conditions for award only since January 1998.

Representative Citation: To understand the award better, a sample recipient would be JC-2195 Subadar Major Roshan, 9th Battalion, Dogra Regiment:

On 18th January 1964, at 1230 hours, a kerosene fire broke out owing to a defective oil heater in the quarters of Jemadar Madan Lal in Deir-el-balah (UAR [now Egypt]). The room was made of wood and Jemadar Madan Lal was trapped inside, the blazing heater blocking the only exit. The first officer to reach the scene was Subadar Major Roshan who rushed into the room, picked up the blazing heater, threw it outside and carried Jemadar Madan Lal to safety, but was himself badly burnt on the face, hands and legs, and fell unconscious. His prompt action, however, saved the life of Jemadar Madan Lal and valuable property of the United Nations Emergency Force.

Subadar Major Roshan displayed exemplary courage, initiative and presence of mind.

(No. 18-Pres./65 of 26 January 1965)

Outline

1023.100 medal.

1024 नौ सेना मैडल / NAO SENA MEDAL / NAVY MEDAL[47]

Awarded to navy personnel for acts of courage or exceptional achievement.

Established: By No. 17-Pres./60 of 26 January 1960 and by No. 32-Pres./60 of 17 June 1960. The statutes were modified by 25-Pres./61 of 15 May 1961, which established the circular medal design.

Obverse: The medal was originally described as a pentagonal silver medal, with concave sides, but it appears this design (1024.100) was never issued (except as specimens and miniatures?).

The design was altered in May 1961. The medal as finally issued is a 35 mm circular silver medal (1024.200) with the naval crest (a naval crown) on the obverse.

Reverse: Originally, to have been a trident, points upward, within a circlet of rope.

In May 1961, this was altered to crossed anchors as shown in figure 1024.200, partially surrounded by a chain cable. Above, 'नौ सेना मैडल' ('Nao Sena Medal').

Ribbon: 32 mm, navy (dark) blue with a 2 mm silver-grey central stripe.

Suspension: The medal is suspended by a fixed ring attached to a 3 mm straight-bar suspender ornamented with Ashoka leaves. The design of the suspension bar makes the task of changing the ribbon nearly impossible.

Naming: Named in engraved capitals along the rim. Until about 1970 the medal was issued with the year of award also on the edge; thereafter this dating seems to have been omitted.

Miniature: Miniatures have been issued.

Background: Awarded to all members of the Indian Navy 'for such individual acts of exceptional devotion to duty or courage as have special significance for the Navy'. The medal may be awarded posthumously and bars are authorized for subsequent awards of the Nao Sena Medal.

The award of a bar is indicated on service ribbons by the addition of a silver rosette. Through 2003, thirteen bars have been awarded.

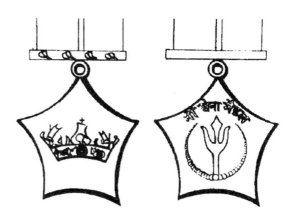

1024.100 Nao Sena Medal, original design

1024.200 Nao Sena Medal

[47] *Encyclopedia of Soldiers with Highest Gallantry Awards*, p. 34; *India's Highest Gallantry Awards*, p. 44; Haynes, 'Medals and Decorations of the Republic of India', pp. 33-34; Das, *Traditions and Customs*, p. 275; Scandaluzzi, *Medal Ribbons of the World*, vol. 3: *India*.

1024A Bar to Nao Sena Medal

In effect, the Nao Sena Medal—in common with the Sena Medal (Army, see 1023) and Vayu Sena Medal (Air Force, see 1025)—serves a dual purpose for the Indian Navy, as a medal for distinguished service and as an award for bravery. There is, however, no distinguishing emblem to differentiate between these two categories of award. Award of the decoration carries the right to use the postnominal abbreviation 'N.M.'.

From 1 February 1999, the central government set a monthly stipend of Rs. 250 for recipients of the award when it is awarded for bravery. The same provincial stipends are awarded for the Nao Sena Medal as for the Sena and Vayu Sena Medals (see Appendix 2).

Through 2003, the award has been bestowed 748 times, with thirteen bars. The notification in the *Gazette of India* has distinguished between the two conditions for award only since January 1998.

Representative Citation: To understand the award better, a sample recipient would be Sub-Lieutenant (SD) (TAS) Anant Ram, Indian Navy:

Sub-Lieutenant Anant Ram has rendered vital diving assistance at national projects and naval tasks since 1961. In September 1964, when a Piper Cub aircraft, belonging to the Bombay Flying Club, crashed while on a flight from Bombay to Ahmedabad, Sub-Lieutenant Anant Ram with a diving team was sent to search for the aircraft. In spite of a rough sea and swift current and very deep water, Sub-Lieutenant Anant Ram decided to undertake the operation and continued the search of a wide area until it was called off as it was evident that the aircraft had sunk in deep mud.

In November 1964, at the request of the Gujarat Electricity Board, Sub-Lieutenant Anant Ram worked with a diving team for the removal of a steel coffer-dam in the river Mahi which was blocking the flow of water into the pump-house of a new power station in Khaira District. The task became very difficult and risky because of the high tide, continous [*sic*] silting, deep mud and complete darkness due to muddy water. Despite all these hazards Sub-Lieutenant Anant Ram led his diving team and successfully conducted the operations of cutting the coffer-dam 8 feet below the datum.

Throughout, Sub-Lieutenant Anant Ram displayed exemplary courage, professional skill and devotion to duty in the best traditions of the Indian Navy.

(No. 23-Pres./66 of 26 January 1966)

Outline

1024.100 original pentagonal design, 1950-51 (never issued?).
1024.200 circular design, post-1951.

1025 वायु सेना मैडल / VAYU SENA MEDAL / AIR FORCE MEDAL[48]

Awarded to air force personnel for acts of courage or exceptional achievement.

Established: By No. 18-Pres./60 of 26 January 1960. Details of the design and the ribbon were published in No. 32-Pres./60 of 17 June 1960. The statutes were amended by No. 62-Pres./68 of 19 August 1968 to include Army Air OP pilots amongst the eligible personnel; and by No. 1-Pres./98 of 19 January 1998.

[48]*Encyclopedia of Soldiers with Highest Gallantry Awards*, p. 35; *India's Highest Gallantry Awards*, p. 45; Haynes, 'Medals and Decorations of the Republic of India', pp. 33-36; Das, *Traditions and Customs*, p. 275; Scandaluzzi, *Medal Ribbons of the World*, vol. 3: *India*.

General Appearance: A 35 mm four-armed silver star with the points shaped like lotus blooms.

Obverse: In the centre, the state emblem appears, surrounded by a wreath.

Reverse: A Himalayan eagle with wings spread, and the legend, above and below, 'वायु सेना मैडल' ('Air Force Medal').

Ribbon: 32 mm, alternating 3 mm diagonal stripes of gray and saffron running diagonally from lower left to upper right. The ribbon has an overall 'woven' appearance. There has been no official change in the ribbon since inception, although variations in the shades as well as textures have been observed.

Suspension: By a fixed ring attached to a 3 mm straight-bar suspender ornamented with Ashoka leaves. The design of the suspension bar makes the task of changing the ribbon a nearly impossible one.

Naming: The medal is normally named on the edge in engraved capitals. Until about 1970 the the year of award was also on the edge; thereafter, this dating seems to have been discontinued.

Miniature: Miniatures have been issued.

Background: Awarded to all members of the Indian Air Force 'in recognition of such individual acts of exceptional devotion to duty or courage as have special significance for the Air Force'. Posthumous awards may be made and a bar is authorized for subsequent awards of the Vayu Sena Medal.

When a bar has been awarded it is indicated on ribbons by the addition of a silver chakra.

In effect, the Vayu Sena Medal—in common with the Sena Medal (Army, see 1023) and Nao Sena Medal (Navy, see 1024)—serves a dual purpose for the Indian Air Force as a medal for distinguished service and as an award for bravery. There is, however, no distinguishing emblem to differentiate between these two categories of award.

From 1 February 1999, the central government set a monthly stipend of Rs. 250 for recipients of the award when it is awarded for bravery. The same provincial stipends are awarded for the Vayu Sena Medal as for the Sena and Nao Sena Medals (see Appendix 2). Award of the decoration carries the right to use the postnominal abbreviations 'V.M.'.

Through 26 January 2003, the award has been bestowed 940 times, with 23 bars (through 2000, probably the last bar to be awarded until 2003). By 26 January 2005, 404 Vayu Sena Medals had been awarded for gallantry, while 575 had been awarded for distinguished service (total of 978). Yet, in the early years, when citations were published, it was not always possible to determine into which category the awards were meant to fall. The notification in the *Gazette of India* has distinguished between the two conditions for award only since January 1998, though citations are no longer published.

Representative Citation: To understand the award better, a sample recipient would be that of the second-award bar to Flight Lieutenant Trevor Keelor (4818), G.D. (P), Indian Air Force:

On the 5th February 1964, Flight Lieutenant Keelor was detailed to

1025.100 Vayu Sena Medal

1025A Bar to Vayu Sena Medal

ferry a Gnat from Poona to Palam in a formation of five aircraft. The last part of the flight had to be undertaken at a height of about 41,000 feet.

While descending to land at Palam, he discovered, at a height of about 15,000 feet, that there was no response from the engine to throttle movements. After informing the leader, Flight Lieutenant Keelor immediately broke off from the formation and attempted to land at Palam, knowing well that previous attempts to force-land a Gnat had resulted in fatal or serious injury to the pilot. With great presence of mind and careful handling, he accomplished the forced-landing successfully without any damage to the aircraft.

Flight Lieutenant Trevor Keelor displayed courage, presence of mind and a high standard of professional skill in the best traditions of the Indian Air Force.

(No. 20-Pres./65 of 13 March 1965)

Outline

1025.100 medal

1026.100 President's Coast Guard Medal

1026 राष्ट्रपति का तटरक्षक मैडल / PRESIDENT'S TATRAKSHAK MEDAL / PRESIDENT'S COAST GUARD MEDAL

Awarded to members of the coast guard to recognize both bravery and distinguished service.

Established: By No. 49-Pres./89 of 7 June 1989. Rules governing the award were published in No. 50-Pres./89 of 7 June 1989.

General Appearance: Circular 35 mm. The statutes specify a circular 35 mm silver medal with gold gilt and such medals have been both awarded and illustrated in coast guard publications, but the ungilded medal—presumably an unfinished example—has also been observed.

Obverse: The Coast Guard crest with 'PRESIDENT'S COAST GUARD MEDAL' above and, separated by stars, the legend 'INDIA' below.

Reverse: The state emblem and motto within a wreath.

Ribbon: 35 mm, silver-white with a broad navy blue centre stripe (equal stripes).

Suspension: By a plain non-swivelling straight-bar suspender.

Naming: The medal is usually named on the edge.

Miniature: Miniatures have been issued.

Background: The Indian Coast Guard was constituted on 19 August 1978 as an independent paramilitary service to protect maritime and other national interests in the maritime zones of India, on 19 August 1978. The coast guard functions under the effective control of the Ministry of Defence.

The medal is awarded to members of the coast guard to recognize such individual acts of exceptional devotion to duty or courage, performed within or without the territory of India, as have special significance for the coast guard. These are categorized as follows:

1. For individual acts of exceptional courage;
2. Success in the conduct of coast guard operations under

difficult conditions such as inclement weather, limitations of ships/boats or equipment;

3. Special service as in the prevention or checking of smuggling, poaching, or safeguarding of national interests in the maritime zones of India;

4. Prolonged service, but only when distinguished by very exceptional ability and merit.

The award may be granted posthumously and a bar worn on the ribbon represents subsequent awards. When such a bar is awarded, it is attached to the ribbon from which the medal is suspended, and is indicated by the addition of a silver rose in gold gilt, to the ribbon bar when ribbons alone are worn. The number of medals for distinguished service is limited to a maximum of two awards in one year. There is no limit to the number of awards for gallantry.

Award of the medal is notified by publication of the name of the recipient in the *Gazette of India*, part 1, section 1. While awards for gallantry are notified as soon as possible after the date on which the act of gallantry was performed, medals for distinguished service are announced on 26 January (Republic Day) and 15 August (Independence Day).

Representative Citation: To understand the award better, a sample recipient in the bravery category of award would be the 1994 award to 4066-D Commandant Abhijit Kumar Dey, Coast Guard Overseeing Team, Goa:

The first Advances [*sic*] Offshore Patrol Vessel SAMAR (Yard 1151), one of the largest and most modern ships to be inducted in the service, is [*sic*] currently in its final stage of outfitting at Goa Shipyard Limited, Goa. On 16th February, 1994 a major fire broke out in the gun bay of the ship. Without caring for his personal safety, Comdt AK Dey immediately rushed to the scene of the fire and fought it relentlessly in spite of the thick smoke which was making it very difficult for any body [*sic*] to enter the compartment. With only minor fire fighting equipment and breathing apparatus available, the officer entered the compartment and evacuated the trapped unconscious workers. Unmindful of the hazards, he also led a search party below decks to other smoke filled compartments to look for casualties. The prompt action taken by the officer prevented further damage to the ship's equipment and compartments. The gallantry, valour and dedication displayed by the officer in the face of grave danger to his life was of an exceptionally high order.

On the 6th June, 1994 a severe cyclonic storm hit the Goa Coast which resulted in the grounding of 5 ships including the 64,000 DWT bulk carrier 'MV SEA TRANSPORTER.' The Coastal area of Goa came under imminent threat of oil pollution from these grounded ships. Regardless of his personal safety, the officer volunteered for embarking the grounded ship by winching down from a helicopter in very heavy seas and adverse weather conditions. The Officer promptly established a two way communication, assessed the damage and took measures for immediate pumping out of the oil from the ship. Without regard to his personal Safety and comfort the officer remained on board the stricken vessel even after a rope way had been established to ensure that the oil is [*sic*] discharged with the least possible delay. This enabled avoidance of a major oil spill and consequential pollution hazards.

Commandant Abijit Kumar Dey's courage, determination, total disregard of his personal safety under very difficult conditions, high

1027.200 Vishisht Seva Medal

1027A Bar to Vishisht Seva Medal

[49]*Encyclopedia of Soldiers with Highest Gallantry Awards*, pp. 36-37; *India's Highest Gallantry Awards*, pp. 46-47; Haynes, 'Medals and Decorations of the Republic of India', pp. 30-32; Das, *Traditions and Customs*, pp. 273-74; Scandaluzzi, *Medal Ribbons of the World*, vol. 3: *India*.

regard for human life, devotion to duty and valour are in keeping with the highest traditions of the Indian Coast Guard Service.

(No. 132-Pres./94 of 15 August 1994)

Outline

1026.100 medal.

1027 विशिष्ट सेवा मैडल / VISHISHT SEVA MEDAL / DISTINGUISHED SERVICE MEDAL[49]

Awarded to armed forces personnel for distinguished service.

Established: By No. 19-Pres./60 of 26 January 1960 and by No. 32-Pres./60 of 2 June 1960, as the 'Vishisht Seva Medal, Class III'. The statutes were revised by No. 34-Pres./62 of 30 April 1962 to clarify the fact that awards were made by the President of India (which had only been implied in the original statutes) and to allow for posthumous awards. The award was further revised, redesigned, and renamed by No. 30-Pres./67 of 27 January 1967. It was later further modified by No. 25-Pres./91 of 14 February 1991.

General Appearance: A 35 mm circular bright bronze medal. At first glance, it can be difficult to distinguish this medal from the Param Vishisht Seva Medal (1007), as the bronze is sometimes brighter than the thin and often elusive gilt of the P.V.S.M..

Obverse: A five-pointed star in the centre.

Reverse: The state emblem with the name of the decoration in Hindi above, 'विशिष्ट सेवा मैडल'. There was, of course, no alteration in this design with the changes that took place in the designs of the Param Vishisht Seva Medal (1007) and Ati Vishisht Seva Medal (1013).

Ribbon: 32 mm, yellow with three 2 mm dark blue stripes. Some sources suggest this design has altered over time: 1960-81, 32 mm with three equally spaced 2 mm dark blue stripes; and after 1981, a darker yellow colour and the blue stripes reduced to 1 mm. There is, however, no evidence that these variations reflect any policy shift and they are, instead, mere manufacturing differences.

Suspension: Suspended from a fixed straight-bar suspender.

Naming: Named on the edge. Early awards (until about 1970), were also inscribed with the date of award.

Miniature: Miniatures have been issued.

Background: The Vishisht Seva Medal is awarded to recognize 'distinguished service of an exceptional order' by all ranks of the armed forces. The award may be granted posthumously and subsequent awards are represented by a bar worn on the ribbon.

The award carries with it the right to use 'V.S.M.' as post-nominal letters.

The Vishisht Seva Medal was originally established as the 'Vishisht Seva Medal, Class III', and only on 27 January 1967 was it renamed as detailed below. This did not, however, result in any change in the design of the medal.

In 1980, the Yuddh Seva Medal (1016) was created to recognize distinguished services in a specified operational environment. Since that date, awards of the V.S.M. have been restricted to peacetime service.

The provincial stipends accompanying this award are detailed in Appendix 2.

Through 26 January 2003, the award has been bestowed 3,699 times. Until 8 October 2002, thirty-nine bars have been awarded.

Representative Citation: To understand the award better, a sample recipient would be the 1990 award to 607094-R Sergeant (now JWO) Bhan Singh Gill, Inst Fit, 129 Helicopter Unit, Indian Air Force:

Sergeant Bhan Singh Gill is on the posted strength of one of the Helicopter Units since 16 Jun 87. He was selected as a member of the Air Force contingent for the 8th Indian Scientific Expedition to Antarctica.

For flying operations at Antarctica, the Pratap helicopters were fitted with Decca Doppler 91 nav system and Primus 500 weather radar. Sgt Gill worked untiringly for long hours and accomplished this complex task of modification well in time. He again carried out transfer of this modification from one helicopter to another at Antarctica working on the ship deck undettered by the sub zero temperature and strong winds. To accomplish the task, the Air Force team was flying round the clock to make full use of the scarce good weather at Antarctica.

For his exceptional devotion to duty and professionalism of the highest order displayed at Antarctica, the President is pleased to award the Vishisht Seva Medal to Sgt Bhan Singh Gill.

(No. 41-Pres/90 of 26 January 1990)

Outline

1027.100 Vishisht Seva Medal, Class III (1960-67). There is no difference between this medal and the one that follows, only the records would reveal the distinction

1027.200 Vishisht Seva Medal (1967-). There is no difference between this medal and the one which precedes, only the records would reveal the distinction

1028 INDIAN POLICE MEDAL FOR GALLANTRY[50]

This medal was awarded for acts of bravery by members of the Indian police. While this medal was awarded in British-ruled India from 1932 until their departure in 1947, this entry deals only with the medal as it was awarded in independent India, during the Dominion and early Republic period.

Established: By a Royal Warrant of 23 February 1932, revised in December 1944 to create separate classes of medals for gallantry and distinguished service. The extension of award under the Dominion of India was authorized by a Royal Warrant of 1 May 1948, published in the *Gazette of India* under Private Secretary to the Governor-General's No. 15-H of 8 June 1948. The medal became obsolete in March 1951 when the Police Medal for Gallantry (1029) was created.

General Appearance: Circular 36 mm bronze.

Obverse: The crowned bust of King George VI, facing left

[50] Abbott and Tamplin, *British Gallantry* Awards, pp. 279-85; *Medal Yearbook 1999*, p. 95.

1028.100 Indian Police Medal for Gallantry

and surrounded by the royal titles 'GEORGIVS VI D: G: BR: OMN: REX ET INDIAE IMP:'. These are, of course, the king's titles prior to the Indian Independence Act. While a strong case might have been made for a redesign of the medal to reflect the new constitutional status, there is no indication that this took place.

Reverse: Within a crowned wreath, the words 'INDIAN / POLICE' and on a ribbon tying the sides of the wreath 'FOR GALLANTRY'.

Ribbon: 34 mm, dark blue with a 10 mm medium red central stripe, and 5 mm white edge stripes. A 1 mm white stripe divides both the blue stripes. The same ribbon is used for the successor medal, the Police Medal for Gallantry (1029).

Suspension: Suspended by a straight-bar suspender

Naming: The medal is named on the edge.

Miniature: Miniatures have been issued.

Background: In the ambiguous constitutional circumstances of the Dominion period, this medal was continued from the period of British rule into the early years of Independence. It thus constituted an anachronistic continuation of royal authority into post-Independence India.

Awards: From 1948 to 1950, the medal was awarded eighty-one times. The first award for a post-Independence action was that to Sub-Inspector of Police Keshav Govind Shidore, Bombay City (PSG-G No. 23-H of 22 June 1948). During this same time period, two bars for second awards were made (presumably to pre-1947 medals), to Deputy Superintendent Shri Lourdu Thomas Mallavarapu (24 July 1948) and to Superintendent Shri S. A. Thomas (29 October 1949).

Representative Citation: To understand the award better, a sample recipient would be Shri Gurdial Singh, Officiating Deputy Superintendent of Police, Hissar, Punjab (I):

Shri Gurdial Singh was specially deputed with an armed force to round up Banwari's gang which had cast a spell of terror in Hissar, Rohtak and Gurgaon Districts and in the Districts of Patiala and East Punjab States Union and elsewhere by kidnapping rich people and holding them for ransom. On the night between 3rd and the 4th June 1949, an informer told him that Shambhu, a lieutenant of Banwari, wanted in connection with cases of murder and dacoity, was likely to visit village Lohani, Shri Gurdial Singh at once organized a raiding party and proceeded to the village. He arrived there with his party at about 4 a.m. and found that Shambhu had left about midnight towards village Kaihrpura. He then set out with his small party to follow his tracks and when he reached village Kaihrpura, they learnt that Shambhu had left with Rameshwar, his relative, on a camel towards village Assalwas. Shri Gurdial Singh continued to follow the tracks and about 2/3 furlongs from village Assalwas noticed a camel of the same description as that of Shambhu outlaw. On seeing the pursuit party, Shambhu mounted his camel which was exceptionally fast, and tried to escape but was pursued by the police party and his camel was disabled. Shambhu then took up his position on a sand dune and opened fire on the Police party at the same time retreating through the sand dunes towards the nearby jungle. The Police party was not able to see where he had gone. Shri Gurdial Singh, thereupon, with two Constables and with a bren gun got into his jeep and circled round the area to find out where he was. After putting a cordon round the area he began to search with a small force when suddenly Shambhu jumped out from behind a thick thorny bush and started firing on them. Shri Gurdial Singh returned fire and ordered one of the Constables who was armed with a bren gun also to fire a burst which caught Shambhu in the middle of the chest with the result that he died instaneously. A .303 rifle, some chargers, a bandolier and a haversack were recovered from his body.

In the encounter Shri Gurdial Singh displayed courage and leadership of a very high order.

(No. 26/48/49-Police-I of 18 March 1950)

Outline

1028.100 medal.

1029 पुलिस पदक वीरता के लिये / POLICE PADAK VIRTA KE LIYE / POLICE MEDAL FOR GALLANTRY[51]

Awarded for acts of bravery by members of the Indian Police.

Established: By No. 3-Pres/51 and No. 4-Pres./51 of 1 March 1951. This was later modified by notifications No. 5-Pres/51 of 9 April 1951 (to correct an error in No. 4-Pres./51), No. 27-Pres./51 of 12 June 1951 (to amend the rules), No. 28-Pres./52 of 17 March 1952 (to amend the rules), No. 59-Pres./52 of 22 September 1952 (to amend the rules), No. 8-Pres,/53 of 17 February 1953 (corrigendum; to amend the rules), No. 50-Pres./54 of 14 December 1954 (to amend the rules), No. 11-Pres./56 of 8 March 1956 (to amend the rules), No. 25-Pres./57 of 1 June 1957 (to alter the rates of monthly allowance), No. 65-Pres./62 of 10 October 1962 (to include members of the Central Intelligence Bureau among the eligible categories), No. 66-Pres./62 of 10 October 1962 (to amend the rules), No. 78-Pres./63 of 17 October 1963 (to include members of the Railway Protection Force among the eligible categories), No. 79-Pres./63 of 17 October 1963 (to amend the rules and increase the permissible limit of awards in one year to 200 [maximum 225]), No. 30-Pres./66 of 10 March 1966 (to amend the rules and increase the permissible limit of awards in one year to 275 [maximum 300]), No. 43-Pres./71 (to amend the eligible categories by replacing the added 'members of the Central Intelligence Bureau and Railway Protection Force with 'Central Police/Security Organizations) and No. 44-Pres./71 (to amend the rules) of 5 August 1971, No. 118-Pres./74 of 1 December 1974 (to amend the rules), No. 42-Pres./75 of 19 May 1975 (to amend the rules), No. 43-Pres./75 of 19 May 1975 (to amend the rules), No. 125-Pres./75 of 24 December 1975 (to amend the rules), No. 42-Pres./82 of 24 September 1982 (to alter the rates of monthly allowance), No. 19-Pres./84 of 13 February 1984 (to amend the rules), No. 77-Pres./87 of 4 November 1987 (to amend the rules), No. 81-Pres./88 of 29 July 1988, No. 99-Pres./90 of 17 December 1990 (to amend the rules), and No. 101-Pres./98 of 18 August 1998 (to alter the rates of monthly allowance). Redesigned by No. 88-Pres./98 of 20 July 1998.

1029.100 Police Medal for Gallantry, first variety

1029.200 Police Medal for Gallantry, second variety

[51]*Encyclopedia of Soldiers with Highest Gallantry Awards*, p. 38; *India's Highest Gallantry Awards*, p. 48; Dorling, *Ribbons & Medals*, pp. 144-45; Scandaluzzi, *Medal Ribbons of the World*, vol. 3: *India*.

General Appearance: Circular 35 mm bronze medal.

Obverse: First variety: The state emblem in the centre, with 'POLICE MEDAL' above and with the State motto 'सत्यमेव जयते' ('Satyameva Jayate' or 'Truth Alone Triumphs') below, separated by a small star. *Second variety:* The state emblem and motto in the centre and the legend 'पुलिस पदक' ('Police Medal') in Hindi above and 'POLICE MEDAL' below, separated by a small star.

Reverse: First variety: Shown above, two horizontal lines, above and below the legend 'Indian /Police' and, in the centre between the lines, 'For Gallantry'. The entire reverse is contained within a wreath. *Second variety:* In 1998, the reverse was modified to include 'भारतीय पुलिस' ('Bharatiya Police' or 'Indian Police') above and 'INDIAN POLICE' below, both legends separated by two horizontal lines with 'वीरता के लिये' ('Virta ke Liye' or 'For Bravery') and 'FOR GALLANTRY'. The entire reverse is contained within a wreath.[52]

Ribbon: 34 mm, dark blue with a 10 mm medium red central stripes, 5 mm white edge stripes and a 1 mm white stripe in the centre of the blue stripes. This is the same ribbon as for the Indian Police Medal for Gallantry (1028).

Suspension: Both varieties are suspended by a non-swivelling straight-bar suspender.

Naming: The medal is named on the edge in engraved running script.

Miniature: Miniatures have been issued of both varieties.

Background: This is a post-Republic revision of the older Indian Police Medal for Gallantry (1028). It is awarded to members of a recognized police force, the Central Intelligence Bureau, or an organized fire service (until 1975 only) who have performed services of conspicuous gallantry. All police personnel of the country irrespective of rank and length of service are eligible for this award. In normal circumstances, no more than 175 police gallantry medals may be awarded in any one year. The recipients of this medal are granted an allowance of Rs.100 per month (or Rs. 50 for a bar) which continues to be paid to them at the same rate even after retirement. After the death of the recipient of the medal, this allowance continues to be paid to his widow at the same rate. Recipients are also eligible to travel free by train in the First Class AC II tier or in the First Class with an attendant. For subsequent acts of gallantry, a bar may be awarded. The bar is of bronze, of an oblong slip-on design, with the recipient's details engraved on the reverse. When service ribbons are worn alone, the possession of a bar is indicated by the addition of a miniature silver rosette to the ribbon bar. Bars to this medal are comparatively common, especially in recent years.

The first award was to No. 278/J Assistant Sub-Inspector of Police S. Hazara Singh, Punjab Police, Gurdaspur District, on 7 May 1951 (No. 14-Pres./51).

There are two varieties. The first was awarded from 1951 to 1998, and the second has been awarded since 1998. In 1975, when the separate Fire Service Medal for Gallantry (1030) was created, fire service personnel ceased to be eligible for this award.

[52] This image, though not high quality, is from the Indian Mint website, http://www.igmint.org/photo1.htm.

Representative Citation: To understand the award better, a sample recipient would be Chanan Singh, Foot Constable No. 617, District Amritsar, Punjab:

Two soldiers Sardul Singh and Mohinder Singh, deserted from Kathua (Jammu State) along with a 303 rifle and ammunition. They were joined by Sardul Singh's brother, Bachan Singh, an ex-Army man. Their declared intention was to kill some of their enemies in the village and, thereafter, to form a dacoit gang for committing dacoities. On the evening of 4th May, 1949, a small police party, consisting of 1 Assistant Sub-Inspector and 3 Foot Constables, while escorting two accused persons from village Mudala to Majitha, were suddenly fired upon by a party of three cyclists. The police party immediately took position and replied with their fire-arms. The culprits fled but were hotly pursued by the police party and had to abandon their cycles and take shelter in the country-side under cover of darkness. The abandoned cycles were recovered as also a haversack which contained a Pay Book which showed that it belonged to Sardul Singh. Raids were then organized at the homes and haunts of the three men and a large scale search commenced. On the morning of the 6th May, one small search party contacted them and a running encounter ensued. An immediate message was also sent to headquarters for assistance from where the mounted police and the Armed Reserve, of which Foot Constable Chanan Singh was a member, rushed to the spot. Finally, the culprits were brought to bay in village Sainsra Khurd, Police Station Majitha. Being trained Army men, they took up an excellent offensive [defensive?] position consisting of a small semi-circular enclosure about a foot and half below ground level and bounded by a low mud parapet. Inside there was thick undergrowth which screened the culprits from sight completely. The enclosure was isolated from the village *abadi* with a few dismantled mud houses on one side. The ground on all sides being open, a straight attack could not be launched. The three culprits, having taken up this position, after a while became quite silent. Tear smoke was used but without effect. The complete silence and lack of response, made the Senior Superintendent of Police, who was conducting the operations, suspect that they may have escaped. There was no way of ascertaining this, except by approaching the *morcha* of the culprits which was a most hazardous undertaking. Foot Constable Chanan Singh No. 617 immediately volunteered to do so. Disguised as a villager and accompanied by an old woman, to strengthen the disguise; he approached the position of the culprits from the rear and was able to see one of them entrenched in the ditch. Having accomplished this 'scouting' job successfully, he returned and volunteered to go again armed with a rifle and take his chance of shooting the culprit whom he had seen. He could not spot the other two. Then he dressed up as a *Mazhabi* woman but hid a loaded rifle under his clothes and proceeded towards the entrenched position again. When he got to a favourable spot he took aim and shot dead the culprit whom he had seen previously and who was still in the same place. This brave action greatly demoralized the remaining two culprits. However, they still did not come out into the open for surrender. Meanwhile, more police reinforcements arrived with Hand Grenades and a Bren Gun. Towards evening, a well planned advance was ordered and Hand Grenades were also used. The culprits, seeing the advance, opened fire and, in doing so exposed themselves. One of them was shot dead with a Bren Gun burst and the other then surrendered.

Foot Constable Chanan Singh displayed outstanding courage and devotion to duty.

(No. 45-Pres/51 of 5 October 1951)

Outline

1029.100 first variety with English only (1951-98).
1029.200 second variety with Hindi (1998-).

1030.100 Fire Services Medal for Gallantry

1030 अग्नि शमन सेवा पदक वीरता के लिये / AGNI SHAMAN SEVA PADAK VIRTA KE LIYE / FIRE SERVICES MEDAL FOR GALLANTRY

Awarded for acts of bravery by members of the fire services.

Established: By No. 40-Pres./75 and No. 41-Pres./75 of 1975. It was further modified by No. 15-Pres./88 of 22 February 1988.

General Appearance: Circular 35 mm bronze medal.

Obverse: The State Emblem and the legend 'FIRE SERVICE MEDAL' अग्नि शमन सेवा पदक'.

Reverse: A wreath bearing a horizontal oval tablet with the legend 'FOR GALLANTRY'. 'वीरता के लिये '.

Ribbon: 32 mm, brown, with 4 mm yellow edge stripes, and a 3 mm black stripe down the centre.

Suspension: By a non-swivelling straight-bar suspender.

Miniature: Miniatures have presumably been issued.

Naming: The medals are named on the edge.

Background: Awarded to fire services personnel for acts of gallantry. The award carries a monthly allowance of Rs. 40 (or of Rs. 20 for a bar). Bars may be awarded for subsequent acts of gallantry. The bars are slip-on bars, oblong-shaped and made of bronze; they have the recipient's details engraved on the reverse. When ribbons are worn alone, a bar is indicated by the addition of a silver rosette.

The first award, 15 August 1975, was to Shri S. Singhajit Singh, Station Officer, Manipur Fire Service (No. 98-Pres./75).

Representative Citation: To understand the award better, a sample recipient would be the posthumous 1985 award to Shri Rajbir Singh, Constable, Industrial Security Force, Madhya Pradesh:

On the 1st March 1985, a serious fire occurred in [the] Indo-Burma Petroleum Complex, a public sector undertaking, located near Korba, Madhya Pradesh. On receiving the request for help from this undertaking, the fire fighting team of Central Industrial Security Force (Fire Wing) was sent to the scene. Shri Rajbir Singh was not included in the team. But on learning that the fire was serious, Shri Rajbir Singh could not stop himself and he volunteered to go for the task. The fire had become more violent since it involved high explosives. Shri Rajbir Singh fought the fire courageously saving life and public property but in the process he got exposes [*sic*] to a sudden gush of products of combustions [*sic*] noxious gases resulting in his death due to asphysia [*sic*].

In this action, Shri Rajbir Singh, Constable, exhibits [*sic*] exemplary courage, initiative and devotion to duty of a high order.

(No. 82-Pres./85 of 15 August 1985)

Outline

1030.100 medal.

1031   CORRECTIONAL SERVICE MEDAL
FOR GALLANTRY

Awarded to correctional service personnel for acts of conspicuous gallantry performed within India.

Established: By No. 62-Pres/1999 of 5 April 1999, with effect from 1 July 1999. The rules governing the award were notified by No. 63-Pres/1999 of 5 April 1999.

Eligible Categories: Awarded to the members of a recognized correctional service.

General Appearance: A 34 mm diameter bronze medal.

Obverse: The state emblem in the centre; and the words 'CORRECTIONAL SERVICE MEDAL FOR GALLANTRY' in Hindi, joined by a wreath. This is surrounded by a six-pointed star, with 'BHARAT' at the bottom. As we have not observed this medal, this descrtiption is based on the rather confusing gazette description.

Reverse: In the centre, a conch, with the English inscription 'FOR GALLANTRY' contained in the middle circle, surrounded by a six-pointed star.

Ribbon: 32 mm, saffron, with a 3 mm yellow stripe in the centre.

Suspension: Suspended by a non-swivelling straight-bar suspender.

Naming: The medal is named on the edge.

Miniature: Miniatures have not been issued.

Background: Awarded to members of a recognized correctional service for performing acts of exceptional gallantry in apprehending or preventing the escape of prisoners, the risk incurred being estimated with regard to the obligations and duties of the concerned officer. The criteria of award of the Correctional Service Medal for Gallantry are identical to those for the award of the President's Correctional Service Medal for Gallantry, the terms 'for acts of exceptional gallantry' and 'for acts of conspicuous gallantry' being used at varying points in both cases. It is therefore difficult to know how these two are distinguished in practice. Subsequent awards of the medal are recognized by addition of a bar to the medal ribbon, each bar being denoted by a small silver lotus emblem on the ribbon of the medal when worn alone. The medal is not authorized to be awarded posthumously and there is no provision either in the instituting gazette or in the rules to this effect; yet, in the sample citation given below, the award is a posthumous award. This practice seems to require refinement and resolution.

Names of personnel awarded the medal are notified in the *Gazette of India* and the Ministry of Home Affairs maintains a register of such names. Grant of the medal and each subsequent bar carries with it a monetary allowance of Rs. 60. All recipients, irrespective of rank, are entitled to the allowance, at a uniform rate. Recipients who may already have been awarded the Police Medal for Gallantry are eligible to the full allowance, in addition to the allowance attached to the earlier award.

There is no limit on the number of Correctional Service Medals for Gallantry that can be awarded in a year. The medal may be forfeited if the holder is held to be guilty of 'disloyalty, cowardice in action or such conduct as in the opinion of the President, brings the force into disrepute'. Awards are announced biannually on the occasions of the Republic Day (26 January) and Independence Day (15 August).

Representative Citation: To understand the award better, a sample recipient would be the posthumous award to Shri Ashok Kumar Gautam, Jailer, District Prison, Lucknow, in 2000:

Shri Ashok Kumar Gautam, while posted as Jailer in the highly sensitive District Jail, Lucknow, made continuous efforts to strengthen the prison administration. He effectively controlled the activities of a group of prisoners who were a part of [the] mafia. Despite threats to his life, he continued in his efforts to strengthen the administration and compelled them to live like other prisoners and helped establish an atmosphere of fearlessness from [the] mafia in the jail. He was brutally killed on 4-10-1997 at the instance of the mafia while he was going home from [the] jail.

While posted as Jailor [*sic*] in the District Jail, Lucknow, Shri Askok Kumar Gautam, thus, displayed exemplary gallantry, courage, and devotion to duty.

(No. 12-Pres./00 of 26 January 2000)

Outline

1031.100 medal.

1032.100 Home Guards and Civil Defence Medal

1032 गृहरक्षा व नागरिक सुरक्षा पदक वीरता के लिये / GRIHRAKSHA WA NAGARIK SURAKSHA PADAK VIRTA KE LIYE / HOME GUARDS AND CIVIL DEFENCE MEDAL FOR GALLANTRY[53]

Awarded for acts of bravery by members of the home guard and civil defence organizations.

Established: By No. 100-Pres./74 of 7 October 1974 (with effect from 15 August 1974), by the President of India. The rules governing the award were published in No. 101-Pres./74 of 7 October 1974 and modified by No. 17-Pres./90 of 27 February 1990.

General Appearance: A circular 35 mm bronze medal.

Obverse: The state emblem and motto, surrounded on either side by the legend 'गृहरक्षा व नागरिक सुरक्षा पदक' ('Grihraksha wa Nagarik Suraksha Padak' or 'Home Guards and Civil Defence Medal') and 'HOME GUARDS AND CIVIL DEFENCE MEDAL'.

Reverse: In the centre, the Home Guards emblem, surrounded on either side by the legend 'वीरता' ('Virta' or 'Gallantry') and 'GALLANTRY'.

Ribbon: 32 mm, five alternating black-and-white stripes (three 8 mm white and two 4 mm black). The colour sequence of the five stripes is white/black/white/black/white. In addition, the central white stripe should have a thin (1 mm) black stripe down the centre. The ribbons that have been observed, however, omit the central black stripe. The same ribbon is apparently used both for gallantry and for distinguished service awards.

Suspension: The medal is suspended from a ring.

Naming: The medal is named on the edge.

[53]*Encyclopedia of Soldiers with Highest Gallantry Awards*, p. 32.

Miniature: Miniatures have (presumably) been issued, although there is no official basis for this in gazette notifications.

Background: Awarded to members of the home guards, civil defence, and mobile civil emergency force for acts of gallantry performed within the territory of India. Gallantry medals were limited to fifty awards per year until 1990, when the statutes were amended and no limit was placed on the number of medals to be awarded for gallantry (No. 17-Pres./90 of 27 Feb. 1990). Subsequent acts of bravery may be recognized by the addition of a bronze bar to the medal ribbon. When a bar has been awarded, it is indicated on service ribbons by the addition of a silver rosette. Posthumous awards are possible. Award of the medal carries with it a lump sum monetary reward. Till 1990, a recipient was entitled to Rs. 500 upon award of the medal, and Rs. 250 for every subsequent bar. This was amended by No. 17-Pres./90 of 27 Feb. 1990 and the amount was raised to Rs. 1,500 for both the medal and the bar.

The first award on 15 August 1975 was the posthumous award to Shri Kalubhai H. Jadav, Platoon Sergeant, Gujarat State Home Guards (No. 100-Pres./75).

Representative Citation: To understand the award better, a sample recipient would be the 1984 award to Shri Purushottamlal Patwa, Sainik Volunteer, Madhya Pradesh:

Shri Purushottamlal Patwa was enrolled as a Home Guard in District Sagar on the 20th October, 1982, and later he was deputed to Police Station, Bina. On the 22nd February 1984, the Station House Officer of Police Station, Bina, received information that Rameshwar Ghosi, a notorious criminal, was housing in Jawahar Ward. He along with Shri Purushottamlal Patwa and a few Police Constables and Home Guards, went to Jawahar Ward in search of the accused person. On seeing the Police party, a person emerged from the back lane and started running away. Shri Purushottamlal Patwa guessed that the person must be the accused and started chasing him. When Shri Patwa was about to overtake him, the accused took out the pistol and threatened him. Unmindful for his personal safety, Shri Purushottamlal Patwa continued advancing towards the accused. When the accused was about to be overpowered, he aimed his loaded pistol at Shri Purushottamlal Patwa but misfired. Shri Purushottamlal Patwa without caring for his life caught hold of the accused who inflicted injuries in the chest and abdomen of Shri Purushottamlal Patwa by pistol in order to free himself and escape, but Shri Patwa did not lose his grip till other police personnel arrived and apprehended the accused.

Shri Purushottamlal Patwa thus displayed exemplary courage and high sense of devotion to duty at a great risk to his life.

(No. 93-Pres./84 of 15 August 1984)

Outline

1032.100 medal.

1033 उत्तम जीवन रक्षा पदक / UTTAM JEEVAN RAKSHA PADAK / BEST LIFESAVING MEDAL[54]

Awarded for lifesaving in conditions of great danger.

Established: By No. 45-Pres./61 of 30 September 1961, as the 'Jeevan Raksha Padak, Class II'. Statutes republished in No.

[54] *Encyclopedia of Soldiers with Highest Gallantry Awards,* p. 39; *India's Highest Gallantry Awards,* p. 49; Das, *Traditions and Customs,* p. 274.

1033.200 Uttam Jeevan Raksha Padak

1033A Comparison of the size of one of the Jeevan Raksha Padaks, with a 'normal' medal

7-Pres./62 of 18 January 1962 and revised and decoration renamed by No. 79-Pres./67 of 26 August 1967.

General Appearance: A 58 mm roughly circular silver medal with a rectangular projection 22.5 × 12.5 mm at the top, and at the bottom, a 42.5 × 10 mm projection. This incredibly large award seems more appropriate for tabletop display than for wearing, and it is believed that most recipients actually wear the half-sized miniature, which would be almost the same size as a normal medal.

To understand the size of this award, the medal may be compared to the President's Police and Fire Services Medal for Gallantry (see Fig. 1033A).

Obverse: In the centre, a hand in the *Abhai Mudra* and, above 'मा भैः' and below 'जीवन रक्षा पदक' ('Jeevan Raksha Padak') (1961-67). The later variety reads 'उत्तम जीवन रक्षा' ('Uttam Jeevan Raksha') (after 1967).

Reverse: The state emblem, with the motto in the lower projection.

Ribbon: 32 mm, red with 4 mm light blue edge stripes and two 1 mm green centre stripes 4 mm apart. These colours are said to symbolize fire (red), water (blue), and life (green).

Suspension: By a ring.

Naming: These medals are issued unnamed.

Miniature: Miniatures are awarded, and are frequently worn if the recipient is in a position where wearing of medals is called for.

Background: Awarded primarily to civilians to recognize acts of lifesaving, including cases of drowning, fire, or mine accidents, 'for courage and promptitude under circumstances of very great danger to the life of the rescue [*sic*]'. The only cases in which members of the armed forces, police, or fire services can be awarded the medal is when such acts take place outside the course of their duty. The medal may be awarded posthumously and subsequent awards are recognized by the addition of a bar to the medal ribbon. When a bar has been awarded, this is indicated on the service ribbon by the addition of a silver miniature of the medal. Through 26 January 2004, one bar had been awarded; in that same period, the U.J.R.P. had been awarded 299 times. At least one bar to this medal has been awarded, to Shri Rambilas Sharma Pahalwan, in 1968 (No. 54-Pres./68).

Recipients of the award are given a cash gratuity of Rs. 45,000.

Like many other Indian awards, the Uttam Jeevan Raksha Padak was originally established as a part of a three-class decoration, the Jeevan Raksha Padak in 1961. The second class of this award was renamed the Uttam Jeevan Raksha Padak in 1967.

Representative Citation: To understand the award better, a sample recipient would be the 1976 award to Shri Parappallil Varkey John, Rangpo, Sikkim:

On 26th November, 1974, Shri Parappallil Varkey John while work-ing as an enumerator for traffic census at Teesta Bridge saw an old man being carried away by the fast current of the Teesta river. He immediately jumped into the river from the bridge which is at a height of about 100 feet from the normal river level, without even removing his clothes, plunged after the drowning man despite the strong current and brought him to the bank after a heroic struggle. He was completely exhausted by the struggle to bring the rescued man towards the bank. In the meantime a number of persons had gathered on the bank and they extended a helping hand to Shri John.

Shri Parappallil Varkey John displayed exceptional courage in saving a drowning man at grave danger to his own life.

(No. 2-Pres./76 of 6 January 1976)

Outline

1033.100 Jeevan Raksha Padak, Class Two (1961-67).
1033.200 Uttam Jeevan Raksha Padak (1967-).

1034 आहत मैडल / AHAT MEDAL / WOUND MEDAL / PARAKRAM PADAK[55]

Awarded for wounds received in combat situations.

Established: By No. 5-Pres./73 of 17 January 1973 (with effect from 15 August 1947) and amended by No. 84-Pres./83 dated 18 November 1983 (to allow for a bar for subsequent awards) and by No. 89-Pres/98 dated 10 July 1998 (extending eligibility to internal security operations). The medal was officially redesignated as the 'Parakram Padak' with immediate effect by No. 107-Pres./00 dated 28 August 2000. The change of name was deemed to be retrospective.

General Appearance: A 35 mm circular silver medal.

Obverse: The state emblem in the centre. To the left, there is the legend 'आहत मैडल' and to the right 'WOUND MEDAL'. There is no indication that the medal was redesigned in any way when it was renamed in 2000.

Reverse: Ashoka Chakra.

Ribbon: 32 mm, white, with a 10 mm red central stripe.

Suspension: The medal is suspended by a ring. In some issues, the ring is especially thin.

Naming: The medal is named on the edge with impressed capital letters.

Miniature: Miniatures have been issued, although they are usually seen with a straight-bar suspender.

Background: Awarded with effect from 15 August 1947 to those who sustain 'wounds as a result of direct enemy action in any type of operations or counter-insurgency actions'. Eligible categories include all ranks of the Indian military, including reserve and territorial forces, and members of the Railway Protection Force, police, home guards, civil defence, or any other organization specified by the government. Aircrews who, in the course of bailing out of an aircraft destroyed by hostile action sustain injuries (and not specifically 'wounds') may be awarded the medal. In a significant extension of the qualifying criteria, personnel wounded during 'internal security' operations were included amongst those eligible for award of the medal, by No. 89-Pres/98 dated 10 July 1998. This notification was also deemed to have effect from 15 August 1947. Somewhat strangely, the medal may not be awarded

1034.100 Wound Medal/Ahat Medal/Parakaram Padak

[55]*Encyclopedia of Soldiers with Highest Gallantry Awards*, pp. 40-41; *India's Highest Gallantry Awards*, pp. 50-51; Das, *Traditions and Customs*, pp. 275-76; Scandaluzzi, *Medal Ribbons of the World*, vol. 3: *India*.

posthumously. No specific provision was made for bars for subsequent awards until 1983; there is no provision to indicate that such a bar has been awarded when ribbons are worn alone.

In 2000, the medal was inexplicably renamed as the 'Parakram Padak', apparently at the behest of the Ministry of Defence, though no changes in the design were instituted due to that change of name.[56] Given this name change, considerable confusion with the Op Parakram Medal (1047) may also be anticipated.

Outline

1034.100 medal.

1035.300 General Service Medal 1947

1035 GENERAL SERVICE MEDAL 1947[57]

A general service campaign medal awarded for military operations, 1947-75.

Established: A draft Royal Warrant was prepared in January 1949 for the possible institution of this award in the name of the British sovereign as, during the Dominion period, such a step would have been necessary to give the award status within the Commonwealth. On consideration, this course was abandoned and the medal was later created by No. 3-Pres./50 of 5 June 1950, by the President of India (with retrospective effect from 15 August 1947). The reverse designs were altered by Presidential amendments No. 30-Pres./54 of 21 June 1954 and by No. 49-Pres./54 of 6 December 1954.

General Appearance: A circular 35 mm cupro-nickel medal.

Obverse: A representation of Bhavani, or the divine sword of justice and true discrimination, point upwards and within a halo.

Reverse: The original design of 1950, which was never issued, described the reverse: in the centre, a lotus flower with buds with the legend above 'The General Service Medal', and, below, '1947'. In June 1954, the lower reverse legends were altered to read '1947' with 'INDIA' just above this. Finally, in December 1954, the design of the reverse as actually issued was specified as having the upper inscription read 'GENERAL SERVICE' and below, 'INDIA'. No specimens have been seen of the first two reverses, though prototypes may exist.

Ribbon: 31 mm, red with five 1 mm dark green stripes. As it has been so common and so widely produced, there is some variability of the precise shades of the colours in this ribbon. These colour variations have no significance (as some have stated). The notifying gazette unusually specified the symbolic significance of the ribbon colours; red representing valour and passion, and green auspiciousness.

Suspension: Suspended by a non-swivelling straight-bar suspender to which the clasp is attached. These clasps (except that for the 'Mizo Hills') are distinguished by having individualized representative emblems on the rose at each end; these are detailed and illustrated below.[58]

[56] The Ministry of Defence apparently suggested the change of nomenclature at the behest of the President of India in August 1998.

[57] *Encyclopedia of Soldiers with Highest Gallantry Awards*, pp. 42-47; *India's Highest Gallantry Awards*, pp. 52-57; Haynes, 'Medals and Decorations of the Republic of India', pp. 36-37; Johnson, 'Medals of the Republic of India', pp. 38-9; Das, *Traditions and Customs*, p. 276; Dorling, *Ribbons & Medals*, p. 144; Scandaluzzi, *Medal Ribbons of the World*, vol. 3: *India*.

[58] In standard phaleristic usage the 'rose' is defined as ornamental florets on the ends of certain clasps serving to conceal rivet fittings; see *Medal Yearbook 2001*, p. 38.

Naming: The medals are named on the edge with impressed capital letters.

Miniature: Miniatures have been issued. Both official and unofficial slip-on clasps are encountered in a wide range of styles.

Background: Ther medal is warded for service with the Indian armed forces (including reserve forces, territorial army, Indian States Forces, militia, nursing services, and enrolled or uniformed civilians) in circumstances of active service. The individual active service events are each represented by a clasp, and these are detailed below. Multiple clasps are, of course, possible. In practice, however, they seem to be quite uncommon. All clasps are inscribed in English rather than in Hindi.

Throughout, and regardless of the specified time periods for qualification, award of a decoration, wounds resulting in evacuation or death in circumstances of active service result in automatic eligibility for the medal and appropriate bar. Likewise, time spent as a prisoner of war is allowed to count towards the qualifying period.

In 1965, the medal was partially replaced by the Samanya Seva Medal (1036), though awards of the two overlapped for a period of time. By 1975, when the qualifying period for the 'Mizo Hills' clasp was closed out, this medal may be considered to have lapsed.

Clasps: The medal was not awarded without a clasp. These clasps are illustrated below.

Outline

1035.100 first reverse (1950-54), 'The General Service Medal' above and '1947' below and in the centre a lotus flower with buds and leaves—never issued (except as prototypes?).

1035.200 second reverse (1954), 'The General Service Medal' above and 'India / 1947' below and in the centre a lotus flower with buds and leaves—never issued (except as prototypes?).

1035.300 third reverse (1954-65), 'GENERAL SERVICE' above and 'INDIA' below and in the centre a lotus flower with buds and leaves:

1035.301 Jammu and Kashmir 1947-48—instituted by No. 4-Pres./50 of 5 June 1950 (as the original clasp for the medal), this clasp was awarded for one day of service in specific battles within the geographical limits of Jammu and Kashmir State in the first Indo-Pakistani conflict over Kashmir, 24 October 1947 to 1 January 1949. Air force personnel would qualify by five operational sorties or twenty hours of flight time. Others who served in the region between these dates qualified by 180 days of service. Service that qualified for this clasp cannot be counted towards the Jammu and Kashmir clasp to the Sainya Seva Medal (see 1047.001). The clasp has chinar leaves at the ends. The following specific battles were included in the qualifying criteria: Battle of Srinagar (27 October 1947 to 30 November 1947), Relief of Kotli (15 November 1947 to 30 November 1947), Battle of Naushera (25 January 1948 to 11 February 1948), Recapture of Jhangar (1 March 1948 to 20 March 1948),

1035.301 Clasp Jammu and Kashmir 1947-48

1035.302 Clasp Overseas Korea 1950-53

1035.303 Clasp Naga Hills

Capture of Rajauri (7 April 1948 to 15 April 1948), Advance from Uri and Capture of Pirkanthi (20 May 1948 to 30 June 1948), Capture of Tithwal (17 May 1948 to 25 August 1948), Zojila operations ('Op Bison') (1 September 1948 to 25 November 1948), Second link-up with Punch ('Op Easy') (18 September 1948 to 25 November 1948), and Capture of Gurais (20 June 1948 to 30 June 1948).

1035.302 Overseas Korea 1950-53—an 'overseas clasp' concept was established in principle by No. 26-Pres./53 of 28 July 1953. The apparent expectation was that there would be a series of clasps for overseas service, paralleling the 'domestic' series of clasps (such as the earlier clasp for service in the Jammu and Kashmir conflict). The specific 'Overseas Korea 1950-53' clasp was separately authorized. As events worked out, this clasp would be the sole 'overseas' clasp to the medal, with such functions passing to the new Videsh Seva Medal (1052) in 1960. This clasp was awarded for one day of service ashore in Korea between 22 November 1952 and 8 July 1953 on the active strength of the 60th Para Field Ambulance Unit, approximately seventeen officers, nine JCOs, and three hundred other ranks. The clasp has a caduceus ascending from a lotus flower at the ends. Some sources indicate that the original intention had been to issue the United Nations' medal for Korea in a Hindi (or Sanskrit?) issue—as it was brought out in the languages of all the participants in the UN operations in Korea (see 3001). Due to emerging Indian policy on the acceptance of such awards, this scheme was never put into place.

1035.303 Naga Hills (1955-75)—Instituted by No. 13-Pres./60 of 26 January 1960 and amended by 43-Pres./80 of 7 July 1980. The clasp was discontinued with effect from 8 May 1975, by No. 41-Pres./80 of 7 July 1980. Awarded for 180 days (90 days for temporary inductees) of operational service as follows: Naga Hills or Tuensang area of north-eastern India between 27 April 1955 and 1 April 1956 ('Op Goli'), or to those operating or located under the operational command of GOC Assam/23 Infantry Div/Op Orchid/GOC Nagaland/8 Mountain Div/GOC 101 Communication Zone area. Aircrew personnel would qualify through five operational sorties or twenty hours of operational flying during this period and in the operational area of GOC Assam/23 Infantry Div/Op Orchid/GOC Nagaland/8 Mountain Div/GOC 101 Communication Zone area from 27 April 1955 onwards. Between 1 January 1968 and 8 May 1975, the General Service Medal, 1947 when awarded with clasps 'Naga Hills' and 'Mizo Hills', was to be worn with the ribbon of the new Samanya Seva Medal, 1965 (No. 43-Pres./80 of 07 July 1980). Later service would be recognized by the 'Nagaland' bar to the Samanya Seva Medal, 1965 (1036.103). The clasp has stalks of bamboo in the roundels at the ends.

1035.304 Goa 1961—Instituted by No. 77-Pres./62 of 22 December 1962 and amended by No. 43-Pres./63 of 22 April 1963. The clasp was awarded for service in 'Operation Vijay', the reunification with India of the remnant Portuguese colonies along India's coast. This clasp was awarded for two days (48 hours) of actual service within the geographical limits of Goa,

Daman, and Diu from 18 to 22 December 1961. Air force personnel would qualify through one operational sortie during this period. The units involved included the 17th Infantry Division Task Force comprising the 17th Infantry Division (48th Infantry Brigade: 5th Guards, 13th Kumaon, and 1st Sikh L.I.; 63rd Infantry Brigade: 3rd Sikhs, 2nd Bihar, and 4th Sikh L.I.; the 17th Artillery Brigade; and support troops), the 50th Parachute Brigade; nine ships of the Indian Navy (*Vikrant, Mysore, Delhi, Rajput, Trishul, Beas, Betwa, Khukri*, and *Kuthar*); and Indian Air Force units. The clasp has a palm tree at the ends.

1035.305 Ladakh 1962—Instituted by No. 41-Pres./65 of 23 June 1965 for services against Chinese forces in Ladakh along India's northern borders. The specific areas and conditions of service were quite detailed (down to the citation of specific map coordinates) but, in brief, the clasp was awarded for one day of service in (1) the battle surrounding Yula 20-23 October 1962, (2) the battles along the southern border of Ladakh 27-29 October 1962, or (3) the battle at Chushul 18-21 November 1962. The bar could also be awarded for fifteen days of service within Ladakh between 20 October 1962 and 21 November 1962. Air force personnel would qualify through one operational sortie in these specific battles, three operational sorties elsewhere in the area, of twelve hours of flying in the area during this period. The clasp has mountains at the ends.

1035.306 NEFA 1962—Instituted by No. 41-Pres./65 of 23 June 1965 and modified by No. 31-Pres./66 of 1966. This clasp was awarded for services against Chinese forces in the North-East Frontier Agency (NEFA), along India's north-eastern borders. The specific areas and conditions of service were quite detailed (down to the citation of specific map coordinates) but, in brief, the clasp was awarded for one day of service in (1) the action at Namkacho, 21 September 1962, (2) the action at Senjangn 10 October 1962, (3) the action at Dhola, 19-25 October 1962, (4) the action at Towang, 21-24 October 1962, (5) the actions at Sela and Bomdi La, 25 October-21 November 1962, (6) the action at Mechuka Lamang, 25-30 October 1962, (7) the actions at Manigong and Lamdola, 23-28 October 1962, (8) the action along the Asafila-Ridding-Henkar line, 23-24 October 1962, (9) the actions at Dichi and Kibithoo, 20-25 October 1962, (10) the action at Walong, 25 October-18 November 1962, (11) the action at Takshing, 21-23 October 1962, (12) the action at Limeking, 17-21 November 1962, (13) the action at Maja, 21/22 October 1962, or (14) the actions at Kepang La and Gelling, 17-21 November 1962. The clasp could also be awarded to army personnel for fifteen days of service between 21 September 1962 and 21 November 1962 in the North-East Frontier Agency and in certain specified areas north and south of the Brahmaputra River. Air force personnel qualified by service in one operational sortie in the actions detailed above, by three other operational sorties, or by twelve hours of flying in areas specified from 20 October to 21 November 1962. The clasp has a leafy tree at the ends.

1035.304 Clasp Goa 1961

1035.305 Clasp Ladakh 1962

1035.306 Clasp NEFA 1962

1035.307 Clasp Mizo Hills

1035.307 Mizo Hills (1966-75)—Instituted by No. 36-Pres./ 70 of 16 July 1970 and amended by Nos. 42-Pres./80 of 7 July 1980 and 43-Pres./80 of 7 July 1980, the bar was discontinued with effect from 8 May 1975, by No. 42-Pres./80 of 7 July 1980. The clasp was awarded for 180 days (90 days for temporary inductees) of operational service in the erstwhile Mizo District of Assam. This included troops deployed for 'Op Orchid' under the operational control of GOC 8 Mountain Division and those for 'Op Battle Axe' under the operational control of GOC 101 Communication Zone area between 20 February 1966 and 8 May 1975. Service with effect from 28 February 1966 in the Mizo Hills region under 'Op Orchid' could not count toward qualifying service for the clasp 'Naga Hills' to the General Service Medal (1035.303), or the 'Bengal-Assam' clasp to the Sainya Seva Medal (see 1048.004). The actual areas of qualifying service are defined in truly excruciating detail, including map coordinates, and are not included here. Later service would be recognized by the 'Mizoram' clasp to the Samanya Seva Medal, 1965 (1036.104). Between 1 January 1968 and 8 May 1975, the General Service Medal, 1947 when awarded with clasps 'Mizo Hills' and 'Naga Hills' was to be worn with the ribbon of the new Samanya Seva Medal 1965 (see 1036.104 and consider this an alternate ribbon of representational 1035.307a) (No. 43-Pres./80 of 7 July 1980). Recipients with multiple-clasp medals do not appear to have been accounted for in issuing these orders. However, the order is a reflection of the slow demise of the venerable system of multi-clasp medals in the Indian military. The 'Mizo Hills' clasp has uniquely plain ends.

1036 सामान्य सेवा मैडल 1965 / SAMANYA SEVA MEDAL 1965 / GENERAL SERVICE MEDAL 1965[59]

A general service campaign medal for military operations since 1965.

Established: By No. 35-Pres./75 of 8 May 1975 (with effect from 26 January 1965). The description of the ribbon was modified by No. 28-Pres./78 of 13 May 1978.

General Appearance: A circular 35 mm cupro-nickel medal.

Obverse: In the centre, the state emblem, and to the left 'सामान्य सेवा मैडल' and to the right 'SAMANYA SEVA MEDAL'. At the bottom, the date '1965'.

Reverse: The Indian elephant badge, drawn from the design of the flag of the Indian President.

Ribbon: 32 mm, dark green with three equally spaced 3 mm stripes of red, dark blue, and light blue. As it has been so common and so widely produced, there is some variability of the precise shades of the colours in this ribbon. These colour variations have no significance. See also the mention of the 'Naga Campaign Ribbon' under 1036.003, below. Some sources suggest that the ribbon colour variations in fact have some significance: 1975-81, 32 mm, dark green with three equally spaced 3 mm stripes of red, dark blue, and light blue; and after 1981, 30 mm and of a darker green but with the same stripes. These variations are, however, merely differences in

1036.100 Samanya Seva Medal 1965

[59]*Encyclopedia of Soldiers with Highest Gallantry Awards*, pp. 48-49; *India's Highest Gallantry Awards*, pp. 58-59; Johnson, 'Medals of the Republic of India', pp. 39-40; Das, *Traditions and Customs*, pp. 276-77; Scandaluzzi, *Medal Ribbons of the World*, vol. 3: *India*.

manufacturing and have no policy basis. While the ribbon colour was indeed redefined in 1978 (No. 28-Pres./78) from 'dark green' to 'Indian Green', this appears to have constituted no more than a change in descriptive vocabulary.

Suspension: The medal is suspended by a straight-bar non-swivelling suspender to which the clasps are attached.

Naming: The naming is impressed on the edge. Hindi naming is also encountered.

Miniature: Miniatures have been issued. Both official and unofficial clasps have been encountered in a wide range of styles.

Background: Intended as a successor for the General Service Medal 1947 (1035, though the time period of some of the operations overlap), the General Service Medal, 1965 (or more properly, to avoid confusion, the Samanya Seva Medal, 1965) was awarded for services rendered by or with the armed forces in specified actions or active service conditions which were represented by clasps attached to the medal. While all but one of the clasps observed have been produced in Hindi rather than English, they will frequently be referred to by their English names.

Throughout, and regardless of the specified time periods for qualification, for award of a decoration wounds resulting in evacuation or death in circumstances of active service result in automatic eligibility for the medal and appropriate bar. Likewise, time spent as a prisoner of war is allowed to count towards the qualifying period.

Clasps: The medal was not awarded without a clasp. All clasps are in Hindi only, except the one for Manipur, which is bilingual. These clasps have been illustrated below.

Outline

1036.100 medal.

1036.101 कच्छ-कारगिल 1965 / Kutch-Kargil 1965—Instituted by No. 36-Pres/75 of 8 May 1975 (as one of the two original clasps for the medal), this clasp was awarded for actions against Pakistani troops in western and northern India from April 1965 to January 1966 in two widely diverse environments: the salt flats of Kutch (in Gujarat state) or in the Kargil sector of the high Himalayas. Kutch: one day of service in battle between 9 April 1965 and 1 May 1965 or ten days of general service in Kutch between 9 April 1965 and 1 July 1965. Aircrew personnel would qualify by one operational sortie or three hours of flight time. Kargil: one day of service in specific battle zones in the Kargil sector between 17 May 1965 and 25 January 1966 or 90 days of active service in the area between 17 May 1965 and 25 January 1966. Aircrew personnel would qualify by three operational sorties or ten hours of flying. The precise zones of qualification are specified in the establishing order in excruciating detail and are not given here.

1036.102 नाथूला-चोला 1967 / Nathula-Chola 1967—Instituted by No. 37-Pres./75 of 8 May 1975 (as one of the two original clasps for the medal). This clasp was awarded for service along the Sino-Indian border for one day of service in the border

1036.101 Clasp Kutch-Kargil 1965

1036.102 Clasp Nathula-Chola 1967

1036.103 Clasp Nagaland

1036.104 Clasp Mizoram

1036.105 Clasp Tirap

incidents at Nathula (11-16 September 1967) or Chola (1 October 1967). Air force personnel would qualify by one operational sortie during these periods.

1036.103 नागालैंड / Nagaland (1975-)—Instituted by No. 45-Pres./80 of 7 July 1980, the conditions of eligibility were modified by No. 71-Pres./86 of 3 September 1986 and awarded for service in Nagaland from 8 May 1975 to date. Earlier service was recognized by the 'Naga Hills' clasp to the General Service Medal, 1947 (1035.303). A ribbon appears in collections which has been identified as the 'Naga Campaign Medal Ribbon'; the ribbon is 32 mm, with seven equal stripes of white, dark green, white, yellow, white, red, and white. No official record can be found of this ribbon or the reasons for its inception. It should be considered an unofficial creation of enterprising military tailors when the new general service medal had been announced but not notified. Early Samanya Seva medals with this clasp were, however, worn briefly on the ribbon for the General Service Medal, 1947 (1035). The clasp was awarded to the following eligible categories: Personnel who had served an aggregate of 180 days under the operational command of the GOC Assam/23 Infantry Division, Op Orchid/Nagaland/8 Mountain Division/101 CZA; personnel who had put in 90 days active service in Nagaland; air and ejection crews who had completed a minimum of 5 operational sorties or 20 flying hours in the operational area. Recipients of decorations or those mentioned in despatches, as well as those killed, wounded or disabled in operations, were eligible irrespective of the time spent in the theatre.

1036.104 मिजोरम / Mizoram (1975-)—Instituted by No. 44-Pres./80 of 7 July 1980 and awarded for service in the erstwhile Mizo areas of Assam (now the State of Mizoram) or in 'Operation Orchid', under the operational control of the 8th Mountain Division, or in 'Op Battle Axe' under 101 CZA, from 8 May 1975 to a date to be determined.[60] Earlier service was recognized by the 'Mizo Hills' clasp to the General Service Medal, 1947 (1035.307). The clasp was awarded to the following eligible categories: personnel who had served an aggregate of 180 days in the operational areas specified; aircrew and ejection crews who had completed a minimum of five operational sorties or twenty flying hours in the qualifying operational area. Recipients of decorations or those mentioned in despatches, as well as those killed, wounded or disabled in operations, were eligible irrespective of the time spent in the theatre. On the clasp Mizoram is misspelled as 'Mijoram'.

1036.105 तिरप / Tirap (1979-)—Instituted by No. 45-Pres./82 of 6 October 1982, it was awarded for service in counter-insurgency operations in the Tirap district of Arunachal Pradesh after 1 June 1979. The clasp was awarded to the following eligible categories: personnel who had served an aggregate of 180 days in the operational areas specified under 51 Mountain Artillery Brigade or 192 Mountain Brigade under 2 Mountain Division (temporary inductees for specific operations qualified in 90 days); aircrew and ejection crews and certain other specified categories who had completed a

[60] Although the insurgency in Mizoram is now officially over and the army has moved out, the clasp has still not been discontinued.

minimum of 5 operational sorties or 20 flying hours in the qualifying operational area. Recipients of decorations or those mentioned in despatches, as well as those killed, wounded or disabled in operations, were eligible irrespective of the time spent in the theatre. Time spent in captivity as a POW was to count toward eligibility for the award.

1036.106 मणिपुर / MANIPUR (1980-)—Instituted by No. 87-Pres./87 of 23 November 1987, the clasp is awarded for service in counter-insurgency operations in Manipur with effect from 27 September 1980. Qualifying criteria are 180 days on the active strength of a unit operating in the geographical limits of the state of Manipur. In the case of aircrew and ejection crew, a minimum of five operational sorties or twenty hours operational flying in Manipur are required to qualify for award of the clasp. Recipients of decorations or those mentioned in despatches, as well as those killed, wounded or disabled in operations, are eligible irrespective of the time spent in the operational area. This is the only bilingual clasp to this medal.

1036.106 Clasp Manipur

1037 विशेष सेवा पदक / VISHESH SEVA PADAK / SPECIAL SERVICE MEDAL

Awarded for operational services by the Indian military. The medal is consistently referenced in the notification by its English name and the Hindi name appears only in the legend on the medal.

Established: By No. 8-Pres/86 of 29 January 1986. The ordinance was deemed to have come into effect from 1 April 1984. Designs were altered as discussed below.

General Appearance: Circular cupro-nickel medal, 35 mm diameter. The medal was originally designed as octagonal, but this was altered to circular by No. 60-Pres./90 of 23 July 1990. No octagonal medals were ever issued. In addition, the obverse and reverse as described in the instituting notification are interchanged on the actual medal. No authority for this reversal in design appears to have been promulgated. We have dealt with the medal in the form in which it has been produced and awarded, not as it was officially notified.

Obverse: A stylized sunburst all around the edge of the medal encircles an inner wreath which in turn surrounds the state emblem and motto. Above and below the state emblem is the legend 'विशेष सेवा पदक / SPECIAL SERVICE MEDAL'.

Reverse: In the centre, within an outer stylized sunburst and an inner wreath, a falcon (which looks more like a dove) flying to the left above a mountain range.

Ribbon: 32 mm, divided into three parts of 8 mm, 16 mm, and 8 mm, the colours being red, steel grey and red, respectively.

Suspension: Suspended by a non-swivelling straight-bar to which the clasp is attached.

Naming: The medal is named on the edge by impressed characters in either English or Hindi.

Miniature: Miniatures have been issued.

Background: Instituted to recognize services rendered under active service conditions, or conditions akin thereto, by the

1037.200 Special Service Medal

Indian military which could not easily be recognized by existing medals. The initial intent seems to have been that this medal would serve as a replacement for the Samanya Seva Medal (1036). While the Hindi name is used on the medal and is employed here, it is nowhere referenced in the governing gazette notifications.

While the medal is specifically instituted to recognize services rendered by the armed forces, the clause listing eligible categories in the instituting notification goes on to include 'civilians of either sex in all walks of life', and all other forces and security forces operating under the operational control of the regular armed forces.

The requirement for a separate medal was felt following the Indian armed forces' involvement in 'Operation Blue Star' on 3 June 1984, the name used to describe the operations conducted against separatist Sikh militants in the Punjab. Since the operations were conducted by the army against a section of Indian citizens, the existing Samanya Seva Medal (1036), which was in a direct line of policy extending over a century to the earlier colonial India general service series of campaign medals, could not be awarded in this case since issues of political expediency which would allow for a campaign medal to be issued for counter-insurgency operations in the remote hill states of the north-east, could not very well extend the same logic to the Punjab from which a large portion of the Indian soldiery is still drawn. In these circumstances, the same political expediency eventually functioned to prevent the issue of a clasp for 'Operation Blue Star', and the first clasp notified for award with the medal was 'Siachen Glacier'. This clasp was, however, never issued, and the clasp was replaced by the Siachen Glacier Medal (1041) in 1987.[61]

The first clasp to be awarded with this medal was 'Sri Lanka', for service with the Indian Peace Keeping Force, 1987-89. Normally such a clasp would have been awarded with the Samanya Seva Medal, but having instituted the medal, the defence establishment would have been hard-pressed not to institute a clasp to be awarded with it. The clasp therefore was significant from two aspects: (1) it effectively overshadowed and heralded the demise of the old general service medal with a lineage stretching back to 1799, and (2) it overlooked the time-honoured principle of not awarding two medals for the same campaign or service (barring the 'War' medal and 'Star' precept established in the two world wars). The 'Suraksha' clasp, awarded in 1995 for operations in Punjab, Assam, and Jammu and Kashmir, signalled a return to the original instituting logic of this medal.

Throughout, and regardless of the specified time periods for qualification, award of a decoration, wounds resulting in evacuation or death in circumstances of active service result in automatic eligibility for the medal and appropriate bar. Likewise, time spent as a prisoner of war is allowed to count toward the qualifying period.

Clasps: The medal is not awarded without a clasp. These clasps have been illustrated at fig. 1037.202 and 1037.203.

[61] It was, however, deemed possible—if not necessarily any more politically expedient—to issue the Garaj Star in the face of strong opposition from the army (see 1042) for 'Operation Black Thunder' in the Punjab in 1988.

Outline

1037.100 original octagonal design—Never issued.

1037.200 Round design.

1037.201 सियाचिन ग्लेशियर / Siachen Glacier—instituted by No. 9-Pres./86 of 3 February 1986. This clasp was never issued and was later replaced by the separate Siachen Glacier Medal (see 1041) in 1987.

1037.202 श्रीलंका / Srilanka / Sri Lanka—instituted by No. 65-Pres./89 of 20 July 1989 and amended by No. 80-Pres./89 of 19 October 1989 and No. 52-Pres./90 of 6 June 1990, the clasp Awarded for 'Operation Pawan', peacekeeping service in northern and eastern Sri Lanka, 1987-89, as a part of the Indian Peace Keeping Force (IPKF). Recipients of this clasp are also awarded the 'Sri Lanka' clasp to the Videsh Seva Medal (1052.310). Around 2,00,000 Indian troops served in 'Operation Pawan'.

1037.203 सुरक्षा / Suraksha—instituted by No. 169-Pres./95 of 3 August 1995, the clasp has been awarded for security service in the Punjab, in Jammu and Kashmir, and in the north-eastern areas of India, since 1984, as follows: (1) Operation 'Rakshak', from 15 November 1989 till termination; (2) Operation 'Tasha', from 21 June 1990 till termination; (3) Operation 'Bajrang' from 27 November 1990 till 10 June 1991; and (4) Operation 'Rhino' from 15 September 1991 till termination. These areas were geographically defined as follows:[62]

(a) Op Rakshak:
    (i) Jammu and Kashmir: State of J&K less area east of the Zoji La.
    (ii) Punjab: The entire State of Punjab including the Union Territory of Chandigarh.
(b) Op Bajrang—the Assam districts of Dhubri, Bongaigaon, Kokrajhar, Barpeta, Nalbari, Goalpara, Kamrup, Darrang, Sonitpur, North Lakhimpur, Morigaon, Nowgaon, Karbi Anglong, Golaghat, Jorhat, Sibsagar, Dhomaji, Tinsukhia, and Dibrugarh.
(c) Op Tasha—the area geographically contained by the sea and land on/off the east coast of India and the east and south coasts of Sri Lanka, south of latitude 17 North and east of longitude 77 East up to 100 nautical miles.
(d) Op Rhino—same areas as Op Bajrang above.

The qualifying period for award was 180 days, except in the case of personnel temporarily inducted for specific operations, who qualified in 90 days. Aircrew and ejection crews and certain other specified categories who had completed a minimum of five operational sorties or 20 flying hours in the operational area qualified; recipients of decorations or those mentioned in despatches, as well as those killed, wounded or disabled in operations, were eligible irrespective of the time spent in the theatre. In order to be eligible for the clasp, personnel should have been granted field service concessions within the respective qualifying areas.

1037.202 Clasp Sri Lanka

1037.203 Clasp Suraksha

[62] Ministry of Defence letter No. 3(11)/92/D(Cer) dated 25 October 1995.

1038.100 Samar Seva Star 1965

1038 समर सेवा स्टार 1956/ SAMAR SEVA STAR 1956[63]

Awarded for combat service in the 1965 Indo-Pakistani conflict.

Established: By No. 15-Pres./67 of 26 January 1967. The statutes were amended by No. 38-Pres./67 of 29 April 1967, by No. 19-Pres./68 of 11 March 1968, and by No. 51-Pres./68 of 22 July 1968. The qualifying areas and battle zones were further amended by MOD Notification No. 1-E of 29 March 1968, published in the *Gazette of India Extraordinary*, part 1, section 3.

General Appearance: A five-pointed 39 mm bright bronze star. Recently, six-pointed tailors' copies of this star have been noted; these are completely unofficial contrivances.

Obverse: In the domed circular centre, the state emblem with the surrounding legend below 'समर सेवा स्टार 1965' ('Samar Seva Star 1965').

Reverse: The naming details are impressed in the centre of the plain reverse.

Ribbon: 30 mm, red, dark blue, and light blue, with five thin white stripes.

Suspension: Suspended by a ring.

Naming: Named on the reverse. Unnamed examples are occasionally encountered.

Miniature: Miniatures have been issued. The miniature is sometimes observed with a totally unofficial clasp 'PAKISTAN 1965'.

Background: The Samar Seva Star, roughly translated as 'Battle Service Star', was awarded for ten days of service in an area defined as a 'battle zone' during the 1965 war between India and Pakistan (1-23 September 1965, but with qualifying dates for the star of 5 August 1965-25 January 1966), or for one day of service in actual combat conditions, or for three operational sorties or three operational flying hours (five hours for air observation post personnel). It was awarded to all members of the Indian armed forces, as well as to reserve, territorial, and militia personnel, as well as to civilians who served in combat areas in support positions.

This star could not be awarded alone and recipients of this star were also awarded the Raksha Medal 1965 (1044).

Outline

1038.100 medal.

[63]*Encyclopedia of Soldiers with Highest Gallantry Awards*, pp. 50-53; *India's Highest Gallantry Awards*, pp. 60-63; Haynes, 'Medals and Decorations of the Republic of India', p. 38; Johnson, 'Medals of the Republic of India', p. 40; Das, *Traditions and Customs*, p. 277; Scandaluzzi, *Medal Ribbons of the World*, vol. 3: *India*.

[64]*Encyclopedia of Soldiers with Highest Gallantry Awards*, pp. 54-56; *India's Highest Gallantry Awards*, pp. 64-5; Johnson, 'Medals of the Republic of India', p. 41; Das, *Traditions and Customs*, p. 277; Scandaluzzi, *Medal Ribbons of the World*, vol. 3: *India*.

1039 –पूर्वी स्टार / POORVI STAR[64]

Awarded for combat service in the eastern theatre during the 1971 Indo-Pakistani conflict.

Established: By No. 2-Pres./73 of 17 January 1973. Amended by No. 46 Pres./73 of 12 September 1973 and No. 68-Pres./81 of 17 November 1981.

General Appearance: A five-pointed 40 mm bright bronze star. Recently, six-pointed tailors' copies of this star have been noted; these are completely unofficial contrivances.

Obverse: In the domed circular centre, the state emblem and motto with a 2 mm wide surrounding band containing the legend 'POORVI STAR / पूर्वी स्टार'.

Reverse: The naming details are impressed in the centre of the plain reverse.

Ribbon: 33 mm, green with an 11 mm central stripe of golden yellow.

Suspension: Suspended by a ring.

Naming: Usually named on the reverse.

Miniature: Miniatures have been issued.

Background: Awarded to all ranks of the Indian armed forces, various police forces, and civilians employed in support of the armed forces during the 1971 Indo-Pakistani conflict, the Poorvi Star was awarded to those who served in the eastern theatre of the war for one day in a battle zone between 3 December and 16 December 1971 in Bangladesh or the Bay of Bengal, or for ten days in another qualifying area (25 March 1971 and 25 March 1972 in specified areas of West Bengal, Bihar, Assam, Meghalaya, Tripura, Mizoram, and specified airfields and ports), or who carried out one operational sortie or three flying hours in the zones and periods specified. In 1981 eligibility of the award was extended to include personnel of India's official intelligence agency, the Research and Analysis Wing (RAW), as well as organizations under the Directorate General of Security, such as the SSB, ARC and SFF.

This star could not be awarded alone and recipients were also awarded the Sangram Medal (1045).

Outline

1039.100 medal.

1040 पश्चिमी स्टार / PASCHIMI STAR[65]

Awarded for combat service in the western theatre during the 1971 Indo-Pakistani conflict.

Established: By No. 3-Pres./73 of 17 January 1973. Amended by No. 46 Pres./73 of 12 September 1973 and No. 69-Pres./81 of 17 November 1981.

General Appearance: A five-pointed 40 mm bright bronze star. Recently, six-pointed tailors' copies of this star have been noted; these are completely unofficial contrivances.

Obverse: In the domed circular centre, the state emblem and motto with a 2 mm wide surrounding band containing the legend 'PASCHIMI STAR / पश्चिमी स्टार'.

Reverse: The naming details are impressed in the centre of the plain reverse.

Ribbon: 31 mm, medium pink (officially described as 'clarot' [claret]) with three 2 mm white central stripes.

Suspension: Suspended by a ring.

Naming: Usually named on the reverse.

Miniature: Miniatures have been issued.

Background: Awarded to all ranks of the Indian armed forces, various police forces, and civilians employed in support of the armed forces during the 1971 Indo-Pakistani conflict, the

1039.100 Poorvi Star

[65]*Encyclopedia of Soldiers with Highest Gallantry Awards*, pp. 56-57; *India's Highest Gallantry Awards*, pp. 66-67; Johnson, 'Medals of the Republic of India', p. 41; Das, *Traditions and Customs*, pp. 277-78; Scandaluzzi, *Medal Ribbons of the World*, vol. 3: *India*.

1040.100 Paschimi Star

Paschimi Star was awarded to those who served in the western theatre of war for one day in a specified battle zone (in Jammu and Kashmir, Punjab, Rajasthan, Gujarat, and the Arabian Sea between 3 December and 16 December 1971) or for ten days in a specified qualifying area (25 March 1971-25 March 1972, in particular areas of Jammu & Kashmir, Punjab, Rajasthan, Gujarat, and specified airfields and ports), or who carried out one operational sortie or three flying hours in the zones and periods specified. In 1981, eligibility of the award was extended to include personnel of India's official intelligence agency, the Research and Analysis Wing (RAW), as well as organizations under the Directorate General of Security, such as the SSB, ARC and SFF.

This star could not be awarded alone and recipients were also awarded the Sangram Medal (1045).

Outline

1040.100 medal.

1041 सियाचिन ग्लेशियर मैडल / SIACHEN GLACIER MEDAL

Awarded for combat service in clashes between India and Pakistan on the Saltoro ridge bordering the Siachen Glacier.

Established: By No. 48-Pres./87 of 17 July 1987 with effect from 1 April 1984.

General Appearance: Circular 36 mm cupro-nickel medal.

Obverse: In the centre, the national emblem, surrounded by the legend 'सियाचिन ग्लेशियर मैडल / SIACHEN GLACIER MEDAL'.

Reverse: A stylized scene of the mountains with standing figures and a helicopter. It is important to compare this reverse to that for the High Altitude Service Medal (1049).

Ribbon: 31 mm, equal stripes of medium granite grey 10 mm, silver-white 11 mm, and granite grey 10 mm.

Suspension: Suspended by a non-swivelling straight-bar.

Naming: The medal is named on the edge and has been seen named in both English and Hindi.

Miniature: Miniatures have been issued.

Background: The medal is awarded for combat service in the ongoing quasi-war ('Operation Meghdoot') between India and Pakistan on the area around 6,600 m (22,000 ft) high Siachen Glacier in northern Jammu and Kashmir, at the intersection of the borders of India, Pakistan, and China. This is an almost unimaginably hostile area in which to conduct any sort of military operations, where temperatures fall as low as –86° C (–122° F) and blizzards swirl up icy 300 kph (190 mph) winds. Also awarded to personnel of the Indian Air Force for activities in support of troops serving in the Siachen Glacier area since April 1984.

This service was originally to have been recognized by a 'Siachen Glacier' clasp to the Special Service Medal (see 1037.100), but in 1987 the award was replaced by this free-standing medal.

Outline

1041.100 medal.

1041.100 Siachen Glacier Medal

1042 गरज स्टार / GARAJ STAR

Awarded to personnel of the National Security Guards who took part in 'Operation Black Thunder' in the Punjab in 1988.

Established: By No. 79-Pres./89 of 6 September 1989 with effect from 3 March 1988.

General Appearance: A five-pointed bronze star with bevelled rays, 40 mm in diameter.

Obverse: In the centre, a commando holding a rifle with a bolt of lightning running diagonally across his chest, within a circular band, 2 mm in width and 20 mm in diameter at the outer edges. On the band, the inscription 'GARAJ STAR' and 'गरज स्टार' The band is broken at the top by the head of the commando. The medal is struck in extremely low relief and of unusually coarse design.

Reverse: Plain, presumably intended for naming. No description is given in the gazette.

Ribbon: 32 mm, black silk, with a 5 mm wide silver-white stripe running diagonally across from the top left corner to the bottom right corner. The ribbon for ribbon bar wear—which, in any case, is difficult to visualize as a suspension ribbon—has been manufactured from what seems to be plasticized paper. It is important to note that although no official order of wearing is indicated for this award, it has been habitually worn as the final medal in ribbon bar groups, following the nine-year long service medal.[66] The medal ribbon seems never to have been produced, leaving us only with the ribbon for ribbon-bar wear.

Suspension: Suspended from a ring attached to the point of the uppermost ray of the star.

Naming: Presumably intended to named on the reverse.

Miniature: A miniature was authorized but has not been observed.

Background: The star was awarded to personnel of the National Security Guards (NSG) who took part in counter-militancy operations in the Punjab from 3 March 1988 to 22 May 1988. A minimum of one day's service in the operational zone was required to qualify for the star. Armed forces personnel are not authorized to wear the medal. 'Op Black Thunder II', was the code name given to the cordon and assault operation against Sikh separatists holed up in the holiest Sikh shrine—the Golden Temple—at Amritsar (Black Thunder I was the futile raid on the temple on 30 April 1986). In no other case has a separate medal or star been sanctioned for any active operations against Indian citizens. Counter-insurgency operations in the north-east were covered by the grant of clasps to the General Service Medal 1947 (1035), and later, the Samanya Seva Medal 1965 (1036). Similar subsequent operations in Kashmir, Punjab, and Assam have been covered by the grant of the clasp 'Suraksha' ('Security') to the Special Service Medal (1037.203). The Ministry of Defence appears to have been quite sensitive to issues of policy in this regard. The institution of this medal at the behest of the Home Ministry presents an unprecedented departure from policy. It was strongly opposed by the armed forces, which rightly argued

1042.100 Garaj Star

[66] But as it constitutes a service star, we have listed it in this location. This does not reflect any official order of wearing, for none includes this award.

that as compared to Op Black Thunder, Op Blue Star (June 1984) was a much bigger operation in terms of degree of opposition, troops employed, and casualties suffered. The question of awarding a general medal for Op Blue Star had been considered and then turned down at the level of the Chiefs of Staff after taking various (and perhaps obvious) considerations into account. However, the Garaj Star was instituted in spite of the objections of the defence establishment, and marked a critical turning point in the manner in which the honours system of the Indian Republic was structured and would henceforth evolve. The progressively feeble military response was blatantly disregarded by an increasingly powerful Home Ministry, which usurped the time-honoured usages of the Indian armed forces and supplanted them as potent symbols of state patronage in the police and paramiltary establishments under its command.

For those not familiar with India's paramilitary forces, the NSG was raised as a federal contingency force in 1984 to meet the emerging threats of terrorism in the country. It has a strength of approximately 7,500 elite personnel, trained in high-risk counter-terrorist and counter-hijack operations.[67]

Outline

1042.100 medal.

1043.200 Op Vijay Star

1043 ओप विजय स्टार / OP VIJAY STAR

Awarded for combat service in the 1999 Indo-Pakistani conflict in Kargil and northern Jammu and Kashmir.

Established: Announced by the prime minister on 26 July 2001 and established by No. 116-Pres./01 of 20 August 2001. The ribbon was modified by No. 98-Pres./03 of 18 June 2003.

General Appearance: A 40 mm six-pointed bronze star with bevelled points. Note the odd departure from the long tradition of five-pointed stars for campaign service awards.

Obverse: In the centre the national emblem surrounded by a band bearing the legend 'ओप विजय स्टार / OP VIJAY STAR' in Hindi and English.

Reverse: Plain, presumably for naming purposes.

Ribbon: The original ribbon was 32 mm, steel grey, divided into equal parts by 4 mm stripes of (left to right) red and light blue. The grey represents the rocks and the red and light blue, respectively, the army and air force. In June 2003, the ribbon was altered to include an additional 4 mm dark blue stripe in the centre to represent the navy. This new ribbon produces a visual effect remarkably similar to that of the Op Vijay Medal (1046); some confusion may be anticipated.

Suspension: Suspended by a ring.

Naming: The star will presumably be named on the reverse.

Miniature: Miniatures exist, though they are not mentioned in the establishing notification.

Background: Awarded for participation in combat against Pakistani infiltrators between 1 May 1999 and 31 October 1999

[67] Government of India, *MHA Annual Report 1999-2000*, p. 61.

in and around Kargil; for the army, the minimum qualifying period was one day and for the air force one operational sortie or three hours of flying in the combat zone. The star was not awarded alone and recipients were also awarded the Op Vijay Medal (1046).

Outline

1043.100 first ribbon.
1043.200 second ribbon.

1044 रक्षा मैडल 1965 / RAKSHA MEDAL 1965 / DEFENCE MEDAL 1965[68]

Awarded for general service in the 1965 Indo-Pakistani conflict.
Established: By No. 14-Pres./67 of 26 January 1967. Amended by No. 51-Pres./68 of 22 July 1968 and by No. 73-Pres./71 of 14 December 1971.
General Appearance: Circular 36 mm cupro-nickel medal.
Obverse: In the centre, the state emblem.
Reverse: The depiction of a rising sun, with a half-wreath below, and above, the legend 'रक्षा मैडल / 1965' ('Raksha Medal/ 1965').
Ribbon: 32 mm, orange with three equally spaced 3 mm stripes of red, dark blue, and light blue. As it is so common and so widely produced, there is some variability in the shades of the colours in this ribbon. These colour variations have no significance. Some sources, however, suggest a significance to colour varieties. Regular forces: 32 mm, orange divided into equal parts by 3 mm stripes of red, dark blue, and light blue; para-military forces: as above, but with the red, dark blue, and light blue stripes only 1 mm in width. There is no actual policy basis for this apparently random ribbon manufacturing difference.
Suspension: Suspended by a straight-bar suspender.
Naming: The medal is usually named on the edge.
Miniature: Miniatures have been issued.
Background: Awarded for service in the 1965 conflict with Pakistan. The medal was awarded to any armed forces personnel, paramilitary forces under military command (including police forces in many cases) who were borne on the effective strength of their unit on 5 August 1965 and who had, as of that date, served for at least 180 days. The medal was also awarded to anyone who qualified for the Samar Seva Star (1038).

Outline

1044.100 medal.

1045 संग्राम मैडल / SANGRAM MEDAL[69]

Awarded for general service in the 1971 Indo-Pakistani conflict.
Established: By No. 1-Pres./73 of 17 January 1973. Modified by No. 23-Pres./76 of 9 March 1976.

1044.100 Raksha Medal 1965

[68]*Encyclopedia of Soldiers with Highest Gallantry Awards*, pp. 58-59; *India's Highest Gallantry Awards*, pp. 68-69; Haynes, 'Medals and Decorations of the Republic of India', p. 38; Johnson, 'Medals of the Republic of India', p. 41; Das, *Traditions and Customs*, p. 278; Scandaluzzi, *Medal Ribbons of the World*, vol. 3: *India*.

[69]*Encyclopedia of Soldiers with Highest Gallantry Awards*, pp. 60-61; *India's Highest Gallantry Awards*, pp. 70-71; Johnson, 'Medals of the Republic of India', p. 42; Das, *Traditions and Customs*, p. 278; Scandaluzzi, *Medal Ribbons of the World*, vol. 3: *India*.

1045.100 Sangram Medal

General Appearance: Circular 35 mm cupro-nickel medal.
Obverse: The state emblem in the centre with the surrounding legend 'संग्राम मैडल / SANGRAM MEDAL'.
Reverse: The depiction of a rising sun with a half wreath below.
Ribbon: 32 mm, maroon-brown with three equally spaced 1 mm white stripes.
Suspension: Suspended from a ring suspender.
Naming: The medal is normally named on the edge. Medals to police and paramilitary forces were largely issued unnamed.
Miniature: Miniatures have been issued, although usually with a straight-bar suspender.
Background: Awarded for service during the 1971 conflict with Pakistan. The medal could be given to all categories of personnel who served in the military, paramilitary forces, police, and civilians in service in the operational areas of Jammu and Kashmir, Punjab, Gujarat, Rajasthan, West Bengal, Assam, Meghalaya, Mizoram, or Tripura between 3 December 1971 and 20 December 1972 (both dates inclusive). Those who had qualified for the Poorvi Star (1039) or the Paschimi Star (1040) automatically qualified for award of this medal.

Outline

1045.100 medal.

1046.100 Op Vijay Medal

1046 ओप विजय मैडल / OP VIJAY MEDAL

Awarded for general service in the 1999 Indo-Pakistani conflict in Kargil and northern Jammu and Kashmir.
Established: By No. 115-Pres./01 of 20 August 2001.
General Appearance: A 35 mm circular cupro-nickel medal.
Obverse: The 'Jai Stambh' or 'Victory Pillar' (apparently, actually the Vijay Stambh at Chittor, Rajasthan) in the centre, surrounded by the legend 'जय स्तम्भ / JAI STAMBH' in Hindi and English. Precisely how a monument in Rajasthan relates to the high Himalayas remains to be established.
Reverse: The state emblem surrounded by the legend 'ऑपरेशन विजय / OPERATION VIJAY'.
Ribbon: 32 mm, grey, divided equally by three 2 mm stripes of (left to right) red, dark blue, and light blue, representing the three branches of services (army, navy, and air force).
Suspension: Suspended by a plain, straight, non-swivelling bar.
Naming: The medal is normally named on the edge.
Miniature: Miniatures have been issued, though they are not mentioned in the establishing notification.
Background: Awarded to all personnel of the armed forces who served in or in support of the operations in Kargil, 1 May 1999 to 31 January 2000, the medal was also awarded to those who had qualified for the Op Vijay Star (1043). The medal was also awarded to a range of paramilitary forces, including the Central Police Forces, Railway Protection Force, Home Guards, and other similar bodies and to civilians serving under military orders. Proposals to award the medal on a special basis to the

then-serving Minister of Defence and Minister of Foreign Affairs have not been implemented.

Outline

1046.100 medal.

1047 ऑपरेशन पराक्रम मैडल / OP PARAKRAM MEDAL

Awarded for deployment as a part of Op Parakram, 2001-2. This is an interesting 'campaign medal' for a deployment, not for a war and not, arguably, even for a campaign.

Established: By No. 16-Pres./05 of 3 May 2005.

General Appearance: Circular 35 mm cupro-nickel medal.

Obverse: A map of India with the legends 'ऑपरेशन पराक्रम' and 'OPERATION PARAKRAM'.

Reverse: The state emblem.

Ribbon: 32 mm, with three equal parts of blue, olive green, and sand colour, with the blue worn toward the right shoulder. The blue and olive green sections are separated by a 2 mm white stripe, while the olive green and sand coloured sections are separated by a 2 mm red stripe.

Suspension: Suspended by a straight-bar suspender.

Naming: The medal will presumably be named on the edge.

Miniature: Miniatures will presumably be issued.

Background: The medal was awarded for 180 days of service by military, paramilitary, and police forces, and attached civilians mobilized and deployed along India's border with Pakistan (and in support of the operation in rear areas as well). Over 5,00,000 troops were deployed in this operation, with 528 casualties. The qualifying dates extend from 14 December 2001 to 18 December 2003 (and to 31 March 2004 for those engaged in demining operations).

While arguably this service could have been commemorated by a clasp to the Special Service Medal or with a clasp to the Sainya Seva Medal, government policy led to the creation of a new award. Though the overall case for this medal seems quite slim, it is important to recall the justifications put forward: this deployment was viewed as 'unprecedented' in the speed with which it was accomplished and the complexity of the task; despite harsh and protracted conditions of service, the armed forces maintained a high level of morale and readiness; and there were 528 fatal casualties and 1,533 non-fatal casualties (all, of course, in the absence of a combatant 'enemy').

Outline

1047.100 medal.

1048 सैन्य सेवा मैडल / SAINYA SEVA MEDAL / SERVICES MEDAL[70]

Awarded to personnel of the armed forces in recognition of services under conditions of special hardship and severe climate.

1047.100 Op Parakaram Medal

[70] *Encyclopedia of Soldiers with Highest Gallantry Awards*, pp. 62-63; *India's Highest Gallantry Awards*, pp. 72-73; Haynes, 'Medals and Decorations of the Republic of India', pp. 38-40; Johnson, 'Medals of the Republic of India', pp. 42-43; Das, *Traditions and Customs*, pp. 278-79; Scandaluzzi, *Medal Ribbons of the World*, vol. 3: *India*.

1048.100 Sainya Seva Medal

1048.101 Clasp Jammu Kashmir

1048.102 Clasp NEFA

Established: By No. 14-Pres./60 of 26 January 1960 with effect from 15 August 1947. Expanded in No. 32-Pres./60 of 2 June 1960 and revised by No. 56/Pres./68 of 3 August 1968.

General Appearance: Circular 36 mm cupro-nickel medal.

Obverse: An image of the Nanda Devi mountain peak with a bamboo clump in the foreground.

Reverse: The gate to a medieval fort (actually the Delhi Gate at Purana Qila in New Delhi). Above, there is the legend 'सैन्य सेवा मैडल' ('Sainya Seva Medal').

Ribbon: 32 mm, orange-saffron, with two 1 mm stripes, white and green; the orange represents renunciation and sacrifice, the white represents the snows, and the green the jungles and forests. As it has been so common and so widely produced, there is some considerable variability of the precise shades of the colours in this ribbon. These colour variations have no significance.

Suspension: Suspended by a straight-bar suspender to which the clasps are attached.

Naming: The medal is normally named on the edge.

Miniature: Miniatures have been issued. Clasps are also seen in a wide range of official and unofficial styles.

Background: Awarded to members of the armed forces in recognition of services under conditions of special hardship and severe climate. The medal may well be said to be the single most common award in the Indian military. Multi-clasps medals, however, are not frequently encountered.

Clasps: The medal is not awarded without a clasp. While all clasps observed have been produced in Hindi rather than English, they will frequently be referred to by their English names. These clasps are illustrated below.

Outline

1048.100 medal.

   1048.101 जम्मू कश्मीर / Jammu Kashmir—Instituted by No. 32-Pres./60 of 17 June 1960. Awarded (a) for an aggregate of one year of service in Jammu and Kashmir after 27 October 1947. Service which qualified for the appropriate bar to the 1947 General Service Medal (see 1035.301) or for the 'Himalaya' bar to the Sainya Seva Medal (see 1048.003) will not be counted; (b) air force personnel who have carried out a minimum of ten sorties or forty hours of flying after 27 October 1947, with the same limits to overlapping service applying here as well. Between the two words on the clasp is a depiction of a *chinar* leaf.

   1048.102 नीफा / NEFA—Instituted by No. 32-Pres./60 of 2 June 1960. The clasp was amended by corrgindum No. 4-Pres./86 of 29 August 1986 (*Gazette of India*, part 1, section 3, 11 October 1986) to rename the clasp 'Arunachal'; no such clasp has to date been observed (though, should it appear, it might be classified as a provisional 1048.002a). While reviewing the proposal of the Chiefs of Staff Committee for the institution of the High Altitude Medal, to replace the 'Himalaya' clasp (below), the Defence Minister suggested that the clasp 'NEFA' should be renamed as 'Arunachal', since the erstwhile agency was about to be incorporated into India as a state, a process completed in 1987. The clasp is awarded: (a) for an aggregate of one year of service in the North-East Frontier Agency (NEFA) to personnel employed in the construction of roads and airfields between 7 October 1952 and 15 November 1958; (b) personnel seconded to the Assam Rifles who have completed an aggregate of one year of service in NEFA (excluding those areas for which the 'Himalaya' clasp was awarded, see [1047.003]) after 15 August 1947; (c) air force personnel who carried out a minimum of ten sorties or forty hours of flying after 7 October 1952. The clasp is designed to look like a horizontal stalk of bamboo.

1048.103 Clasp Himalaya

1048.103 हिमालया / Himalaya—Instituted by No. 32-Pres./ 60 of 2 June 1960 and amended by No. 56-Pres./68 or 3 August 1968 (to alter the Devanagari nomenclature to read हिमालय instead of हिमालया—though all clasps observed to date have been in the latter spelling, the revised हिमालय spelling could be viewed as 1048.003a) and by MoD notification No. 3033 of 20 November 1965 (listing additional qualifying areas). Awarded (a) for an aggregate of one year of service in the mountainous northern areas (roughly: portions of NEFA, the Tibet borders in Himachal Pradesh, Uttar Pradesh, Jammu and Kashmir, and Sikkim) and time periods specified by the government; (b) air force personnel who carried out a minimum of ten sorties or forty hours of flying in areas and time periods specified by the government. Between the two partial words on the clasp (indicated above by the space in the Hindi) is a depiction of a pine (cedar?) tree. Award of this clasp was terminated with the creation of the High Altitude Medal (see 1049) in 1986. A total of 2,27,000 clasps had been issued through September 1988 (late issues extending well beyond the termination date of the clasp).

1048.104 Clasp Bengal-Assam

1048.104 बंगाल-असम / Bengal-Assam—Instituted by MoD Notification No. 1398 dated 22 July 1960; amended by MoD Notification No. 1913 of 23 June 1967 (to amend the qualifying areas). Awarded (a) for an aggregate of one year of service in specified areas on West Bengal and Assam after 26 October 1962; (b) for ten sorties or forty hours of flying over specified areas of West Bengal and Assam after 26 October 1962. The clasp is unornamented.

1048.105 Clasp Andaman and Nicobar

1048.105 अंडमान और निकोबार / Andaman and Nicobar— Authorized by A.I. 34/67 of 1 July 1967. Awarded (a) for one year of aggregate service in the Andaman and Nicobar Islands after 20 May 1966; (b) for fifty hours of flying in the Andaman and Nicobar Islands after 20 May 1966. At either end of the unusually ornate clasp, there is a lotus flower. This is the only clasp to this medal for which there are a significant number of naval recipients.

1048.106 मरुस्थल/ Marusthal (Desert)—Instituted by MoD Notification No. 12 dated 20 July 1984. Awarded (a) for one year of aggregate service in the qualifying desert areas; (b) to aircrew to ten sorties or forty hours of flying over specified areas in the western Rajasthan and western Haryana desert. The clasp is unornamented.

1048.106 Clasp Marusthal

1049.100 High Altitude Medal

1049 उच्च तुंगता मैडल / UCCHH TUNGTA MEDAL / HIGH ALTITUDE MEDAL

Awarded for service in harsh high-altitude areas.

Established: Established by No. 72-Pres./86 of 12 September 1986 to have effect from 1 April 1984 and amended in No. 168-Pres./95 of 19 September 1995.

General Appearance: Circular 35 mm cupro-nickel medal.

Obverse: The state emblem and motto in the centre. On either side, the legend 'उच्च तुंगता मैडल / UCCHH TUNGTA MEDAL'.

Reverse: A somewhat stylized scene of the Himalayan mountains. The reverse is similar to that of the Siachen Glacier Medal (see 1041), although these mountains are unpopulated (as opposed to the Siachen medal, where there are troops and a helicopter).

Ribbon: 32 mm, medium blue with a series of 1½ mm white chevrons, approximately 6 mm apart. The ribbon is observed with a great deal of variation, but never of consistent high quality. Many specimens are produced from what seems to be thin plasticized paper, while others are made from a coarse, almost plastic, material (where the medium blue seems almost to have been spray-painted on); all are distinctly one-sided. Early in the life of the medal, it was worn from a medium grey-blue ribbon with traditional vertical white stripes; this ribbon is shown in the ribbon charts towards the end of this volume; in fact, this ribbon is from Sri Lanka, and is the ribbon for the Sri Lankan Navy's 25th Anniversary Medal, 1975.

Suspension: Suspended from a non-swivelling straight-bar suspender.

Naming: Named on the edge. Naming has been observed in both English and Hindi.

Miniature: Miniatures have been issued with the same unfortunate range in ribbon quality as is seen with the full-size medal.

Background: The medal is awarded for 180 days of service in the high Himalayas, above 9,000 feet (approximately 2,700 m). Transport and helicopter aircrew are awarded the medal for carrying out a minimum of 10 sorties or 40 hours of flying on transport support roles at high altitude DZs. Personnel who died or were evacuated due to wounds are eligible for the medal irrespective of the time limit. This medal replaces the earlier 'Himalaya' clasp to the Sainya Seva Medal (see 1048.003) which was cancelled from the date of institution of this medal.

Outline

1049.100 medal.

1050 पुलिस कठिन सेवा पदक / POLICE KATHIN SEVA PADAK / POLICE (SPECIAL DUTY) MEDAL[71]

Awarded to the police forces for service in harsh environmental conditions and/or conditions of other special difficulty.

[71] *Encyclopedia of Soldiers with Highest Gallantry Awards*, pp. 64-65; *India's Highest Gallantry Awards*, pp. 74-75; Scandaluzzi, *Medal Ribbons of the World*, vol. 3: *India*.

Established: No. 29-Pres./62 and No. 30-Pres./62 of 23 February 1962 (as corrected in the *Gazette of India*, 24 March 1962, p. 87), with effect from 1 January 1959. This was amended by No. 32-Pres./62 of 28 April 1962. The statute was completely redrafted in No. 25-Pres./64 and No. 26-Pres./64 of 18 February 1964. The terms of award were further revised by No. 34-Pres./73 of 22 May 1973 and by No. 10-Pres./88 of 28 January 1988. There seem to be no orders formally establishing the various clasps or laying out the qualifying conditions for their award.

General Appearance: Circular 39 mm cupro-nickel medal.

Obverse: The state emblem within an ornate wreath.

Reverse: A low-relief depiction of the high Himalayas, labelled below left as 'GANGOTRI'. Above, the curved legend 'पुलिस कठिन सेवा पदक' ('Police Kathin Seva Padak') appears.

Ribbon: 34.5 mm, white, with a series of 4 mm stripes: red, yellow, green, red, yellow, green. As it has been so common and so widely produced, there is some variability of the precise shades of the colours in this ribbon. These colour variations have no significance. Although, some sources have attributed significance to these designs: regular police, as described above but with orange stripes rather than yellow; Central Reserve Police, first type, as described above with yellow stripes; Central Reserve Police, second type, six equal alternate stripes of dark red, orange, and dark green, separated by very thin white stripes and with white edges. Again, these inventive systematizations seem to be without any basis in policy or in fact.

Suspension: Suspended by an ornate fixed straight-bar suspender to which the clasps are attached.

Naming: The medal is issued unnamed, though some unofficially and privately named specimens have been observed.

Miniature: Miniatures have been issued, though no clasps have been observed.

Background: The Police (Special Duty) Medal is an area service medal and is awarded to those personnel who have completed an aggregate of one year's service in areas of harship after 1 January 1959. Orginally, this seems to have been conceived of as a police equivalent to the Sainya Seva Medal. The rules were amended in 1988 to recognize service under conditions of broader hardship and/or climate, intentionally including one year of service in the 'politically harsh' conditions of Punjab and Chandigarh after 1 January 1983. The recipients of this award are presented with their medals in ceremonies arranged by the state governments. The statute requires that all awards be published, by name and number, in the *Gazette of India*—see, for example, Home Department No. 24/3(11)/64-Police in the *Gazette of India*, pt. 1, sect. 1, of 15 October 1966, pp. 680-4. While it seems strange for an award issued unnamed to be published by name—and at great length—this is the mandated practice.

Unlike what may be termed a 'normal' procedure, subsequent awards of the medal are not affected by adding additional clasps to the existing medal, but are instead commemorated by the award of an additional medal. This is

1050.100 Police (Special Duty) Medal

even extended to a repeat qualification for a clasp already received. In these cases a second (or subsequent) medal with the same clasp is awarded. This can result, to cite one observed example, in a policeman wearing among his other awards the Kathin Seva Jammu & Kashmir, Kathin Seva Punjab, Kathin Seva Punjab, Kathin Seva Jammu & Kashmir, and Kathin Seva Punjab (three 'Punjab' medals and two 'Jammu & Kashmir' medals!). Multi-clasp medals can, therefore, safely be assumed not to exist. This is just one more example of some of the deviances from normal standards and practices present in police policies towards awards. Such awards are gazetted as a second (or third) 'bar' to the medal (see, for example, No. F/9/12/66-P.IV in the *Gazette of India*, pt. 1, sect. 1 of 26 February 1966).

Additionally, in almost all cases, these medals have not been officially manufactured and issued, but are instead made locally by independent manufacturers. This has given rise to extraordinary variability in manufacture and even in design details. This process seems also to have given rise to considerable 'inventiveness' with regard to clasps and unofficial clasps for this medal may have proliferated. All clasps observed have been inscribed in English rather than in Hindi and the medals are issued unnamed.

Some police personnel have been observed wearing the High Altitude Service Medal (1049) in addition to this award. It is difficult to see the legitimate statutory basis for this.

Clasps: The medal was not awarded without a bar. It has been extraordinarily difficult to trace these clasps, and the list below should be taken merely as something between tentative and representative. In reality, we can list with certainty only those clasps we have seen. It has proved impossible to trace the provisions by which each clasp has been created, as there seems to be little central coordination over this process.

Outline

1050.100 medal.
  1050.101 Andaman and Nicobar
  1050.102 Arunachal Pradesh
  1050.103 Assam (believed to exist)
  1050.104 Chandigarh
  1050.105 Gujarat
  1050.106 Himachal Pradesh
  1050.107 Indo-Tibetan Border (believed to exist)
  1050.108 J&K—this version of the 'Jammu & Kashmir' clasp is believed to exist; see also 1050.109.
  1050.109 Jammu & Kashmir—see also 1050.108.
  1050.110 Manipur
  1050.111 Meghalaya
  1050.112 Mizoram
  1050.113 Nagaland
  1050.114 Punjab
  1050.115 Rajasthan
  1050.116 Tripura

1051.100 Police (Internal Security) Medal

1051 पुलिस आन्त्रिक सुरक्षा सेवा पदक / POLICE ANTRIK SURAKSHA SEVA PADAK / POLICE (INTERNAL SECURITY) MEDAL

Awarded to police forces for internal security duties.

Established: By No. 142-Pres/2000 of 20 September 2000, with effect from 1 January 1989. This was altered by No. 109-Pres./2003 of 27 October 2003 to require the maintenance in the Ministry of Home Affairs, of a register recording the names of all recipients of this medal.

General Appearance: A 38 mm circular cupro-nickel medal. As the official medal has not appeared, we have been forced to illustrate a tailor's copy.

Obverse: A soldier aiming a rifle against the geographical outline of the map of India. The Hindi inscription 'पुलिस (आन्त्रिक सुरक्षा सेवा) पदक—भारत' appears along the upper rim while the words 'POLICE (ANTRIK SURAKSHA SEVA) PADAK—INDIA' are inscribed along the lower half, separated by a star on either side.

Reverse: The reverse shows the state emblem in the centre with the national motto, encircled by a decorative wreath with 37 spokes placed at equal distance from each other. The state emblem has superscribed the words 'पुलिस बलों के लिए' ('Pulis Balon ke Liye') above and 'FOR POLICE FORCES' below in semi-circular shapes. A star separates the upper and lower semi-circles on either side.

Ribbon: 35 mm, navy blue and red in colour. (In the *Gazette*: 'Navy blue portion shall be double the size of the red colour vertically.') In practice, this was first rendered as a ribbon half navy blue and half red, with the blue worn to the wearer's right. In the apparent awareness that this was not what the vaguely drafted statute intended, a second unsymmetrical ribbon was introduced, 35 mm, with a 23 mm blue stripe to the left and a 12 mm stripe to the right; this ribbon seems most closely to approximate the intent of the notification. The third ribbon being worn is one of six alternating stripes of blue and red, three of each, of equal width, with a blue stripe coming first. There is tremendous confusion over this ribbon (and this medal) and the ribbon descriptions we have given here represent our best efforts at disentangling a muddled situation.

Suspension: Suspended by a 38 mm long horizontal non-swivelling bar with the inscription 'Police (Antrik Suraksha Seva) Padak' (existing tailors' copies do not include this feature). While there is no specific mention of any clasps in the instituting notification, the phrase 'to which the clasps are attached' used in describing the suspension suggests that clasps—similar to those of the Special Duty Medal?—are contemplated. It is hard to say for certain.

Naming: The medal is not expected to be named.

Miniature: Miniatures have not apparently been issued.

Background: The medal is awarded to police personnel, including the central police organizations and other security organizations, for services in internal security operations in India. It may be awarded posthumously. Names of personnel awarded the medal are, unbelievably, to be notified in the

Gazette of India and a register of such names is to be maintained by the Ministry of Home Affairs. This medal continues the unfortunate trend of instituiting medals for police and para-military forces.

Clasps: There may well be a series of clasps for this medal eventually. There is much uncertainty and confusion here as well.

Outline

1051.100 medal.

1052.100 Videsh Seva Medal (Original design)

1052 विदेश सेवा मैडल / VIDESH SEVA MEDAL / OVERSEAS MEDAL[72]

Awarded to armed forces personnel for overseas service.

Established: By No. 15-Pres./60 of 26 January 1960, with effect from 15 August 1947. The design of the medal, ribbon and clasps was notified in No. 32-Pres./60 of 2 July 1960. The first clasps as well as eligible categories of personnel were notified in MoD Notification No. 1399, dated 22 July 1960.[73] Ministry of Defence notifications in the *Gazette of India* part 1, section 3, at varying times commencing from Notification No. 1399 of 22 July 1960 have authorized additional clasps. The authority for each, whenever available, is listed below against the individual entry for each clasp. The design of the medal itself was modified by No. 52-Pres./68 of 22 July 1968.

Eligible Categories: (a) Commissioned Officers, Junior Commissioned Officers, Other Ranks and Non-Combatants (enrolled) of the regular Army, embodied Auxiliary and Reserve Forces or any other lawful constituted Armed Forces. (b) Nursing Officers and other members of Nursing Services in the Armed Forces.

General Appearance: A 35 mm circular cupro-nickel medal.

Obverse: The original design specifications called for the obverse to show an ancient Indian warship; this was never issued except as miniatures.

The final design was of the state emblem, and below 'विदेश सेवा मैडल' ('Videsh Seva Medal') in Hindi.

Reverse: The original design specifications called for the reverse to show 'a swelling ocean in the centre and the Hindi inscription "विदेश सेवा मैडल" or "Videsh Seva Medal" along the upper rim'.

The issued variety shows an attractive rendering of an ancient Indian ship on the open stormy seas.

Ribbon: 32 mm, cobalt blue with five equally spaced 1 mm white stripes. The five white stripes represent Prime Minister Nehru's five principles of non-alignment (*panchsheel*), while the blue is United Nations' blue. Earlier ribbons appear to have been produced in a darker blue which is seen with contemporary samples.

Suspension: Suspended by a non-swivelling straight-bar suspender to which the clasps are attached.

Naming: The medal is named on the edge.

[72] *Encyclopedia of Soldiers with Highest Gallantry Awards*, pp. 67-68; *India's Highest Gallantry Awards*, pp. 77-78; Haynes, 'Medals and Decorations of the Republic of India', pp. 39-42; Johnson, 'Medals of the Republic of India', pp. 43-45; Das, *Traditions and Customs*, p. 279; Scandaluzzi, *Medal Ribbons of the World*, vol. 3: *India*.

[73] Published in the *Gazette of India*, pt. 1, sect. 3, 30 July 1960.

Miniature: Miniatures have been issued. There is a wide range of official and semi-official clasps.

Background: The medal is awarded to military personnel for services outside of India. Personnel assigned on the regular staff of diplomatic missions in the countries where clasps have been authorized are excluded from awards. In many cases, the clasps are awarded either for service with the United Nations or other multi-national missions or for detached service on loan to foreign governments. In May 1970 it was decided that the following categories of service were in future to be recognized for the institution of a clasp to the medal *irrespective of the number of personnel involved*:

(a) campaign service or service in peace-keeping roles with the UN; and

(b) deputation with other countries in various capacities as trainers, as advisors, and to fill up specific posts for temporary periods, etc.

1052.200 Videsh Seva Medal

As will be seen, this has resulted in some extremely small numbers of qualifying personnel. Qualifying periods for clasps have been largely standardized as follows: peacekeeping operations, 90 days; observers/training missions, 180 days; aircrew, three sorties or twelve flying hours. Exceptions are made for special cases. The medal may be awarded posthumously. Moreover, personnel who died or were evacuated due to wounds or other disabilities attributable to service in the countries and during the service specified or who was awarded a gallantry award in the course of such service would qualify automatically for the award of a clasp even if they did not meet the minimum stipulated qualifying service period.

Although the second clause of the instituting notification stipulated that the medal was to be awarded 'for such service abroad . . . which has not been considered for any other Indian medal', on at least one occasion the Videsh Seva Medal (with clasp Sri Lanka) has been awarded in conjunction with another medal, the Special Service Medal with clasp 'Sri Lanka' (1037.203), awarded for service with the Indian Peace Keeping Force. However, this relaxation of the instituting ordinances was specially notified by a President's Secretariat Notification (No. 66-Pres./89 of 20 July 1989). As the instituting notification implies, non-India medals are frequently bestowed for the same service as the Videsh Seva Medal, most commonly for United Nations or other multinational peacekeeping operations. For further details of Indian participation see the section on UN medals in Chapter 3.

Awards to police personnel for similar services seem to have taken place, though the authorization for this is elusive and obscure. Under normal circumstances an amending notification under presidential authority should have been issued, officially extending entitlement to this medal to police forces, but this seems not to have taken place.

Clasps: The medal is not awarded without a clasp. Clasps are 32 mm long with a frosted background and burnished

1052.201 Clasp Korea

borders. While all clasps have been produced in Hindi rather than English, they will frequently be referred to by their English names, as that has been the description used in the authorizing gazette entry. It has not always been possible to determine the actual Hindi rendering of the name of the bar, given in English in the authorizing notifications. Where possible, these clasps have been illustrated here.

Outline

1052.100 Original design, never issued (except as miniatures?). 1052.200 medal.

1052.201 कोरिया / Koriya / Korea (1950-54)—Instituted by MoD Notification No. 1399 of 22 July 1960. For 90 days of service with the Neutral Nations Repatriation Commission (NNRC) or the Indian Custodial Force in Korea, 22 November 1950-17 March 1954. The war ended on 27 July 1953, with the signing of the armistice agreement, which provided for the creation of the Neutral Nations Repatriation Commission (NNRC) and the Custodian Force India (CFI) for the supervision of the armistice and the disposal of the prisoners of war (POWs). The NNRC was formed with Lieutenant General K.S. Thimayya, DSO, as the chairman, to deal with the question of those POWs, who had refused repatriation to their countries of origin. The CFI was made up of 2 Para, 5 Rajputana Rifles, 6 Jat, 3 Dogra, 3 Garhwal Rifles and ancillary services grouped under the 190th Infantry Brigade. Major General S.P.P. Thorat, DSO, was nominated GOC of the force. Subsequently, one more battalion was added to the brigade. Altogether, 6,130 Indian troops (231 officers, 203 JCOs and 5,696 NCOs) went to Korea. The force left India in five batches in August-September 1953. On arrival in Korea, the CFI gathered the POWs into camps built in Korea's Demilitarized Zone between the UN and the Communist lines. They were then taken one at a time to explanation booths. Each POW was told his rights and privileges by men from his homeland. The POW then could choose to go home or to remain with the side that had captured him. The NNRC was limited to 120 days in which to ascertain the desires concerning repatriation of nearly 23,000 prisoners: 22,604 of the UN and, 359 of both North Korea and China. In the process of hearing explanations that at times were themselves contrary, some of these POWs resorted to violence and it was obvious that there were political pressures on them. However, the CFI maintained control, with minimum casualties. There was a deadline for explanations (23 Dec. 1953) and if some unrepatriated POWs were left, a political conference was to be convened. If within thirty days of the conference, some POWs still refused repatriation, they were to be given civilian status and allowed to go to any neutral country that they wished to. Many POWs refused repatriation and the POWs of the UN command threatened to free themselves, if they were not released on 23 January 1954. The two commands put up conflicting demands with regard to the release of the POWs, but Lieutenant General Thimayya took a truly neutral decision whereby the POWs from both sides were to be handed back to their respective commands. Ultimately, the UN command took over their prisoners, while the Communist command refused to take over theirs. On this, the general ordered the CFI to leave the prisoners alone and withdraw from the camp. After some lapse of time, the Communist command took them away. Subsequently, both the commands conveyed their deep appreciation for the impartiality and efficiency of the Indian Army. Out of the repatriated prisoners, eighty-eight were brought to India and finally eleven of them chose to settle there. A person who had received the clasp 'Overseas Korea—1950-53' to the General Service Medal 1947 (1035.002) was not eligible for this award. NNRC service would not have been eligible for the UN Korea medal, even if it had been produced and accepted for wear in India (see 3001).

1052.202 नेपाल / Nepal (1952-)—Instituted by MoD Notification No. 1399 of 22 July 1960, awarded for (a) for 180 days of service on the effective strength of any unit employed in the construction of Tribhuvan Rajpath or airfields in Nepal, 15 April 1952-15 April 1958; (b) 90 days of service providing signal communications during the Nepali elections, 26 November 1958-3 May 1959; (c) for 180 days of service with the Indian Military Training Mission or the Military Advisory Training Group, 1 August 1952 or thereafter; (d) six sorties or twenty-four flying hours as a member of the ejection crew of an air despatch unit on transport support roles in Nepal commencing 1 April 1962 or thereafter.

1052.203 हिन्दचीन / Hindchin / Indochina (1954-70)—Instituted by MoD Notification No. 1399 of 22 July 1960, for 90 days of service on the staff of the International Commission for Supervision and Control in Vietnam, Laos, and Cambodia (ICSC, whose medal they also would have received, see 3002), 7 August 1954-70.

1052.204 इंडोनेशिया / Indoneshiya / Indonesia (1955-??). Instituted by MoD Notification No. 1399 of 22 July 1960. Awarded for service on loan to the government of Indonesia, 25 November 1955 or thereafter.

1052.205 संयुक्त अरब गणराज्य / Sanyukt Arab Ganrajya / United Arab Republic (1956-??)—The clasp, named 'Egypt' in many official documents, was instituted by MoD Notification No. 1399 of 22 July 1960. It was awarded for (a) 180 days of UN service with UNEF (see 3003), 2 November 1956-18 May 1967 (3 Para, 1 Para, 2 Grenadiers, 4 Kumaon, 4 Rajput, 2 Maratha L.I., 9 Dogra, 4 Guards, 3 Punjab, 1 Sikh L.I. were all eligible units); (b) to personnel on loan to the government of Egypt/U.A.R. commencing 21 February 1956. Some 12,000 clasps were awarded.

1052.206 इथिओपिया / Ethiopia (1957- , 1961- , 1970-)—Instituted by MoD Notification No. 1399 of 22 July 1960. Awarded: (a) for 180 days of service on the staff of the Haile Selassie I Military Academy, 3 May 1957 or thereafter; (b) 180 days of service on deputation to the Ethiopian government for service in the Imperial Body Guard Training Centre, after

1052.202 Clasp Nepal

1052.203 Clasp Indochina

1052.205 Clasp United Arab Republic

1052.206 Clasp Ethiopia

1052.209 Clasp Iraq

1052.210 Clasp Sri Lanka

1052.211 Clasp Congo

24 September 1961; and (c) in May 1970 award of the Clasp 'Ethiopia' to Videsh Seva Medal was extended to naval officers on deputation to the government of Ethiopia or on loan service to the Imperial Ethiopian Navy.

1052.207 लेबनान / Lebanon (1958, 1998-)—Instituted by MoD Notification No. 1399 of 22 July 1960. For 90 days of UN service with UNOGIL (see 3004), 19 June 1958-12 December 1958. Approximately twenty Indian military observers were awarded the clasp. The clasp was reinstituted by MoD Notification No. 7 of 5 October 2002[74] for 180 days of service with the United Nations Interim Force in Lebanon (UNIFIL, see 3026) from 19 November 1998. Approximately 5,716 clasps have been awarded till date.

1052.208 घाना / Ghana (1959-)—Instituted by MoD Notification No. 1399 of 22 July 1960, the clasp was awarded for 180 days of service on loan to the government of Ghana, after 23 March 1959.

1052.209 इराक / Iraq (1959-)—Instituted by MoD Notification No. 1399 of 22 July 1960. For 180 days of service on loan to the government of Iraq, after 10 November 1959.

1052.210 श्रीलंका / Sri Lanka (1960-)—Instituted as clasp 'Ceylon' by MoD Notification No 1804 dated 28 June 1971.[75] This was amended to 'Sri Lanka' by MoD Notification No. 32, dated 29 August 1973.[76] Eligibility was extended to Indian Peace Keeping Force (IPKF) personnel by President's Secretariat Notification No. 66-Pres./89 of 20 July 1989[77] which also permitted relaxation of the second clause of No. 15-Pres/60 which prohibited award of a clasp for services which had been recognized by another medal. First awarded for (a) services on deputation to the government of Sri Lanka or on loan to the Sri Lankan Navy after 13 June 1960, or (b) for two days of service in Sri Lanka 12 April-25 May 1971. Most awards of this clasp, however, are for 'Operation Pawan,' peacekeeping service in northern and eastern Sri Lanka, 1987-90, as a part of the IPKF. The clasp is awarded to army, navy, and air force personnel for services in Sri Lanka; around 2,00,000 Indian troops served in 'Operation Pawan' starting 28 July 1987. Recipients of the clasp under these conditions also received the Special Service Medal with clasp for Sri Lanka (1037.202).

1052.211 कांगो / Congo (1960-64, 1999-)—Instituted by No. 15-Pres./60 of 26 January 1960, it was awarded for 180 days of UN service with ONUC (see 3005), 2 August 1960–June 1964, or for six sorties or twenty-four hours of flying transport missions over the Congo, 2 August 1960–June 1964. Approximately 12,000 clasps were awarded. The clasp was reinstituted for 180 days of service with the United Nations Mission in the Democratic Republic of the Congo (3029), from 9 September 1999. Approximately 3,322 of these clasps were awarded for that service.

1052.212 भूटान / Bhutan (1961-)—Instituted by No. 15-Pres./60 of 26 January 1960. Awarded for: (a) service with the

[74] Published in the *Gazette of India,* pt. 1, sect. 3, of 10 September 2002. We cannot explain the discrepancy of dates here, though they are correct.

[75] Published in the *Gazette of India,* of 31 July 1971.

[76] Published in the *Gazette of India,* pt. 1, sect. 3, 22 September 1973.

[77] Amended by No. 81-Pres/89. of 19 October 1989 and 53-Pres/90 of 06 June 1990.

Indian army team in Bhutan, 27 May 1961-22 September 1962; (b) 180 days of service with the Indian Military Training Team, 27 August 1962- ; (c) 180 days of service with a unit employed on road construction in Bhutan, 3 April 1961- ; (d) 90 days of other temporary duty in Bhutan.

1052.213 New Guinea (1962-63)—For UN service with UNTEA and UNSF (see 3006) in West New Guinea (West Irian), October 1962-April 1963. Current evidence suggests that only twelve of these clasps were awarded.

1052.214 यमन / Yemen (1963-64)—Instituted by MoD Notification No. 1709 of 28 June 1971.[78] For 90 days of UN service with UNYOM (see 3007), 4 September 1963-4 September 1964. Only approximately twenty-five of these clasps were awarded.

1052.215 नाइजीरिया / Nigeria (1963-)—Authorized by A.I. 51/73, it was awarded for 180 days of service on deputation to the Nigerian government after 28 December 1963.

1052.216 Algeria (1963-)—For 180 days on service on deputation to the government of Algeria, 28 December 1963- .

1052.217 Cyprus (1964-)—For UN service with UNFICYP (see 3008). Current evidence suggests that only three of these clasps were awarded.

1052.218 मलेशिया / Malaysia (1966-)—Instituted by MoD Notification No 1804 dated 28 Jun 1971.[79] Awarded for service on deputation to the Government of Malaysia or on loan to the Royal Malaysian Navy commencing from 11 April 1966 or thereafter.

1052.219 अफ़गानिस्तान / Afghanistan (1970-)—Authorized by A.I. 61/73 and awarded for services on deputation to the government of Afghanistan after 23 June 1970.

1052.220 बंगलादेश / Bangladesh (1972)—Authorized by A.I. 67/75. Awarded for (a) one day of minesweeping operations in the waters surrounding Bangladesh, 26 March–30 November 1972, or (b) one day of service in the Chittagoing Hills operations on or after 26 March 1972.

1052.221 मारिशस / Mauritius (1973-)—Authorized by A.I. 51/73. Awarded for (a) service on deputation to the government of Mauritius after 25 February 1973, or (b) service in post-cyclone restoration of power and telecommunications, 21 February-17 June 1975.

1052.222 बोत्स्वाना / Botswana (1973-)—Awarded for services on deputation to the Government of Botswana for service with the Indian training mission in Botswana, after 2 August 1973.

1052.223 जाम्बिया / Zambia (1973- , 1994-)—Authorized by A.I. 51/73 and reinstiututed by MoD Notification No. 2 of 8 January 1999.[80] (The clasp has, apparently, been instituted twice.) Awarded for (a) service on deputation to the government of Zambia after 8 October 1973; (b) for service on deputation to the government of Zambia after 28 February 1994.

1052.224 सूडान/Sudan (1976-)—Authorized by A.I. 83/77,

1052.212 Clasp Bhutan

1052.214 Clasp Yemen

1052.215 Clasp Nigeria

1052.218 Clasp Malaysia

1052.220 Clasp Bangladesh

1052.222 Clasp Botswana

[78] Published in the *Gazette of India*, pt. 1, sect. 3, 24 July 1971.
[79] Ibid., 31 July 1971.
[80] Ibid., 6 February 1999.

1052.224 Clasp Sudan

1052.225 Clasp Oman

awarded for (a) service on loan to the government of the Sudan from 25 November 1976 and (b) service in UNMIS (3033) from July 2004.

1052.225 ओमान/ Oman (1976-)—For service on deputation to the Government of Oman after 25 November 1976.

1052.226 Qatar (1988-)—Instituted by MoD Notification No. 2 of 8 January 1999.[81] Awarded for service on deputation to the Government of Qatar with effect from 28 February 1988 or thereafter for a minimum of 180 days aggregate service.

1052.227 तंज़ानिया / Tanzania (1988-)—Instituted by MoD Notification No. 3 of 3 August 1989.[82] Awarded for service on deputation to the Government of United Republic of Tanzania with effect from 12 April 1988 or thereafter for minimum of 180 days aggregate service.

1052.228 इरान-इराक / Iran-Iraq (1988-91)—For a minimum of 180 days of service with UNIIMOG (see 3009), August 1988-April 1991. Current evidence suggests that only six of these clasps were awarded.

1052.229 Maldives (1988)—For service in 'Operation Cactus' in which Indian troops were deployed to the Maldives from 3-6 November 1988 in response to a request from the government for assistance in the face of a mercenary invasion. Army, navy, and air force troops were deployed. This service should rightly have been commemorated by a clasp to the Videsh Seva medal, although such a clasp seems never to have been formally authorized. Due to the ambiguity of this situation, we have provisionally listed this clasp here though its existence is far from certain.

1052.230 शेसैल्स / Seychelles (1989-)—Instituted by MoD Notification No. 1 of 24 May 1993.[83] For 180 days of service on deputation to the Government of the Seychelles with the Indian training mission in Seychelles, after 1 January 1989.

1052.231 अंगोला / Angola (1989-)—For service with the United Nations Angola Verification Mission (UNAVEM I, UNAVEM II, and UNAVEM III), 4 January 1989-June 1997 (see 3010) or with the United Nations Observer Mission in Angola (MONUA), July 1997 (see 3025). For UNAVEM, current evidence suggests that 2,348 of these clasps were awarded. The clasp was further extended for service with the United National Mission Angola (UNMA, no UN medal issued to date) from 2002, where it is estimated that two more clasps were awarded.

1052.232 नामीबिया / Namibia (1989-90)—For 180 days of service with the United Nations Transitional Assistance Group (UNTAG), 13 March 1989-March 1990 (see 3011). Current evidence suggests that only two of these clasps were awarded.

1052.233 Nicaragua (1990-92)—Instituted by MoD Notification No. 2 of 8 January 1999.[84] For 180 days of service in Nicaragua with ONUCA (see 3012), 30 May 1990-January 1992. Approximately five of these clasps were awarded.

1052.234 Honduras (1990-92)—Instituted by MoD

[81] Published in the *Gazette of India*, pt. 1, sect. 3, 6 February 1999.

[82] Ibid., 12 August 1989.

[83] Ibid., 12 June 1993.

[84] Ibid., 6 February 1999.

Notification No. 2 of 8 January 1999.[85] For 180 days of in Honduras service with ONUCA (see 3012), 30 May 1990-January 1992.

1052.235 Guatemala (1990-92)—Instituted by MoD Notification No. 2 of 8 January 1999.[86] For 180 days of service in Guatemala with ONUCA (see 3012), 30 May 1990-January 1992.

1052.236 Costa Rica (1990-92)—Instituted by MoD Notification No. 2 of 8 January 1999.[87] For 180 days of service in Costa Rica with ONUCA (see 3012), 30 May 1990-January 1992.

1052.237 El Salvador (1990-95)—Instituted by MoD Notification No. 2 of 8 January 1999.[88] For 180 days of service with the United Nations Observer Mission in El Salvador (ONUSAL), 30 May 1990-April 1995 (see 3013). Approximately four of these clasps were awarded.

1052.238 Iraq-Kuwait (1991-)—Instituted by MoD Notification No. 2 of 8 January 1999.[89] For 180 days of service with the United Nations Iraq-Kuwait Observation Mission (UNIKOM), 15 April 1991— (see 3014). Current evidence suggests that only sixty-six of these clasps were awarded.

1052.239 Western Sahara (1991-)—For UN service with MINUSRO, after September 1991 (see 3015).

1052.240 Cambodia (1991-93)—Instituted by MoD Notification No. 2 of 8 January 1999.[90] For service with the United Nations Advance Mission in Cambodia (UNAMIC, November 1991-March 1992) or the United Nations Transitional Authority in Cambodia (UNTAC, March 1992-September 1993) (see 3016 and 3018). For UNTAC, current evidence suggests that 1,719 of these clasps were awarded.

1052.241 Yugoslavia (1992-95)—For UN service with UNPROFOR, 2 March 1992-December 1995 (see 3017). Current evidence suggests that only two of these clasps were awarded.

1052.242 New York (1993-)—Instituted by MoD Notification No. 2 of 8 January 1999.[91] For 180 days of service at the United Nations' headquarters in New York, NY, USA, after 1 July 1993. The United Nations Headquarters medal (3034) would also be awarded for this service.

1052.243 सोमालिया / Somalia (1993-95)—Instituted by MoD Notification No. 2 of 8 January 1999.[92] For 180 days of service with the United Nations Operations in Somalia (UNOSOM I and UNOSOM II), 28 August 1993-March 1995 (see 3019). Approximately 7,000 of these clasps were awarded.

1052.244 Mozambique (1993-94)—Instituted by MoD Notification No. 2 of 8 January 1999.[93] For 180 days of service with the United Nations Operation in Mozambique (ONUMOZ), May 1993-December 1994 (see 3020). Approximately 600 of these clasps were awarded.

1052.245 Haiti (1993-96)—For service with the United Nations Mission in Haiti (UNMIH), September 1993-June 1996 (see 3021). Approximately fifty of these clasps were awarded to the police.

1052.246 Liberia (1994-)—Instituted by MoD Notification

[85] Published in the *Gazette of India*, 6 February 1999.
[86] Ibid.
[87] Ibid.
[88] Ibid.
[89] Ibid.
[90] Ibid.
[91] Ibid.
[92] Ibid.
[93] Ibid.

No. 2 of 8 January 1999.[94] For 180 days of service with the United Nations Observer Mission in Liberia (UNOMIL), 15 August 1994- (see 3022). Current evidence suggests that only seventeen of these clasps were awarded.

1052.247 Rwanda (1994-96)—Instituted by MoD Notification No. 2 of 8 January 1999.[95] For 180 days of service with the United Nations Assistance Mission in Rwanda (UNAMIR), 10 November 1994-March 1996 (see 3023). Approximately 1,000 of these clasps were awarded.

1052.248 Laos (1995-)—For 180 days of service with the Indian training team in Laos from August 1995.

1052.249 Bosnia-Herzegovina (1995- , 1998-)—Instituted by MoD Notification No. 7 of 5 October 2002 (for UNMAC). For service (a) with the United Nations Mission in Bosnia and Herzegovina (UNMIBH), December 1995 (see 3024), and (b) with the United Nations Mine Action Centre (UNMAC) from 12 February 1998. Approximately 135 of these clasps were awarded.[96]

1052.250 Sierra Leone (1998-)—Instituted by MoD Notification No. 7 of 5 October 2002. For 180 days of UN service with UNOMSIL or UNAMSIL, after 31 July 1998 (see 3027). Approximately thirty-one of these clasps were awarded.

1052.251 Kosovo (1999-)—For UN service with UNMIK, after 1999 (see 3028). Approximately 538 of these clasps were awarded to the police.

1052.252 Northern Iraq (2000-)—For UN service with the United Nations Guards Coningent Iraq (UNGCI), after 2 June 2000. Approximately two of these clasps were awarded.

1052.253 Lesotho (2000-)—For service with the Indian training mission in Lesotho, after 10 September 2000.

1052.254 Ethiopia and Eritrea (2000-)—For UN service with UNMEE, after 11 November 2000 (see 3030). Approximately 5,293 of these clasps were awarded.

1052.255 Ivory Coast (2000-)—For UN service with UNOIC (3031). Approximately thirteen of these clasps were awarded.

1052.256 Burundi (2004-)—For UN service with ONUB (3032), after July 2004. Approximately eight of these clasps were awarded.

1053 तटरक्षक मैडल / TATRAKSHAK MEDAL / COAST GUARD MEDAL

Awarded to coast guard personnel for acts of conspicuous devotion to duty and courage.

Established: By No. 49-Pres./89 of 7 June 1989. Rules governing the award were published in No. 50-Pres./89 of 7 June 1989.

General Appearance: Circular 35 mm bronze medal.

Obverse: The coast guard crest with 'COAST GUARD MEDAL' above and, separated by stars, the legend 'INDIA' below.

Reverse: The state emblem within a wreath.

---

[94] Published in the *Gazette of India*, 6 February 1999.

[95] Ibid.

[96] The notification given here covers only military service in UNMAC. Indian service with UNMIBH, entirely police service, is not addressed in this MoD notification and the authority for this UNMIBH qualification is presently unknown.

Ribbon: 35 mm, nine equal stripes, five dark blue and four white.

Suspension: By a plain straight non-swivelling bar suspender.

Naming: The medal is usually issued named on the edge.

Miniature: Miniatures have been produced.

Background: The medal is awarded to members of the coast guard to recognize such individual acts of conspicuous devotion to duty or courage, performed within or without the territory of India, as have special significance for the coast guard. These are categorised as follows:

1. For conspicuous acts of gallantry. These awards are to be made as soon as possible after the event occasioning the grant.
2. For valuable service characterized by resourcefulness and devotion to duty including prolonged service of ability and merit.

The medal may also be awarded to aircrew who have completed the following minimum flying hours within a single tenure of two years or less:

Medium range surveillance aircraft	800 hours.
Light surveillance aircraft	800 hours.
Helicopters	500 hours.

The medal may be granted posthumously. Subsequent awards are represented by a bar worn on the ribbon. When such a bar is awarded, it is attached to the ribbon from which the medal is suspended, and is indicated by the addition of a small silver rose to the ribbons when worn alone. The award of medals for distinguished service is limited to a maximum of five awards in one year. There is no limit on the number of awards for gallantry.

Award of the medal is notified by publication of the name of the recipient in the *Gazette of India*, part 1, section 1. While awards for gallantry are notified as soon as possible after the date on which the act of gallantry was performed, medals for distinguished service are announced on 26 January (Republic Day) and 15 August (Independence Day).

Representative Citation: To understand the award better, a sample recipient in the bravery category of the award would be the 1995 award to 01568-R Uttam Navik (ME) Shri Gurdev Singh, Coast Guard Ship *Varaha*:

At about 1000 hours on 19th August 1994, a major fire broke out in the DA compartment of the CGS VARAHA. Shri Gurdev Singh being a member of the fire fighting party rushed to the spot immediately and made several daring attempts to approach the seat of the fire. The rising flames and excessive smoke prevented his approach. The sailor, thereafter, volunteered and went down in the compartment with a fire suit to attempt activation of the halon fire fighting system from local control due to the malfunction of the remote mode. His action in reaching the halon fire fighting equipment inside the compartment full of flames and smoke was at a grave and serious risk to his life.

Shri Gurdev Singh, Uttam Navik (ME) continued to fight the fire with the fire party till the fire was extinguished by the early hours of

1053.100 Coast Guard Medal

20th August 1994 having worked in excessively hot areas for hours without any respite. The sailor's penetration deep inside the compartment prevented spreading of the fire to adjoining compartments. His conduct and action in this accident displayed his immense courage and highest sense of dedication to duty against heavy odds.

Shri Gurdev Singh's courage, determination, total disregard for his personal safety, devotion to duty, perseverance and valour are in keeping with the highest traditions of the Indian Coast Guard Service.'

(No. 90-Pres./95 of 26 January 1995)

Outline

1053.100 medal.

1054.100 King's Police and Fire Services Medal for
Distinguished Service

1054 KING'S POLICE AND FIRE SERVICES MEDAL FOR DISTINGUISHED SERVICE

Awarded to the police and fire services to recognize distinguished service. While this medal was awarded in British-ruled India from 1909 until their departure in 1947, this entry deals only with the medal as it was awarded in independent India, during the Dominion period.

Established: Originally instituted by King Edward VII by Royal Warrant on 7 July 1909. The design was subsequently modified for succeeding monarchs and the design and structure of the award were changed to establish separate distinguished service and gallantry distinctions in what had previously been a single-division award. The medal continued to be awarded in India, without a distinct notification allowing this, from India's Independence on 15 August 1947 until the creation of the President's Police and Fire Services Medal for Distinguished Service (1055) on 1 March 1951.

General Appearance: Circular silver medal, 35 mm in diameter. Generally, it is similar to the King's Police and Fire Services Medal for Gallantry (1017), with only an alteration to the reverse legend.

Obverse: The crowned bust of King George VI, facing left and surrounded by the royal titles 'GEORGIVS VI D: G: BR: OMN: REX ET INDIAE IMP:'. These are, of course, the king's titles prior to the Indian Independence Act. While a strong case might have been made for a redesign of the medal to reflect the new constitutional status, there is no indication that this took place.

Reverse: A standing robed figure, with sword and shield. The shield carries the legend 'TO GUARD / MY / PEOPLE' and in the exergue below the figure the legend 'FOR DISTINGUISHED SERVICE' appears. Behind this figure there is a monumental construction (representing the police) and behind them an urban skyline.

Ribbon: 36 mm, white with two broad dark blue stripes.
Suspension: A ring.
Naming: Named and dated on the edge.
Miniature: Miniatures have been issued.
Background: In the ambiguous constitutional circumstances

of the Dominion period, this medal was continued from the time of British rule into the early years of Independence. This medal, which had been awarded widely throughout the empire, thus constituted an anachronistic continuation of royal authority into post-Independence India.

While very few awards of this medal took place in the Dominion period, it is not always possible to determine which of these awards were for post-Independence service.

Outline

1054.100 medal.

1055 राष्ट्रपति का पुलिस और अग्नि शमन सेवा पदक विशिष्ट सेवा के लिए / RASHTRAPATI KA POLICE AUR AGNI SHAMAN SEVA PADAK VISHISHT SEVA KE LIYE / PRESIDENT'S POLICE AND FIRE SERVICES MEDAL FOR DISTINGUISHED SERVICE[97]

Awarded to the police and fire services to recognize distinguished service.

Established: By No. 3-Pres/51 and No. 4-Pres./51 of 1 March 1951, replacing the King's Police and Fire Services Medal for Distinguished Service (1054). This was later modified by No. 5-Pres./51 of 9 April 1951, No. 27-Pres./51 of 12 June 1951, No. 18-Pres./52 of 31 January 1952, No. 8-Pres./53 of 17 February 1953, No. 11-Pres./56 of 8 March 1956, No. 65-Pres./62 and No. 66-Pres./62 of 10 October 1962, No. 78-Pres./63 and No. 79-Pres./63 of 17 October 1963, No. 43-Pres./71 of 5 August 1971, and No. 44-Pres./71 of 5 August 1971. In 1973 (No. 34-Pres./73 of 22 May 1973), the medal was split into separate police (1056) and fire services (1057) medals.

General Appearance: Circular gold-gilt medal, 35 mm in diameter. The gilt is very thin and is often absent.

Obverse: In the centre the coat of arms of the President of India on a shield and the legend 'PRESIDENT'S POLICE AND FIRE SERVICES MEDAL' above and 'INDIA' below. Five-pointed stars separate these two legends.

Reverse: The state emblem in the centre with 'FOR DISTINGUISHED SERVICE' below and a wreath above.

Ribbon: 32 mm, half dark blue, half white.

Suspension: A non-swivelling straight-bar suspender.

Naming: Named on the edge.

Miniature: Miniatures have been issued.

Background: Awarded to those in the organized police and fire services or Central Intelligence Bureau who have performed acts of conspicuous devotion to duty. The medal may be awarded posthumously, but was limited to forty-five awards per year. Bars may be awarded for subsequent acts of gallantry. These bars are silver slip-on bars and have the details of the awardee engraved on the reverse. When the ribbon is worn alone, the possession of a bar is indicated by the addition of a silver gilt rosette. In 1973 this medal was separated into the President's Police Medal for Distinguished Service (1056) and

1055.100 President's Police and Fire Services Medal for Distinguished Service (obverse)

[97] *Encyclopedia of Soldiers with Highest Gallantry Awards*, p. 66; *India's Highest Gallantry Awards*, p. 76; Haynes, 'Medals and Decorations of the Republic of India', p. 48; Dorling, *Ribbons & Medals*, p. 144.; Scandaluzzi, *Medal Ribbons of the World*, vol. 3: *India*.

the President's Fire Services Medal for Distinguished Service (1057).

The first award came on 15 August 1951, to Barrister-at-Law S. N. Reddy, M.A., Commissioner of Police, Hyderabad, Deccan (No. 35-Pres/51).

Outline

1055.100 medal.

1056 राष्ट्रपति का पुलिस पदक विशिष्ट सेवा के लिए / RASHTRAPATI KA POLICE PADAK VISHISHT SEVA KE LIYE / PRESIDENT'S POLICE MEDAL FOR DISTINGUISHED SERVICE[98]

Awarded to police personnel to recognize distinguished service.

Established: By No. 34-Pres./73 of 22 May 1973. This was modified by No. 42-Pres./75 and No. 43-Pres./75 of 19 May 1975, No. 64-Pres./79 of 4 December 1979, No. 42-Pres./82 of 24 September 1982, No. 19-Pres./84 of 13 February 1984, No. 77-Pres./87 of 4 November 1987, No. 81-Pres./88 of 29 July 1988, No. 99-Pres./90 of 17 December 1990, No. 131-Pres./94 of 8 July 1994, and No. 101-Pres./98 of 18 August 1998. Redesigned by No. 88-Pres./98 of 20 July 1998.

General Appearance: A 35 mm circular silver gilt medal.

Obverse: First variety: In the centre, the coat of arms of the President of India on a shield and the legend 'PRESIDENT'S POLICE MEDAL' above and 'INDIA' below. These two legends are separated by five-pointed stars. *Second variety:* A five-pointed star with the inscription 'राष्ट्रपति का पुलिस पदक —भारत' along the upper edge, and 'PRESIDENT'S POLICE MEDAL—INDIA' along the lower edge. Both inscriptions are separated by a small star at the 3 and 9 o'clock positions.

Reverse: First variety: The state emblem in the centre. The inscription 'FOR DISTINGUISHED SERVICE' appears below the emblem with a half wreath above. *Second variety:* Within a wreath, the state emblem with motto below, surrounded by the words 'विशिष्ट सेवा के लिए' and 'FOR DISTINGUISHED SERVICE' along the upper and lower edges, respectively.

Ribbon: 32 mm, half dark blue, half white.

Suspension: Both varieties are suspended by a non-swivelling straight-bar suspender.

Naming: Named on the edge in running script.

Miniature: Miniatures have been issued.

Background: A revision of the earlier President's Police and Fire Services Medal for Distinguished Service (1055). An annual maximum of seventy-five medals are awarded on Independence and Republic Days in recognition of a specially distinguished record in police service or in the central police or other security organization. All police personnel in the country with at least twenty-one years of service are eligible for this award.

The first award was to Shri Srinivasa Anandaram, Director, Anti-Corruption Bureau, Hyderabad, Andhra Pradesh, on 15 August 1975 (No. 94-Pres./75).

There have been two varieties of this medal awarded since

1056.100 President's Police Medal for Distinguished Service, first variety

1056.200 President's Police Medal for Distinguished Service, second variety

[98] Scandaluzzi, *Medal Ribbons of the World*, vol. 3: *India*.

the change in name. The first variety was simply an alteration in name and legends from the earlier police and fire services medal (1057). The second variety, consisting of a redesigned medal, was established in 1998.

Outline
1056.100 first variety (1973-98).
1056.200 second variety (1998-).

1057 राष्ट्रपति का अग्नि शमन सेवा पदक विशिष्ट सेवा के लिए / RASHTRAPATI KA AGNI SHAMAN SEVA PADAK VISHISHT SEVA KE LIYE/PRESIDENT'S FIRE SERVICES MEDAL FOR DISTINGUISHED SERVICE

Awarded to fire services personnel to recognize distinguished service.

Established: By by No. 40-Pres./75 and No. 41-Pres./75 of 19 May 1975. This was modified by No. 75-Pres./76 of 31 August 1976 to allow for posthumous awards. It was further modified by No. 103-Pres./84 of 26 September 1984 and No. 15-Pres./88 of 22 February 1988.

General Appearance: A 35 mm silver gilt medal.

Obverse: The state emblem and motto and the legend 'PRESIDENT'S FIRE SERVICE MEDAL' above and 'राष्ट्रपति का अग्नि शमन सेवा पदक' below.

Reverse: The Ashoka Chakra in the centre, with a half wreath above and the bilingual legend 'FOR DISTINGUISHED SERVICE विशिष्ट सेवा के लिए' below.

Ribbon: 32 mm, half brown, half yellow.

Suspension: Suspended by a non-swivelling straight-bar suspender.

Naming: Named on the edge.

Miniature: Miniatures have been issued.

Background: A successor to the earlier President's Police and Fire Services Medal for Distinguished Service (1055), the medal is awarded to recognize outstanding service by members of the fire services. Awards are limited to twenty-five per year. There is no monetary award for this medal. The medal may be awarded posthumously and bars may be awarded for additional distinguished service.

In 1975, the previous President's Police and Fire Services Medal for Distinguished Service (1055) was divided into separate police (1056) and fire service equivalents.

Outline
1057.100 medal.

1058 PRESIDENT'S CORRECTIONAL SERVICE MEDAL FOR DISTINGUISHED SERVICE

Awarded to personnel engaged in prison administration for distinguished service performed within India.

Established: By No. 62-Pres/1999 of 5 April 1999, with effect from 1 July 1999. The rules governing the award were notified by No. 63-Pres/1999 of 5 April 1999.

1057.100 President's Fire Services Medal for Distinguished Service

General Appearance: A 35 mm silver gilt circular medal.

Obverse: The gazette notification describes this medal as four elevated pairs of trapezium designs along the rim. In the centre of the middle circle, the state emblem and motto; and the Devanagari inscriptions 'PRESIDENT'S CORRECTIONAL SERVICE MEDAL FOR DISTINGUISHED SERVICE' and 'INDIA', separated by flowers on either side. This description is difficult to translate into a clear sense of this award, especially as it is not a medal we have seen.

Reverse: The notification describes four elevated pairs of trapezium designs along the rim and a circle with vertical lines inside surrounded by the inscription 'PRESIDENT'S CORRECTIONAL SERVICE MEDAL FOR DISTINGUISHED SERVICE' in English.

Ribbon: One and three-eighths inches wide, half green and half saffron, the two colours being separated by a 1/8 inch wide yellow vertical line. There is apparently no distinction in the ribbons of the medals for gallantry and distinguished service.

Suspension: Suspended by a non-swivelling straight-bar suspender.

Naming: The medal is named on the edge.

Miniature: Miniatures have not been issued.

Background: Awarded to members of the correctional services and state prison administrators for exhibiting conspicuous devotion to duty or for performing acts of exceptional skill within India. The rules governing the award qualify such acts as follows:

1. For a specially distinguished record in correctional service;
2. For success in organizing correctional service or maintaining the administration in special difficulties like mass admission of prisoners;
3. For outstanding ability in suppressing riots, preventing the escape of prisoners, rescuing officials, sportsmanship, public work and exemplary service marked by efficiency, devotion to duty, integrity, loyalty, high sense of discipline and spirit of self-sacrifice.

There is no provision for award of a bar to recognize subsequent awards of the medal. The medal may be awarded posthumously. Names of personnel awarded the medal are notified in the *Gazette of India* and the Ministry of Home Affairs maintains a register of such names. The medal carries no monetary allowance. A maximum of twenty-five awards of the President's Correctional Service Medal for Distinguished Service may be made in one year. The medal may be forfeited if the holder is held to be guilty of 'disloyalty, cowardice in action or such conduct as in the opinion of the President, brings the force into disrepute'. Awards are announced biannually on the occasions of the Republic Day (26 January) and Independence Day (15 August).

Outline

1058.100 medal.

1059 राष्ट्रपति का गृह रक्षा व नागरिक सुरक्षा पदक सराहनीय सेवा के लिए / RASHTRAPATI KA GRIH RAKSHA WA NAGARIK SURAKSHA PADAK SARAHANIYA SEVA KE LIYE / PRESIDENT'S HOME GUARDS AND CIVIL DEFENCE MEDAL FOR DISTINGUISHED SERVICE[99]

Awarded to recognize distinguished service by members of the home guards and civil defence.

Established: By No. 100-Pres./74 of 7 October 1974 with effect from 15 August 1974. The rules governing the award were published in No. 101-Pres./74 of 7 October 1974. These were modified by No. 75-Pres./76 of 31 August 1976 to allow for posthumous awards.

General Appearance: A circular 35 mm silver medal.

Obverse: The state emblem and motto in gilt and, below, the emblem of the Home Guards, surrounding it the legends 'राष्ट्रपति का गृह रक्षा व नागरिक सुरक्षा पदक' ('Rashtrapati ka Grih Raksha wa Nagarik Suraksha Padak' or 'President's Home Guards and Civil Defence Medal') and 'PRESIDENT'S HOME GUARDS AND CIVIL DEFENCE MEDAL'.

Reverse: The Ashoka Chakra in the centre, surrounded by the legend 'सराहनीय सेवा' ('Sarahaniya Seva' or 'Distinguished Service') and 'DISTINGUISHED SERVICE'.

Ribbon: 32 mm, black with an 8 mm white centre, these stripes are separated by thin 4 mm saffron-orange stripes. The same ribbon appears to be used both for gallantry and for distinguished service (cf. 1022).

Suspension: Suspended by a fixed non-swivelling straight bar suspender.

Naming: The medal is named on the rim.

Miniature: Miniatures have been issued.

Background: Awarded to those members of the home guards, civil defence, and mobile civil defence emergency forces who have exhibited conspicuous devotion to duty these awards are limited to twenty-five per year. There is no monetary allowance with this medal. Subsequent acts of similar service may be recognized by the addition of a bar to the medal ribbon. The bar is oblong with a laurel-leaf design and is engraved on the reverse with the recipient's details. When ribbon bars are worn alone, the receipt of a bar is indicated by the addition of a miniature silver gilt rosette to the ribbon. It is unclear whether posthumous awards are possible.

The first award of this medal was to Shri Krishan Kumar Malhotra, Director, National Defence College, Nagpur (No. 99-Pres./75 of 15 August 1975).

Outline

1059.100 medal.

1060 सराहनीय सेवा मैडल / SARAHANIYA SEVA MEDAL / MERITORIOUS SERVICE MEDAL[100]

Awarded to selected non-commissioned armed forces personnel for eighteen years (fifteen years from 1970) of distinguished service.

[99] *Encyclopedia of Soldiers with Highest Gallantry Awards*, pp. 31-32.

[100] *Encyclopedia of Soldiers with Highest Gallantry Awards*, pp. 69-70; *India's Highest Gallantry Awards*, pp. 79-80; Haynes, 'Medals and Decorations of the Republic of India', pp. 42-44; Das, *Traditions and Customs*, p. 280; Scandaluzzi, *Medal Ribbons of the World*, vol. 3: *India*.

1060.100 Meritorious Service Medal, with first ribbon

1060.200 Meritorious Service Medal

Established: By No. 19-Pres./57 of 26 February 1957 with effect from 25 March 1953. Amended by No. 55-Pres./69 of 18 September 1969 to revise the ribbon and by No. 48-Pres./70 of 17 September 1970 to reduce the qualifying period.

General Appearance: A circular 36 mm silver medal.

Obverse: The state emblem within an ornate rim.

Reverse: Within an ornate lotus wreath, the legend 'FOR / MERITORIOUS /—SERVICE— / सराहनीय / सेवा के लिये'.

Ribbon: First ribbon: 34 mm, medium brown grey with 1.5 mm white edge stripes and three 1.5 mm stripes, dark blue, red, and light blue (displaying the British precedence of services). *Second ribbon:* 34 mm, medium brown grey with 1.5 mm white edge stripes and three 1.5 mm stripes, red, dark blue, and light blue (the Indian service precedence). However, very often, the pre-1947 ribbon was used until today: 33 mm, claret, with 3 mm white edges and a 3 mm white centre stripe. This ribbon will presumably continue in use into the future.

Suspension: Suspended from an ornate swivelling scroll suspender.

Naming: The medal is named on the edge and naming has been seen in both Hindi and English.

Miniature: Miniatures are not authorized and have not been observed.

Background: The medal is awarded biannually (on 26 January and 15 August) to non-commissioned officers of the rank of dafadar/havildar, chief petty officer/petty officer, or warrant officer, flight sergeant/sergeant for eighteen years of distinguished service. In 1970, the requisite period of service was reduced to fifteen years. An annuity of Rs. 100 is paid to the recepients of this medal. The medal is currently issued at a rate of four medals for each eight hundred eligible personnel in the service concerned. Service that qualifies for this award duplicates the service that qualifies for the various post-1971 long service medals (1075, 1076, and 1077).

Outline

1060.100 first ribbon (1957-69).
1060.200 second ribbon (1969-   ).
1060.300 pre-1947 ribbon.

1061 दीर्घ सेवा और सदाचरण मैडल / DIRGH SEVA AUR SADACHARAN MEDAL / LONG SERVICE AND GOOD CONDUCT MEDAL[101]

Awarded to selected personnel in the armed forces for specified periods of service.

Established: By No. 20-Pres./57 of 26 February 1957 with effect from 25 March 1953. Amended by No. 49-Pres./70 of 17 September 1970 to reduce the qualifying period.

General Appearance: Circular 36 mm silver medal.

Obverse: The state emblem with motto below, enclosed within an ornate ring of lotus buds along the rim.

Reverse: Within an ornate lotus wreath, the circular legend

[101] *Encyclopedia of Soldiers with Highest Gallantry Awards,* pp. 71-72; *India's Highest Gallantry Awards,* pp. 81-2; Haynes, 'Medals and Decorations of the Republic of India', pp. 43-45; Das, *Traditions and Customs,* p. 280; Scandaluzzi, *Medal Ribbons of the World,* vol. 3: *India.*

'FOR LONG SERVICE AND GOOD CONDUCT' with a small five-pointed star at the bottom and, within this circular legend, the Hindi legend 'दीर्घ सेवा /– और –/ सदाचरण के /– लिये–' ('Dirgh seva / - aur - / sadacharan ke / - liye -').

Ribbon: 32 mm, brown with 2.5 mm white edge stripes and narrow (2 mm) edge stripes (reading inwards) of red, dark blue, and light blue. In practice, the pre-1947 ribbon of the Indian Long Service and Good Conduct Medal (32 mm, claret with 4 mm white edge stripes) continues to be worn unofficially as well.

Suspension: Suspended from an ornate swivelling scroll suspender.

Naming: The medal is named on the edge and naming has been seen in both Hindi and English.

Miniature: Miniatures have not been authorized and have not been observed.

Background: This medal is awarded to personnel below the rank of dafadar/havildar/petty officer/sergeant and to enrolled non-combatant personnel for distinguished service. When originally established in 1957, the requirements for the award were eighteen years in the army and air force and only fifteen years for the navy; in 1970, the requisite period of service was standardized across services at fifteen years. The award is currently granted with a one-time gratuity of Rs. 100, at the rate of four medals for each eight hundred men in service. These provisions have altered over time, and awards without gratuity were once possible. Service that qualifies for this award duplicates the service that qualifies for the various post-1971 long service medals (1073, 1074, and 1075).

Outline

1061.100 medal (1957-).
1061.200 pre-1947 ribbon.

1061.100 Long Service and Good Conduct Medal

1062 INDIAN POLICE MEDAL FOR MERITORIOUS SERVICE

Awarded to police personnel for meritorious service.

Established: By a Royal Warrant of 23 February 1932, revised in December 1944 to create separate classes of medals for gallantry and distinguished service. The extension of the award under the Dominion of India was authorized by a Royal Warrant of 1 May 1948, published in the *Gazette of India* under Private Secretary to the Governor-General's No. 15-H of 8 June 1948. The medal became obsolete in March 1951 when the Police Medal for Meritorious Service (1063) was created.

General Appearance: Circular 36 mm bronze medal.

Obverse: The crowned bust of King George VI, facing left and surrounded by the royal titles 'GEORGIVS VI D: G: BR: OMN: REX ET INDIAE IMP:'. These are, of course, the king's titles prior to the Indian Independence Act. While a strong case might have been made for a redesign of the medal to reflect the new constitutional status, there is no indication that this took place.

1062.100 Indian Police Medal for Meritorious Service

Reverse: Within a crowned wreath, the words 'INDIAN / POLICE' and on a ribbon tying the sides of the wreath 'FOR DISTINGUISHED CONDUCT' changed in 1944 to 'FOR MERITORIOUS SERVICE'.

Ribbon: 35 mm, dark blue, with 5 mm white edge stripes and a 13 mm claret central stripe. This is the same as for the post-1951 Police Medal for Meritorious Service (1063).

Suspension: A non-swivelling straight-bar suspender.

Naming: The medal is named on the edge.

Miniature: Miniatures have been issued.

Background: In the ambiguous constitutional circumstances of the Dominion period, this medal was continued from the time of British rule into the early years of Independence. This medal thus constituted an anachronistic continuation of royal authority into post-Independence India.

Outline

1062.100 medal.

1063.100 Police Medal for Meritorious Service, first variety

[102] *Encyclopedia of Soldiers with Highest Gallantry Awards*, p. 73; *India's Highest Gallantry Awards*, p. 83; Haynes, 'Medals and Decorations of the Republic of India', pp. 48-49; Dorling, *Ribbons & Medals*, pp. 144-45; Scandaluzzi, *Medal Ribbons of the World*, vol. 3: *India*.

1063 पुलिस पदक सराहनीय सेवा के लिये / POLICE PADAK SARAHANIYA SEVA KE LIYE / POLICE MEDAL FOR MERITORIOUS SERVICE[102]

Awarded to police personnel for meritorious service.

Established: By No. 3-Pres/51 and No. 4-Pres./51 of 1 March 1951. This was later modified by notifications No. 27-Pres./51 of 12 June 1951 (to amend the rules), No. 8-Pres,/53 of 17 February 1953 (corrigendum; to amend the rules), No. 11-Pres./56 of 8 March 1956 (to amend the rules), No. 65-Pres./62 of 10 October 1962 (to include members of the Central Intelligence Bureau among the eligible categories), No. 66-Pres./62 of 10 October 1962 (to amend the rules), No. 78-Pres./63 of 17 October 1963 (to include members of the Railway Protection Force among the eligible categories), No. 79-Pres./63 of 17 October 1963 (to amend the rules and increase the permissible limit of awards in one year to 200 [maximum 225]), No. 30-Pres./66 of 10 March 1966 (to amend the rules and increase the permissible limit of awards in one year to 275 [maximum 300]), No. 43-Pres./71 (to amend the eligible categories by replacing the added 'members of the Central Intelligence Bureau and Railway Protection Force' with 'Central Police/Security Organisations') and No. 44-Pres./71 (to amend the rules) of 5 August 1971, No. 42-Pres./75 of 19 May 1975 (to amend the statutes), No. 43-Pres./75 of 19 May 1975 (to amend the rules), No. 19-Pres./84 of 13 February 1984 (to limit the number of awards for meritorious service in a year to 500), No. 81-Pres./88 of 29 July 1988, and No. 99-Pres./90 of 17 December 1990 (to limit the number of awards for meritorious service to 740 per year). The medal was redesigned by No. 88-Pres./98 of 20 July 1998. The number of annual awards was further increased by No. 35-Pres./73 of 22 May 1973.

General Appearance: Circular 35 mm bronze medal.

Obverse: First variety: Shown 1063.100, the state emblem in the centre, with 'POLICE MEDAL' above and with the State motto 'सत्यमेव जयते' ('Satyameva Jayate' or 'Truth Alone Triumphs') below, separated by a small star. *Second variety:* Shown 1063.200, the state emblem and motto in the centre and the legend 'पुलिस मैडल' ('Police Medal') in Hindi above and 'POLICE MEDAL' below, separated by a small star.

Reverse: First variety: Shown 1063.100, two horizontal lines, above and below the legend 'Indian / Police' and, in the centre between the lines, 'For Meritorious Service'. The entire reverse is contained within a wreath. *Second variety:* In 1998, the reverse (shown 1063.200) was modified to include 'भारतीय पुलिस' ('Bharatiya Police' or 'Indian Police') above and 'INDIAN POLICE' below, both legends separated by two horizontal lines with 'सराहनीय सेवा के लिये' ('Sarahaniya Seva ke Liye' or 'For Meritorious Service') and 'FOR MERITORIOUS SERVICE'. The entire reverse is contained within a wreath.

Ribbon: 35 mm, dark blue, with 5 mm white edge stripes and a 13 mm claret central stripe.

Suspension: Both varieties are suspended by a non-swivelling straight-bar suspender.

Naming: The medals are named on the edge in engraved running script.

Miniature: Miniatures have been issued.

Background: A direct continuation of the pre-1947 Indian Police Medal for Meritorious Service (1062), this medal is awarded every year on the occasion of Independence Day and Republic Day to members of a recognized police force, the Central Intelligence Bureau, or an organized fire service (until a separate medal was created in 1975), who have performed services of conspicuous merit. All police personnel in the country with at least fifteen years of service are eligible for this award. The number of medals to be awarded in a year was fixed at 400 until 1973 when it was inflated to 740. In the *Gazette* these notifications run on for page after page. For ongoing meritorious service, a bar may be awarded. Although quite surprisingly, given the large number of awards, very few repeat awards (bars) have been noted. The bar is of bronze, of an oblong slip-on design, with the recipient's details engraved on the reverse. When ribbons are worn alone, the possession of a bar would be indicated by the addition of a miniature silver gilt rose (chakra?).

The first recipient was Officiating Deputy Inspector-General of Police Vaiyavur Rajagopala Rajaratnam, Madras (No. 36-Pres/51 of 15 August 1951).

This medal has been issued in two varieties, the first issued from 1951 to 1998, and a second variety from 1998 to the present. These are described in detail above.

Outline

1063.100 first variety with only English on the reverse (1951-98).

1063.200 second variety with both English and Hindi on the reverse (1998-).

1063.200 Police Medal for Meritorious Service, second variety

1064.100 Fire Services Medal for Meritorious Service

1064 अग्नि शमन सेवा पदक सराहनीय सेवा के लिए / AGNI SHAMAN SEVA PADAK SARAHANIYA SEVA KE LIYE / FIRE SERVICES MEDAL FOR MERITORIOUS SERVICE

Awarded to fire services personnel for meritorious service.

Established: Created by No. 40-Pres./75 and No. 41-Pres./75 of 19 May 1975. This was modified by No. 75-Pres./76 of 31 August 1976 to allow for posthumous awards. It was further modified by No. 15-Pres./88 of 22 February 1988.

General Appearance: Circular 35 mm bronze medal.

Obverse: The state emblem and motto with the legend 'FIRE SERVICE MEDAL'. above and 'अग्नि शमन सेवा पदक' below.

Reverse: A wreath bearing a horizontal oval tablet with the bilingual legend 'FOR MERITORIOUS SERVICE' 'सराहनीय सेवा के लिए'.

Ribbon: 32 mm, brick red (maroon) with 4 mm golden yellow edge stripes and three 3 mm black (notified as navy blue) stripes.

Suspension: By a non-swivelling straight-bar suspender.

Naming: The medals are named on the edge.

Miniature: Miniatures were not authorized and have not been observed.

Background: Awarded for meritorious service to members of the fire services. The awards are limited to one hundred awards per year, there is no monetary award for this medal. Bars may be awarded for subsequent services. These are oblong-shaped slip-on bars, made of bronze with the recipient's details engraved on the reverse. When ribbon bars are worn alone, a bar is indicated by the addition of a silver rosette.

The first award was to Shri Meppiladath Subrama Iyer Subramaniam, Divisional Fire Officer, Tamil Nadu Fire Service (No. 97-Pres./75 of 15 August 1975).

Outline

1064.100 medal.

1065 CORRECTIONAL SERVICE MEDAL FOR MERITORIOUS SERVICE

Awarded to correctional service personnel for acts of conspicuous merit performed within India.

Established: By No. 62-Pres/1999 of 5 April 1999, with effect from 1 July 1999. The rules governing the award were notified by No. 63-Pres/1999 of 5 April 1999.

General Appearance: A 35 mm diameter bronze medal.

Obverse: The *Gazette* notification describes the medal as having the state emblem in the centre, and the words 'CORRECTIONAL SERVICE MEDAL' in English and Hindi, joined by a wreath and surrounded by a six pointed-star, with the word 'BHARAT' at the bottom. As we have not seen this award, it is difficult to describe the design based only on the confused gazette notification.

Reverse: In the centre, a conch with the English inscription 'FOR MERITORIOUS CORRECTIONAL SERVICE' contained in the middle circle, surrounded by a six-pointed star.

Ribbon: 32 mm wide, green, with a 3 mm yellow stripe in the centre.

Suspension: Suspended by a non-swivelling straight-bar suspender.

Naming: The medal is named on the edge.

Miniature: Miniatures have not been issued.

Background: Awarded to members of recognized Correctional Services:

- For a specially distinguished record in correctional service;
- For success in organizing correctional service or maintaining the administration in special difficulties, such as mass admission of prisoners;
- For outstanding ability in putting down riots, preventing the escape of prisoners, rescuing officials, sportsmanship, public work, and exemplary service marked by efficiency, devotion to duty, integrity, loyalty, high sense of discipline, and spirit of self-sacrifice.

These, however, appear to be exactly the same qualifications that are applied for the award of the President's Correctional Service Medal for Distinguished Service (1058), so there is clearly a good deal of confusion and imprecision here.

Subsequent awards of the medal for meritorious service are recognized by the addition of a bar to the medal ribbon. When the ribbon is worn alone, award of the bar is indicated by a small silver lotus stitched to the ribbon. The statutes do no allow for posthumous awards. Names of personnel awarded the medal are notified in the *Gazette of India* and a register of such names is maintained by the Ministry of Home Affairs. Grant of the medal carries with it no monetary allowance. A maximum of seventy-five awards (excluding bars) of the Correctional Service Medal for Meritorious Service may be made in one year. The medal may be forfeited if the holder is held to be guilty of 'disloyalty, cowardice in action or such conduct as in the opinion of the president, brings the force into disrepute.' Awards are announced bi-annually on the occasions of the Republic Day (26 January) and Independence Day (15 August).

Outline

1065.100 medal.

1066 गृहरक्षा व नागरिक सुरक्षा पदक सराहनीय सेवा के लिए / GRIHRAKSHA WA NAGARIK SURAKSHA PADAK SARAHANIYA SEVA KE LIYE / HOME GUARDS AND CIVIL DEFENCE MEDAL FOR MERITORIOUS SERVICE[103]

Awarded to home guards and civil defence personnel for meritorious service.

Established: By No. 100-Pres./74 of 7 October 1974 with effect from 15 August 1974. The rules governing the award were published in No. 101-Pres./74 of 7 October 1974. These were

[103] *Encyclopedia of Soldiers with Highest Gallantry Awards,* p. 32.

1066.100 Home Guards and Civil Defence Medal for Meritorious Service

modified by No. 75-Pres./76 of 31 August 1976 to allow for posthumous awards.

General Appearance: A circular 35 mm bronze medal.

Obverse: The state emblem and motto, surrounding which are the legend 'गृहरक्षक व नागरिक सुरक्षा पदक' ('Grihrakshak wa Nagarik Suraksha Padak' or 'Home Guards and Civil Defence Medal') and 'HOME GUARDS AND CIVIL DEFENCE MEDAL'. (Note the difference in the Devanagari rendering of 'Grihraksha' between the medal and the gazette notification.)

Reverse: In the centre, the Home Guards emblem, surrounded by the legends 'सराहनीय सेवा' ('Sarahaniya Seva') and 'MERITORIOUS SERVICE'.

Ribbon: 32 mm, five stripes, three 8 mm white and two 4 mm black. Apparently the same ribbon is used for both gallantry and distinguished service.

Suspension: The medal is suspended from a non-swivelling straight-bar suspender.

Naming: The medal is named on the edge.

Miniature: Miniatures have presumably been issued.

Background: Awarded to members of the home guards, civil defence, and mobile civil emergency force for meritorious service. There is no monetary award for this medal. Subsequent acts of similar service may be recognized by the addition of a bar to the medal ribbon. When a bar has been awarded, it is indicated on ribbons when worn alone by the addition of a silver rosette. It is unclear whether posthumous awards are possible.

The first award was to Shri Vyankatesh Krishna Bhandarkar, Commandant, Home Guards, Maharashtra (No. 101-Pres./75 of 15 August 1975).

Outline

1066.100 medal.

1067 जीवन रक्षा पदक / JEEVAN RAKSHA PADAK / LIFESAVING MEDAL[104]

Awarded for acts of lifesaving.

Established: By No. 45-Pres./61 of 30 September 1961, as the 'Jeevan Raksha Padak, Class III.' The statutes were republished in No. 7-Pres./62 of 18 January 1962 and revised and the decoration renamed in No. 79-Pres./67 of 26 August 1967.

General Appearance: A 58 mm roughly circular bronze medal with a rectangular projection 22.5 × 12.5 mm at the top, and at the bottom, a 42.5 × 10 mm projection. This incredibly large award seems more appropriate for table-top display than for wearing, and it is believed that most recipients who wear the award actually wear the half-sized miniature, which would be almost the same size as a normal medal.

Obverse: In the centre, a hand in the *Abhai Mudra* and, above 'मा भैः' and below 'जीवन रक्षा' ('Jeevan Raksha'). The design is the same for both varieties.

Reverse: The state emblem with the motto in the lower projection.

[104] *Encyclopedia of Soldiers with Highest Gallantry Awards,* p. 74; *India's Highest Gallantry Awards,* p. 84; Das, *Traditions and Customs,* pp. 274-75.

Ribbon: 32 mm red with 4 mm light blue edge stripes and three 1 mm green centre stripes. These colours are said to symbolize fire (red), water (blue), and life (green).

Suspension: By a ring.

Naming: The medal is not named.

Miniature: Miniatures have been issued.

Background: Awarded to civilians to recognize acts of lifesaving, including cases of drowning, fire, or mine accidents 'for conspicuous courage under circumstances of very danger of grave bodily injury to the rescue'. The only cases in which members of the armed forces, police, or fire services can be awarded the medal is when such acts take place outside the course of their duty. The medal may be awarded posthumously and subsequent awards are recognized by the addition of a bar to the medal ribbon. When a bar has been awarded, this is indicated on the service ribbon by the addition of a silver miniature of the medal. Through 26 January 2004, one bar had been awarded (to Shri C.P. Meharwal, Rajasthan, on 31 March 1994); in that same period, the J.R.P. had been awarded 1,104 times.

Recipients of the award are granted a lump sum payment of Rs. 30,000.

The medal was originally established as a part of a three-class decoration, the Jeevan Raksha Padak in 1961. The third class of this award was renamed the Jeevan Raksha Padak, in 1967. This act, however, resulted in no alteration in the design of this class of the decoration and the precise award can only be determined from the records.

Representative Citation: To understand the award better, a sample recipient would be the 1974 award to Shri Nollu Poliah, Vishakhapatnam, Andhra Pradesh:

1067.200 Jeevan Raksha Padak

On the 29th October 1971, the Hopper Barge 'Kailas' was taken out to sea despite cyclonic weather for dumping the loaded material dredged from Barge Bert II of the Outer Harbour Project at Vishapatnam. While the dumping operation was going on, two Lascars, Sarvashri K. Ch. Appalanaidu and K. Thatarao met with an accident and fell overboard due to heavy swell and cyclonic weather conditions prevailing in the Bay. Shri Nollu Poliah who was in the barge, immediately jumped into the water and saved Shri K. Ch. Appalanaidu who was at the point of drowning. Shri K. Thatarao who did not sustain any injury swam ashore.

By his courageous act, Shri Nollu Poliah had not only saved the life of his colleague but also set an example of devotion to duty without caring for his own personal safety.

(No. 88-Pres./73 of 17 December 1973)

Outline

1067.100 Jeevan Raksha Padak, Class Three (1961-67)—This badge is the same as the one that follows and the precise award can only be determined from the records.

1067.200 Jeevan Raksha Padak (1967-)—This badge is the same as the preceding one and the precise award can only be determined from the records.

1068.100 Territorial Army Decoration

1068 TERRITORIAL ARMY DECORATION[105]

Awarded to officers of the Territorial Army for twenty years of service.

Established: By No. 19-Pres./52 of 31 January 1952 with effect from 15 August 1951. Amended in No. 10-Pres./53 of 27 March 1953 (to fix the order of precedence) and No. 73/Pres./63 of 24 September 1963. Generally revised by No. 84-Pres./64 of 4 December 1964 and further amended in No. 29-Pres./65 of 8 April 1965. Revised again by No. 53-Pres./74 of 10 April 1974. Further revised (the statutes being republished in their entirety) by No. 84-Pres./80 of 10 December 1980.

General Appearance: Oval silver medal, 42 × 33 mm.

Obverse: A five-pointed gilt star in the centre, surrounded by an oblong wreath and surmounted by the state emblem. The gilt is very thin and is frequenty absent.

Reverse: The legend 'अच्छी सेवा के लिये' ('Achhi seva ke liye' or 'For good service') with a lotus stalk below.

Ribbon: 32 mm, dark blue with a 10 mm central orange stripe; the blue stripes have 1 mm white stripes at the centre and between the blue and orange parts. To the ribbon is attached a rectangular bar 36 × 9 mm, with the legend 'TERRITORIAL'. The colours of the ribbon have an attributed significance; the orange denoting renunciation and sacrifice, the blue devotion, and the white purity.

Suspension: Suspended by a ring which is shielded by the state emblem in gilt.

Naming: Named on the edge.

Miniature: Miniatures have been issued.

Background: The medal is awarded to officers of the Territorial Army for twenty years of efficient service. Service is actually computed by a rather elaborate formula but in general, active service during wartime or any other emergency condition counts as double.

Outline

1068.100 medal.

1069 TERRITORIAL ARMY MEDAL[106]

Awarded to non-commissioned officers and enlisted personnel of the Territorial Army for twelve years of service.

Established: By No. 19-Pres./52 of 31 January 1952 with effect from 15 August 1951. Amended by No. 10-Pres./53 of 27 March 1953 (to fix the order of precedence) and by No. 73-Pres./63 of 24 September 1963. Generally revised by No. 84-Pres./64 of 4 December 1964 and further amended by No. 29-Pres./65 of 8 April 1965. Revised again by No. 53-Pres./74 of 10 April 1974. The statutes were republished in their entirety in No. 84-Pres./80 of 10 December 1980.

General Appearance: An oval 42 mm × 32 mm silver medal.

Obverse: The state emblem in the centre.

Reverse: Around the upper edge of the medal, the legend

[105] *Encyclopedia of Soldiers with Highest Gallantry Awards,* pp. 75-79; *India's Highest Gallantry Awards,* pp. 85-90; Haynes, 'Medals and Decorations of the Republic of India', pp. 45-46; Das, *Traditions and Customs,* p. 280.

[106] *Encyclopedia of Soldiers with Highest Gallantry Awards,* pp. 80-85; *India's Highest Gallantry Awards,* pp. 91-97; Haynes, 'Medals and Decorations of the Republic of India', pp. 45-46; Das, *Traditions and Customs,* p. 280.

'अच्छी सेवा के लिये' ('Achhi Seva ke liye' or 'For Good Service'). The lower portion of the reverse is blank.

Ribbon: 32 mm, dark blue, with a 1 mm orange central stripes and, on each side, two equally spaced 1 mm white stripes. Differing colour schemes have been described by some sources, with the dark blue varying towards black. Despite assertions to the contrary, these are merely manufacturing variations.

Suspension: Suspended from an ornate straight-bar suspender embellished with two leaves and bearing the legend 'TERRITORIAL'.

Naming: The medal is named on the edge.

Miniature: Miniatures have been produced.

Background: The medal is awarded to junior commissioned officers, non-commissioned officers, and enlisted personnel of the Territorial Army for twelve years of efficient service during which they have attended a minimum of twelve training sessions; recipients also must be specifically recommended for the award. A bar is awarded for eighteen years of service and a second bar may be awarded for twenty-four years of service. The bar is made of silver and bears the Ashoka Chakra in the centre. When service ribbons alone are worn, the bar is indicated by a silver rosette.

Service is actually computed by a rather elaborate formula, but in general, active service during wartime or any other emergency condition counts for double, but that service may not be counted toward any other long service award such as the Long Service and Good Conduct Medal (1061).

Outline

1069.100 medal.

1069.100 Territorial Army Medal

1070 INDIAN INDEPENDENCE MEDAL 1947[107]

Awarded to commemorate India's Independence on 15 August 1947.

Established: Created by King George VI in Private Secretary to the Governor-General No. 27-H of 18 September 1948 (*Gazette of India*, 18 September 1948, pp. 1148-9), it was modified by A.I. 13/49 of 1949; amended by A.I. 137/49 of 1949 and A.I. 350/49 of 1949. It was also published in British Army Council Instruction 337 of October 1949, as amended by British Army Council Instruction 767 of 1949.

General Appearance: Circular 36 mm cupro-nickel medal.

Obverse: Ashoka Chakra, crowned (for the last time) with the surrounding legend: 'GEORGIUS : VI D : G : BRITT : OMN : RED : FID : DEF' (apparently the first usage of the new royal titles, omitting any reference to Emperor of India). The original proposals used this as the reverse of the medal.

Reverse: The national emblem, without motto, and the legend 'INDIAN INDEPENDENCE / 15TH AUGUST 1947'. The original proposals used this as the obverse of the medal.

Ribbon: 30 mm, three equal saffron, white, green stripes, representing the Indian national flag. The overall impact of the ribbon is similar to that of the British King's South Africa

1070.100 Indian Independence Medal 1947

[107] *Encyclopedia of Soldiers with Highest Gallantry Awards*, p. 86; *India's Highest Gallantry Awards*, p. 98; Haynes, 'Medals and Decorations of the Republic of India', pp. 37, 42; Poulson, *Catalogue of Medals*, p. 112; Das, *Traditions and Customs*, p. 281; Dorling, *Ribbons & Medals*, no. 228, p. 143; Scandaluzzi, *Medal Ribbons of the World*, vol. 3: *India*.

Medal, but with the order of the colours reversed. The original proposals for the ribbon included a blue-embroidered chakra in the centre or, alternatively, a metal chakra device; these schemes were never adopted except in test productions. The metal chakras—which had been manufactured—were recycled as the first insignia for mentions in despatches (see 1084) and subsequently used to denote the award of a bar to Presidential decorations for gallantry/distinguished service.

Suspension: Suspended by a straight non-swivelling bar.

Naming: The medal is normally named on the edge, but was also issued unnamed.

Miniature: Miniatures have been issued. Most period miniatures were manufactured in silver with a ring suspension.

Background: The medal was awarded to all members of the Indian armed forces (including those of the rulers and state forces of the 'Princely' states that had acceded to India before 1 January 1948) who were serving on 15 August 1947. It was also awarded to British service personnel who remained in India after Independence to assist in the reformulation of the armed forces of India after Partition and who were still serving on 1 January 1948.

The conditions and details of award are somewhat complex and deserve citation in full here. The medal was awarded to:

a. All Indian nationals, male and female, on the strength of units/formations of the Indian Armed Forces on the 15th August, 1947 and the Ruling Princes and State Forces of States acceding to the Dominion of India by the 1st January, 1948.

b. British Officers, Ratings, Other ranks and Airmen, male and female:

    (1) Serving on the 1st January, 1948, with the Armed Forces of the Dominion of India;

    (2) Serving on the 1st January, 1948, on the Active List of a Government House or in the Central and Provincial Governments (in civil employment);

    (3) Who proceeded on leave before 1st January, 1948 pending retirement but had volunteered and were serving with the Indian Forces between 15th August, 1947 and the 1st January, 1948.

    (4) Officers and Other Ranks of the Transport Squadrons and Communication Flights of the Royal Air Force which had been lent to and were serving with the Dominion of India.[108]

Outline

1070.100 medal.

1071 INDEPENDENCE MEDAL 1950[109]

Awarded to police personnel to commemorate India's attainment of republic status on 26 January 1950. Although the medal has nothing to do with independence, this word and misattribution are part of the name.

[108] 'Regulations Relating to the Award of the Indian Independence Medal', No. 27-H of 18 September 1948, *Gazette of India*, 18 September 1948, p. 1149. The notification as published in the *London Gazette* made it clear that clause (a) also included Gorkhas.

[109] *Encyclopedia of Soldiers with Highest Gallantry Awards*, p. 87; *India's Highest Gallantry Awards*, p. 99; Dorling, *Ribbons & Medals*, no. 229, p. 144; Scandaluzzi, *Medal Ribbons of the World*, vol. 3: *India*.

Established: By No. 9-Pres./51 of 4 May 1951.

General Appearance: A circular 36 mm cupro-nickel medal.

Obverse: The state emblem and motto in the centre surrounded by the legend 'INDEPENDENCE MEDAL / 26th JANUARY 1950'.

Reverse: Within a lotus wreath, the chakra and, below, the legend 'POLICE'.

Ribbon: 32 mm, red with a 9 mm light saffron central stripe; a 2 mm dark blue stripe separates the red and saffron on each side. The overall impact of the ribbon is similar to that of the British Queen's South Africa Medal.

Suspension: Suspended by a non-swivelling straight-bar suspender.

Naming: The medal was issued unnamed, although some recipients subjected it to unofficial naming procedures.

Miniature: Although miniatures were not authorized in the establishing notification, they have been observed.

Background: Awarded to all members of the Indian police forces who were serving on 26 January 1950, the date of the proclamation of India's status as a Republic (and, in effect, of full Independence, as India had been a Dominion since 15 August 1947). The medal, unfortunately misnamed, was awarded as a token of recognition of the magnificent manner in which the police forces had borne unprecedented strain during the days of Partition and thereafter.

Outline

1071.100 medal.

1071.100 Independence Medal 1950

1072 पचीसवी स्वतंत्रता जयन्ती मैडल / PACHISVI SWATANTRATA JAYANTI MEDAL / 25TH INDEPENDENCE ANNIVERSARY MEDAL[110]

Awarded to commemorate the twenty-fifth anniversary of India's Independence on 15 August 1972.

Established: By No. 4-Pres./73 of 17 January 1973. Modified to extend eligibility to fire services, jail personnel, industrial security force, etc., by No. 110-Pres./75 of 10 November 1975 and further modified by No. 8-Pres./79 of 21 February 1979.

General Appearance: Circular 35 mm cupro-nickel medal.

Obverse: The state emblem with motto in the centre. Surrounded on either side along the rim by the legend '25th INDEPENDENCE ANNIVERSARY MEDAL / पचीसवी स्वतंत्रता जयन्ती मैडल'.

Reverse: The chakra with the dates '1947' above and '1972' below.

Ribbon: 32 mm, maroon with central stripes of saffron, white, and green (4 mm each).

Suspension: Suspended by a ring.

Naming: Issued both named and unnamed.

Miniature: Miniatures have been issued, though usually with a straight-bar suspender.

1072.100 25th Independence Anniversary Medal

[110] *Encyclopedia of Soldiers with Highest Gallantry Awards,* pp. 88-89; *India's Highest Gallantry Awards,* p. 100; Das, *Traditions and Customs,* p. 281; Scandaluzzi, *Medal Ribbons of the World,* vol. 3: *India.*

Background: Awarded to commemorate the twenty-fifth anniversary of Indian Independence in 1972. The medal was awarded to the following categories of personnel who were serving on 15 August 1972:

(i) all members of the armed forces, reserves, territorial army, J&K Militia;

(ii) all ranks of the railway protection force, police forces, home guards and civil defence and other specified organizations;

(iii) certain categories of national cadet corps officers;

(iv) uniformed personnel of the fire services, jails, central industrial security force, intelligence bureau (technical staff only), Calcutta special police force;

(v) directorate general, security—SSB, ARC/SFF;

(vi) civilians holding honourary military rank.

Along with the Sangram Medal it also was the first medal to be 'outsourced' for manufacture by the Mint.

Outline

1072.100 medal.

1073.100 50th Independence Anniversary Medal

1073 स्वतंत्रता की स्वर्ण जयन्ती पदक / SWATANTRATA KI SWARAN JAYANTI PADAK / 50TH ANNIVERSARY OF INDEPENDENCE MEDAL

Awarded to commemorate the fiftieth anniversary of India's Independence on 15 August 1997.

Established: By No. 87-Pres./98 of 24 June 1998.

General Appearance: Circular-35 mm cupro-nickel.

Obverse: The Lahori Gate of the Red Fort in Delhi with the legend above '50th INDEPENDENCE ANNIVERSARY' above and '1947-1997' below. The inscription differs from that specified in the statutes which reads '50th Anniversary of Independence 1947-1997'.

Reverse: A pebbled map of India with the legend '50वीं स्वतन्त्रता वर्षगांठ' ('50th Swatantrata Varshganth' or '50th Anniversary of Independence') above and '1947-1997' below. This differs from the statutes, which state that the inscription willl read स्वतंत्रता की स्वर्ण जयन्ती पदक ('Golden Jubilee of Independence Medal').

Ribbon: 32 mm, gold with central 3 mm stripes of saffron, white, and green, signifying the Indian tricolour.

Suspension: Suspended by a cast non-swivelling straight-bar suspender.

Naming: The medal was issued unnamed by the medal section, naming being left to regimental arrangements. It would appear that medals are named on the edge when awarded to officers, but generally unnamed for other ranks.

Miniature: Miniatures have been issued.

Background: Instituted to commemorate the fiftieth anniversary of India's Independence, 15 August 1997. This medal was not struck at the government mint, but was manufactured under contract by private firms. It was awarded to all military, paramilitary, police and fire service personnel, including Territorial Army and Home Guards and Civil Defence, who were borne on the effective strength on 15 August 1997.

Outline

1073.100 medal.

1074 तटरक्षक रजत जयन्ती पदक / TATRAKSHAK RAJAT JAYANTI PADAK / COAST GUARD SILVER JUBILEE MEDAL

Awarded to commemorate twenty-five years of the coast guard.
   Established: By 123-Pres./2002 of 10 June 2002.
   General Appearance: A circular 35 mm cupro-nickel medal.
   Obverse: The coast guard crest with 'COAST GUARD SILVER JUBILEE MEDAL' above, and below separated by stars, '1977-2002'.
   Reverse: The state emblem in the centre with the inscription 'तटरक्षक रजत जयन्ती पदक' above and '1977-2002' below.
   Ribbon:. 32 mm, two equal parts of silver white and navy blue.
   Suspension: Suspended by a non-swivelling straight bar suspender.
   Naming: The medal is named on the edge.
   Miniature: Miniatures have been issued.
   Background: Awarded to all coast guard personnel borne on the strength on 1 February 2002, the medal, instituted to recognize '25 years of dedicated service of the coast guard to the nation', represents a major departure from established norms whereby only national jubilees are commemorated by award of a medal. As of the time of writing, the armed forces have protested the institution of this medal as setting an unfortunate precedence which is likely to open the floodgates for similar awards by other organizations; it is therefore possible that this award may be withdrawn.

Outline

1074.100 medal.

1075 त्रिंशत् वर्ष दीर्घ सेवा मैडल / TRINSHAT VARSH DIRGH SEVA MEDAL / 30 YEARS LONG SERVICE MEDAL[111]

Awarded to all armed forces personnel (including territorial army) for thirty years of unblemished service.
   Established: By No. 38-Pres./80 of 8 May 1980. Qualifications revised by 88-Pres./86, dated 10 December 1986.
   General Appearance: Circular 35 mm cupro-nickel medal.
   Obverse: The state emblem in the centre with the motto beneath, surrounded by the legend 'दीर्घ सेवा / LONG SERVICE' above and, below, 'त्रिंशत् वर्ष / 30 YEARS'.
   Reverse: A depiction of the armed forces tri-service emblem of crossed swords, anchor, and eagle with a rising sun above.

1074.100 Coast Guard Silver Jubilee Medal

[111] Das, *Traditions and Customs*, pp. 281-82.

1075.100 30 Years Long Service Medal

Ribbon: 32 mm, orange, with central stripes of red, dark blue, light blue (each 2 mm).

Suspension: Suspended by a plain non-swivelling straight-bar suspender.

Naming: The medal is issued named on the edge.

Miniature: Miniatures have been issued.

Background: The medal is awarded to all personnel of the army, navy and air force on completion of thirty years of un-blemished service. The term 'unblemished service' is clarified as: 'service that counts for pension or gratuity; the period of blemished service, viz., imprisonment or conviction may be excluded for reckoning the prescribed length of service for the award of the medal; and there may be no more than eight red-ink entries in the service record, and no red-ink entry during the last one year preceding the award'.

In 1988 the ordinances relating to eligibility criteria of the thirty years long service medal were amended to include all Territorial Army personnel who had completed thirty years or more of unblemished service (both embodied and non-embodied) and who had attended thirty or more training camps (including forty-six days training in case of urban TA units) with effect from 20 November 1986, or thereafter.

Outline

1075.100 medal.

1076 विंश वर्ष दीर्घ सेवा मैडल / VINSH VARSH DIRGH SEVA MEDAL / 20 YEARS LONG SERVICE MEDAL[112]

Awarded to all armed forces personnel for twenty years of service.

Established: By No. 25-Pres./71 of 19 April 1971.

General Appearance: Circular 35 mm cupro-nickel medal.

Obverse: The state emblem in the centre with the motto beneath, surrounded by the legend 'दीर्घ सेवा / LONG SERVICE' above and, 'विंश वर्ष / 20 YEARS' below.

Reverse: A depiction of the armed forces tri-service emblem of crossed swords, anchor, and eagle with a rising sun above.

Ribbon: 32 mm, equal stripes of red, dark blue, light blue.

Suspension: Suspended by a non-swivelling straight-bar suspender.

Naming: Usually named on the edge.

Miniature: Miniatures have been issued.

Background: The medal is awarded to all personnel of the army, navy and air force on completion of twenty years of unblemished service. The term 'unblemished service' is defined as: 'service that counts for pension or gratuity; the period of blemished service, viz., imprisonment or conviction may be excluded for reckoning the prescribed length of service for the award of the medal; and there may be no more than eight red-ink entries in the service record, and no red-ink entry during the last one year preceding the award.'

1076.100 20 Years Long Service Medal

[112] *Encyclopedia of Soldiers with Highest Gallantry Awards*, pp. 90-91; *India's Highest Gallantry Awards*, p. 101; Das, *Traditions and Customs*, p. 282; Scandaluzzi, *Medal Ribbons of the World*, vol. 3: *India*.

Outline

1076.100 medal.

1077 नव वर्ष दीर्घ सेवा मैडल / NAV VARSH DIRGH SEVA MEDAL / 9 YEARS LONG SERVICE MEDAL[113]

Awarded to all armed forces personnel for nine years of service.

Established: By No. 24-Pres./71 of 19 April 1971.

General Appearance: Circular 35 mm cupro-nickel medal.

Obverse: The state emblem in the centre, with the national motto beneath, surrounded by the legend 'दीर्घ सेवा / LONG SERVICE' above and, 'नव वर्ष / 9 YEARS' below.

Reverse: A depiction of the armed forces tri-service emblem of crossed swords, anchor, and eagle with a rising sun above.

Ribbon: 32 mm, green with nine equally spaced 1 mm black stripes.

Suspension: Suspended by a non-swivelling straight-bar suspender.

Naming: Named on the edge.

Miniature: Miniatures have been issued.

Background: The medal is warded to all personnel of the army, navy and air force on completion of nine years of unblemished service. The term 'unblemished service' is defined as: 'service that counts for pension or gratuity; the period of blemished service, viz., imprisonment or conviction may be excluded for reckoning the prescribed length of service for the award of the medal; and there may be no more than eight red-ink entries in the service record, and no red-ink entry during the last one year preceding the award.'

Outline

1077.100 medal.

1077.100 9 Years Long Service Medal

1078 उन्नत रक्षा सुरक्षा कोर मैडल / UNNAT RAKSHA SURAKSHA CORPS MEDAL / HIGHER DEFENCE SECURITY CORPS MEDAL[114]

Awarded to members of the Defence Security Corps for long and distinguished service.

Established: By No. 54-Pres./64 of 10 July 1964 as the 'Defence Security Corps Medal, Class I,' renamed as the 'Unnat Raksha Suraksha Corps Medal' by No. 26-Pres./69 of 18 November 1968. Revised under No. 85-Pres./71 of 21 December 1971.

General Appearance: Circular 35 mm silver medal.

Obverse: The state emblem, with the national motto beneath. In the pre-1969 'Class I' version, the motto was omitted.

Reverse: Two crossed swords above a circular Indian shield with a five-pointed star above and the legend indicating the name of the medal (which was altered in 1968). See 1078.200. In the earlier 'Class I' version, the swords depicted were much thinner, and appeared below the shield. The inscription 'रक्षा सुरक्षा कोर मैडल' was only in Devanagari and placed around the lower edge from the 9 o'clock to the 3 o'clock position (1078.100).

Ribbon: 32 mm, light blue with two 1 mm yellow stripes, 2 mm apart, towards each edge.

First variety medal:
1078.100 Defence Security Corps Medal, Class I

[113] *Encyclopedia of Soldiers with Highest Gallantry Awards*, pp. 92-93; *India's Highest Gallantry Awards*, p. 102; Das, *Traditions and Customs*, p. 282; Scandaluzzi, *Medal Ribbons of the World*, vol. 3: *India*.

[114] *Encyclopedia of Soldiers with Highest Gallantry Awards*, pp. 94-5; *India's Highest Gallantry Awards*, p. 103-04; Das, *Traditions and Customs*, p. 282; Scandaluzzi, *Medal Ribbons of the World*, vol. 3: *India*.

Second variety medal:
1078.200 Unnat Raksha Suraksha Corps Medal

Suspension: Suspended from a swivelling ornate straight-bar suspender.

Naming: Named on the edge.

Miniature: Miniatures are not known to have been issued.

Background: The medal is awarded annually to enlisted personnel of the Defence Security Corps (DSC) who have served for a minimum of seven years in the corps and for a total of fifteen years combined armed forces service and corps service. The medal is awarded on a scale of two per thousand enlisted personnel in the Defence Security Corps. It carries with it a gratuity of Rs. 25 per year. Personnel who meet the qualifications but are not awarded this medal and are due to retire may be awarded the Raksha Suraksha Corps Medal (1079).

The DSC has a strength of around 31,000 personnel and provides security at Defence Ministry sites. Raised in 1947 as the Defence Department Constabulary, its task was to afford a higher degree of protection to certain armed forces installations in India. The armed constabulary was meant to protect defence installations against minor sabotage and pilfering. They could also be used as gate guards, searchers, or checkers and as mobile patrols by day or night. The new corps was intended to replace regular army, navy, and air force personnel employed until then in the protection of service installations. It was to subsequently absorb the Armed Forces Headquarters (India) Security Police, as well as the Royal Indian Navy Dockyard Police.[115]

Outline

1078.100 Defence Security Corps Medal, Class I (1964-69)—reverse legend 'रक्षा सुरक्षा कोर मैडल' ('Raksha Suraksha Corps Medal').

1078.200 Unnat Raksha Suraksha Corps Medal (1969-)—reverse Devanagari legend 'उन्नत रक्षा सुरक्षा कोर मैडल' on the left, and 'Unnat Raksha Suraksha Corps Medal' in English, on the right. Although the actual medal carries the bilingual legend, the instituting notification allows for only the Hindi inscription.

1078.201 There is a spelling error in the Hindi name of the medal on the reverse: 'कोर'(actually 'kear', a non-word which cannot easily be reproduced) rather than 'कोर'—so far, all specimens of this medal which have been encountered have this spelling error.

1079 रक्षा सुरक्षा कोर मैडल/ RAKSHA SURAKSHA CORPS MEDAL / DEFENCE SECURITY CORPS MEDAL[116]

Awarded to members of the Defence Security Corps for long and distinguished service.

Established: By No. 54-Pres./64 of 10 July 1964 as the 'Defence Security Corps Medal, Class II', renamed as the 'Raksha Suraksha Corps Medal' by No. 26-Pres./69 of 18 November 1968. Revised under No. 85-Pres./71 of 21 December 1971.

General Appearance: Circular 35 mm bronze medal.

Obverse: The state emblem, with the national motto beneath. In the earlier 'Class II' version, the motto was omitted.

[115] *Journal of the United Service Institution of India (JUSI)*, 78, p. 564.

[116] *Encyclopedia of Soldiers with Highest Gallantry Awards*, p. 96; *India's Highest Gallantry Awards*, p. 105; Das, *Traditions and Customs*, pp. 282-83; Scandaluzzi, *Medal Ribbons of the World*, vol. 3: *India*.

Reverse: Two crossed swords above a circular Indian shield with a five-pointed star above and the legend 'रक्षा सुरक्षा कोर मैडल' along the edge to the left, and 'Raksha Suraksha Corps Medal' to the right. In the earlier 'Class II' version, the swords depicted were much thinner, and placed below the shield. The inscription 'रक्षा सुरक्षा कोर मैडल' was only in Devanagari and placed around the lower edge from the 9 o'clock to the 3 o'clock position.

Ribbon: 32 mm, light blue with a 1 mm yellow stripe towards each edge.

Suspension: Suspended from a swivelling ornate straight-bar suspender.

Naming: Named on the edge.

Miniature: Miniatures are not believed to have been issued.

Background: The medal is awarded annually to enlisted personnel of the Defence Security Corps who have served for a minimum of seven years in the Defence Security Corps and for a total of fifteen years in combined armed forces service and corps service. This medal is awarded to those who have met the conditions of award for the Unnat Raksha Suraksha Corps Medal (1078) but have not received that medal (and its pension). The medal is awarded on a scale of two per thousand enlisted personnel in the Defence Security Corps.

It is possible to determine from the design of the medal whether it is the pre-1969 or post-1969 award. (See *Reverse* above.)

Outline

1079.100 Defence Security Corps Medal, Class II (1964-69).
1079.200 Raksha Suraksha Corps Medal (1969-).

1080 राष्ट्रीय केडट कोर द्वादश वर्ष दीर्घ सेवा मैडल / RASHTRIYA KADET CORPS DWADASH VARSH DIRGH SEVA MEDAL / NATIONAL CADET CORPS TWELVE YEARS LONG SERVICE MEDAL

Awarded for twelve years of service as a cadet instructor or NCC comissioned officer with the National Cadet Corps (NCC).

Established: By No. 32-Pres./79 of 19 July 1979.

General Appearance: A circular 35 mm cupro-nickel medal.

Obverse: The state emblem with, above 'NATIONAL CADET CORPS / राष्ट्रीय केडट कोर' and below 'द्वादश वर्ष दीर्घ सेवा मैडल / TWELVE YEARS LONG SERVICE MEDAL'

Reverse: In the centre, a small domed wreathed circle with 'NCC' and below 'एकता और अनुशासन' ('Ekta aur Anushasan' or 'Unity and Discipline').

Ribbon: 32 mm, light pink, with 3 mm stripes of red (left edge), dark blue (centre), and light blue (right edge).

Suspension: Suspended by a non-swivelling straight-bar suspender.

Naming: The medal is named on the edge.

Miniature: While provided for in the *Gazette* notification, no miniatures have been observed.

Background: This medal is awarded to cadet instructors and

1079.100 Defence Security Corps Medal, Class II

The second variety medal:
1079.200 Raksha Suraksha Corps Medal

1080.100 National Cadet Corps Twelve Years
Long Service Medal

lecturers of NCC companies and troops—known as Associated NCC Officers (ANO) (usually university professors)—who have been seconded to the National Cadet Corps, for twelve years of unblemished service, and who have attended no less than seven annual training camps and two refresher courses. The Indian Parliament passed the National Cadet Corps Act in 1948, thus creating the National Cadet Corps. The NCC has an army wing, an air wing, and a naval wing. A 'C' certificate enables direct entry into the corresponding military academy, with only the requirement for an interview. The National Cadet Corps can be considered as a successor of the University Officers Training Corps that was established by the British in 1942.

Outline

1080.100 medal.

1081.100 National Cadet Corps Seven Years
Long Service Medal

1081 राष्ट्रीय केडट कोर सप्त वर्ष दीर्घ सेवा मैडल / RASHTRIYA KADET KOR SAPT VARSH DIRGH SEVA MEDAL / NATIONAL CADET CORPS SEVEN YEARS LONG SERVICE MEDAL

Awarded for seven years of service as a cadet instructor or NCC comissioned officer with the National Cadet Corps.

Established: By No. 32-Pres./79 of 19 July 1979.

General Appearance: A circular 35 mm cupro-nickel medal.

Obverse: The state emblem with, above 'NATIONAL CADET CORPS / राष्ट्रीय केडट कोर' and below 'सप्त वर्ष दीर्घ सेवा मैडल / SEVEN YEARS LONG SERVICE MEDAL

Reverse: In the centre, a small domed wreathed circle with 'NCC' and below 'एकता और अनुशासन' ('Ekta aur Anushasan' or 'Unity and Discipline').

Ribbon: 32 mm, nine equal repeating stripes of red, dark blue, and light blue, the light blue being nearest the left shoulder.

Suspension: Suspended by a non-swivelling straight-bar suspender

Naming: The medal is named on the edge.

Miniature: While provided for the the gazette notification, no miniatures have been observed.

Background: The medal is awarded to lecturers of NCC companies and troops—known as Associated NCC Officers (ANO) (usually university professors)—who have been seconded to the National Cadet Corps for seven years of unblemished service, and having attended not less than four annual training camps and one refresher course. For background on the NCC, see the note with 1080, above.

Outline

1081.100 medal.

1082 20 YEARS COAST GUARD SERVICE MEDAL

Awarded for twenty years of service in the coast guard.

Established: By No. 132-Pres/2004 of 17 November 2004, with effect from the date of notification.

General Appearance: A circular 35 mm cupro-nickel medal.

Obverse: The state emblem and the inscriptions '20 Years TATRAKSHAK SEVA' in Hindi and English above and below it along the rim.

Reverse: The crest of the coast guard and its motto in the centre.

Ribbon: 32 mm wide, silk, navy blue with two horizontal silver-white waves (similar to a sine curve) of 2 mm width in the centre. This is one of the most amazing ribbons in use in India, requiring separate and careful treatment when worn on the ribbon bar and on the medal. This replicates the unfortunate problems of the proposed first ribbon of the Indian Independence Medal (1070).

Suspension: By a fixed non-swivelling straight bar.

Naming: It will be issued named.

Miniature: Miniatures have been authorized.

Background: The medal is awarded for twenty years of service in the coast guard. This is apparently the first paramilitary force to create its own long service awards. Given the plethora of such organizations, this is likely to set an unfortunate precedent for similar medals.

Outline

1082.100 medal.

1082.100 20 Years Coast Guard Service Medal

1083 09 YEARS COAST GUARD SERVICE MEDAL

Awarded for nine years of service in the coast guard.

Established: By No. 132-Pres/2004 of 17 November 2004, with effect from the date of notification.

General Appearance: A circular 35 mm cupro-nickel medal.

Obverse: The state emblem and the inscriptions '09 Years TATRAKSHAK SEVA' in Hindi and English above and below it along the rim.

Reverse: The crest of the coast guard and its motto in the centre.

Ribbon: 32 mm wide, silk, sky-blue background with one horizontal silver-white wave (similar to a sine curve) of 2 mm width in the centre. This ribbon shares the same problems as the twenty year medal.

Suspension: By a fixed non-swivelling straight-bar suspender.

Naming: It will be issued named.

Miniature: Miniatures have been authorized.

Background: The medal is awarded for nine years of service in the coast guard.

Outline

1083.100 medal.

1083.100 9 Years Coast Guard Service Medal

1084 MENTION IN DESPATCHES[117]

Awarded to recognize distinguished or meritorious service in operational areas which is not of sufficient magnitude to warrant the award of a decoration.

[117] *Encyclopedia of Soldiers with Highest Gallantry Awards*, pp. 97-98; *India's Highest Gallantry Awards*, pp. 106-07; Das, *Traditions and Customs*, p. 283.

1084.200 Mention in Despatches Emblem,
on illustrative ribbon

Established: It was originally proposed to use the chakras manufactured for use as ribbon devices on the Indian Independence Medal, 1947 (1070) for 'mention in despatches' emblems. While this seems to have been done, there also appears to have been no formal notification regarding this scheme. The final leaf design was instituted in No. 15-Pres./50 of 21 November 1950. The terms of award were modified by 61-Pres./64 of 1 August 1964 to reflect alterations in organizational terminology within the Indian armed forces.

Obverse: A very small dark bronze lotus leaf, 15 × 5 mm, worn on the medal ribbon or ribbon bar of the appropriate campaign medal.

Shown here illustratively on the ribbon for the Paschimi Star (1040).

Background: Initially proposed as a circular bronze chakra, this was never formally used or notified. The use of a horizontal bronze lotus leaf was established in 1950, to take effect from 15 August 1947. The leaf design is very small, almost undetectable when worn on a medal, and is worn at the uppermost edge of the appropriate medal ribbon or on the ribbon when ribbon bars are worn alone; the same leaf, in the same size, is employed for both purposes. The device may be added to the ribbons of:

- General Service Medal, 1947 (1035)
- Samanya Seva Medal 1965 (1036)
- Special Service Medal (1037)
- Samar Seva Star 1965 (1038)
- Poorvi Star (1039) or Paschimi Star (1040) for 1971
- Siachen Glacier Medal (1041)
- Op Vijay Star (1043)
- Op Parakram Medal (1047)
- Videsh Seva Medal (1052)

In exceptional cases, where the campaign star might not have been awarded, there exists the theoretical possibility that the device might be worn on the Raksha Medal (1044), Sangram Medal (1045), or Op Vijay Medal (1046); this would normally be a highly irregular practice.

A certificate in the following form is also issued to each recipient:

'Under the orders of the President of the Republic of India the mention of _____ 's name in a despatch by the Chief of the Army Staff/Chief of the Naval Staff/Chief of the Air Staff, was published in the *Gazette of India* on _____ .

By order,
Secretary to the Government of India
Ministry of Defence.'

Even though an individual may be mentioned in despatches more than once during a particular campaign, only one emblem is worn on the ribbon. A few provinces offer awards to recipients of the mention in despatches. These are detailed in Appendix 2.

Outline

1084.100 chakra insignia—possibly never issued.
1084.200 leaf insignia.

1085 COMMENDATION BADGES AND CARDS[118]

Awarded for individual acts of gallantry, distinguished service, or devotion to duty in operational or non-operational areas, which are not of sufficient magnitude to warrant the award of a decoration.

Established: These represent one of the few non-presidential awards discussed in this chapter. For the Army, the Chief of Staff's commendation badges were introduced in the 1980s, though the corresponding card predates the badges by a considerable time. The Vice Chief of Army Staff badges were instituted on 9 August 2002. For the Air Force, the Chief of Air Staff badges were instituted on 8 October 1982. The Vice Chief of Air Staff and Air Officer Commanding-in-Chief badges were introduced from 11 June 1997. It is not known when the Navy badges were instituted. In all cases, the issue of commendation cards predates the badges. Two commemoration cards are illustrated as examples at 004 and 005.

Obverse: A pin-back badge, worn on the pocket flap. As these badges vary considerably in design, they are described in detail under *Outline.*

Reverse: Pin backed.

Naming: The badges are unnamed and unnumbered.

Background: These badges are awarded to all military and civilian personnel working under the supervision, direction, and control of the respective service. Patterned on the line of the various army commanders' commendation cards, and later the King's Commendations for Brave Conduct awarded during WW II, these commendations are the easiest manner in which a commander can exercise his discretion to reward personnel serving under his command. The earliest known Chief's Commendations were issued by the IAF during the 1962 Sino-Indian conflict, although the practice may date back to the J&K operations of 1947-48. The date when commendations were formally institutionalized is not known.

In 1987, the COAS approved of 'Engineer-in-Chief's Commendation' to be awarded by the E-in-C to deserving civilian personnel of the MES. The award of the E-in-C's commendations was discontinued from 1 September 1991 following extension of the COAS Commendation for award to all deserving army personnel including civilians.

Commendations awarded by the chief of staff of a particular service are worn on the left pocket flap, while those awarded by commanders-in-chief of various commands are worn on the left flap (army and navy) and on the right flap (air force).

Awards are announced twice a year, once on 15 August (Independence Day) for the army and navy and 26 January (Republic Day) for the air force; and for a second time on Army Day (15 January) for the army, Navy Day (4 December) for the navy, and Air Force Day (8 October) for the air force. Commendations may not be awarded posthumously.

Within the armed forces, these badges have profilerated in the last decade. Moreover, in recent years, the award of these badges has been extended beyond the armed forces, and paramilitary forces have adopted similar awards. The Coast

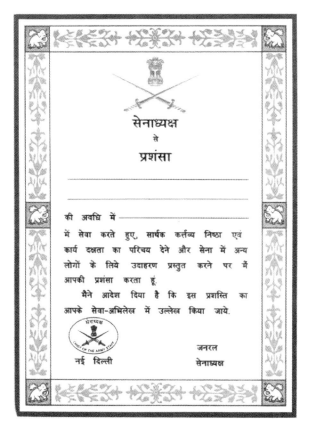

004. COAS Commendation Card

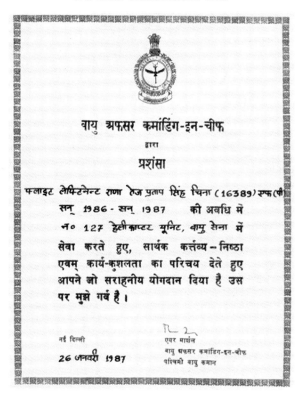

005. AOC-in-C Commendation Card

[118] *Encyclopedia of Soldiers with Highest Gallantry Awards,* p. 99; *India's Highest Gallantry Awards,* p. 108; Das, *Traditions and Customs,* p. 283.

1085.110 CIDS

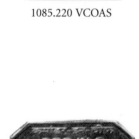

1085.210 COAS

1085.220 VCOAS

1085.231 GOC-in-C Northern Command

1085.232 GOC-in-C Eastern Command

Guard, Central Reserve Police, and Border Security Force badges are illustrated at 1085.500, 1085.600 and 1085.700 as examples.

Outline

1085.100 HQ Integrated Defence Staff Awards.

1085.110 Chief of Integrated Defence Staff Commendation Card and Badge. In the centre the tri-service emblem in gold against a maroon background. The English legend 'CHIEF OF INTEGRATED DEFENCE ST AFF' ab ove and b elow 'प्रशंसा/ COMMENDATION'.

1085.200 Army Awards.

1085.210 'थल सेना अध्यक्ष प्रशंसा'Thal Sena Adhyaksh Prashansa/ Chief of the Army Staff Commendation Card and Badge—A 36 × 25 mm oval bronze badge with the chief of staff's badge in the centre and, above 'थल सेना अध्यक्ष/ CHIEF OF THE ARMY STAFF' and below 'प्रशंसा / COMMENDATION'. The reverse has a horizontal pin.

1085.220 Vice Chief of the Army Staff Commendation Card and Badge—This badge was established on 11 June 1997.

1085.230 Ge neral Offic er C ommanding-in-C hief C ommendation C ard and B adges—These w ere estab lishe d o n 11 June 1997. Originally oval bronze, the badge is now a 34 × 21.5 mm sil vered sq uare w ith c lipped c orners. P resumably, this c hange was int roduced t o r emove the p revious v isual confusion between the regional commendation badges and the chief of staff's badge. In the centre there is a device representing the regional command; above, there is the le gend 'कमांडर-इन- चीफ / GOC-in-C' and below 'प्रशंसा / COMMENDATION'. The reverse has a horizontal pin.

1085.231 Northern Command—In the c entre an e mblem depicting geographic north.

1085.232 Eastern Command—In the centre is a rising sun.

1085.233 Southern Command—In the centre is the constellation of the Southern Cross.

1085.233 GOC-in-C Southern Command

1085.234 Western Command—In the centre is an emblem illustrative of the sun.

1085.234 GOC-in-C Western Command

1085.235 Central Command—In the centre is a chakra.

1085.235 GOC-in-C Central Command

1085.300 Navy Awards.

1085.310 नौ सेना अध्यक्ष प्रशंसा/Nao Sena Adhyaksh Prashansa/Chief of the Naval Staff Commendation Card and Badge—A 36 × 25 mm bronze badge with the naval badge in the centre and, above 'नौ सेना अध्यक्ष / CHIEF OF THE NAVAL STAFF' and below 'प्रशंसा / COMMENDATION'. The reverse has a horizontal pin.

1085.310 CNS

1085.320 Vice Chief of the Naval Staff Commendation Card and Badge

1085.320 VCNS

1085.330 Flag Officer Commanding-in-Chief Commendation Card and Badge

1085.400 Air Force Awards.

1085.410 वायु सेना अध्यक्ष प्रशंसा/Vayu Sena Adhyaksh Prashansa/Chief of the Air Staff Commendation Card and Badge—

1085.330 FOC-in-C

1085.411 CAS Bronze

1085.412 CAS Silver

1085.414 CAS Silver with two stars

1085.420 VCAS

1085.430 AOC-in-C

1085.510 DG Coast Guard

1085.520 Coast Guard Regional Commander

A 36 × 25 mm badge with the air force badge in the centre and, above 'वायु सेना अध्यक्ष / CHIEF OF THE AIR STAFF' and below 'प्रशंसा / COMMENDATION'. The reverse has a horizontal pin.

1085.411 First award—Until 1999, the badge was in bronze.

1085.412 Second (and subsequent) award—Until 1999, the badge was silvered.

1085.413 Since 1999, when the air force changed its badges from brass to white metal, the badge for the first award has been in silver; this is the same badge as 1085.412, above.

1085.414 Since 1999, the second and subsequent awards are denoted by a similar silver badge with the addition of two stars upon it.

1085.420 Vice Chief of the Air Staff Commendation Card and Badge.

1085.430 Air Officer Commanding-in-Chief Commendation Card and Badge—A 34 × 21 mm silvered square, slightly domed blue enamel, with clipped corners. In the centre, is the air force crest; above, there is the legend 'वायु आफिसर कमांडिंग-इन-चीफ / AOC-in-C' and below 'प्रशंसा / + COMMENDATION +'. The reverse has a horizontal pin. The same badge is awarded for all air force regional commands. A similar badge is awarded to personnel posted at Air HQ in Delhi, who have been commended by the Vice Chief of the Air Staff, except that the letters 'AOC-in-C' are replaced by 'VCAS'.

1085.500 Coast Guard Awards.

1085.510 Director General Coast Guard Commendation Card and Badge.

1085.520 Coast Guard Regional Commander Commendation Card and Badge.

1085.600 Central Reserve Police Awards.

1085.610 महानिदेशक प्रशंसा / Director General Commendation Card and Badge—A 36 × 25 mm oval bronze badge (though they are alos seen in silver) with the CRP emblem in the centre and, above 'महानिदेशक' and 'DIRECTOR GENERAL'; below 'प्रशंसा' and 'COMMENDATION'. The reverse has a horizontal pin.

1085.610 DG CRPF

1085.700 Border Security Force Awards.

1085.710 Border Security Force Director General's Commendation Card and Badge.

1085.710 DG BSF

1086 PRIME MINISTER'S LIFE SAVING MEDAL[119]

Awarded to police personnel for saving life.

Established: In 1958, not established by normal presidential authority, but by the prime minister himself. The constitutional position of this award is, therefore, vague.

General Appearance: Circular bronze medal, 35 mm (1-3/8 inches). While all specimens observed match this description, there is some indication that a gilt variety of the medal may also exist.

Obverse: The state emblem with a raised border with the legend 'PRIME MINISTER'S POLICE MEDAL' with a lotus flower and buds below.

Reverse: A traditional Indian shield, surrounded by a raised border with the legend 'FOR SAVING LIFE' above, and 'जीवन रक्षणार्थ' ('Jivan Rakshanarth' or 'Life Saving' in very Sankritized Hindi) below. The two legends are separated by lotus bud designs.

Ribbon: The ribbon is 35 mm, half red, half green, with 5 mm central stripes of blue (left) and yellow-saffron (right). A second reported unofficial ribbon variation is 32 mm, yellow, with 5 mm central stripes (reading left to right) of black and white; while we have illustrated this variant, we can find no authority for its usage.

Suspension: Suspended by a straight non-swivelling bar.

Naming: The medal is named on the rim.

Miniature: No evidence of a miniature has been traced.

Background: This medal was instituted in 1958 to encourage policemen of all ranks to bring help and aid to the afflicted and is awarded to police personnel within the territory of India who have done outstanding work in saving life. The recipients are presented medals with their medals by the prime minister in the All-India Police Duty Meet. From 1 November 2002, an allowance of Rs. 200 per month has been extended to recipients

1086.100 Prime Minister's Life Saving Medal

[119] Scandaluzzi, *Medal Ribbons of the World*, vol. 3: *India*.

of this award. There seems to be no provision for the award of bars to this medal or for posthumous awards. The constitutional basis of this medal seems to be somewhat suspect, as most hounors would normally come forward under at least nominal presidential authority.

At the time this medal was instituted, the Jeevan Raksha Padak series of medals had not yet come into existence and the police forces had been excluded from elegibility for the awards of the Ashoka Chakra Medal series (though this limitation has since been ignored). Within this context, the institution of this medal can be better understood. With the instiution of the Jeevan Raksha Padak, there would appear to have been a strong case for ending this award, but that was not to be.

Outline

1086.100 medal.

1087 एशियाड विशिष्ट ज्योति /ASIAD VISHISHT JYOTI / SPECIAL ASIAD FLAME

Awarded for distinguished service to the IX Asian Games, held in New Delhi, 20 November-3 December 1982.

Established: By No. 11-Pres./84 of 28 January 1984.

General Appearance: A 35 mm circular gold medal.

Obverse: In the centre, the IX Asiad symbol, with 'नवम एशियाड खेल 1982' above and 'IX Asian Games 1982' below.

Reverse: The Asiad torch with 'एशियाड विशिष्ट ज्योति' above and 'Asiad Vishisht Jyoti' below.

Ribbon: Initially notified as having a 32 mm green silk ribbon (the colour of the IX Asiad Games) the ribbon was subsequently changed to blue and green by No. 16-Pres./85 of 18 February 1985.

Suspension: Suspended by a ring.

Naming: Unknown.

Miniature: None reported.

Background: Twenty-two medals were awarded to officials for distinguished and meritorious services in connection with the successful organization and conduct of the Games (Notification No. 60-Pres./84 of 28 January 1984). The award is an oddity; there were no such awards given for the first Asian Games held in Delhi in 1951.

Outline

1087.100 first ribbon, solid green.
1087.200 second ribbon, half blue, half green.

1088 एशियाड ज्योति / ASIAD JYOTI / ASIAD FLAME

Awarded for meritorious service to the IX Asian Games, held in New Delhi, 20 November-3 December 1982.

Established: By No. 11-Pres./84 of 28 January 1984. The ribbon was redesigned by No. 16-Pres./85 of 18 February 1985.

General Appearance: A 35 mm circular silver medal.

Obverse: In the centre, the IX Asiad symbol, with 'नवम एशियाड

खेल 1982' above and 'IX Asian Games 1982' below.

Reverse: The Asiad torch with 'एशियाड ज्योति' above and 'Asiad Jyoti' below.

Ribbon: Initially notified as a 32 mm green silk ribbon (the colour of the IX Asiad Games) the ribbon was subsequently changed to blue and green by No 16-Pres./85 of 18 February 1985.

Suspension: Suspended by a ring.

Naming: Unknown.

Miniature: Not reported.

Background: Thirty-two medals were awarded to officials for meritorious services in connection with the successful organization and conduct of the Games. (Notification No. 61-Pres./84 of 28 January 1984.) The award is an oddity; as no such awards were given for the first Asian Games, held in Delhi in 1951.

Outline

1088.100 first ribbon, solid green.

1088.200 second ribbon, half blue, half green.

1089 MACGREGOR MEMORIAL MEDAL[120]

Awarded by the United Service Institution of India (USI) for outstanding deeds of military reconnaissance which have produced information of value for the defence of India.

Established: By the United Service Institution of India in 1888 as a memorial to the late Major-General Sir Charles Metcalfe MacGregor, KCB, CSI, CIE, founder of the USI in 1870. The medal has been continued in India since Independence and enjoys official sanction.

General Appearance: There are three types of the medal: (a) The standard size large circular silver medal, 70 mm in diameter awarded to officers, including JCOs; (b) a reduced-size silver medal awarded to an NCO or soldier, and (c) a reduced size gold medal which might be awarded to an officer for especially valuable work.

Obverse: MacGregor's profile facing left, surrounded by the inscription 'Major General Sir Charles Metcalfe MacGregor, KCB, CSI, CIE. In Memoriam 1887'

Reverse: The striking reverse depicts figures of army personnel belonging to various communitiues.

Ribbon: The complex 40 mm wide ribbon is made up of the colours of the MacGregor tartan-red, green, black, and white.

Suspension: Suspended in post-1947 awards by a ring from a ribbon and worn around the neck.

Naming: The medals are named on the edge followed by 'for valuable reconnaissance' or 'for valuable work', along with the year of the award. The word 'especially' is added for gold medals.

Miniature: Miniatures have not been issued.

Background: The MacGregor Memorial Medal was instituted by the United Service Institution of India in 1888 as a memorial to the late Major-General Sir Charles Metcalfe MacGregor, KCB,

1089.100 MacGregor Memorial Medal, gold

1089.300 MacGregor Memorial Medal, silver

[120] Hamond, *MacGregor Memorial Medals.*

CSI, CIE who had founded the Institution in 1870. It is the only medal instituted before Independence that is still awarded to the armed forces of independent India.

It was intended that the medal should be awarded annually for the best military reconnaissance, journey of exploration, or survey in remote areas of India, or in countries bordering or under the jurisdiction of India, which produced new information of value for the defence of India. In some areas it was in fact the characteristic medal of 'The Great Game'.

Personnel of the Indian armed forces, Territorial Army, reserve force, Assam Rifles, and militias are eligible for the awards. Recommendations are received by the USI through the Joint Planning Committee. However, recommendations for awards that do not fall into the category of military reconnaissance can also be sent directly to the USI.

Personal risk to life during these journeys was not a necessary qualification for the award but, in the event of two journeys being of equal value, the man who incurred the greater risk would be considered to have the greater claim to the award. Most journeys, especially in the remote areas of the Himalayas and Tibet, in the deserts of Persia and Afghanistan, and in the jungle regions of Burma, Assam, and Tibet/China/Thailand borders, carried an in-built physical risk. Some areas had additional hazards in the form of hostile inhabitants, brigands, and dacoits, as well as dangers from wild animals and lethal diseases. A few medals were awarded in times of war for reconnaissance in, or escapes from, enemy-occupied territory and for these medallists there were additional dangers.

In some years no medal was awarded; in others more than one were given. A medal would sometimes be awarded several years after the journey had been made. Historically, a medal would have been available for award each year for (a) a standard-sized silver medal to an officer, British or Indian (including VCOs/JCOs), and (b) a reduced size silver medal to an NCO or soldier, British or Indian, plus a gratuity, usually of Rs 100. For especially valuable work a gold medal might be awarded, either in place of one of the above silver medals or in addition to the two silver medals awarded for that year. Similarly, if an additional NCO or soldier was also considered to have done valuable work, the Council might make a special award of an extra reduced size silver medal for that year but this special award did not carry a gratuity.

While initially the award was to be given only for significant military reconnaissance or journey of exploration, subsequently, on 22 October 1986, the USI Council expanded the scope to include mountain/desert expeditions, river rafting, world cruises, polar expeditions, running/trekking across the Himalayas, and adventure flights. First priority, however, was to be given to military reconnaissance. This decision regarding the expanded scope was again confirmed by the Council in its meeting held on 22/23 December 1994. No awards in this category have yet been made.

In the past 114 years, from 1889-2003, the following awards have been made: seven gold medals, all awarded to officers, five were in place of the standard size silver medals awarded in those years; in the same period sixty-two standard size silver medals were awarded to sixty-one officers (one officer gaining two awards in 1938 and 1946, and including four VCOs and one JCO). From 1889-1944 forty-eight reduced size silver medals, with ribbon, were awarded to NCOs and soldiers. Eleven of these were 'special awards' which did not carry a gratuity. No awards of the small size silver medal have been made since 1944. Among the well-known pre-Independence British recipients have been Captain F. E. Younghusband (1890) and Major-General O.C. Wingate (1943).

The medal may be worn around the neck in uniform on ceremonial occasions prescribed by the respective services. It is the only medal not instituted by the President of India to be accorded this privilege.

Awards: Since Independence, there have been fourteen awards of the medal, including one gold medal:

Major Z.C. Bakshi, Vr.C., 2/5th Gorkha Rifles (F.F.)—1949
Colonel I.C. Katoch, M.B.E., 6/5th Gorkha Rifles (F.F.)—1951
Captain M.S. Jarg, 3rd Bn, Jat Regiment—1956
2/Lieutenant I.B. Goel, Bengal Engineers Group—1956
Captain V. Badhawar, 5/5th Gorkha Rifles (F.F.)—1957
Captain S.L. Tugnait, Air OP Squadron, Regiment of Artillery—1958
Brigadier M.L. Whig, M.V.C., 2/5th Gorkha Rifles (F.F.)—1969
Major Prem Chand, V.S.M., 13th Bn, Dogra Regiment—1970
Colonel C.S. Nugyal, 6th Bn, Sikh Regiment—1971 (gold medal)
Captain Ravindra Misra, 4/3rd Gorkha Rifles—1972
Subadar Bel Bahadur Pun, 4/3rd Gorkha Rifles—1972
Squadron Leader R.K. Makar, IAF—1986
Flight Lieutenant R.T.S. Chhina, IAF—1986
Lieutenant Colonel N.J. Korgaokar, S.M., Garhwal Rifles—1997

While the small silver medal has not been awarded since 1944, it is still available for award.

Outline

1089.100 small gold medal
1089.200 large silver medal
1089.300 small silver medal

1090 MOUNT EVEREST EXPEDITION MEDAL, 1953[121]

Awarded to the expedition leader and to the two successful expedition members for the first conquest of Mt. Everest, 23 May 1953.

Established: Apparently established in May 1953, though there seem to have been no formal orders involved. The President of India presented the medals.

General Appearance: A large circular gold medal, approximately 70 mm in diameter.

[121] 'Gold Medals for Everest Heroes', *Fauji Akhbar*, 19 July 1953.

1090.100 Mount Everest Expedition Medal 1953

Obverse: The state emblem with the name of the recipient in capital letters above and the Sanskrit legend 'साहसे श्री प्रतिवासाथी' ('Sahase Shri Prativasathi', or 'Courage is the Abode of Glory') below.

Reverse: A high-relief depiction of Mt. Everest.

Ribbon: Plain white moiré neck ribbon (most likely very similar if not identical to the Bharat Ratna ribbon [1001]).

Suspension: Swivelling ring suspension. The medal was worn around the neck.

Naming: The medal is named, as described above, as a part of the obverse design.

Miniature: There was almost surely no miniature involved.

Background: Awarded by the Republic of India to Sir Edmund Hillary and Tenzing Norkay (as his name is spelled on the medal), the first conquerors of Mt. Everest, and to the expedition leader, Sir John Hunt. The medals were presented in New Delhi on 29 June 1953.

Awards: As discussed above, the special medal was awarded only three times.

Outline

1090.100 medal.

OTHER NATIONAL AWARDS

As it has been our intention here to focus on official, traditional, wearable awards created and bestowed in an official or semi-official fashion by the Republic of India, and especially those awards instituted under formal presidential authority, we have somewhat arbitrarily excluded a range of other awards, some of them wearable and some quite nicely produced. A few words on some of these would be in order.

Badge of Sacrifice and Certificate of Honour

A Badge of Sacrifice and a Certificate of Honour was instituted by the army in 1999 for presentation to war widows/next of kin of all soldiers who have laid down their lives during various military operations since 15 August 1947. The badge is a 52 × 36 mm bright bronze badge with a torch in the centre with 'INDIAN ARMY' above and 'BADGE OF SACRIFICE' below, and 'FOR YOUR TOMORROW HE GAVE HIS TODAY' behind the torch. (A new design is, apparently, under consideration.) The Area HQs/Sub Area HQs and respective Regimental Centres have been asked to organize central functions for presentations to the widows. The state governments have been approached to recognize the Badges and Certificates and accord a special priority to the holders when they interact with various government agencies for their essential requirements like allotment of land, educational and medical facilities, etc. Some of the state governments have already issued instructions to all their concerned departments to honour the holders of the Badges of Sacrifice and Certificates of Honour and provide necessary assistance on priority.[122] It is not known if these awards have been notified or not, though we suspect this has not been the case.

006. Badge of Sacrifice

[122] Law Relating to Disability Benefits in the Armed Force, p. 274. In many ways, these awards recall the plaques issued to next-of-kin of deceased soldiers in WW I.

Presidential Medals

Following on the old personal medals awarded by the Viceroys to their staff and bodyguard, similar wearable medals have continued to be awarded by the Governors-General and Presidents since Independence. These differ immensely and interestingly from President to President. We have only illustrated a single representative specimen, that awarded by President Rajendra Prasad (1950-62).

Academic Awards

Before 1947, titles (Mahamahopadhyaya and Shans-ul-Ulema) were awarded by the government for achievement in 'traditional' fields of learning. While titles are no longer permitted under the new constitution, annual awards have continued to be presented by the President for special achievement in Sanskrit, Arabic, and Persian scholarship. These awards were begun from 1958. These occasional awards comprise certificates and monetary awards.

Krishi Pandit

Created in 1949, this title has been awarded by the Indian Council of Agricultural Research for outstanding contributions to Indian agriculture. As this is a title, its status under the constitutional ban on titles seems somewhat suspect.

Bharat Samman Award (Pravasi Bharatiya Samman)

Instituted by the President in 1998 and awarded for special achievement by the Indian diaspora, by Non-Resident Indians (NRIs), and Persons of Indian Origin (PIOs). (See MHA notification no.1/7/98-Public.) While originally proposed in three classes (Bharat Vishisht Samman, Bharat Priya Samman, and Bharat Samman), these were later collapsed into a single award. The award, which is in the form of a citation (*sanad*) is given annually to foreign nationals including NRIs and PIOs who have contributed towards fostering a better understanding of India abroad and for their support to the cause of India and for promotion of India's interests internationally. It appears this was created, in part, to remove pressure on the 'Padma awards' with regard to recognizing achievements by NRIs and PIOs. There is no accompanying medal.

Sports Awards

The Arjuna Award has been awarded to outstanding sports-persons of the year since 1961. The Dronacharya Award is similarly awarded for excellence in athletic coaching. These are large trophies rather than wearable awards.

Census Medals

Commencing at least from the first census of independent India in 1951, wearable medals have been awarded for meritorious service with each decennial Indian census. The sample medal illustrated is from the 1961 census.

007. Presidential Medal (Dr Rajendra Prasad)

008. Census Medal

2

Provincial Medals

As we have conducted the research for this book, we have encountered a range of provincial and other quasi-official medals. Setting aside the major constitutional issues that such non-presidential awards pose—they are precisely the sort of awards the bestowal of which would have been promptly terminated in the years before 1947—we have also been frusrtrated by the almost universal absence of any reliable information on these awards. Our efforts to prepare any comprehensive list—much less a catalogue—of these local decorations have proved impossible. Perhaps at a future stage in our ongoing researches we may be able to discuss these provincial awards with some assertion of comprehensive treatment, but that day is now some distance away. We have decided, therefore, simply to cite a few examples of these awards to indicate the *sorts* or provincial and other local awards that exist.

We have not attempted to illustrate these awards but some of their ribbons are shown in the ribbon chart, as referenced below.

'PRINCELY' STATE AWARDS

The first category of non-central awards to develop historically represent a logical continuation from the pre-Independence awards granted by India's 'princes' to their own subjects. Until their legal status was modified by Prime Minister Indira Gandhi, these monarchs had asserted their right to issue such medals. While the British opposed this practice before 1947 and—one presumes—the Dominion and the Republic did so as well after this date, such awards existed—and flourished—nevertheless.[1]

As they are relevant to this present work, these post-1947 medals exist in two general categories: (1) awards commemorating India's Independence and the integration of the states into the union, and (2) a range of dynastic events, mostly the coronation of new rulers, which took place in the years immediately following the integration of the states. In the former category, there are the Accession to India Medal of Dhrangadhra State (2001),[2] the Integration Medal of Jind State (2002),[3] and the King's Medal of Jawahar State.[4] In the latter category we should make note of the 1948 Coronation Medal of Jind State (2003)[5] and the 1948 Coronation Medal of Tonk State (2004).[6] Some evidence exists that some states continued

[1] A masterful treatment of the full scope of these fascinating awards is provided in Tony McClenaghan's *Indian Princely Medals.*

[2] McClenaghan, *Princely Medals*, no. 114, pp. 127-28.

[3] Ibid., no. 176, p. 178.

[4] Ibid., no. 171, pp. 174-75.

[5] Ibid., no. 175, p. 178.

[6] Ibid., no. 243, p. 251.

to award their orders, either in the Dominion period or later, for example, Jaipur State's Most Eminent Order of the Star of Dundhar, or Dhrangadhra's Shaktimat Order of Jhalavada.

While these awards were, as has been discussed in the previous chapter, allowed to be worn (as expressed in Independent India's first, though unpublished, order of wearing directives), they are rarely encountered and represent, in their own way, another form of survival of a decentralized authority system into the Dominion period and beyond.

COLONIAL SURVIVALS

While we might, in a sense, include the King's Police Medal for Gallantry, the Indian Police Medal for Gallantry, the King's Police Medal for Distinguished Service, and the Indian Police Medal for Meritrorious Service in this category as they comprise pre-Independence holdovers into the Dominion period, we have in mind here a different class of awards: the awards by non-British colonial powers in India whose awards were continued after Independence, until the integration of these territories into the Indian union in 1961 (for the Portuguese possessions in Goa, Daman, and Diu), and in 1962 (for the French possessions in Pondicherry, though de facto unified since 1954).

Probably the best example of these colonial survivals is the Dupliex Medal (2005), awarded for meritorious service to the French administration in Pondicherry. As such awards terminated with the integration of the French and Portuguese possessions into the Indian union, and as they may no longer be worn (at least in India), such awards may be, in effect, no more than an interesting footnote.

PROVINCIAL AWARDS

The awards by the provincial governments of the Republic of India present an interesting, complex, and somehwhat disturbing picture. In theory, in law, and in terns of the Indian Constitution, they probably ought not to exist. Yet they do exist, and in some cases seem to thrive with profligate abandon.

In the course of researching this volume, a number of such awards were discovered and documented in a very limited fashion. Had it been possible to present these in more than a superficially representative fashion, it may have been an interesting exercise, valuable in demonstrating the downward percolation of symbolic authority—far removed from any nod towards legitimate presidential authority—in the provinces of India. But without more information, it has proved to be impossible to discuss these awards in the rigorous level of consistent detail we would like to employ. The best we can do is to suggest several arenas in which these local awards seem especially common.

Provincial Awards for Gallantry or Lifesaving

The Assam government awards a Governor's Medal in gold and silver, apparently for gallantry and meritorious service; several such awards are known to the Assam Rifles. In Bengal, the 'Dr Harendra Coomer Mookerjee Silver Medal' is awarded by the governor for lifesaving; unusually, the receipt and wearing of this medal by serving military personnel is a documented possibility (Army Order 530/65).

Provincial Police Awards

We suspect, and are not especially surprised to note, that many provinces have awards for their police forces, mirroring in a way the proliferation of police awards, we have noted, at the centre. For example, we have noted ribbons (though the existence of medals is unestablished), for the 'Utkrisht Seva Samman Chinh' (roughly translated from the very Sanskritized Hindi as 'Distinguished Service Emblem' [2006]) and 'Sarahaniya Seva Samman Chinh' (roughly, 'Meritorious Service Emblem' [2007]), locally awarded to and worn by the Uttar Pradesh police. The Andhra Pradesh police have a full set of five provincial medals for their police and fire services: A.P. Mukhyamanthri Shaurya Pathakam (2008), A.P. Police Mahonnatha Seva Pathakam (2009), A.P. Police Uttama Seva Pathakam (2010), A.P. Police Kathina Seva Pathakam (for police only, [2011]), and A.P. Police Seva Pathakam (2012).[7] Likewise, Tamil Nadu, Karnataka, and Kerala have multiple medals for their police. Tamil Nadu, for example, enjoys the Tamil Nadu Chief Minister's Medal for Excellence in Public Service, the Tamil Nadu Chief Minister's Police Medal for Excellence in Investigation, the Tamil Nadu Chief Minister's Prison Service Medal for Meritorious and Gallantry and Good Service [sic], the Tamil Nadu Chief Minister's Police Medal for Gallantry, Bravery, and Heroic Action, the Tamil Nadu Chief Minister's Special Task Force Injury Medal, the Tamil Nadu Chief Minister's Special Task Force Participation Medal, the Chief Minister's Constabulary Medal, the Mahatma Gandhi Police Medal for Outstanding Work in Curtailing Illicit Liquor Menace, the Chief Minister's Police Medal 2003 (Anna Medal), and the Tamil Nadu Chief Minister's Police Medal (Outstanding Devotion to Duty). Sikkim also seems to have a police medal for high-altitude service. If the pattern holds, it may be safely predicted that most provinces have created a set of focused police medals that parallel, duplicate, and transcend national awards, but lurk in invisibility.

Provincial Jubilee Medals

We have observed an anniversary medal for Madhya Pradesh, 1956-81, although few details are forthcoming on this well-produced cupro-nickel award. This suggests the possible existence of other provincial medals.

National Cadet Corps Medals

As might be expected, a number of states seem to have medals for the National Cadet Corps (NCC). We have noted medals (in gold and silver) awarded by both the governor (2013) and

---

[7] 'Andhra Pradesh Police: Pathakams', http://www.apstate police.org/AboutUs/Pathakams/Pathakams.htm, June 2004.

the chief minister (2014) of Kerala and Lakshadweep for the NCC.

Awards of Ministries and Other Bodies

Examples of medals established by various governmental and non-governmental bodies have been unearthed. For example, long service medals are issued to civilian personnel of the ordnance corps.

AWARDS OF SIKKIM

Sikkim presents a unique case. Until its integration into India in 1975, it enjoyed a separate history for over four centuries which leads to a distinctive form of treatment here. Under independent Sikkim, the kings (Mi-dbang Chos-rgyal-chen-po or, put more simply, 'Chogyal') of the rNam dynasty since 1947 were: bKra-shis rNam-rgyal (Tashi Namgyal) (1914-63) and dPaldan Don-grub rNam-rgyal (Palden Thondup Namgyal) (1963-75).

During the reign of Chogyal Palden Thondup Namgyal, a state order (the Order of the Jewel of Sikkim) was established (in five classes [2015]), a decoration (the Pema Dora) was awarded (including to at least two Indian officers), and a medal commemorated the Chogyal's accession to the throne (2016). With the integration of Sikkim into India in 1975, these awards became obsolete.

3

Non-Indian Awards

Most of the non-Indian awards will be medals of the United Nations. As most United Nations medals are identical, with differences only in the ribbons, this generic peacekeeping medal will be illustrated but once, for the United Nations Observation Group in Lebanon (3004). Ribbons are shown in the ribbon chart at the end of this volume.

In 1990, the President of India accorded blanket sanction to the acceptance and wearing of United Nations medals by personnel of the Indian defence services who had served on deputation or as members of a peacekeeping force or otherwise with the UN. The medals are to be worn in the order in which they were earned, among 'other awards'.[1]

3001 UNITED NATIONS: KOREA SERVICE MEDAL, 1950-53[2]

Awarded for United Nations service in Korea, 1950-53.

Established: December 1950, but never authorized for Indian manufacture or wear.

General Appearance: Circular 35 mm bronze medal. (The standard US and British variety is illustrated.)

Obverse: The United Nations emblem within a wreath. Suspended from a straight-bar suspender with a bar reading (in the British variety) 'KOREA'. Though, tellingly and relevantly, the official UN description reads: 'A bronze medallion bearing on the obverse the representation of the UN symbol in bas-relief. . . . The medallion is attached to the ribbon by means of a bar that bears the name "KOREA" in bas-relief. The wording shown may be in English, French, Spanish, Danish, Greek, Italian, Dutch, Swedish, *Sanskrit* or Turkish.' [Emphasis added.]

Reverse: In the British variety, the legend 'FOR SERVICE IN DEFENCE OF THE PRINCIPLES OF THE CHARTER OF THE UNITED NATIONS'. Relevantly to this study, the official UN description reads: '. . . on the reverse, the wording 'FOR SERVICE IN THE DEFENCE OF THE PRINCIPLES OF THE CHARTER OF THE UNITED NATIONS', also in bas-relief. . . . The wording shown may be in English, French, Spanish, Danish, Greek,

3001.100 United Nations Korea Service Medal, 1950-53

[1] MoD No. 3(19)/90/D (Ceremonials), dated 31 October 1990.
[2] See *Indian Army: Peacekeeping Operations*, pp. 8-13, 114, 116-17.

Italian, Dutch, Swedish, *Sanskrit* or Turkish.' [Emphasis added.]

Ribbon: 35 mm, seventeen narrow stripes, alternating light blue (outermost) and white. The ribbon bears alternate narrow stripes of white and blue, the colours of the UN.

Suspension: By a straight non-swivelling bar with an integral clasp reading 'Korea' in the appropriate language.

Naming: Awarded unnamed.

Miniature: Miniatures have been issued, though none have been encountered in the Indian variety.

Background: The story of this medal as awarded to Indian forces serving in the Korean War is both complex and cloudy.

This medal was awarded for service in Korea with United Nations forces, from 1950 to July 1953. Service in Korea after this date (as with the Neutral Nations Repatriation Commission) did not earn this award. Personnel were eligible to receive the medal after a period of thirty days' service in the mission. The following countries provided troops to this mission: Australia, Belgium, Canada, Columbia, Denmark, Ethiopia, France, Greece, Italy, Luxembourg, the Kingdom of the Netherlands, New Zealand, Norway, the Philippines, South Africa, Sweden, Thailand, Turkey, the United Kingdom of Great Britain and Northern Ireland, and the United States of America. Indian troops also served in Korea, and it is the convoluted tale of their involvement in Korea that leads to this medal's presence here.

The medal appeared in a number of national varieties, as the bar and reverse legend were supposed to be rendered in the language of the nation making the award. It was clearly the intent of the UN that this medal would be issued by India, but it seems to have run afoul of government policy which discouraged foreign awards to Indian nationals. There is at least circumstantial evidence that at least the ribbon of this medal has at times been worn by Indian troops.[3]

Service which would have qualified for this award was also recognized with the 'Overseas Korea 1950-53' bar to the General Service Medal, 1947 (1035.302). Service with the Neutral Nations Repatriation Commission (NNRC) or the Indian Custodian Force 1950-54—recognized by the 'Korea' bar to the Videsh Seva Medal (1052.201)—specifically did not qualify for this medal.

Thus, Indian service which would have qualified for this medal would have been limited to those personnel of the 60th Para Field Ambulance (17 officers, 9 JCOs, and 300 other ranks) who served in Korea in 1950-53. As a function of prevailing policy that mitigated strongly against Indian acceptance of foreign awards—and this UN medal was seen as a 'foreign' award—the medal was never manufactured in a Hindi version and acceptance and wearing of the medal, even in English, was disallowed.

After all these years, and as other UN medals are now commonly accepted by Indian forces, this decision seems ripe for reassessment. It is our understanding that this issue is under consideration, even as we write, and we can only hope for a

[3] See, for example, the picture of Captain A.N. Jatar who can be seen wearing this ribbon in the photo in *Stories of Heroism*, p. 212.

fair resolution for these aging deserving veterans of India's first UN service.

Outline

3001.100 'KOREA'—The standard British/Commonwealth variety of the medal.
3001.200 'कोरिया' ('Korea' in Hindi)—Possibly prepared, but to date never awarded.

3002.100 ICSC Medal

3002 INTERNATIONAL COMMISSION FOR SUPERVISION AND CONTROL IN INDO-CHINA: SERVICE MEDAL, 1954-70[4]

Awarded for service with the ICSC in Indochina, 1954-70.

Established: The medal was instituted by the International Commission for Supervision and Control (ICSC) in 1967 and awarded for service between 7 August 1954 and 28 January 1973. Wearing of this medal was authorized by AO 330/69, citing Ministry of Defence Letter No. F3/40/D (Ceremonials) of 1 August 1969.

General Appearance: A circular bright bronze medal, 26 mm in diameter.

Obverse: It depicts the emblem of the ICSC—crossed flags, a maple leaf on the left one and a central horizontal line on the right one, with a dove of peace where the flag staffs cross, and lions between the flags facing left and centre. Around the edge are the words 'INTERNATIONAL COMMISSION FOR SUPERVISION AND CONTROL—PEACE', with the word PEACE at the bottom and in larger, more widely spaced letters. Red portions of the flags are properly enamelled. (This describes the medal as issued to Indian troops; other national issues differ slightly in design details and presentation.)

Reverse: A map of Vietnam, Laos, and Cambodia with the names of the countries properly inscribed.

Ribbon: 32 mm, three equal stripes of dark green, white, and red. Often this has been incorrectly replaced by the Indian Independence Medal 1947 ribbon (1070), reversed to green, white, and orange (King's South Africa design).

Suspension: A plain non-swivelling straight bar.

Naming: Named on the edge of the medal.

Miniature: Miniatures were issued.

Background: The medal was awarded for ninety days of service as an Assistant Delegate with the International Commission for ICSC in Vietnam, Laos, and Cambodia, 1954-70, calculated from the date the member came under the command of the commission; or less than ninety days if such service was terminated by death, injury or any disability received in carrying out official duties, and a certificate is given to this effect by the Senior Military Advisor.

The ICSC was established to supervise the implementation of the provisions of Chapter VI of the July 1954 Geneva Conference in the former states of French Indochina (Vietnam, Laos, and Cambodia). India had played a vital role at the UN

Geneva Conference that brought about an end to the war in Indochina. Therefore, she was requested to assist in supervising the implementation of the Agreement. For the purpose of supervision, three separate commissions were set up, one each for Vietnam, Cambodia, and Laos. Each commission had India as chairman and Canada and Poland as members.

From September 1954, detachments of Indian, Canadian, and Polish troops were dispatched to Indochina to comprise six-member teams (with two members from each delegated state) to supervise the ceasefire.

The mandate of the ICSC in Vietnam was to supervise the ceasefires, withdrawal of French troops, and the movement of refugees. The ICSC Laos was to supervise the ceasefire and promote negotiations between the Royal Laotian government and the Pathet Lao. The ICSC Cambodia monitored the Geneva Accords and helped the Khmer resistance forces disband and return home and the Viet Minh to leave the country. Much of the work was done from 1954. The commission withdrew completely in 1969.

In addition to delegates and headquarters staff drawn from a range of Indian units, an initial detachment from the 2nd Guards was dispatched to the region to serve as a security team for the commission. As the work of the commission lasted for many years, a turnover policy, under which officers and personnel were replaced every year with fresh staff from India, was followed. The 'Indochina' bar to the Videsh Seva Medal (see 1052.203) also recognized this service.

Gradually, there was a decrease in the number of teams and a proportionate decrease in the number of troops. Indian troops were pulled out in 1968, 1969, and 1970, leaving only four officers and three other ranks with the Commissions in Vietnam and Laos. Subsequently, the commission in Vietnam was also wound up.

Outline

3002.100 medal.

3003 UNITED NATIONS EMERGENCY FORCE I (UNEF I), NOVEMBER 1956-MAY 1967[5]

Awarded for service in the Middle East with UNEF, 1956-67.

Established: 7 November 1956. The medal was authorized for Indian troops by AO 390/65.

General Appearance: Bronze, circular, 37 mm.

Obverse: The United Nations symbol within a wreath. Above 'UNEF'.

Reverse: The inscription 'IN THE SERVICE / OF PEACE'. This is the same as the ubiquitous UN peacekeeping medal (although the obverse differs).

Ribbon: 36 mm, tan-yellow ('sand'), central medium blue stripe, two black and green stripes toward each edge: 2 mm tan-yellow, 1 mm black, 2 mm tan-yellow, 1 mm green, 7 mm tan-yellow, 10 mm medium blue, 7 mm tan-yellow, 1 mm green, 2 mm tan-yellow, 1 mm black, 2 mm tan-yellow. The

[5] *Indian Army: Peacekeeping Operations*, pp. 16-23, 121.

3003.100 UNEF Medal

ribbon has a background of a sand or buff colour symbolizing the Sinai with a wide centre band of UN blue. Two thin lines in dark blue and green appear at either end of the ribbon, the blue representing the Suez Canal, and the green, the Nile Valley.

Suspension: Suspended from a ring.

Naming: Awarded unnamed.

Miniature: Miniatures have been issued.

Background: Israel invaded Egypt on 29 October 1956. As Britain and France had their interests in the Suez Canal, they issued an ultimatum to both sides to withdraw their forces 16 km from the canal and to allow their own forces (British and French) to be located alongside the canal. While Israel accepted, Egypt refused, when British and French troops landed in the canal area on 5 November 1956.

On 6 November the UN intervened and brought about a ceasefire. A UN Emergency Force (UNEF) was constituted under Major-General E.L.M. Burns of Canada to supervise the ceasefire. India was invited to provide troops for peacekeeping in the Suez Canal area. India's participation in the peacekeeping mission was code-named Operation Shanti ('Peace'). UNEF's mission was to secure and to supervise the cessation of hostilities, including the withdrawal of the armed forces of France, Israel and the United Kingdom of Great Britain and Northern Ireland from Egyptian territory, and after the withdrawal, to serve as a buffer between the Egyptian and Israeli Forces. The mission was terminated at the request of Egypt in June 1967.

The medal is awarded for ninety days of service in the United Nations Emergency Force (Egypt) (UNEF) between 7 November 1956 and 19 May 1967. This emergency force was established to restore order in the aftermath of the British, French, and Israeli invasion of Egypt in the context of the Suez Canal Crisis of October 1956. The following nations provided troops: Brazil, Canada, Columbia, Denmark, Finland, Indonesia, India, Norway, Sweden, and Yugoslavia.

The first batch of Indian troops left by air on 16 November 1956. But their actual participation in peacekeeping operations started in early December when 3rd Para entered the buffer zone that separated the Anglo-French and Egyptian forces. Subsequently, it followed the Israeli withdrawal along the Suez Road. Annual relief brought in 2nd Grenadiers, 4th Kumaon, 4th Rajput, 2nd Sikh, 2nd Maratha LI, 9th Dogra, 4th Guards, 3rd Punjab, and 1st Sikh LI. In addition, there was a platoon from the Army Service Corps, and detachments from the Corps of Signals, Ordinance Corps, Medical Corps, Military Police, and Army Postal Service. Later the Indian troops concentrated at El Arish, to take over its area of responsibility in the Gaza Strip. The main task of the UNEF was to guard the Armistice Demarcation Line (ADL) and to protect the UN establishments. With this end in view, the Indian battalion established twenty-seven observations posts in its sector, extending over an area of 13 km.

The Indian Army served in Gaza until 1967. On 18 May 1967, Egypt served quit orders on UNEF. On 5 June, war erupted between Israel and Egypt. This disrupted the evacuation plan of Indian troops. Caught in the war, they suffered fourteen killed and twenty-five wounded.

Indian service was also recognized with the 'United Arab Republic' bar to the Videsh Seva Medal (1052.205).

Outline

3003.100 medal.

3004 UNITED NATIONS OBSERVATION GROUP IN LEBANON (UNOGIL), JUNE-DECEMBER 1958[6]

Awarded for service with UNOGIL in Lebanon.

Established: By the United Nations General Assembly on 30 July 1959.

General Appearance: Bronze, circular, 36 mm. This is the ubiquitous UN peacekeeping medal. It will be consistently so referenced below throughtout this chapter.

Obverse: The United Nations emblem with 'UN' above. This is the ubiquitous UN peacekeeping medal. This is the same as the obverse of other UN peacekeeping medals.

Reverse: The inscription 'IN THE SERVICE / OF PEACE'. This is the ubiquitous UN peacekeeping medal. This is the same as the reverse as for other UN peacekeeping medals.

Ribbon: 35 mm, medium blue, thin white stripes towards each edge.

Suspension: Suspended from a ring in all its varieties.

Naming: All UN medals are awarded unnamed.

Miniature: Miniatures have been issued for all these UN peacekeeping medals.

Background: Lebanon was caught in an internal strife in the 1950s and this led to growing communal tensions and to US military intervention. This external involvement was widely resented by the Arab states; the UN General Assembly passed a resolution calling for US withdrawal. Further, as growing communal tensions had threatened the stability of Lebanon, the UN Security Council voted at the request of the Lebanese president to dispatch an observer mission.

The UN Security Council decided to station an Observer Group in Lebanon to prevent the entry of foreigners and smuggled arms and to ensure free and fair elections. Countries providing troops to UNOGIL included Canada, Ecuador, India, Norway, and the United States of America. The UNOGIL headquarters was in Beirut and, at its peak, UNOGIL posted 591 observers at 49 posts throughout Lebanon. The crisis entered a new phase and UNOGIL was withdrawn when the United States deployed combat troops to the region in 1958. Colonel Ranbir Singh of the Indian Army led the observer group. It arrived in Lebanon on 19 June 1958. The elections were held in a peaceful manner and the president took office on September 28th. The last batch of UN troops was withdrawn from Lebanon on 25 October 1958.

The medal was awarded for thirty days of service with UNOGIL between 11 June 1958 and 9 December 1958. Indian

3004.100 United Nations Medal, generic issue (with UNOGIL ribbon)

---

[6] *Indian Army: Peacekeeping Operations*, pp. 24-25.

service was also recognized with the 'Lebanon' bar to the Videsh Seva Medal (1052.207).

This is the same medal as was awarded for service with the United Nations Truce Supervisory Organization (UNTSO), although India did not participate in this peacekeeping mission. The medal is also seen with a clasp 'CONGO' for service with ONUC (see 3005).

Outline

3004.100 medal.

3005 OPERATIONS DES NATIONS UNIES AU CONGO (ONUC), JULY 1960-JUNE 1964[7]

Awarded for service with ONUC in the Congo, 1960-64.

Established: ONUC was established by S/RES/143 (1960) of 14 July 1960. The 'CONGO' bar was authorized in July 1960; the revised ribbon was approved in 1963.

General Appearance: This is the standard UN peacekeeping medal (see 3004 for a description).

Ribbon: Originally, the medal awarded for service in the Congo was a UN blue and white ribbon with a clasp indicating Congo service. In 1963 it was decided that a distinctive ribbon should be issued. The ribbon subsequently awarded carries a broad centre band of green, symbolic of hope, which was thought to be appropriate for a young nation, and also to represent the Congo Basin. The centre band is flanked by two narrow white bands, representing the UN Mission, and at either end are two bars of UN blue.

Background: In 1960, Belgium terminated her seventy-eight years of rule in the Congo and Patrice Lumumba formed the first national government. Soon, violence erupted in the Congo and the provinces of Katanga and Kasai seceded. To save the Congo from a disastrous civil war, the UN Security Council by its resolution of 21 February 1961, decided upon military intervention in that country.

ONUC was established initially in July 1960 to ensure the withdrawal of Belgian forces, to assist the government in maintaining law and order, and to provide technical assistance. The function of ONUC was subsequently modified to include maintaining the territorial integrity and the political independence of the Congo, preventing the occurrence of civil war, and securing the removal from the Congo of all foreign military, paramilitary, and advisory personnel not under the United Nations Command, and all mercenaries. On completion of the mandate, the mission was withdrawn in June 1964.

Countries that provided troops to ONUC included Argentina, Austria, Brazil, Burma (now Myanmar), Canada, Ceylon (now Sri Lanka), Congo, Denmark, Ecuador, Ethiopia, Ghana, Greece, Guinea, India, Indonesia, Iran, Ireland, Italy, Liberia, Malaya, the Federation of Mali (now Mali and Senegal), Morocco, the Netherlands, Nigeria, Norway, Pakistan, the Philippines, Sierra Leone, Sudan, Sweden, Tunisia, the United Arab Republic (later Egypt and Syria), and (former) Yugoslavia.

India initially provided some logistics support units to the

[7] *Indian Army: Peacekeeping Operations,* pp. 26-35, 113-17, 121.

UN Command at Congo: the 152nd General Hospital; a signal company; supply and composite platoons, and detachments of air dispatch; military police; and Army Postal Service. Subsequently, this contribution was enhanced to a brigade on request from the United Nations. The 99th Infantry Brigade Group under Brigadier K.A.S. Raja was sent to Leopoldville, the capital, in the period from March to June 1961.

To end the secession of Katanga, UN forces launched two important operations codenamed Rumpunch and Marthor in August-September 1961. The 99th Inf. Bde. consisting of the 1st Dogra, 2nd Jat, 3/1st Gurkha Rifles, a squadron of 63rd Cavalry, 120th Heavy Mortar Battery, 13th Field Company of engineers, a company from 4th Mahar (Machine Gun), and 95th Field Ambulance made substantial contribution in these operations. The last and most important act of the brigade in Katanga was the launching of Operation Grand Slam on 28 December 1962. It aimed at freeing Elisabethville and Jadotville from gendarmerie (Katanga groups) menace. Although Operation Grand Slam was a success, Indian forces suffered seven dead and forty-nine wounded.

There was a turnover of Indian troops subsequently and Brigadier R.S. Noronha took over as the Commander of the 99th Infantry Brigade. The replacements were 4th Madras, 4th Rajputana Rifles (Outram's), 2/5th Gorkha Rifles, and fresh sub-units of 63rd Cavalry and 4th Mahar. The 121st Heavy Mortar Battery and 22nd Field Company of engineers also joined the brigade. Major General Dewan Prem Chand was appointed commander of the Katanga area. The Indian Air Force also contributed substantially towards the success of the UN troops in the Congo, with Canberras from No. 5 Squadron IAF participating in these operations. The repatriation of the Indian brigade which started on 1 March 1963 was completed on 30 June 1964.

In all, thirty-nine units of the Indian Army participated in the Congo operations during 1961-64. During their three-year service with the UN, 142 Indian Army officers and men won awards for gallantry or distinguished service. The Indian forces earned tremendous goodwill from the UN headquarters and the world at large.

Thirty-nine Indians were killed while serving in ONUC and 108 were wounded. Indian service was also recognized with the 'Congo' bar to the Videsh Seva Medal (1052.211).

The first medal was a simple adaptation of the medal and ribbon (UN blue with two thin white edge stripes) awarded for the United Nations Observation Group in Lebanon (UNOGIL) (see 3004) and the United Nations Truce Supervisory Organization (UNTSO) with the addition of a clasp reading 'CONGO'. In 1963 a new ribbon was authorized, and this is described above.

Outline

3005.100 UNOGIL medal with clasp 'CONGO'.
3005.200 ONUC medal—The common UN medal with Congo-specific ribbon.

3006 UNITED NATIONS TEMPORARY EXECUTIVE AUTHORITY (UNTEA) AND UNITED NATIONS SECURITY FORCE (UNSF), OCTOBER 1962-APRIL 1963[8]

Awarded for service in Cambodia with UNTEA and UNSF, 1962-63.

General Appearance: This is the standard UN peacekeeping medal (see 3004 for a description).

Ribbon: The medal ribbon has a background of UN blue with three centred narrow stripes in dark green, white and light green. The dark green represents the jungle and the swampland, the white indicates the snow-capped mountains, and the pale green represents the coral beaches of the region.

Background: When Indonesia became independent in 1949, a dispute arose over the status of West Irian between the governments of Netherlands and Indonesia. The United Nations undertook to resolve the dispute and this led to the establishment of the United Nations Temporary Executive Authority (UNTEA) and the UN Security Force (UNSF) in 1962.

UNSF was established in October 1962 to maintain peace and security in the territory under the United Nations Temporary Executive Authority established by agreement between Indonesia and the Kingdom of the Netherlands. UNSF monitored the ceasefire and helped ensure law and order during the transition period, pending transfer to Indonesia. By 21 September 1962, all Indonesian forces were located and concentrated and 500 Indonesian political detainees had been repatriated. Upon completion of the mandate, the mission was withdrawn in April 1963.

The countries of Brazil, Canada, Ceylon (now Sri Lanka), India, Ireland, Nigeria, Pakistan, Sweden, and the United States of America provided troops to this mission. Arrangements for a ceasefire were supervised by a UN military observer team led by Brigadier I.J. Rikhye. India provided two military observers from its contingent serving in Congo with ONUC at that time. Indian service was also recognized with the 'New Guinea' bar to the Videsh Seva Medal (1052.213).

Outline

3006.100 medal.

3007 UNITED NATIONS YEMEN OBSERVER MISSION (UNYOM), JUNE 1963-SEPTEMBER 1964[9]

Awarded for service with UNYOM in Yemen, 1963-64.

Established: By the United Nations General Assembly on 30 July 1959.

General Appearance: This is the standard UN peacekeeping medal (see 3004 for a description).

Ribbon: 34 mm, a 5 mm brown centre shading out to yellow towards each edge, where there are abrupt thin (2 mm) blue edge stripes. The centre of the ribbon is a wide bar filled with varying shades of brown indicating the dry and rugged mountainous mass in Yemen, while the lighter shades represent

[8] *Indian Army: Peacekeeping Operations*, pp. 42-43.
[9] Ibid., pp. 36-37.

the desert. The centre is flanked by two stripes of UN blue.

Background: A civil war broke out in Yemen in September 1962. To bring peace, a UN Yemen Observer Mission (UNYOM) was established on 13 June 1963 in order to assist in the disengagement of Egyptian forces from their involvement in the Yemeni civil war and to supervise the 20 km demilitarized zone between Yemen and Saudi Arabia. This mission ended its activities and was withdrawn in September 1964.

Countries that provided troops to UNYOM included Australia, Austria, Canada, Denmark, Ghana, India, Italy, the Netherlands, New Zealand, Norway, Pakistan, Sweden, the United States of America, and Yugoslavia. The mission consisted of 200 personnel with 25 military observers, including military personnel from India. Major-General P.S. Gyani and Brigadier I.J. Rikhye of India commanded the mission at different periods. Indian service was also recognized with the 'Yemen' bar to the Videsh Seva Medal (1052.214).

The UN medal was awarded for sixty days of service with UNYOM from 11 June 1963 to 4 September 1964.

Outline

3007.100 medal.

3008 UNITED NATIONS FORCE IN CYPRUS (UNFICYP), MARCH 1964- [10]

Awarded for service in Cyprus with UNFICYP since 1964.

General Appearance: This is the standard UN peacekeeping medal (see 3004 for a description).

Ribbon: The medal has three equal bars, one of white in the centre and two of UN blue at either end. The bars are separated by two narrow bands of dark blue symbolizing the Mediterranean Sea.

Background: Cyprus, a British colony in the Mediterranean, became independent in 1960. It had a predominantly Greek Cypriot population of about 80 per cent and a Turkish minority population of about 20 per cent. Continuing tension between the two communities came to a head in March 1964 and the UN Security Council established a peacekeeping force— UNFICYP—to police the green line between the communities in Nicosia. UNFICYP was to use its best efforts to prevent the recurrence of fighting between the Greek Cypriots and Turkish Cypriots and, as necessary, to contribute to the maintenance and restoration of law and order and a return to normal conditions. Since the hostilities of 1974, the mandate has included supervising the ceasefire and maintaining a buffer zone between the lines of the Cyprus National Guard and of the Turkish and Turkish Cypriot forces. The mission continues to the present date.

The following countries have provided troops to this mission: Austria, Argentina, Brazil, Canada, Denmark, Finland, Hungary, India, Ireland, the Kingdom of the Netherlands, Slovenia, Sweden, and the United Kingdom. The following countries provided civilian policemen: Australia,

[10] *Indian Army: Peacekeeping Operations*, pp. 38-41, 121.

Austria, Denmark, New Zealand, and Sweden.

On 17 January 1964, Lieutenant General P.S. Gyani was appointed personal representative of the UN Secretary-General, and was later appointed as force commander of the 6,400-strong UN contingent deployed in Cyprus. General K.S. Thimayya took over from him in June 1964 and did an outstanding job till his death in December 1965. Major-General Dewan Prem Chand was appointed as the force commander in December 1965, and he held the appointment for six years. These three force commanders represent the only Indian participation and there was no Indian contingent in UNFICYP *per se*, so only these three officers would have qualified for this medal. They would also have received (one posthumously) the 'Cyprus' bar to the Videsh Seva Medal (1052.217).

Outline

3008.100 medal.

3009 UNITED NATIONS IRAN-IRAQ MILITARY OBSERVER GROUP (UNIIMOG), AUGUST 1988-APRIL 1991[11]

Awarded for service on the Iran-Iraq border with UNIIMOG, 1988-91.

General Appearance: This is the standard UN peacekeeping medal (see 3004 for a description).

Ribbon: The ribbon has a broad central band of UN blue flanked on the left end by three equal stripes in green, white, and red to represent the Iranian flag, and on the right end, by three equal stripes of red, white, and black to represent the Iraqi flag.

Background: A war between Iran and Iraq started in September 1980, over the control of the Shatt-al-Arab water channel. Subsequently, it assumed territorial and religious overtones. As a result of UN efforts, a ceasefire became effective on 20 August 1988.

The Security Council Resolution provided a UN International Military Observation Group to supervise the Cease-Fire Agreement (CFA). Some 350 officers formed the group. This mission was established in August 1988 to verify, confirm, and supervise the ceasefire and withdrawal of all forces to the internationally recognized boundaries agreed to between Iran and Iraq. The mission ceased in April 1991. Ninety days of service in the mission were required to qualify for the medal.

Military observers from Argentina, Australia, Austria, Bangladesh, Canada, Denmark, Finland, Ghana, Hungary, India, Indonesia, Ireland, Italy, Kenya, Malaysia, New Zealand, Nigeria, Norway, Peru, Poland, Senegal, Sweden, Turkey, Uruguay, Yugoslavia, and Zambia served in UNIIMOG.

Indian service included the Assistant Chief Military Observer (Iraq) and National Senior Brigadier V.M. Patil and fourteen other officers (one colonel and thirteen majors). The Indian contingent contributed substantially in the peacekeeping efforts

[11] *Indian Army: Peacekeeping Operations*, pp. 44-47.

on the ceasefire line. Their service was also recognized with the 'Iran-Iraq' bar to the Videsh Seva Medal (1052.228).

Outline

3009.100 medal.

3010 UNITED NATIONS ANGOLA VERIFICATION MISSION, UNAVEM I, JANUARY 1989-JUNE 1991, UNAVEM II, JUNE 1991-FEBRUARY 1995, AND UNAVEM III, FEBRUARY 1995-JUNE 1997[12]

Awarded for service with UNAVEM in Angola, 1989-97.

Established: UNAVEM was established by the United Nations Security Council Resolution S/RES/696 (1988) of 20 December 1988, with the mission expanded in S/RES/696 (1991) of 30 May 1991, S/RES/747 (1992) of 24 March 1992, and S/RES/976 (1995) of 8 February 1995.

General Appearance: This is the standard UN peacekeeping medal (see 3004 for a description).

Ribbon: Yellow, light blue centre stripe edged with thin stripes (reading inwards) of red, white, and blue. 8 mm yellow, 2 mm red, 2 mm white, 1 mm black, 9 mm UN blue, 1 mm black, 2 mm white, 2 mm red, 8 mm yellow. The yellow, red, and black represent the Angolan national flag.

Background: Angolan independence merged into civil war between the Soviet- and Cuban-supported Popular Movement for the Liberation of Angola (MPLA), and the South African- and US-supported National Union for the Total Independence of Angola (UNITA). The people of Angola became pawns in the artificial East-West confrontation. With the 1988 agreement on Cuban withdrawal and the beginning of implementation of the Namibian independence process, it looked as if this artificial construct had served its purpose and that Angola might be able to contemplate peace after thirty years of armed struggle against the Portuguese.

The UN Angola Verification Mission (UNAVEM I) was established by the Security Council in 1988 to certify the northward redeployment and withdrawal of the 50,000-strong Cuban contingent. In March 1992, the Security Council agreed to a plan whereby UNAVEM II would observe and verify the forthcoming elections, to supervise the ceasefire, and to conduct general peacekeeping operations after the termination of UNAVEM I. The elections were conducted, but UNITA cried foul and resumed the war. Nearly 3.5 million people were displaced, drought-affected, or in need of various forms of aid as a consequence of the war. Appalling reports of sieges and massacres proliferated. By February 1995, UNAVEM III came into being in an ongoing effort to restore peace in Angola. UNAVEM III terminated operations in June 1997.

The medal was awarded for ninety days of service with the UNAVEM (I, II, or III). Countries providing troops to UNAVEM included Algeria, Argentina, Bangladesh, Brazil, Bulgaria, Canada, Colombia, Congo, Czechoslovakia (former), Egypt, Fiji, France, Guinea Bissau, Hungary, India, Italy, Ireland,

[12] *Indian Army: Peacekeeping Operations*, pp. 98-108.

Jordan, Kenya, Korea (South), Malaysia, Mali, Morocco, Namibia, the Netherlands, New Zealand, Nigeria, Norway, Pakistan, Poland, Portugal, Romania, Russia, Senegal, Singapore, Slovakia, Spain, Sweden, Tanzania, Ukraine, the United Kingdom, Uruguay, Yugoslavia (former), Zambia, and Zimbabwe.

India provided some military observers to UNAVEM I during the period 1989-91. India again sent a few observers to monitor elections in UNAVEM II, and later sent a contingent of an infantry battalion (14th Punjab relieved by 16th Guards a year later) supported by an engineer company (417th Field Coy, later replaced by 386th Field Coy) and other elements totalling 1,014 all ranks. The unit was deployed in Angola's northern region for peacekeeping. In addition, nineteen military observers and forty-nine staff officers were also sent and were deployed in Zaire, Uige and Bengo provinces. Indian service was also recognized by the 'Angola' bar to the Videsh Seva Medal (1052.231).

Outline

3010.100 medal.

3011 UNITED NATIONS TRANSITION ASSISTANCE GROUP (UNTAG), APRIL 1989-MARCH 1990[13]

Awarded for service with UNTAG in Namibia, 1989-90.

Established: UNTAG was established by S/RES/632 (1989) of 16 February 1989.

General Appearance: This is the standard UN peacekeeping medal (see 3004 for a description).

Ribbon: Gold-yellow, with broad UN-blue edge stripes. In the centre, five thin stripes (left to right): black, gold-yellow, red, light blue, dark blue. The centre of the UNTAG ribbon contains five equal stripes in black, yellow, red, green and royal blue, the colours of the five Olympic Rings and representing the five continental regions of the world, all of which were represented in either the military or the civilian police components of UNTAG. The centre is flanked by equal bars of a buff or sand colour to represent the Kalahari and Namib deserts with equal bands of UN blue appearing at each end.

Background: Despite a UN Resolution, Namibia was one of the last of the African countries to gain independence from colonial rule. It was under the WWI-era mandate of South Africa, which had been exploiting the natural resources of the country for a long time. The South-West African People's Organisation (SWAPO) under Sam Nujoma and certain other local organizations were fighting for independence. Some of them were functioning from the neighbouring countries and were assisted by Cuban troops. South Africa on its part tried to put down the SWAPO forces by all possible methods, but could not succeed. Ultimately, they agreed to implement the UN Resolution. The UN took over the administration of Namibia to start with, with the idea of preparing and training the Namibians for administration. UNTAG was established to

[13] *Indian Army: Peacekeeping Operations,* pp. 48-53.

ensure the early independence of Namibia through free and fair elections under the supervision and control of the United Nations. The mission was established in April 1989 with a mandate for one year and finally closed in May 1990.

The medal was awarded for ninety days of service with the UNTAG from April 1989 to March 1990. Countries providing troops to UNTAG included Australia, Austria, Bangladesh, Barbados, Belgium, Canada, China, Congo, Costa Rico, Czechoslovakia (former), Denmark, Egypt, Fiji, Finland, France, German Democratic Republic (former), Federal Republic of Germany (former), Ghana, Greece, Guyana, Hungary, India, Indonesia, Ireland, Italy, Jamaica, Japan, Kenya, Malaysia, the Netherlands, New Zealand, Nigeria, Norway, Pakistan, Panama, Peru, Poland, Portugal, Senegal, Singapore, Spain, Sudan, Sweden, Switzerland, Thailand, Togo, Trinidad and Tobago, Tunisia, the USSR (former), the United Kingdom, and (former) Yugoslavia.

Indian service included the force commander Lieutenant General Dewan Prem Chand, fifteen military observers (mostly communications experts), police monitors, and civilian electoral supervisors. Indian service included members of the Border Security Force (BSF) during 1989. During this period, Brajesh Mishra of India was appointed as UN Commissioner for Namibia and helped the Namibians a great deal in preparing for independence.

Indian service was also recognized with the 'Namibia' bar to the Videsh Seva Medal (1052.232).

Outline

3011.100 medal.

3012 ORGANISATION DE NATIONS UNIES AU CENTRAL AMERICA (ONUCA), DECEMBER 1989-JANUARY 1992[14]

Awarded for service with ONUCA in Central America, 1989-92.

General Appearance: This is the standard UN peacekeeping medal (see 3004 for a description).

Ribbon: The medal ribbon contains five narrow green stripes to represent the five countries involved. These five green stripes are separated by four equal white stripes. The central group is flanked by two equal bands of sea blue to represent the Pacific Ocean and the Caribbean Sea, flanked in turn by two broad bands of UN blue to represent the United Nations' presence in the area.

Background: Established in December 1989 to conduct on-site verification of termination of aid to irregular forces and insurrectionist movements, and the non-use of the territory of one state for attacks on other states in the countries of Costa Rica, El Salvador, Guatemala, Honduras, and Nicaragua. The mission terminated in January 1992. Ninety days of service in the mission were required to qualify for the medal. The countries of Argentina, Brazil, Canada, Colombia, Ecuador,

[14] *Indian Army: Peacekeeping Operations*, pp. 54-57.

India, Ireland, Spain, Sweden and Venezuela provided observers and troops to ONUCA.

Indian service was also recognized with the appropriate country-clasp to the Videsh Seva Medal, 'Nicaragua' (1052.233), 'Honduras' (1052.234), 'Guatemala' (1052.235), or 'Costa Rica' (1052.236).

Outline

3012.100 medal.

3013 UNITED NATIONS OBSERVER MISSION IN EL SALVADOR (ONUSAL), JULY 1991-APRIL 1995[15]

Awarded for service with ONUSAL in El Salvador 1991-95.

Established: Medal was authorized in January 1992. ONUSAL was created by United Nations Security Council resolution 693 of 20 May 1991.

General Appearance: This is the standard UN peacekeeping medal (see 3004 for a description).

Ribbon: The medal has five equal bars, the centre being white, flanked by dark blue, and, at either end, by UN blue. The dark blue and white represent the national flag of El Salvador.

Background: In El Salvador, a left-wing rebel movement, the FMLN (Farabundo Marti Liberation Front) challenged the right-wing government with varying degrees of success, in spite of the American policy of linking military and economic aid with efforts aimed at democratization. As far as Washington was concerned, the rebellion in El Salvador was linked to the Sandinistas in Nicaragua and through them to Cuba and Moscow. From the late 1970s to the late 1980s, the Salvadoran civil war is said to have cost up to 70,000 lives, mainly civilian. From early in the 1980s, Latin American governments were coming together to promote peace in Central America. They formulated the Esquipelas Agreements which addressed Central America as a whole, dealt with national reconciliation, an end to hostilities, democratization, free elections, termination of aid to insurgents, non-use of territory to attack another state, control and limitation of weapons, and international inspection.

In early 1990, the Salvadoran government and the FMLN began peace negotiations under the auspices of the UN. This was followed by the establishment of an observer group (ONUCA, see 3012) to verify security arrangements. However, the Security Council continued to extend ONUCA's mandate until it was subsumed under ONUSAL, created by the Council in May 1991 to monitor agreements reached between the Salvadoran government and the FMLN to resolve the civil war, to promote democratization, guarantee human rights, and reunify Salvadoran society. ONUSAL began by monitoring the Agreement on Human Rights, investigating violations and following up action taken by the parties to correct them.

This mission was established on 20 May 1991 to monitor all agreements between the Government of El Salvador and Frente

Farabundo Marti para la Liberacion Nacional (FMLN). This mission was subsequently expanded in January 1992 to assume the verification of all aspects of the ceasefire and separation of forces and the agreement on the National Civil Police that saw ONUSAL monitoring the maintenance of public order during the transitional period while a new National Civil Police was set up.

A medal was established in January 1992 for which ninety days of service was required for qualification. It was instituted to supervise the ceasefire and to conduct general peacekeeping operations in El Salvador between the government and the FMLN. Countries providing troops to ONUSAL included Austria, Brazil, Canada, Chile, Columbia, Ecuador, France, Guyana, India, Ireland, Italy, Mexico, Norway, Spain, Sweden, the United States of America, Uruguay, and Venezuela.

India provided seven military observers in the period from 1991 to 1993. Indian service was also recognized with the 'El Salvador' bar to the Videsh Seva Medal (1052.237).

Outline

3013.100 medal.

3014 UNITED NATIONS IRAQ-KUWAIT OBSERVATION MISSION (UNIKOM), APRIL 1991- [16]

Awarded for service along the Iraq-Kuwait border with UNIKOM since 1991.

Established: By the United Nations General Assembly on 30 July 1959.

General Appearance: This is the standard UN peacekeeping medal (see 3004 for a description).

Ribbon: 34 mm, light canary-tan, 4 mm central medium blue stripe. The ribbon contains a narrow central stripe of UN blue, surrounded by two broad bands of a buff or desert colour.

Background: In the aftermath of the Gulf War, a UN observer force (UNIKOM) was deployed in a demilitarized zone straddling the Kuwait-Iraq border to ensure the inviolability, demarcation and guarantee of the frontier between the two states. UNIKOM was established in April 1991 to monitor a demilitarized zone established along the boundary between the states of Iraq and Kuwait and the Khor Abdullah.

The UNIKOM was authorized by United Nations Security Council Resolutions 689 (1991) of 9 April 1991, 687 (1991), and 806 (1993). The UNIKOM was established to patrol and supervise the demilitarized zone (DMZ) between Iraq and Kuwait (extending 10 km into Iraq and 5 km into Kuwait) in the aftermath of Gulf War II and to remove unexploded ordnance and clear mines. As of November 1994, UNIKOM had experienced three fatalities.

The medal is awarded for ninety days of service with UNIKOM after 3 April 1991. Nations providing troops to UNIKOM have been Argentina, Austria, Bangladesh, Canada, Chile, China, Denmark, Fiji, Finland, France, Germany, Ghana, Greece, Hungary, India, Indonesia, Ireland, Italy, Kenya,

[16] *Indian Army: Peacekeeping Operations*, pp. 58-59, 122.

Malaysia, Nigeria, Norway, Pakistan, Poland, Romania, Russia, Senegal, Singapore, Sweden, Switzerland, Syria, Thailand, Turkey, United Kingdom, United States of America, Uruguay, and Venezuela.

Indian involvement included a detachment of six military observers. One Indian has been killed while serving with UNIKOM (Major Ramani Shankar). As of 31 October 2001, six Indian observers were serving with this mission. Indian service was also recognized with the 'Iraq-Kuwait' bar to the Videsh Seva Medal (1052.238).

Outline

3014.100 medal.

3015 MISSION DES NATIONS UNIES POUR LE REFERENDUM DANS LE SAHARA OCCIDENTAL (MINURSO), SEPTEMBER 1991-

Awarded for service with MINURSO in the Western Sahara since 1991.

Established: MINURSO was established by S/RES/690 (1991) of 29 April 1991.

General Appearance: This is the standard UN peacekeeping medal (see 3004 for a description).

Ribbon: Light tan with edge stripes of medium blue, 4 mm UN blue, 26 mm tan, 4 mm UN blue. The medal has a very wide central band of a sandy brown colour, representing the Sahara Desert, with two narrow bands of UN blue at either end.

Background: MINURSO was established in May 1991, to enable the people of Western Sahara to choose freely between integration with Morocco or independence. It is awarded for ninety days of service after September 1991 with the Mission des nations unies pour le referendum dans le Sahara Occidental (or United Nations Mission for the Referendum in Western Sahara, MINURSO). MINURSO was established by the United Nations to supervise the ceasefire between Morocco and the POLISARIO (Frente Popular para la Liberacion de Saguia el-Hamra y Rio de Oro) and to monitor the transitional period to a referendum in the Western Sahara.

Troops have been provided by Argentina, Australia, Austria, Bangladesh, Belgium, Canada, China, Egypt, El Salvador, France, Germany, Ghana, Greece, Guinea, Honduras, Hungary, India, Ireland, Italy, Kenya, Malaysia, Nigeria, Norway, Pakistan, Peru, Poland, Portugal, the Republic of Korea, Russia, Switzerland, Togo, Tunisia, the United States of America, Uruguay, and Venezuela.

Indian service was also recognized with the 'Western Sahara' bar to the Videsh Seva Medal (1052.239).

Outline

3015.100 medal.

3016 UNITED NATIONS ADVANCE MISSION IN CAMBODIA (UNAMIC), NOVEMBER 1991-MARCH 1992[17]

Awarded for service with UNAMIC in Cambodia, 1991-92.

Established: UNAMIC was established by S/RES/717 (1991) of 16 October 1991.

General Appearance: This is the standard UN peacekeeping medal (see 3004 for a description).

Ribbon: UN Blue, with central stripes of broad red, narrow yellow, broad dark blue, medium white, broad dark blue, narrow yellow, and broad red. The medal ribbon contains a white central stripe flanked by dark blue, gold and red stripes, representing the Cambodian flags. These are bordered on either side by a band of UN blue.

Background: UNAMIC was established in October 1991 to assist the Cambodian Parties to facilitate communications between the military headquarters of the four Cambodian Parties in matters relating to the ceasefire and to undertake a mine-awareness training role. Subsequently, this mandate was extended to include training in mine clearance and the initiation of a de-mining programme. The mandate for this Mission expired in March 1992 with the establishment of the United Nations Transitional Authority in Cambodia.

The medal was awarded for ninety days of service with the UNAMIC between November 1991 and March 1992. UNAMIC was instituted to maintain the ceasefire in Cambodia, to initiate 'mine-awareness' among the populace, and to prepare for the deployment of UNTAC. Countries providing troops to UNAMIC included Algeria, Argentina, Australia, Austria, Bangladesh, Belgium, Canada, China, France, Germany, Ghana, India, Indonesia, Ireland, Malaysia, the Netherlands, New Zealand, Pakistan, Poland, Russia, Senegal, Thailand, Tunisia, the United Kingdom, the United States of America, and Uruguay.

Indian service was also recognized with the 'Cambodia' bar to the Videsh Seva Medal (1052.240).

Outline

3016.100 medal.

3017 UNITED NATIONS PROTECTION FORCE (UNPROFOR), MARCH 1992-DECEMBER 1995[18]

Awarded for service with UNPROFOR in former Yugoslavia, 1992-95.

Established: By S/RES/743 (1992) of 21 February 1992. This mandate was expanded by S/RES/758 (1992) of June 1992, S/RES/762 (1992) of 30 June 1992, S/RES/769 (1992) of 7 August 1992, S/RES/776 (1992) of September 1992, S/RES/779 (1992) of 6 October 1992, S/RES/781 (1992) of November 1992, S/RES/795 (1992) of December 1992, S/RES/816 (1993) of March 1993, S/RES/819 (1993) of April 1993, S/RES/824 (1993) of May 1993, S/RES/836 (1993) of June 1993, S/RES/

[17] *Indian Army: Peacekeeping Operations*, pp. 65-73, 116-17, 122.
[18] Ibid., pp. 60-63.

908 (1994) of March 1994, and S/RES/959 (1994) of November 1994. The final mandate of the force came to an end with the creation of the NATO-led Multinational Implementation Force (IFOR) in S/RES/1031 (1995) of 20 December 1995.

General Appearance: This is the standard UN peacekeeping medal (see 3004 for a description).

Ribbon: Medium blue, with green and brown stripes towards each edge and a red central stripe edged with thin white stripes. 2.5 mm UN blue, 5 mm dark green, 3 mm UN blue, 1 mm white, 8 mm red, 1 mm white, 3 mm UN blue, 5 mm dark brown, 2.5 mm UN blue. The colour combination of the ribbon for the medals and bars consists of a background of UN blue, with a central wide band of red representing the United Nations Protected Areas (UNPAs), flanked by thin stripes of white. On the left side there is a narrow band of green, representing forests, and on the right side a narrow band of brown, repre-senting the mountains.

Background: Since the Second World War, President Tito had preserved the Yugoslav state by a complicated balancing act between the three major nationalities—Serbs, Croats, and Slovenes—and lesser minorities. During 1990, the federal authority in Yugoslavia ceased to function. Serbia's attempts to re-establish a more central authority based in Belgrade with the ultimate aim of creating a greater Serbian state were opposed by Croatia and Slovenia and provoked their declarations of independence on 25 June 1990. The Croatian president gave no guarantees for the protection of minority rights. The pursuit of independent statehood placed the Muslim dominated and encircled presidency of Bosnia-Herzegovina in a dilemma leading to the subsequent declaration of its independence. These events led to ethnic conflict and civil war in the area. The European Community managed a ceasefire and a UN peacekeeping force was inducted in March 1992 with Lieutenant General Satish Nambiar of India as the Overall Force Commander. He stayed for a year and on completing his tenure returned to India. The UN force blamed the UN Headquarters for lack of a suitable directive for the force, whilst the UN noted a marked hesitancy on the part of their troops deployed in the field to force a way. The inability of the European Union to project a united policy or implement an effective response to the conflict discredited the Union and arguably encouraged the continuation of the conflict.

UNPROFOR was established in February 1992 as an interim arrangement to create the conditions of peace and security required for the negotiation of an overall settlement of the Yugoslavian crisis. The role of the UN troops was to ensure that areas designated as the UNPA's became and remained demilitarized and that all persons residing in these areas were protected from fear of armed attack. The role of UN police monitors was to ensure that local police forces carried out their duties without discriminating against persons of any nationality or abusing any human rights. The force also assisted the humanitarian agencies of the UN in the return of all displaced persons who so desired. There were several extensions of the original UNPROFOR covering the following purposes: reopening of the Sarajevo airport for humanitarian purposes; establishing a security zone encompassing Sarajevo and its airport; protection of convoys of released detainees in Bosnia and Herzegovina as requested by the International Committee of the Red Cross; monitoring arrangements for the complete withdrawal of the Yugoslavian Army from Croatia; the demilitarization of the Prevlaka peninsula and the removal of heavy weapons from neighbouring areas of Croatia and Montenegro; monitoring compliance with the ban on military flights; and the establishment of the United Nations presence in the former Yugoslav Republic of Macedonia. UNPROFOR also monitored the implementation of a ceasefire agreement requested by the Bosnian Government and Bosnian-Croat Forces in February 1994. In addition, UNPROFOR monitored ceasefire arrangements, negotiated between the Bosnian Government and Bosnian Serb forces, which became effective on 1 January 1995. On 31 March 1995, the Security Council decided to restructure UNPROFOR, replacing it with three separate but interrelated peacekeeping operations: UNCRO (United Nations Confidence Restoration Operation in Croatia), UNPREDEP (United Nations Preventive Deployment Force) under the joint theatre headquarters known as UNPF (United Nations Peace Forces) located in Zagreb. Eventually, following positive developments in the former Yugoslavia and the establishment of two new United Nations Missions in Bosnia-Herzegovina and Croatia, UNPF-HQ was phased out in January 1996.

The medal is awarded for ninety days of service with the United Nations Protection Force (Yugoslavia) (UNPROFOR) from March 1992 to December 1995. UNPROFOR was instituted to supervise the ceasefire and to conduct general peacekeeping operations in the former Socialist Federal Republic of Yugoslavia (full operations in Bosnia and Herzegovina, Croatia, Macedonia, Montenegro, and Serbia, with only a liaison presence in Slovenia). In addition, the operation was to provide security patrols, establish checkpoints, provide route maintenance, clear minefields, and construct and maintain shelters in Croatia and Bosnia-Herzegovina. Two phases of action were represented under UNPROFOR: Phase 1—March 1992 to spring 1994; Phase 2—spring 1994 to December 1995. UNPROFOR was subdivided into three operational units: UNPROFOR Croatia (later UNCRO, S/RES/981 [1995] of 31 March 1995), UNPROFOR Bosnia and Herzegovina (later UNMIBH, S/RES/1035 [1995] of 21 December 1995), and UNPROFOR Macedonia (later UNPREDEP, S/RES/983 [1995] of March 1995).

Countries providing troops to the full UNPROFOR included Argentina, Australia, Bangladesh, Belgium, Brazil, Canada, Colombia, Congo, the Czech Republic, Denmark, Egypt, Finland, France, Germany, Ghana, Indonesia, India, Ireland, Jordan, Kenya, Lithuania, Luxembourg, Malaysia, Nepal, the Netherlands, New Zealand, Nigeria, Norway, Pakistan, Poland, Portugal, the Russian Federation, Senegal, the Slovak Republic,

Spain, Sweden, Switzerland, Thailand, Tunisia, Turkey, the Ukraine, the United Kingdom, the United States of America, and Venezuela.

Indian service included only the first head of mission, Lieutenant-General Satish Nambiar, and a staff officer. Indian service was also recognized with the 'Yugoslavia' bar to the Videsh Seva Medal (1052.241).

Outline

3017.100 medal.

3018 UNITED NATIONS TRANSITIONAL AUTHORITY IN CAMBODIA (UNTAC), MARCH 1992-SEPTEMBER 1993[19]

Awarded for service with UNTAC in Cambodia, 1992-93.

Established: UNTAC was authorized by S/RES/745 (1992) of 28 February 1992.

General Appearance: This is the standard UN peacekeeping medal (see 3004 for a description).

Ribbon: Dark green, with a central stripe of medium blue, edged with thin black stripes; in the centre, thin red, white, red strips. 9 mm dark green, 1 mm dark blue, 4 mm UN blue, 1 mm red, 3 mm white, 1 mm red, 4 mm UN blue, 1 mm dark blue, 9 mm dark green. The medal ribbon and bars feature green, to depict the paddy fields that cover most of the country. The white central stripe is flanked by red stripes representing all the factions' flags. These are bordered on either side by a band of UN blue and Supreme National Council blue.

Background: The UNTAC was set up to organize and conduct elections, including writing the electoral law, registering voters and supervising the polls. UNTAC's military role was to stabilize the security situation and build confidence among the parties to the conflict. Verification of the withdrawal of foreign forces, supervision of the ceasefire, including regroupment, cantonment, disarming and demobilization, weapon control and mine clearance, were specific military tasks.

UNTAC was established in February 1992, incorporating the existing Mission, UNAMIC. The mandate for this Mission relates to human rights, the organization and conduct of free and fair elections, military arrangements, civil administration, the maintenance of law and order, the repatriation and resettlement of the Cambodian refugees and displaced persons, and the rehabilitation of essential Cambodian infrastructures during the transitional period. After the elections, the Mission was closed on 15 November 1993 and replaced by the United Nations Military Liaison Team (UNMLT), consisting of twenty military observers, whose task was to maintain close liaison with the Cambodian government, to report to the Secretary-General on matters affecting security in Cambodia and to assist the government in dealing with residual military matters related to the Paris Agreement. UNMLT was established for a single period of six months. Military observers are eligible to receive the UNTAC medal.

[19] *Indian Army: Peacekeeping Operations,* pp. 65-73, 116-17, 122.

UNTAC was a success of restraint and tactful diplomacy of UN peacekeeping. The Khmer Rouge were to have been disarmed as per the UN treaty, but they kept their weapons and remained in their strongholds. Consequently, other factions had to be given their surrendered weapons for their self-defence. The atmosphere was tense, punctuated by violence and intimidation, and obstacles that often seemed insuperable. Despite the dice being heavily loaded against UNTAC, elections took place as scheduled and all the participants accepted the results.

The medal is awarded for ninety days of service with the UNTAC, March 1992 to December 1993. UNTAC was set up (absorbing UNAMIC) to monitor the implementation of a constitution and supervise elections (May 1993) in Cambodia. UNTAC included troops from Algeria, Argentina, Australia, Austria, Bangladesh, Belgium, Brunei Darussalam, Bulgaria, Cameroon, Canada, Chile, China, Columbia, Egypt, Fiji, France, Germany, Ghana, Hungary, India, Indonesia, Ireland, Italy, Japan, Jordan, Kenya, Malaysia, Morocco, Namibia, Nepal, the Netherlands, New Zealand, Nigeria, Norway, Pakistan, the Philippines, Poland, Russia, Senegal, Singapore, Sweden, Thailand, Tunisia, the United Kingdom, the United States of America, and Uruguay.

India provided a contingent of 1,373 all ranks, from 1992-94, for the military tasks. This consisted of an infantry battalion (1st Assam followed by 4th J&K Rifles on relief), a field ambulance company, a mine training team, sixteen staff personnel, and seventeen military observers. Indian service was also recognized with the 'Cambodia' bar to the Videsh Seva Medal (1052.240).

Outline

3018.100 medal.

3019 UNITED NATIONS OPERATIONS IN SOMALIA, UNOSOM I, APRIL 1992-APRIL 1993, AND UNOSOM II, MAY 1993-MARCH 1995, AND THE UNIFIED TASK FORCE (UNTIAF), APRIL 1993-MAY 1993[20]

Awarded for service in Somalia with UNOSOM and UNTIAF, 1993-95.

Established: UNOSOM I was authorized by S/RES/751 (1992) of 24 April 1992. This original mission was augmented by S/RES/794 (1991) of 28 August 1992 (the Security Council augmented UNOSOM I's mission with the creation of the Unified Task Force [UNITAF]). By S/RES/814 (1993) of 26 March 1993, the Security Council reverted UNITAF's armed mission to the original peacekeeping focus, and constituted UNOSOM II. UNOSOM II's mission was clarified and expanded under S/RES/837 (1993) of June 1993 and S/RES/886 (1993) of 1993. The mission of UNISOM was ended with S/RES/897 (1994) of 4 February 1994.

General Appearance: This is the standard UN peacekeeping medal (see 3004 for a description).

[20] *Indian Army: Peacekeeping Operations*, pp. 78-91, 116-17, 121-22.

Ribbon: 34 mm, tan-yellow ('sand'), medium blue centre with green edges. 10 mm light yellow, 2 mm light green, 10 mm UN blue, 2 mm light green, and 10 mm light yellow. The background of the ribbon is sand or buff coloured symbolizing the desert, with a wide centre band of UN blue flanked by narrow stripes of dark green symbolizing hope.

Background: Somalia occupies a strategic location in the Horn of Africa. Due to war with Ethiopia over Ogaden and the corrupt dictatorship of Said Barre, Somalia's political and economic situation deteriorated steadily through the 1950s. Said's overthrow led to the emergence of some fifteen political leaders (including General Aided and Alt Mahdi) which resulted in clan wars, famine, and total lawlessness. Relief efforts failed despite UN deployment (UNOSOM I) due to armed gangs, either associated with Somali factions or operating independently, who looted relief agencies. In early December 1992, the UN approved a large-scale deployment of troops in Somalia (about 37,000) which finally took the shape of Operation Continue Hope in May 1993 (UNOSOM II).

UNOSOM was established on 24 April 1992 by Security Council Resolution 751. In accordance with the agreements reached with the two main Somali factions in Mogadishu, the ceasefire in the capital was to be monitored by a group of fifty unarmed, uniformed United Nations military observers. The observers were to be deployed along the demarcation line separating Mogadishu into two zones. As regards humanitarian assistance, the security personnel envisaged in the agreements were to provide protection and security for United Nations personnel, equipment and supplies at the port of Mogadishu and escort deliveries of humanitarian supplies from there to distribution centres in the city and its immediate environs. They were also to provide security for United Nations personnel, equipment and supplies at the airport in Mogadishu. They were to provide the United Nations convoys of relief supplies with a sufficiently strong military escort to deter attack; they were authorized to fire in self-defence as a last resort if deterrence should not prove effective. On 28 August, the Security Council, by its Resolution 775 authorized an increase in strength of UNOSOM by four additional UN security units, for the protection of the humanitarian convoys and distribution centres throughout Somalia. Several of the Somali de facto authorities refused to agree to the deployment of United Nations troops and only one battalion and military observers were deployed to Mogadishu. Relief ships were blocked from docking and even shelled. Air and seaports came under fire resulting in the non-delivery of relief supplies to areas where the need was most acute. On 3 December 1992, the Security Council authorized the use of all necessary means to establish, as soon as possible, a secure environment for humanitarian and relief operations in Somalia. The first elements of the Unified Task Force, spearheaded by the United States of America, were deployed in Mogadishu on 9 December 1992. Once their task was accomplished, the military command was handed over to the United Nations. Meanwhile, UNOSOM remained fully responsible for the political aspects and for humanitarian assistance to Somalia. In February 1994, after several violent incidents and attacks on United Nations soldiers, the Security Council revised UNOSOM II's mandate to exclude the use of coercive methods. UNOSOM II was withdrawn in early March 1995.

The medal is awarded for ninety days of service with the United Nations Operation in Somalia (UNOSOM) from April 1992 to March 1995. The United Nations authorized UNOSOM—including UNOSOM I (24 April-28 August 1992), UNITAF (28 August 1992-26 March 1993), and UNISOM II (26 March 1993-March 1995)—to protect aid-delivery agencies, to ensure the delivery of relief supplies to Somalia, and to oversee the establishment of peace and stable government in the country. These operations were carried out by the United Nations in close cooperation with the League of Arab States, the Organization of the Islamic Conference, the Organization of African Unity, the Standing Committee of the Countries of the Horn, and the Non-Aligned Movement.

The nations providing troops included Argentina, Australia, Austria, Bangladesh, Belgium, Botswana, Canada, Czechoslovakia (former), Egypt, Fiji, Finland, France, Germany, Ghana, Greece, Hungary, India, Indonesia, Ireland, Italy, Jordan, the Republic of Korea, Kuwait, Malawi, Malaysia, Morocco, Namibia, Nepal, the Netherlands, New Zealand, Nigeria, Norway, Pakistan, the Philippines, Romania, Saudi Arabia, Sweden, Tunisia, Turkey, the United Arab Emirates, the United States of America, Zambia, and Zimbabwe.

Indian service included Indian troops which arrived in Mogadishu on 23 August 1993; the last Indian troops left on 23 December 1994. For UNTIAF, three naval ships (INS *Deepak*, INS *Kuthar*, and INS *Cheeta*) were contributed, the first Indian Navy deployment on UN service. For UNOSOM II, more troops were deployed in the form of the 66th (Independent) Brigade Group, consisting of the 1st Bihar, 5th Mahars, 2nd J&K Light Infantry, 3rd Mechanized Infantry (former 1/8th Gorkha Rifles), one squadron of the 7th Cavalry, the 8722nd Light Battery, the 6th Reconnaissance and Observation Flight of the Army Aviation Corps, and an IAF helicopter detachment, a detachment from the Remount and Veterinary Corps, and associated logistical units. In sum, troops from all three branches, from the Indian Army, Navy, and Air Force, took part in this mission. The brigade reached Mogadishu in August-September 1993. The formation was to receive much praise in the ensuing year, both from the Somalis and from the UN, for the manner in which it carried out its mission. Its commander was Brigadier M.P. Bhagat.

By March 1994 it was decided to send an Indian naval task force to bring back the brigade. The Indian Navy played a major part in the Indian contribution to the UN task force in Somalia. During induction in 1993, three ships, including the INS *Survana*, had brought 66th (Independent) Brigade to Mogadishu from India. On 6 December 1994, another Indian naval task force set-off from India to bring back the formation.

It consisted of the frigates INS *Ganga*, INS *Godavari*, and a logistics ship, INS *Shakti*, under Commodore P. Kaushiva.

Members of the naval staff and commanding officers from the brigade met regularly and problems were settled as they arose, on board INS *Ganga*. On December 9 and 10, the *Ro Ro* ship and the cargo ship from Bombay berthed at Kismayu. The task force sailed north from Kismayu on the night of 11/12 December and arrived in Mogadishu the following afternoon. Here it provided support for the other troops of the brigade until the final evacuation on 23 December. The meticulous planning and organization of the Indian task force gave 66th (Independent) Brigade complete protection during their evacuation. There were no casualties, nor damage to equipment. This was the first instance in the history of the United Nations that a naval task force from Asia had been deployed for such a task.

Decorations were awarded for this service as follows: 1 Param Vishisht Seva Medal, 2 Shaurya Chakras, 2 Sena Medals, 1 UN Force Commander's Citation. Fourteen Indians were killed while serving with UNOSOM II. Indian service was also recognized with the 'Somalia' bar to the Videsh Seva Medal (1052.243).

Outline

3019.100 medal.

3020 OPERACAO DAS NACOES UNIDAS EM MOCAMBIQUE (ONUMOZ), DECEMBER 1992-DECEMBER 1994[21]

Awarded for service with ONUMOZ in Mozambique, 1992-94.

Established: ONUMOZ was authorized by S/RES/797 of 16 December 1992.

General Appearance: This is the standard UN peacekeeping medal (see 3004 for a description).

Ribbon: Medium blue with (reading inwards) light green and white edge stripes. 5 mm light green, 5 mm white, 13 mm UN blue, 5 mm white, 5 mm light green. The colour combination for the ribbon and bars consists of a central wide band of UN blue flanked by two narrow bands of white, representing Peace, and two bands in green on the sides, representing the tropical climate of Mozambique.

Background: After the collapse in 1974 of almost five centuries of Portuguese colonial rule in Africa, Mozambique entered one year of transitional government before gaining independence in June 1975. This was followed by a split in the main freedom party that led to sixteen years of civil war. The economy was devastated and almost 1.5 million Mozambicans fled to neighbouring countries.

Towards the late 1980s, Mozambique, formerly a Marxist-Leninist state, steadily moved towards liberalization and democratization. Mediation by the Catholic Church led to a General Peace Agreement being signed in Rome in October

[21] *Indian Army: Peacekeeping Operations*, pp. 74-77, 122.

1992, between the warring factions. Pursuant to the agreement a UN force, ONUMOZ was inducted in the beginning of 1993 with the mandate of monitoring peace, leading to free and fair presidential and parliamentary elections. By April 1993, the military component comprising the contingent for 'peace-keeping' and the 'observer group for demobilizing the two Armies and monitoring of the ceasefire' had been deployed.

The ONUMOZ mission was established by Security Council Resolution 782 of 13 October 1992 to monitor and verify the ceasefire, the separation and concentration of forces, their demobilization and the collection, storage, and destruction of weapons; to monitor and verify the complete withdrawal of foreign forces; to monitor and verify the disbanding of private and irregular armed groups; to authorize security arrangements for vital infrastructures; to provide security for the United Nations and other international activities in support of the peace process, especially in the corridors; to provide technical assistance and monitor the entire electoral process; to co-ordinate and monitor all humanitarian assistance operations, in particular those related to refugees, internally displaced persons, demobilized military personnel, and the affected local population, and to facilitate the implementation of the general peace agreement for Mozambique. Upon completion of the task, the mission was terminated in January 1995.

The medal was awarded for ninety days of service with ONUMOZ, December 1992 to December 1994. ONUMOZ was set up to monitor the ceasefire, oversee mine clearing operations, and conduct the subsequent peace negotiations between the government of Mozambique and RENAMO (Resistência Nacional Moçambicana). ONUMOZ included troops from Argentina, Australia, Austria, Bangladesh, Botswana, Brazil, Canada, Cape Verde, China, the Czech Republic, Egypt, Ghana, Guinea-Bissau, Guyana, Hungary, India, Indonesia, Ireland, Italy, Japan, Jordan, Malaysia, Nepal, the Netherlands, New Zealand, Nigeria, Norway, Pakistan, Portugal, Russia, Spain, Sri Lanka, Sweden, Switzerland, Togo, the United States of America, Uruguay, and Zambia.

On establishment of ONUMOZ, the Indian Army contributed eighteen military observers, twenty-one staff officers, two engineer companies, one logistics company and one headquarters company. After a year, these troops returned home. The engineer companies had carried out combat engineering tasks and various civic action schemes. The logistics company provided transportation and supply cover, whilst the headquarters company provided provost and clerical support. Indian service also included members of the BSF during 1994. Two Indians were killed while serving with ONUMOZ. Indian service was also recognized with the 'Mozambique' bar to the Videsh Seva Medal (1052.244).

Outline

3020.000 medal.

3021 UNITED NATIONS MISSION IN HAITI (UNMIH), SEPTEMBER 1993-JUNE 1996

Awarded for service in Haiti with UNMIH, 1993-96, this medal also covers service with UNTMIH (United Nations Transition Mission in Haiti) in 1997 and UIPONUH (United Nations Civilian Police Mission in Haiti) 1997-2000.

Established: By S/RES/867 (1993) of 22 September 1993; the status of UNMIH was extended by S/RES/940 (1994) of 19 September 1994.

General Appearance: This is the standard UN peacekeeping medal (see 3004 for a description).

Ribbon: UN blue, with broad centre stripes of blue (left) and red (right), these stripes are edged off from the UN blue edges by thin white stripes. The colour combination for the ribbon consists of the royal blue and red of the Republic of Haiti, bordered by the UN blue with two white lines denoting friendship between the two.

Background: It was originally established to help implement certain provisions of the Governors Island Agreement signed by the Haitian parties on 3 July 1993. In 1993, UNMIH's mandate was to assist in modernizing the armed forces of Haiti and establishing a new police force. That mandate could not be carried out due to the non-cooperation of the Haitian military authorities. Later, The Security Council by its Resolution 940 of 31 July 1994 approved the establishment of an advance team of UNMIH to institute the appropriate means of coordination with the multinational force, to carry out the monitoring of the operations of the force, to assess requirements and to prepare for the deployment of UNMIH upon completion of the mission of the multinational force.

The medal was awarded for ninety days of service with the United Nations Mission in Haiti (UNMIH) between September 1993 and June 1996. UNMIH was instituted to supervise the elections and conduct general peacekeeping operations in Haiti. Countries which provided troops to UNMIH included Algeria, Antigua and Barbuda, Argentina, Austria, Bahamas, Bangladesh, Barbados, Belize, Benin, Canada, Djibouti, France, Guatemala, Guinea-Bissau, Guyana, Honduras, India, Ireland, Indonesia, Jamaica, Jordan, Madagascar, Mali, Nepal, the Netherlands, New Zealand, Pakistan, the Philippines, Russia, St. Kitts and Nevis, St. Lucia, Senegal, Spain, Surinam, Switzerland, Togo, Trinidad and Tobago, Tunisia, the United States of America, and Venezuela.

UNTMIH was the third in the series of UN Peacekeeping Operations in Haiti. It was established by Security Council Resolution 1123 of 30 July 1997 for a single four-month period ending on 30 November 1997. It was established to assist the Government of Haiti by supporting and contributing to the professionalization of the Haitian National Police (HNP). The countries of Argentina, Benin, Canada, France, India, Mali, Niger, Pakistan, Senegal, Togo, Tunisia and the United States of America provided civilian police and military personnel to this mission.

UNTMIH was succeeded in December 1997 by the United Nations Civilian Police Mission in Haiti (MIPONUH). The Security Council established MIPONUH by its Resolution 1141 (1997) of 28 November 1997. Unlike the three previous missions, MIPONUH had no military component. Its mandate was to continue the work of the United Nations to support the Haitian National Police and to contribute to its professionalization. These countries provided civilian police personnel: Argentina, Benin, Canada, France, India, Mali, Niger, Senegal, Togo, Tunisia and the United States of America. Indian service included members of the BSF during 1997.

Indian service was also recognized with the 'Haiti' bar to the Videsh Seva Medal (1052.245).

Outline

3021.100 medal.

3022 UNITED NATIONS OBSERVER MISSION IN LIBERIA (UNOMIL), SEPTEMBER 1993-[22]

Awarded for service with UNOMIL in Liberia after 1993.

Established: The medal was authorized in March 1994. UNOMIL was established by S/RES/ 866 (1993) of 22 September 1993. The mandate of UNOMIL was expanded by S/RES/1020 (1995) of 1995.

General Appearance: This is the standard UN peacekeeping medal (see 3004 for a description).

Ribbon: A UN blue centre stripe, with broad edge stripes on the left (reading inwards) of green and white and, on the right (also reading inwards) of red and white. The ribbon contains one centred stripe of United Nations blue that is flanked by white stripes on either side representing peace. On the left there is a stripe of deep blue representing the Atlantic Ocean littoral with its reliefs, heights, greens, and rains. On the right, the red stripe represents the sacrifice of human blood in the terrible carnage.

Background: Liberia, the second oldest black republic in the world (after Haiti), survived the decolonization of its neighbours without disturbance. The American-Liberian elite had maintained control since the nineteenth century and they continued for most of the twentieth century. In 1980, the American-Liberian rulers were overthrown by a bloody military coup led by Master Sergeant Doe who turned out to be a military dictator and nine years later some of his colleagues rebelled.

The subsequent civil war destroyed the central government and law and order throughout the country. The UN showed no disposition to involve itself in the bloody struggle as Liberia tore itself to pieces. However, the lead was taken by the Economic Community of West African States (ECOWAS), which created a military observer group (ECOMOG) and set about the task of peacemaking and peacekeeping. ECOWAS consists of sixteen states, the most important being Liberia's three neighbours plus Nigeria, Ghana, and Senegal.

[22] *Indian Army: Peacekeeping Operations*, pp. 96-97.

In July 1993, the UN Secretary General's representative, the Executive Secretary of ECOWAS, and the President of the OAU chaired a meeting at which the parties signed an agreement on a series of steps leading to elections, starting with a ceasefire on 1 August to be monitored by ECOMOG and UN observers.

UNOMIL was established on 22 September 1993 by Security Council Resolution 866 (1993) to receive and investigate all reports of alleged incidents of violations of the ceasefire agreement and, if the violation could not be corrected, to report its findings to the Violations Committee and to the Secretary General. In addition, the mission was to monitor compliance with the embargo on the delivery of arms and military equipment to Liberia and the cantonment, to monitor disarmament and demobilization of combatants, and to observe and verify the election process. The United Nations Military Observers have been working in close cooperation with a peacekeeping force (ECOMOG) provided by a sub-regional community, ECOWAS.

Countries that have provided troops to UNOMIL include Austria, Bangladesh, Belgium, Brazil, China, the Czech Republic, Egypt, Guinea-Bissau, Hungary, India, Jordan, Kenya, Malaysia, Nepal, the Netherlands, Pakistan, Poland, Russia, Slovakia, Sweden, and Uruguay. As of 1998, UNOMIL comprised 500 personnel, including 300 military observers. The medal is awarded for ninety days of service with the UNOMIL after September 1993.

Indian service included a detachment of twenty military observers in 1994. Indian service was also recognized with the 'Liberia' bar to the Videsh Seva Medal (1052.246).

Outline

3022.000 medal.

3023 UNITED NATIONS ASSISTANCE MISSION IN RWANDA (UNAMIR), OCTOBER 1993-MARCH 1996[23]

Awarded for service with UNAMIR in Rwanda, 1993-96.

Established: The medal was authorized in December 1993 by United Nations Security Council Resolution 872 of 5 October 1993.

General Appearance: This is the standard UN peacekeeping medal (see 3004 for a description).

Ribbon: The ribbon contains a wide centred stripe of UN blue flanked by a narrow stripe of white and three equal stripes of black, green, and red. The black colour represents the volcanic lava and the world famous gorillas of the area; green is the colour of the local bush vegetation; and red represents the African soil.

Background: In Rwanda, the majority of the population belongs to the agriculturist Hutu tribe, but historically power has rested with the pastoralist Tutsis. Fighting broke out between the predominantly Hutu-Rwandese Armed Forces and the Rwandese Patriotic Front (RPF) across the Ugandan border. In 1990 ceasefires were arranged, however, warfare resumed in early 1993 while Organisation for African Unity (OAU) and

[23] *Indian Army: Peacekeeping Operations*, pp. 92-95, 117.

Tanzanian sponsored negotiations were in progress between the combatants.

Rwanda and Uganda addressed the Security Council and a UN Observer Mission Uganda-Rwanda (UNOMUR) was deployed. In October, the Council authorized the establishment of a UN Assistance Mission for Rwanda (UNAMIR) that was to work towards the secure installation and subsequent operation of a transitional government. It would provide for repatriation of about 900,000 Rwandese refugees and displaced persons.

UNAMIR was established by Security Council Resolution 872 (1993) of 5 October 1993 to monitor the ceasefire, security situation, process of repatriation of refugees, to assist with mine clearance, the coordination of humanitarian assistance, and to contribute to the security of the city of Kigali. UNAMIR also contributed to the security of personnel of the International Tribunal for Rwanda and of human rights offices in Rwanda and assisted in the establishment and training of a new, integrated national police force. On 6 April 1994, the president of Rwanda (a Hutu) was killed in a missile attack on his aircraft. This led to the murder of the prime minister who was a Tutsi. Thereupon, an organized massacre of the minority Tutsi community and moderate Hutus started. At this time, the UN had about 2,500 personnel in Kigali but the force did not have the mandate, or the numbers, or the equipment to quell what amounted to a sudden nationwide explosion of internecine violence which saw a mass exodus and the killing of more than 250,000 people. The UNAMIR mandate came to an end in March 1996.

A medal was established in December 1993. UNAMIR was instituted to supervise the ceasefire and to conduct general peacekeeping operations in Rwanda (this is a Rwanda-side sibling operation to UNOMUR). Ninety days of service is required for qualification. Countries which provided troops to UNAMIR included Argentina, Australia, Austria, Bangladesh, Belgium, Canada, Chad, Congo, Djibouti, Egypt, Ethiopia, Fiji, Ghana, Guinea, Guinea-Bissau, Guyana, India, Jordan, Malawi, Mali, the Netherlands, Niger, Nigeria, Poland, Romania, the Russian Federation, Senegal, Togo, Tunisia, the United Kingdom, Uruguay, and Zimbabwe.

Indian service included a battalion group of the 1/3rd Gorkhas, a signal company, an engineer company, nine staff officers, and a detachment of twenty military observers. The 1/3rd Gorkha Rifles assisted in the move of over 70,000 internally displaced persons as also the movement of about 7,000 prisoners to other areas. It looked after eight orphanages, several schools and gave much needed medical assistance to the locals. Both the signal and the engineer companies earned high praise for their devoted service. One award of the Sena Medal was granted for this service (to Major Abhay Krishna, 6th Rajputana Rifles). Indian service was also recognized with the 'Rwanda' bar to the Videsh Seva Medal (1052.247).

Outline

3023.100 medal.

3024 UNITED NATIONS MISSION IN BOSNIA AND HERZEGOVINA (UNMIBH), DECEMBER 1995-

Awarded for service in Bosnia and Herzegovina with UMBIBH after 1995.

Established: The medal was authorized in August 1996. UNMIBH was established by S/RES/1035 (1995) of 21 December 1995.

General Appearance: This is the standard UN peacekeeping medal (see 3004 for a description).

Ribbon: Five equal bars, left to right: light green, UN blue, white, UN blue, red. The centre is white, representing peace, flanked by UN blue on either side; on the left is a stripe of light green representing the forests in spring in Bosnia-Herzegovina, and, on the right, a red colour symbolizing the sunrise over the mountains of this country.

Background: This mission was established in December 1995 under the Resolution 1035 (1995) for a period of one year from the transfer of authority from the United Nations Protection Force (UNPF) to the multinational implementation force (IFOR). The main tasks of the United Nations civilian police force include monitoring, observing and inspecting law enforcement activities; training and advising law enforcement personnel; facilitating within the International Police Task Force mission of assistance, the parties' law enforcement activities; and ensuring the existence of conditions for free and fair elections.

The medal was awarded for ninety days of service with United Nations Mission in Bosnia and Herzegovina (UNMIBH) after March 1995. UNMIBH was instituted to oversee the full implementation of the Dayton Peace Agreement in Bosnia and Herzegovina. Countries providing troops to UNMIBH include Argentina, Austria, Bangladesh, Bulgaria, Canada, Chile, Denmark, Egypt, Estonia, Fiji, Finland, France, Germany, Ghana, Greece, Hungary, Iceland, India, Indonesia, Ireland, Italy, Jordan, Kenya, Malaysia, Nepal, the Netherlands, Nigeria, Norway, Pakistan, Poland, Portugal, Russia, Senegal, Spain, Sweden, Switzerland, Thailand, Turkey, the Ukraine, the United Kingdom, and the United States of America. Indian service included members of the BSF during 1996-99.

Indian service was also recognized with the 'Bosnia-Herzegovina' bar to the Videsh Seva Medal (1052.249). Approximately 135 of these medals are beleived to have been awarded.

Outline

3024.100 medal.

3025 UNITED NATIONS OBSERVER MISSION IN ANGOLA (MONUA), JULY 1997-

Awarded for service in Angola with MONUA after 1997.

Established: To date, no medal has been established though it is expected. MONUA was established by S/RES/1118 (1997) of 30 June 1997.

General Appearance: This is expected to be the standard UN peacekeeping medal (see 3004 for a description).

Ribbon: Unknown at present.

Background: To date, no medal has been issued for the United Nations Observer Mission in Angola (MONUA), but one is expected to be forthcoming, along normal UN lines. MONUA, the immediate successor body to UNAVEM III (3010), was instituted to encourage peace and national reconciliation in Angola after January 1997, in the context of the 31 May 1991 and the Lusaka Protocol of 20 November 1994. Countries providing troops to MONUA include Bangladesh, Brazil, Bulgaria, Congo, Egypt, France, Guinea Bissau, Hungary, India, Jordan, Kenya, Malaysia, Mali, Namibia, the Netherlands, New Zealand, Nigeria, Norway, Pakistan, Poland, Portugal, Romania, Russia, Senegal, the Slovak Republic, Sweden, Tanzania, the Ukraine, Uruguay, Zambia, and Zimbabwe.

Indian service included the force commander, Brigadier V.K. Saksena, an infantry battalion group (of the 14th Punjab and 16th Guards), and engineer company (417th Independent Field Company and 386th Independent Field Company), and a detachment of military observers. It also included members of the BSF during 1995. Indian service was also recognized with the 'Angola' bar to the Videsh Seva Medal (1052.231).

Outline

3025.100 medal.

3026 UNITED NATIONS INTERIM FORCE IN LEBANON (UNIFIL), MARCH 1978-

Awarded for ninety days of service with UNIFIL since 19 March 1978.

General Appearance: This is the standard UN peacekeeping medal (see 3004 for a description).

Established: UNIFIL was established by S/RES 425 (1978) and 426 (1978) of 19 March 1978.

Ribbon: 33 mm, 9 mm UN medium blue, 11 mm green centre stripe edged with 3 mm white stripes with 1 mm red centre stripes; 9 mm UN medium blue, 1 mm white, 1 mm red, 1 mm white, 11 mm green, 1 mm white, 1 mm red, 1 mm white, 9 mm UN medium blue. The ribbon bears three equal bands of the UN colours: blue, green and UN blue. The bands are separated by two equal sized white stripes, each bisected by a narrow red line. The colours represent the UN and Lebanese flags.

Background: This mission was established in March 1978 to confirm the withdrawal of Israeli forces from southern Lebanon, to restore international peace and security, and to assist the Government of Lebanon in ensuring the return of its effective authority in the area. The mission continues to the present date.

The medal is awarded for ninety days of service with UNIFIL since 19 March 1978. The United Nations Interim Force in Lebanon was authorized by United Nations Security Council Resolutions 425 (1978) and 426 (1978), both of 19 March 1978.

UNIFIL was created to supervise the Israeli withdrawal after their invasion of Lebanon on the night of 14/15 March 1978; to date this mission has not been fully accomplished.

As of 31 October 2001, 810 Indian troops were serving with UNIFIL. Indian service was also recognized with the 'Lebanon' bar to the Videsh Seva Medal (1052.207).

Outline

3026.100 medal.

3027 UNITED NATIONS OBSERVER MISSION IN SIERRA LEONE (UNOMSIL) AND UNITED NATIONS MISSION IN SIERRA LEONE (UNAMSIL), JULY 1988-

Awarded for service with UNOMSIL and UNAMSIL in Sierra Leone after 1988.

General Appearance: This is the standard UN peacekeeping medal (see 3004 for a description).

Established: UNOMSIL was established by Security Council Resolution 1181 (1998) of 13 July 1998. UNAMSIL was established by Security Council Resolution 1270 (1999) of 22 October 1999.

Ribbon: Medium blue, with broad edge stripes (reading inwards) or dark blue, white, and green.

Background: After a few years of civil war, in June 1998 the Secretary General reported to the Council (S/1998/486) that the priority task in Sierra Leone was to promote stability and security by disarming and demobilizing former combatants. The United Nations could render immediate assistance by deploying a limited number of unarmed military observers. The Security Council welcomed this proposal and established UNOMSIL for an initial period of six months. UNOMSIL's purpose is to monitor the military and security situation in the country as a whole, as security conditions permit; monitor the disarmament and demobilization of former combatants concentrated in secure areas of the country; assist in monitoring respect for international humanitarian law, including at disarmament and demobilization sites, where security permits; advise, in coordination with other international efforts, the Government of Sierra Leone and local police officials on police practice, training, re-equipment and recruitment, in particular on the need to respect internationally accepted standards of policing in democratic societies. Qualifying time for the medal is ninety days of service in the mission.

Personnel contributors are China, Egypt, India, Kenya, Kyrgysztan, New Zealand, Pakistan, the Russian Federation, the United Kingdom, and Zambia.

On 22 October 1999, the Security Council authorized the establishment of UNAMSIL by its resolution 1270 (1999), a new and much larger mission with a maximum of 6,000 military personnel, including 260 military observers, to assist the government and the parties in carrying out provisions of the Lome peace agreement. At the same time, the Council decided to terminate UNOMSIL.

Personnel contributors include Bangladesh, Bolivia, Canada, China, Croatia, Czech Republic, Denmark, Egypt, France, Gambia, Ghana, Guinea, India, Indonesia, Jordan, Kenya, Kyrgyzstan, Malaysia, Mali, Namibia, Nepal, New Zealand, Nigeria, Norway, Pakistan, Russian Federation, Senegal, Slovak Republic, Sweden, Thailand, Ukraine, United Kingdom, United Republic of Tanzania, Uruguay, Zimbabwe, and Zambia.

As of 31 October 2001, Indian troops were serving with UNAMSIL. Indian service was also recognized with the 'Sierra Leone' bar to the Videsh Seva Medal (1052.250).

Outline

3027.100 medal.

3028 UNITED NATIONS INTERIM ADMINISTRATION MISSION IN KOSOVO (UNMIK), JUNE 1999-

Awarded for six months of service with UNMIK in Kosovo after 1999.

Established: In September 1999.

General Appearance: This is the standard UN peacekeeping medal (see 3004 for a description).

Ribbon: The ribbon has two outer bands of light UN blue, symbolizing the presence of the United Nations. The inner band in dark blue symbolizes the International Security presence and the cooperation and support received from it. The two bands in white symbolize the overall objective to promote peace for all the people in Kosovo.

Background: UNMIK was established on 10 June 1999 by adoption of the Security Council Resolution 1244. The goal of the mission is the resolution of the grave humanitarian situation in Kosovo, through the implementation of the return of refugees and the prevention of escalation of the conflict between parties in the region.

Countries that have contributed are Argentina, Austria, Bangladesh, Belgium, Benin, Bolivia, Bulgaria, Canada, Chile, Côte D'Ivoire, Czech Republic, Denmark, Dominican Republic, Egypt, Estonia, Fiji, Finland, France, Gambia, Germany, Ghana, Greece, Hungary, Iceland, India, Ireland, Italy, Jordan, Kenya, Kyrgyztan, Lithuania, Malawi, Malaysia, Nepal, Netherlands, New Zealand, Niger, Nigeria, Norway, Pakistan, Philippines, Poland, Portugal, Romania, Russian Federation, Senegal, Slovenia, Spain, Sweden, Switzerland, Tunisia, Turkey, Ukraine, United Kingdom of Great Britain and Northern Ireland, United States of America, Zambia, Zimbabwe.

As of 31 October 2001, 538 Indian police were serving with this mission. Indian service was also recognized with the 'Kosovo' bar to the Videsh Seva Medal (1052.251).

Outline

3028.100 medal.

3029 UNITED NATIONS OBSERVER MISSION IN THE DEMOCRATIC REPUBLIC OF THE CONGO (MONUC), FEBRUARY 2000-

Awarded for ninety days of service with MONUC in the Democratic Republic of the Congo after 2000.

Established: 2 May 2000.

General Appearance: This is the standard UN peacekeeping medal (see 3004 for a description).

Ribbon: The ribbon has two outer bands of UN blue, representing the UN presence in the Democratic Republic of Congo (DRC). Inside the two bands, there are two equal bars in yellow; they represent the dawn of peace and prosperity. The dark blue in the middle of the yellow represents the Congo River.

Background: The mission was established on 24 February 2000 by the adoption of the Security Council Resolution 1291. The main goals of the mission are to monitor the implementation of the ceasefire agreement and to investigate violations of the ceasefire, to work with the parties to obtain the release of all prisoners of war, and to supervise and verify the disengagement and redeployment of the parties' forces.

Personnel contributors are Algeria, Bangladesh, Belgium, Benin, Bolivia, Burkina Faso, Canada, Czech Republic, Denmark, Egypt, France, Ghana, India, Jordan, Kenya, Libya, Malaysia, Mali, Morocco, Nepal, Niger, Nigeria, Pakistan, Peru, Poland, Romania, Russian Federation, Senegal, South Africa, Sweden, Switzerland, Tunisia, Ukraine, United Kingdom, United Republic of Tanzania, Uruguay, and Zambia.

As of 31 October 2001, Indian troops serving with this mission: 4 troops and 25 observers. Indian service was also recognized with the 'Congo' bar to the Videsh Seva Medal (1052.211).

Outline

3029.100 medal.

3030 UNITED NATIONS MISSION IN ETHIOPIA AND ERITREA (UNMEE), FEBRUARY 2000-

Awarded for ninety days of service with UNMEE in Ethiopia and Eritrea after 2000.

Established: January 2001.

General Appearance: This is the standard UN peacekeeping medal (see 3004 for a description).

Ribbon: The ribbon has two outer bands of UN blue, symbolizing the presence of the United Nations. The inner band in green symbolizes hope and fertility of the land. The two bands in tan symbolize religious freedom and the ruggedness of the country.

Background: The mission was established on 15 September 2000 by the adoption of the Security Council Resolution 1320. The main goals of the mission are to monitor the cessation of hostilities, to assist in ensuring the observance of the security commitments agreed to by the parties, to monitor and verify the redeployment of Ethiopian forces from positions taken, to monitor the positions of Ethiopian forces once redeployed, and the positions of Eritrean forces.

The countries that have provided personnel are Algeria, Austria, Bangladesh, Canada, China, Finland, Ghana, India, Italy, Jordan, Kenya, Malaysia, Nepal, the Netherlands, Norway, Peru, Poland, Romania, Spain, Sweden, Switzerland, Tunisia, Ukraine, the United Republic of Tanzania, Uruguay, and Zambia.

As of 31 October 2001, there were 1,316 Indian troops and 5 observers serving with this mission. Indian service was also recognized with the 'Ethiopia and Eritrea' bar to the Videsh Seva Medal (1052.254).

Outline

3030.100 medal.

3031 UNITED NATIONS OPERATION IN CÔTE D'IVOIRE (UNOIC), FEBRUARY 2004-

Awarded for ninety days of service with UNOIC in Côte d'Ivoire after 2004.

Established: UNOIC was established by the Security Council by its Resolution 1528 of 27 February 2004.

General Appearance: This is expected to be the standard UN peacekeeping medal (see 3004 for a description).

Ribbon: Unknown at present.

Background: To date, no medal has been issued for UNOIC but one is expected to be forthcoming along normal UN lines. UNOIC replaced the United Nations Mission in Côte d'Ivoire (MINUCI), a political mission set up by the Council in May 2003 with a mandate to facilitate the implementation by the Ivorian parties of the peace agreement signed by them in January 2003.

Military personnel have been provided by Bangladesh, Benin, Bolivia, Brazil, Burkina Faso, Chad, China, Congo, Croatia, the Dominican Republic, Ecuador, El Salvador, France, Gambia, Ghana, Guatemala, Guinea, India, Ireland, Jordan, Kenya, Moldova, Morocco, Namibia, Nepal, Niger, Nigeria, Pakistan, Paraguay, Peru, Philippines, Poland, Romania, the Russian Federation, Senegal, Serbia and Montenegro, Togo, Tunisia, Uruguay, Yemen, and Zambia. Civilian police have been provided by Argentina, Bangladesh, Benin, Cameroon, Canada, Chad, Djibouti, El Salvador, France, Ghana, Lebanon, Niger, Nigeria, Portugal, Senegal, Sri Lanka, Togo, Turkey and Uruguay.

Indian service was also recognized with the 'Ivory Coast' bar to the Videsh Seva Medal (1052.255).

Outline

3031.100 medal.

3032 UNITED NATIONS OPERATION IN BURUNDI (ONUB), MAY 2004-

Awarded for ninety days of service with ONUB in Burundi after 2004.

Established: ONUB was established by the Security Council, by its Resolution 1545 of 21 May 2004.

General Appearance: This is expected to be the standard UN peacekeeping medal (see 3004 for a description).

Ribbon: Unknown at present.

Background: To date, no medal has been issued for ONUB, but one is expected to be forthcoming, along normal UN lines. The mission was established to support and help to implement the efforts undertaken by Burundians to restore lasting peace and bring about national reconciliation, as provided under the Arusha Agreement.

Countries contributing military personnel are Algeria, Bangladesh, Belgium, Benin, Bolivia, Burkina Faso, Chad, China, Egypt, Ethiopia, Gabon, Gambia, Ghana, Guatemala, Guinea, India, Jordan, Kenya, Kyrgyzstan, Malawi, Malaysia, Mali, Mozambique, Namibia, Nepal, the Netherlands, Niger, Nigeria, Pakistan, Paraguay, Peru, Philippines, Portugal, Republic of Korea, Romania, Russia, Senegal, Serbia and Montenegro, South Africa, Spain, Sri Lanka, Thailand, Togo, Tunisia, Uruguay, Yemen, and Zambia. Civilian police have been provided by Benin, Burkina Faso, Cameroon, Chad, Côte d'Ivoire, Guinea, Madagascar, Mali, Niger, Nigeria, Senegal, and Turkey.

Indian service was also recognized with the 'Burundi' bar to the Videsh Seva Medal (1052.256).

Outline

3032.100 medal.

3033 UNITED NATIONS MISSION IN THE SUDAN (UNMIS), MARCH 2005-

Awarded for ninety days of service with UNMIS in Sudan after 2005.

Established: UNMIS was established by Security Council Resolution 1590 of 24 March 2005.

General Appearance: This is expected to be the standard UN peacekeeping medal (see 3004 for a description).

Ribbon: Unknown at present.

Background: To date, no medal has been issued for UNMIS, although one is expected to be forthcoming, along normal UN lines. The mission was established to support implementation of the Comprehensive Peace Agreement signed by the Government of Sudan and the Sudan People's Liberation Movement/Army on 9 January 2005; and to perform certain functions relating to humanitarian assistance, and protection and promotion of human rights.

Military personnel have been provided by Bangladesh, Canada, Croatia, Denmark, Egypt, Finland, India, Italy, Jordan, Kenya, Malaysia, Nepal, Norway, Pakistan, Spain, Sweden,

Switzerland, Turkey, the United Kingdom, and Zambia. Police forces have been provided by Finland, India, Jordan, Kenya, Malaysia, Nigeria, Philippines, Sri Lanka, Sweden, Tanzania, Turkey, and the United Kingdom.

Indian service was also recognized by the 'Sudan' bar to the Videsh Seva Medal (1052.224).

Outline

3033.100 medal.

3034 UNITED NATIONS HEADQUARTERS

Awarded for ninety days of service at the UN Headquarters at New York, NY, USA.

Established: 16 June 1997.

General Appearance: This is the standard UN peacekeeping medal (see 3004 for a description).

Ribbon: The ribbon is of solid UN blue.

Background: From time to time countries may provide, on a secondment basis, staff trained, military officers to serve in staff positions at United Nations Headquarters in New York to assist with the planning and implementation of new missions. This medal is awarded to Indian forces serving on this assignment.

Indian service was also recognized with the 'New York' bar to the Videsh Seva Medal (1052.242).

Outline

3034.100 medal.

4

Awards of the Provisional Government of Azad Hind, 1941-1945

These decorations were awarded, first, by the 'Free Indian Government' under the leadership of Netaji Subhas Chandra Bose in Europe during World War II and, later, by that government as it acted in concert with the Japanese Empire in the latter days of the war. These decorations were primarily awarded to members of the 'Indian Legion' in Europe, to the 'Indian National Army' in Asia, and to German and Japanese officers and others serving with these units. It is not clear to what degree the awards transplanted exactly or identically from Europe to Asia. It is, however, known that when Bose relocated from Europe to Asia, specimens of the medals made in Europe came along on his submarine voyage. Described here are primarily the European awards, manufactured by the Vienna firm of Rudolf Souval.[1] No authentic examples of any medals made in South-East Asia have been found.

While these awards may arguably fall outside the scope of this volume, it seems to us that they deserve treatment and recollection as part of the pre-independence phaleristic history of Independent India.

4001 SHAHEED-I-BHARAT / MARTYR OF INDIA

Awarded posthumously to those who gave their lives in India's fight for freedom.

Established: 1942.

Obverse: 36 mm circular bronze medal with the legend 'AZAD HIND' or 'Free India' (actually displayed with 'German-style' quotation marks: "AZAD HIND"). Above is a tiger's head, facing left, and below a stylized lotus with what appears to be a spear emerging from it. Attached to the top of the medal are two crossed sabres.

Reverse: On a cross-hatched and rayed background, the legend (in German) 'INDIENS FREIHEITS KAMPF' or 'India's Freedom Struggle'.

Ribbon: 37 mm, moiré, green with 4 mm edge stripes (reading inward) of orange and white.

Suspension: Suspended by a ring.

Naming: Unnamed.

[1] Throughout, see: St. Martin, 'Auszeichenungen der Prov. Regierung "Azad Hind"', Kleitmann, 'Awards of the Provisional Government of "Azad Hind"', O'Toole, 'Indian National Army', and Singh, *Formation and Growth of the Indian National Army*, pp. 38-40. As the master dies of this firm survived the war, restrikes are common.

Miniature: No miniatures have been reported and it is unlikely that authentic miniatures exist.

Background: Awarded posthumously to all Indian soldiers who gave their lives in the armed struggle for Indian Independence, 1942-45, the medal is sometimes seen without swords, and this is almost certainly a fantasy manufacture. It is estimated that only about 300 of these decorations were manufactured in Europe; South-East Asian manufacturing has not been established. Known to have been awarded four times in South-East Asia.

Representative Citation: To understand the award better, a sample recipient would be Naik Molar Singh:

It was a night of April 1944, when in Kaladan sector [in Burma], Naik Molar Singh's unit was marching to attack a powerful centre of the enemy on a hill. During the attack, it so happened, that an enemy machine gun started firing from very close quarters.

It was clear as day, that in order to achieve our objective, our unit should invariably check this open fire. And this hard job necessitated a man's sacrifice. Fortunately time selected its own hero.

Naik Molar Singh, determined as he was to demolish the enemy post, not caring for his own life rushed to charge the post all alone. And he went on till he had stopped the machine-gun; but his chest was, by then no less that [*sic*] a sieve—every inch of it pierced by bullets. The stake of his life got his unit their objective. But he could not survive this victory.[2]

Outline:

4001.100 medal.

4002 APOCRYPHAL ORDER

In a number of wartime and postwar pictures, Netaji Subhas Chandra Bose is depicted as wearing an elaborate order and other medals.

While there is absolutely no evidence that such an order was ever established, manufactured, or worn, and there is no photographic evidence for its existence, it is worth recording this apocryphal order here.

The order, if it ever existed, would appear to have been constructed along standard European (or, for that matter, Japanese lines), with a collar and collar badge, sash (of orange, white, green, worn over the left shoulder) with a possible—though unrecorded and undepicted—sash badge, breast star, and neck badge (with unknown ribbon). These awards have been described and sketched by Squadron Leader E. O'Toole and his descriptions and sketches are a basic reference for what follows.[3] In suspension of disbelief, we shall describe these awards as if they actually existed. It is, however, important to stress that there is absolutely no evidence that these were wartime awards and that they were anything more than artistic inventions.

The other medals depicted as being worn by *Netaji* all appear identical, circular, and all suspended from orange, white, and green tricolour ribbons. They seem to be no more than artistic fantasies, most likely post-Independence creations.

4001.100 Shaheed-i-Bharat

4002.000 Apocryphal Order

[2] Giani, *Indian Independence Movement in East Asia*, p. 122.
[3] O'Toole, 'Indian National Army', pp. 93-94.

Outline:

4002.100 collar and collar badge—A number of links, enamelled in orange, white, and green with small medallions between. The central medallion bears the head of the Indian nationalist leader G.K. Gokhale, and it may be reasonable to suggest that the others bore depictions of other prominent nationalist figures. The pendant badge has a sunburst and two crossed national flags. Below, some sort of precious gem seems to be suspended.

4002.200 breast star—An eight-pointed rayed star with a red-enamelled map of India in the centre with the legend 'Azad Hind Fauj', or 'Indian National Army' above in Hindi; the Urdu legend below is illegible but may be assumed to repeat the Hindi inscription. This legend seems strange, for it had been the ongoing policy of Bose's movement, both in Europe and in Asia, to use Hindustani in Roman script and to avoid, thereby, the Hindi/Urdu distinction.

4002.300 neck badge—A slightly oval gold medallion with a floral border and ring suspender; overall, the general impression recalls the Bharat Ratna (1001) that was created in 1950. In the centre, the raised legend 'Jai Hind', or 'Victory to India', the slogan of Bose's movement.

4003 SHER-I-HIND / TIGER OF INDIA

Awarded for the very highest degree of bravery or distinguished service.

Established: 1942, though the first documented award came only in 1944.[4]

Obverse: A 60 mm silvered rayed star

Reverse: Plain, but sometimes with a central plaque bearing the manufacturer's name.

Ribbon: 37 mm, moiré, green with 4-mm edge stripes (reading inwards) of orange and white. The ribbon is worn around the neck.

Suspension: Suspended by a ring and loop from a neck ribbon.

Naming: Unnamed.

Miniature: No miniatures have been reported and it is unlikely that authentic miniatures exist.

Background: The medal was awarded to soldiers in the Indian Legion or Indian National Army or civilians, already in possession of the Sardar-i-Jang (4004) medal for additional or ongoing acts of bravery (with swords) or distinguished service (without swords). In this sense, the award was generally patterned on the German Iron Cross. This decoration carried with it an annual stipend of Rs. 300 when awarded with swords. It is estimated that only about one hundred of these decorations were manufactured in Europe; South-East Asian manufacturing has not been established.

Representative Citation: To understand the award better, a sample recipient would be Naik Kehar Singh (presumably an award with swords, but the citation does not specify this):

On the 18th of May 1944, a unit of the I.N.A. was picqueting a hill in

4003.100 Sher-i-Hind

the central sector of the Indo-Burma frontier. Of those on duty, Naik Kehar Singh was one. On an early morning the enemy made an unprecedented pre-planned attack on our picquet.

One of our comrades, who was working a light machine-gun against the enemy was fatally wounded by enemy fire. He signalled to his comrades to come and occupy his machine-gun. But the man who was to relieve him had already been shot dead by enemy fire. Naik Kehar Singh was witnessing all this from a short distance. He made a spontaneous decision.

The enemy was firing uninterruptedly. But caring not for his own safety, he rushed through the pouring bullets to occupy the machine gun post. By the time he reached the post, the enemy had approached him to as close as ten yards. With a smile on his lips, Kehar Singh picked up the machine gun and resting it against his hip opened fire on the enemy who were shooting at him with a tommy gun.

Neglecting the enemy fire, Naik Kehar Singh went on working his own machine gun, so much that the enemy had to retreat. At this he put the machine gun in position and went on firing to push the enemy back to complete retreat.[5]

This medal—as well as the others—was also awarded to German (and, one presumes, Japanese) officers and others involved with the Indian Legion and Indian National Army. For example, the famous German medal expert, the late Dr. K.-G. Kleitmann, was awarded the Sher-i-Hind with swords.[6] It is estimated that only perhaps twenty-five Sher-i-Hind medals were awarded, including two awards for South-East Asia.

Outline:

4003.100 with swords.
4003.200 without swords.

4004 SARDAR-I-JANG / WAR LEADER

Awarded for high degrees of bravery or distinguished service.

Established: 1942, although there is no sound evidence of awards prior to 1944.[7]

Obverse: A 60 mm silvered rayed star

Reverse: A pin-back clasp for wearing. Plain, but sometimes with a central plaque bearing the manufacturer's name.

Ribbon: No suspension ribbon, but it used the same ribbon as the Sher-i-Hind and Vir-i-Hind on ribbon bars: 37 mm, moiré, green with 4 mm edge stripes (reading inwards) of orange and white.

Suspension: Pin-back.

Naming: Unnamed.

Miniature: No miniatures have been reported and it is unlikely that authentic miniatures exist.

Background: Awarded to soldiers in the Indian Legion or Indian National Army or civilians, already in possession of the Vir-i-Hind (4005) medal for additional or ongoing acts of bravery (with swords) or distinguished service (without swords), in this sense, the award was generally patterned on the German Iron Cross. There is good evidence that, at least in this case, the European and Asian awards differed substantially. The South-East Asian variety existed in two classes and it is

4004.100 Sardar-i-Jang

[5] Giani, *Indian Independence Movement in East Asia*, p. 122.
[6] Letter from Dr. K.G. Kleitmann to E.S. Haynes, 12 June 1971.
[7] 'Regierung Bose Stiftet Auszeichunungen.'

unclear how these relate—if at all—to the structure of the European award.

This decoration carried with it an annual stipend of Rs. 250 when awarded with swords. It is estimated that only about one hundred of these decorations were manufactured in Europe; South-East Asian manufacturing has not been established. Known to have been awarded 12 times in South-East Asia.

Representative Citation: To understand the award better, a sample recipient would be Major Pritam Singh (presumably awarded the medal with swords, though the citation does not specify this):

Major Pritam Singh was commanding one unit of the A.H.F. [Azad Hind Fauj = Indian National Army] in Central Sector [of Burma]. This unit had instructions to penetrate the enemy positions and reconnoiter the enemy. He organized his unit and went on his errand early in May [1944?].

When Major Pritam Singh and his party reached near their objective, the enemy opened fire on them with machine-guns and mortars. Not caring for the fire, they marched forward and with loud should [*sic*] of 'Chalo Delhi' [roughly, 'On to Delhi'] charged the enemy. After fulfilling the duty, with which he was entrusted, he ordered his men to retreat. But it was not an easy job to escape from so heavy fire. With a marvellous strategy, Major Pritam Singh was successful in bringing back his unit, with a very little loss. He also inflicted losses on the enemy.[8]

Outline

4004.100 with swords.
4004.200 without swords.

4005 VIR-I-HIND / HERO OF INDIA

Awarded for moderate degrees of bravery or distinguished service.

Established: 1942.

Obverse: A 60 mm silvered rayed star with a circular gilt centre with a tiger's head, facing left, surrounded by the legend 'AZAD HIND'.

Reverse: Plain, but sometimes with a central plaque bearing the manufacturer's name.

Ribbon: 37 mm, moiré, green with 4 mm edge stripes (reading inwards) of orange and white.

Suspension: A ring.

Naming: Unnamed.

Miniature: No miniatures have been reported and it is unlikely that authentic miniatures exist.

Background: The medal was awarded to soldiers in the Indian Legion or Indian National Army or civilians for acts of bravery (with swords) or distinguished service (without swords). This decoration carried with it an annual stipend of Rs. 200 when awarded with swords. It is estimated that only about one hundred of these decorations were manufactured in Europe; South-East Asian manufacturing has not been established. It is known to have been awarded eleven times in South-East Asia.

4005.100 Vir-i-Hind

[8] Giani, *Indian Independence Movement in East Asia*, p. 130.

Representative Citation: To understand the award better, a sample recipient would be S.O. Gurbachan Singh (who was, presumably, awarded the decoration with swords, though the description of his deed does not indicate this):

In 1944 by the end of May S.O. Gurbachan Singh was going in a boat with some Burmese boatmen to a certain place in Northern Burma.

At some sound in the river, the enemy by chance opened fire and a bullet struck him just below his knee. One of the boatmen was also injured and the other two having lost their senses left rowing.

Thirteen American soldiers fell upon the Sub-Officer to arrest him. S.O. Gurbachan Singh plunged into water and lying in concealment behind the boat, began to fire with his pistol. He fatally injured two of the enemy. All his four fingers with which he was resting on the boat got injured, but in spite of that he reloaded his pistol and opened fire again. Just then a bullet crushing his pistol went through the palm of his right hand injuring further his face and brow.

Still he kept up his courage. With his wounded hand he shifted the boat slightly to the left and with this act saved the life of the two boatmen. After this, when he rowed across to the left bank, he discovered three dead bodies of the enemy soldiers—the rest having fled.[9]

For this deed, S.O. Gurbachan Singh was also awarded the Tamgha-i-Shatru Nash, first class (4007.100).

Outline:

4005.100 with swords.
4005.200 without swords.

4006 TAMGHA-I-BAHADURI / MEDAL OF BRAVERY

Awarded for bravery or distinguished service.

Established: 1942.

Obverse: 36 mm circular bronze-gilt medal with the legend 'AZAD HIND' or 'Free India' (actually displayed with 'German-style' quotation marks: "AZAD HIND"). Above is a tiger's head, facing left, and below a stylized lotus with what appears to be a spear emerging from it. The medal with swords is identical to that of Shaheed-i-Bharat (4001, except, of course, for the metal); the Tamgha-i-Bahaduri without swords is illustrated above.

Reverse: On a cross-hatched and rayed background, the legend (in German) 'INDIENS FREIHEITS KAMPF' or 'India's Freedom Struggle'.

Ribbon: 37 mm, moiré, green with 4 mm edge stripes (reading inwards) of orange and white.

Suspension: Suspended by a ring.

Naming: Unnamed.

Miniature: No miniatures have been reported and it is unlikely that authentic miniatures exist.

Background: The medal with swords was awarded for bravery, while the medal without swords was awarded for distinguished service to the Indian Legion or to the Free Indian Government. This decoration carried with it an annual stipend of Rs. 150 when awarded with swords. It is estimated that only about 300 of each division of these decorations were manufactured in Europe; South-East Asian manufacturing has not been

4006.100 Tamgha-e-Bahaduri

[9] Giani, *Indian Independence Movement in East Asia,* pp. 124-25.

established. It is known to have been awarded twenty-one times in South-East Asia.

Representative Citation: To understand the award better, a sample recipient would be Naik Sultan Singh (presumably, an award with swords, though the account does not specify this):

During military work in the central sector [of Burma], Naik Sultan Singh preached the British Indian Army in a very able way. But one day, he was arrested by the enemy and he was handed over to a British Indian Coy.

He convinced the Indian Commander of that Coy. about our I.N.A. and Independence movement in such a way, that next day, when the soldiers of this unit became inclined towards I.N.A. not only Sultan Singh came [to] our rank[s] but he also brought four men, who were placed as guards on him. In addition to this, that Coy. Commander (Subadar) and his Coy. started propaganda work in British Army for the I.N.A.[10]

Outline

4006.100 with swords, crossed sabres attached to the top of the medal.
4006.200 without swords.

4007 TAMGHA-I-SHATRU NASH / MEDAL FOR DESTROYING THE ENEMY[11]

Awarded for the killing or capture of enemy troops.
Established: Unknown.
Obverse: Unknown.
Reverse: Unknown.
Ribbon: Unknown, but it might be expected to have been the same as for the other awards, viz., 37 mm, moiré, green with 4 mm edge stripes (reading inwards) of orange and white.
Suspension: Unknown.
Naming: Unknown, though almost certainly unnamed.
Miniature: No miniatures have been reported and it is unlikely that authentic miniatures exist.
Background: Awarded to members of the Indian National Army or to civilians for the killing or capture of a British or American officer or an enlisted man under conditions where individual bravery and initiative were involved, this appears to be the only Free Indian award distinctive to the Asia theatre.

The award came in two classes: first class, for those members of the I.N.A. who exhibited conspicuous gallantry and devotion to duty in killing or capturing alive any British or American officer or other rank, either in single combat or in group fighting, where qualities if individual initiative and bravery came into play; and second class, for those members of the I.N.A. who killed or captured alive any British or American officer or other rank, either in single combat or in group fighting, where qualities of individual initiative and bravery came into play.[12]

Representative Citation: To understand the award better, sample recipients would be the awards in the second class to Havildar Pir Mohammed and Havildar Hakim Ali:

[10] Giani, *Indian Independence Movement in East Asia*, p. 126.
[11] Palat, *My Adventures with the I.N.A.*, pp. 124-25, and Singh, *Formation and Growth of the Indian National Army*, pp. 38-40.
[12] Palat, *My Adventures*, pp. 124-25.

In the Arakan Sector [of Burma], Hav. Pir Mohd. and Hav. Hakim Ali, along with other men, were sent on patrol duty on February 5 [1944?]. On the way they came across a small unit of the 30th Indian Cavalry. Our patrol tried hard to persuade this unit to join the Azad Hind Fauj [Indian National Army], but as they were under command of a British N.C.O., they did not respond. Upon this Hav. Pir Mohd. and Hav. Hakim Ali fired at them with Tommy guns and killed a British officer and a soldier. The enemy unit who was on patrol took to his heels.[13]

Outline

4007.100 first class—Known to have been awarded three times in South-East Asia.
4007.200 second class—Known to have been awarded twelve times in South-East Asia.

4008 TAMGHA-I-AZADI / MEDAL OF FREEDOM

Awarded for eighteen months of service.
Established: 1942.
Obverse: 36 mm circular silvered medal with the legend 'AZAD HIND' or 'Free India' (actually displayed with 'German-style' quotation marks: "AZAD HIND"). Above, a tiger's head facing left, and below a stylized lotus with what appears to be a spear emerging from it. Attached to the top of the medal are two crossed sabres. The medal is identical to that of Shaheed-i-Bharat (4001, except, of course, for the metal).
Reverse: On a cross-hatched and rayed background, the legend (in German) 'INDIENS FREIHEITS KAMPF' or 'India's Freedom Struggle'.
Ribbon: 37 mm, moiré, green with 4 mm edge stripes (reading inwards) of orange and white.
Suspension: Suspended by a ring.
Naming: Unnamed.
Miniature: No miniatures have been reported and it is unlikely that authentic miniatures exist.
Background: Awarded to all soldiers in the Indian Legion who had served for a year and a half in the unit, the medal is sometimes seen without swords, but this appears to be a fantasy fraudulent post-war restrike. It is estimated that only about 300 of these decorations were manufactured in Europe; South-East Asian manufacturing and award has not been established.

Outline:

4008.100 medal

4008.100 Tamgha-e-Azadi

4009 SANAD-I-BAHADURI / CERTIFICATE OF BRAVERY

Awarded for low levels of bravery not warranting the award of a higher decoration, in essence, a mention in despatches award. Sources are unclear whether this is a certificate alone, with or without a representative ribbon, or whether it was even issued at all.

[13] Giani, *Indian Independence Movement in East Asia*, p. 129.

Established: Unknown.

Ribbon: Unknown, but in the (unlikely) event that one was associated with it, it might be expected to have been the same as for the other awards, viz., 37 mm, moiré, green with 4 mm edge stripes (reading inwards) of orange and white.

Background: It was awarded to those who rendered meritorious service in the field but fell short of qualifying for a decoration. While it appears to have been a sort of mention-in-despatches award, some sources suggest some sort of medal accompanied the award. It is known to have been awarded twelve times in South-East Asia.

Representative Citation: To understand the award better, a sample recipient would be 2/Lieutenant Dura Bahadur:

In March [1944?], in the Central Sector [of the Burma front] 2/Lt. Dura Bahadur was sent to contact a Gurkha unit of the British army. Dura Bahadur, risking his life, reached the Gurkha unit, through the enemy lines, and talked with them for half an hour.

The Gurkha unit promised to do propaganda for the I.N.A. in other Gurkha units. 2/Lt. Dura Bahadur also told them that I.N.A. wants to capture that position and that it is an important point for the I.N.A. from the military standpoint.

The same day, a few hours later another I.N.A. officer met those people and they surrendered that place according to the instructions of the I.N.A. officers.[14]

Outline

4009.100 certificate (and possible medal?).

[14] Giani, *Indian Independence Movement in East Asia*, p. 126.

Ribbon Chart

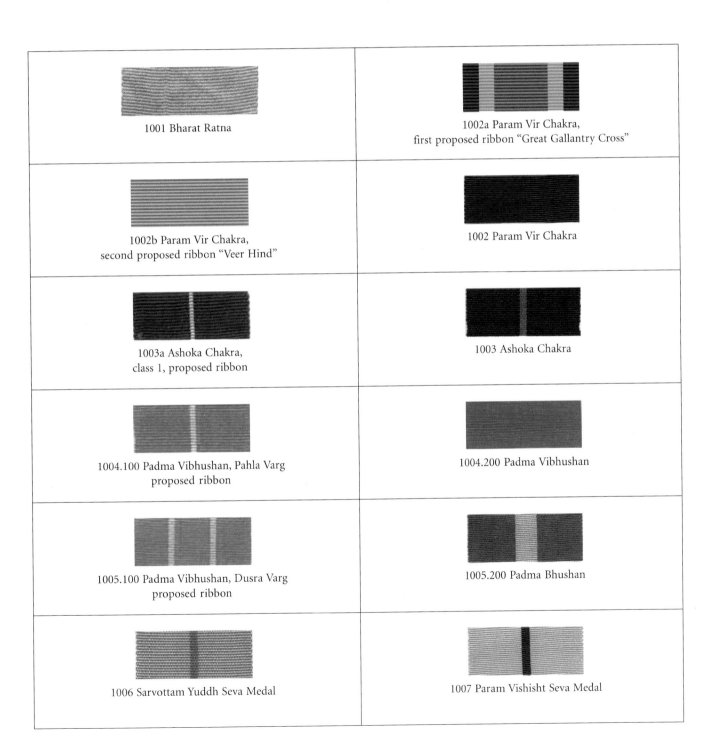

1001 Bharat Ratna	1002a Param Vir Chakra, first proposed ribbon "Great Gallantry Cross"
1002b Param Vir Chakra, second proposed ribbon "Veer Hind"	1002 Param Vir Chakra
1003a Ashoka Chakra, class 1, proposed ribbon	1003 Ashoka Chakra
1004.100 Padma Vibhushan, Pahla Varg proposed ribbon	1004.200 Padma Vibhushan
1005.100 Padma Vibhushan, Dusra Varg proposed ribbon	1005.200 Padma Bhushan
1006 Sarvottam Yuddh Seva Medal	1007 Param Vishisht Seva Medal

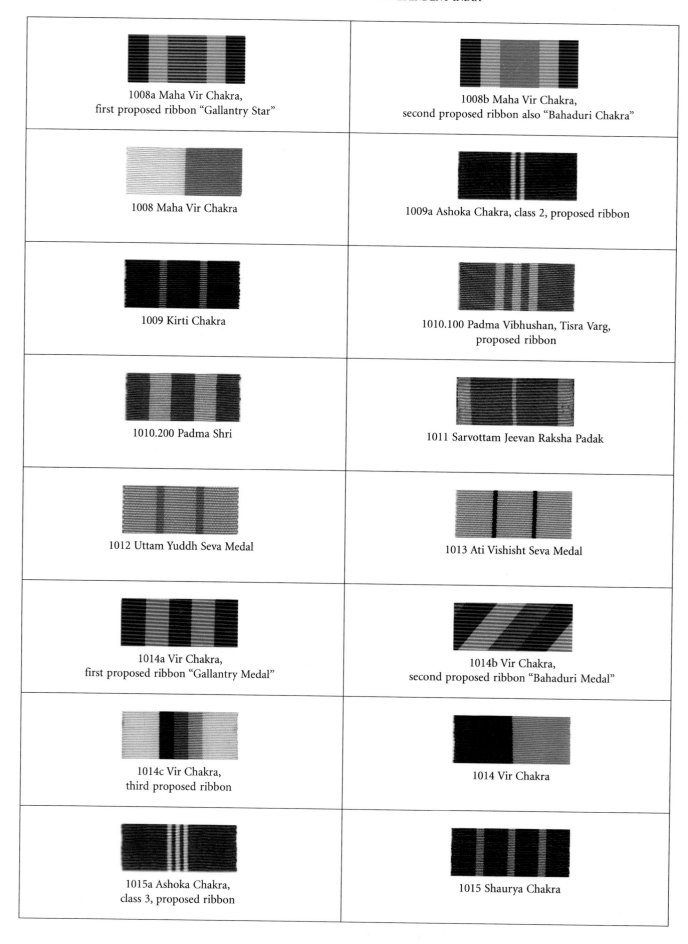

1008a Maha Vir Chakra,
first proposed ribbon "Gallantry Star"

1008b Maha Vir Chakra,
second proposed ribbon also "Bahaduri Chakra"

1008 Maha Vir Chakra

1009a Ashoka Chakra, class 2, proposed ribbon

1009 Kirti Chakra

1010.100 Padma Vibhushan, Tisra Varg,
proposed ribbon

1010.200 Padma Shri

1011 Sarvottam Jeevan Raksha Padak

1012 Uttam Yuddh Seva Medal

1013 Ati Vishisht Seva Medal

1014a Vir Chakra,
first proposed ribbon "Gallantry Medal"

1014b Vir Chakra,
second proposed ribbon "Bahaduri Medal"

1014c Vir Chakra,
third proposed ribbon

1014 Vir Chakra

1015a Ashoka Chakra,
class 3, proposed ribbon

1015 Shaurya Chakra

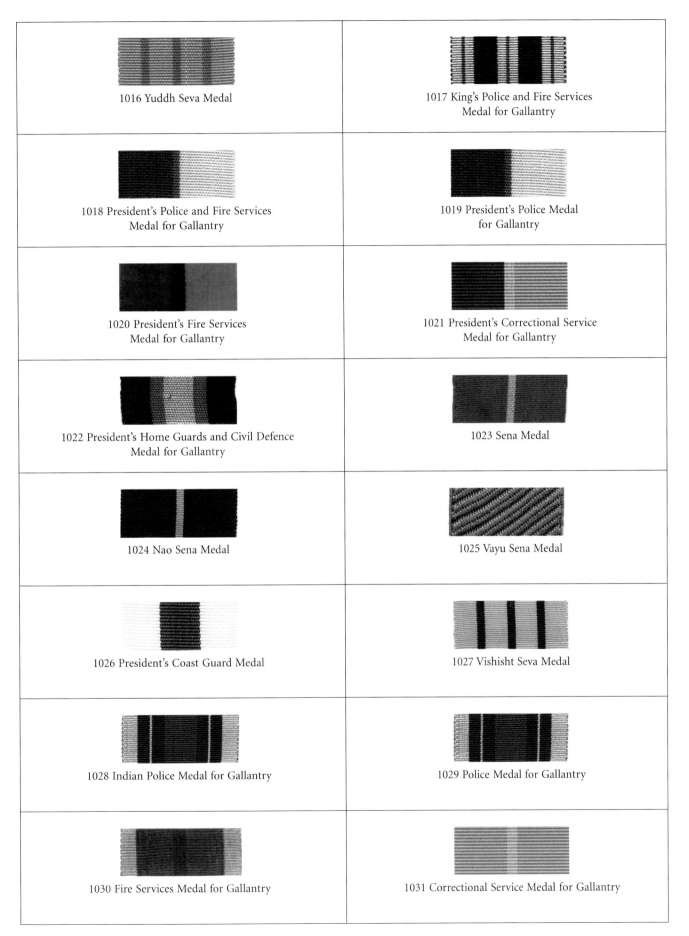

1016 Yuddh Seva Medal

1017 King's Police and Fire Services
Medal for Gallantry

1018 President's Police and Fire Services
Medal for Gallantry

1019 President's Police Medal
for Gallantry

1020 President's Fire Services
Medal for Gallantry

1021 President's Correctional Service
Medal for Gallantry

1022 President's Home Guards and Civil Defence
Medal for Gallantry

1023 Sena Medal

1024 Nao Sena Medal

1025 Vayu Sena Medal

1026 President's Coast Guard Medal

1027 Vishisht Seva Medal

1028 Indian Police Medal for Gallantry

1029 Police Medal for Gallantry

1030 Fire Services Medal for Gallantry

1031 Correctional Service Medal for Gallantry

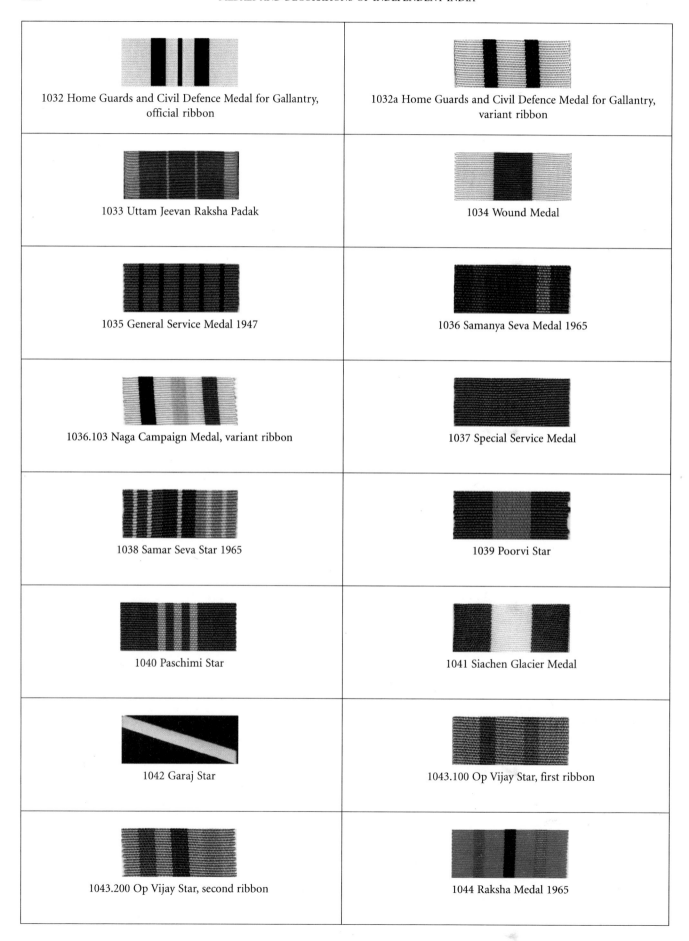

1032 Home Guards and Civil Defence Medal for Gallantry, official ribbon

1032a Home Guards and Civil Defence Medal for Gallantry, variant ribbon

1033 Uttam Jeevan Raksha Padak

1034 Wound Medal

1035 General Service Medal 1947

1036 Samanya Seva Medal 1965

1036.103 Naga Campaign Medal, variant ribbon

1037 Special Service Medal

1038 Samar Seva Star 1965

1039 Poorvi Star

1040 Paschimi Star

1041 Siachen Glacier Medal

1042 Garaj Star

1043.100 Op Vijay Star, first ribbon

1043.200 Op Vijay Star, second ribbon

1044 Raksha Medal 1965

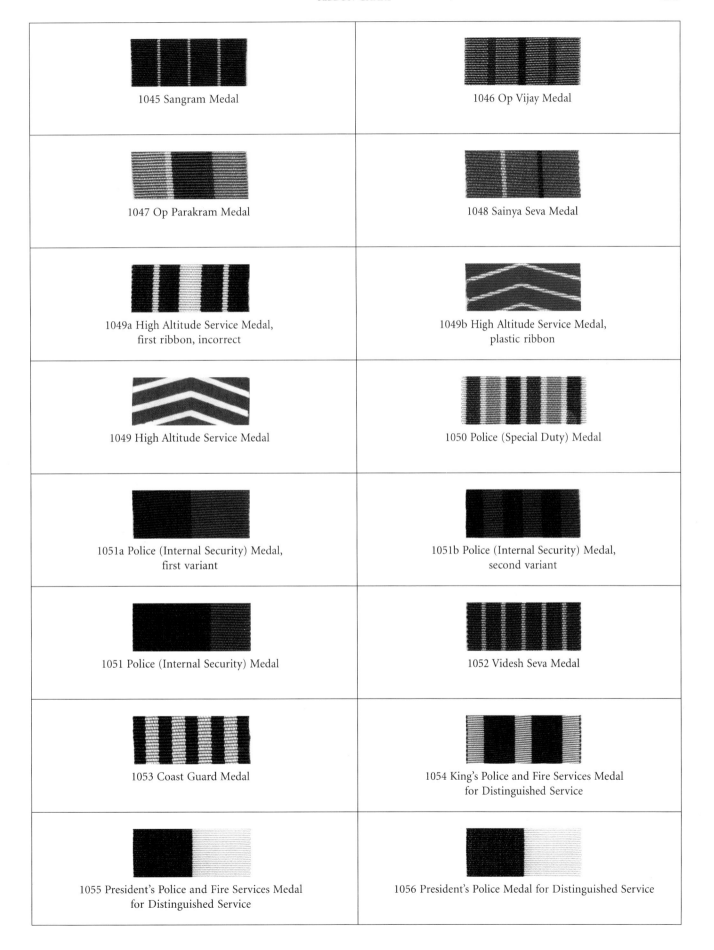

1045 Sangram Medal

1046 Op Vijay Medal

1047 Op Parakram Medal

1048 Sainya Seva Medal

1049a High Altitude Service Medal,
first ribbon, incorrect

1049b High Altitude Service Medal,
plastic ribbon

1049 High Altitude Service Medal

1050 Police (Special Duty) Medal

1051a Police (Internal Security) Medal,
first variant

1051b Police (Internal Security) Medal,
second variant

1051 Police (Internal Security) Medal

1052 Videsh Seva Medal

1053 Coast Guard Medal

1054 King's Police and Fire Services Medal
for Distinguished Service

1055 President's Police and Fire Services Medal
for Distinguished Service

1056 President's Police Medal for Distinguished Service

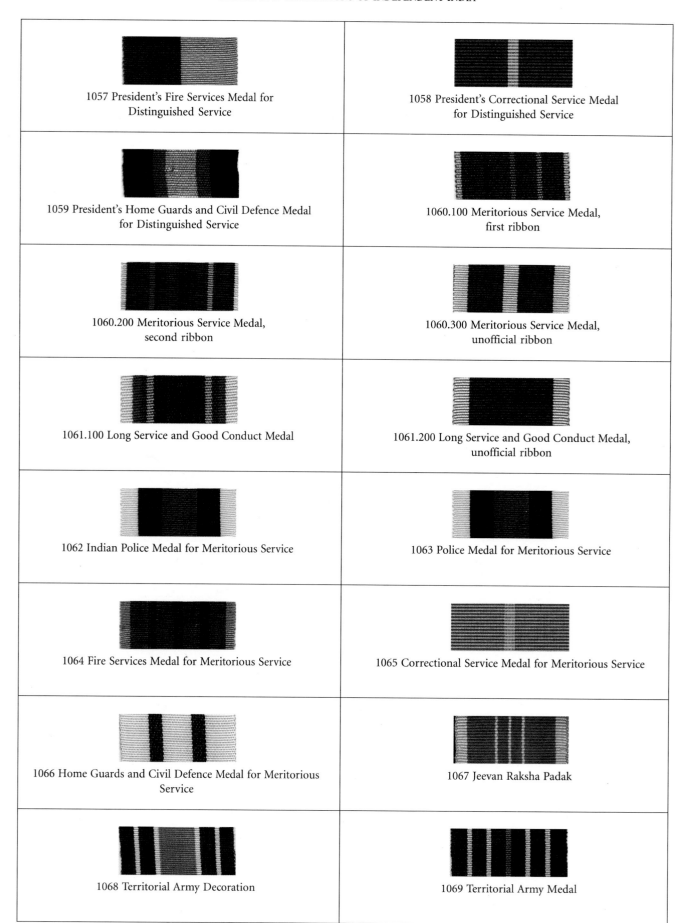

1057 President's Fire Services Medal for
Distinguished Service

1058 President's Correctional Service Medal
for Distinguished Service

1059 President's Home Guards and Civil Defence Medal
for Distinguished Service

1060.100 Meritorious Service Medal,
first ribbon

1060.200 Meritorious Service Medal,
second ribbon

1060.300 Meritorious Service Medal,
unofficial ribbon

1061.100 Long Service and Good Conduct Medal

1061.200 Long Service and Good Conduct Medal,
unofficial ribbon

1062 Indian Police Medal for Meritorious Service

1063 Police Medal for Meritorious Service

1064 Fire Services Medal for Meritorious Service

1065 Correctional Service Medal for Meritorious Service

1066 Home Guards and Civil Defence Medal for Meritorious
Service

1067 Jeevan Raksha Padak

1068 Territorial Army Decoration

1069 Territorial Army Medal

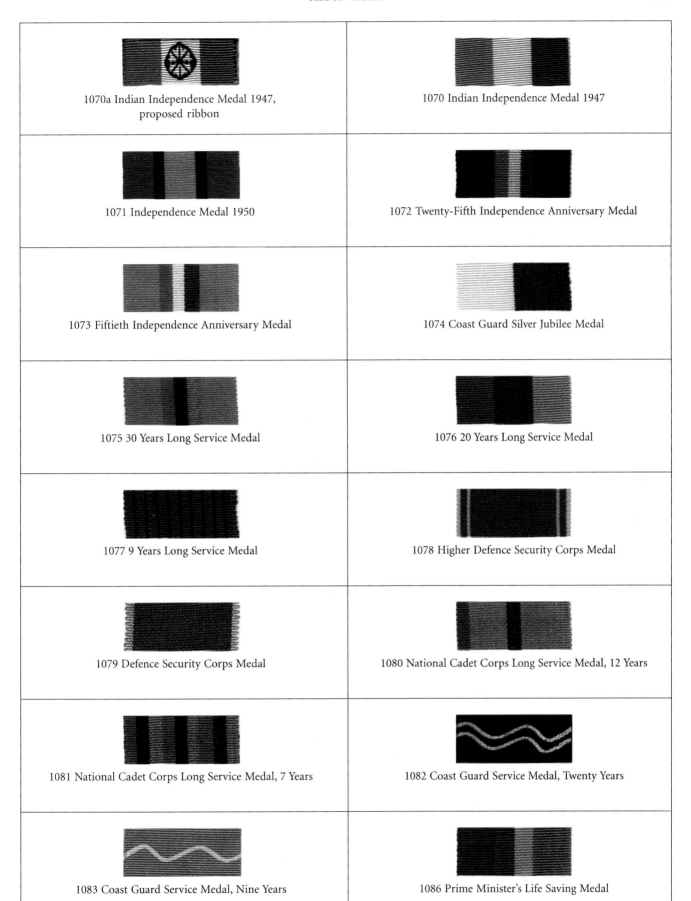

1070a Indian Independence Medal 1947, proposed ribbon

1070 Indian Independence Medal 1947

1071 Independence Medal 1950

1072 Twenty-Fifth Independence Anniversary Medal

1073 Fiftieth Independence Anniversary Medal

1074 Coast Guard Silver Jubilee Medal

1075 30 Years Long Service Medal

1076 20 Years Long Service Medal

1077 9 Years Long Service Medal

1078 Higher Defence Security Corps Medal

1079 Defence Security Corps Medal

1080 National Cadet Corps Long Service Medal, 12 Years

1081 National Cadet Corps Long Service Medal, 7 Years

1082 Coast Guard Service Medal, Twenty Years

1083 Coast Guard Service Medal, Nine Years

1086 Prime Minister's Life Saving Medal

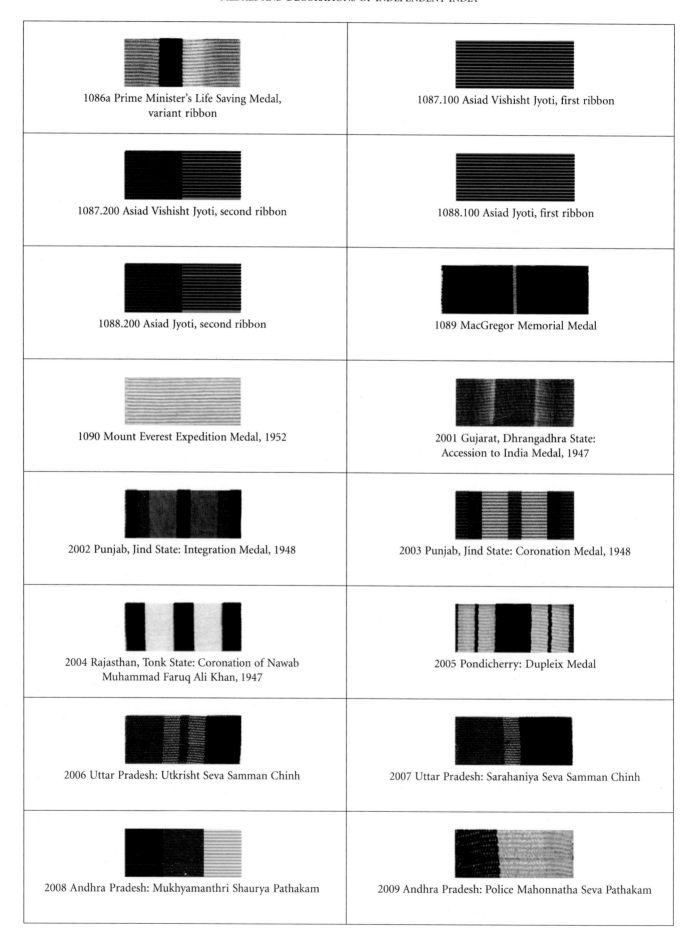

1086a Prime Minister's Life Saving Medal, variant ribbon

1087.100 Asiad Vishisht Jyoti, first ribbon

1087.200 Asiad Vishisht Jyoti, second ribbon

1088.100 Asiad Jyoti, first ribbon

1088.200 Asiad Jyoti, second ribbon

1089 MacGregor Memorial Medal

1090 Mount Everest Expedition Medal, 1952

2001 Gujarat, Dhrangadhra State: Accession to India Medal, 1947

2002 Punjab, Jind State: Integration Medal, 1948

2003 Punjab, Jind State: Coronation Medal, 1948

2004 Rajasthan, Tonk State: Coronation of Nawab Muhammad Faruq Ali Khan, 1947

2005 Pondicherry: Dupleix Medal

2006 Uttar Pradesh: Utkrisht Seva Samman Chinh

2007 Uttar Pradesh: Sarahaniya Seva Samman Chinh

2008 Andhra Pradesh: Mukhyamanthri Shaurya Pathakam

2009 Andhra Pradesh: Police Mahonnatha Seva Pathakam

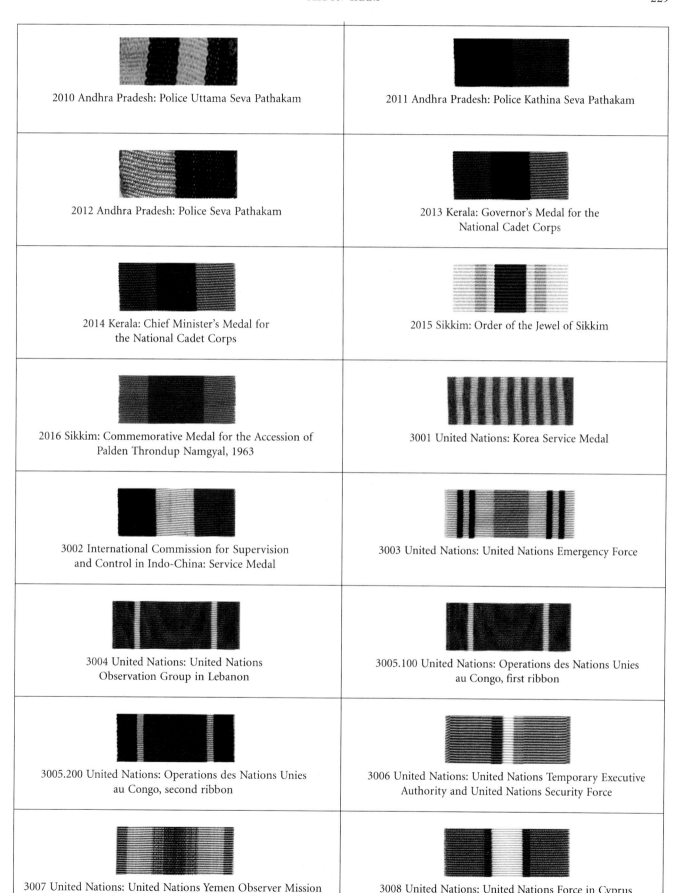

2010 Andhra Pradesh: Police Uttama Seva Pathakam

2011 Andhra Pradesh: Police Kathina Seva Pathakam

2012 Andhra Pradesh: Police Seva Pathakam

2013 Kerala: Governor's Medal for the
National Cadet Corps

2014 Kerala: Chief Minister's Medal for
the National Cadet Corps

2015 Sikkim: Order of the Jewel of Sikkim

2016 Sikkim: Commemorative Medal for the Accession of
Palden Throndup Namgyal, 1963

3001 United Nations: Korea Service Medal

3002 International Commission for Supervision
and Control in Indo-China: Service Medal

3003 United Nations: United Nations Emergency Force

3004 United Nations: United Nations
Observation Group in Lebanon

3005.100 United Nations: Operations des Nations Unies
au Congo, first ribbon

3005.200 United Nations: Operations des Nations Unies
au Congo, second ribbon

3006 United Nations: United Nations Temporary Executive
Authority and United Nations Security Force

3007 United Nations: United Nations Yemen Observer Mission

3008 United Nations: United Nations Force in Cyprus

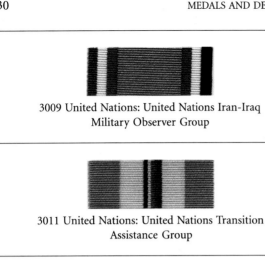

3009 United Nations: United Nations Iran-Iraq
Military Observer Group

3010 United Nations: United Nations Angola
Verification Mission

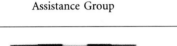

3011 United Nations: United Nations Transition
Assistance Group

3012 United Nations: Organisation de Nations Unies
au Central America

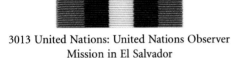

3013 United Nations: United Nations Observer
Mission in El Salvador

3014 United Nations: United Nations Iraq-Kuwait
Observation Mission

3015 United Nations: Mission des Nations Unies pour le
Referendum dans le Sahara Occidental

3016 United Nations: United Nations Advance
Mission in Cambodia

3017 United Nations: United Nations Protection Force

3018 United Nations: United Nations Transitional
Authority in Cambodia

3019 United Nations: United Nations Operations
in Somalia

3020 United Nations: Operacao das Nacoes Unidas
em Mocambique

3021 United Nations: United Nations Mission in Haiti

3022 United Nations: United Nations Observer
Mission in Liberia

3023 United Nations: United Nations Assistance
Mission in Rwanda

3024 United Nations: United Nations Mission in
Bosnia and Herzegovina

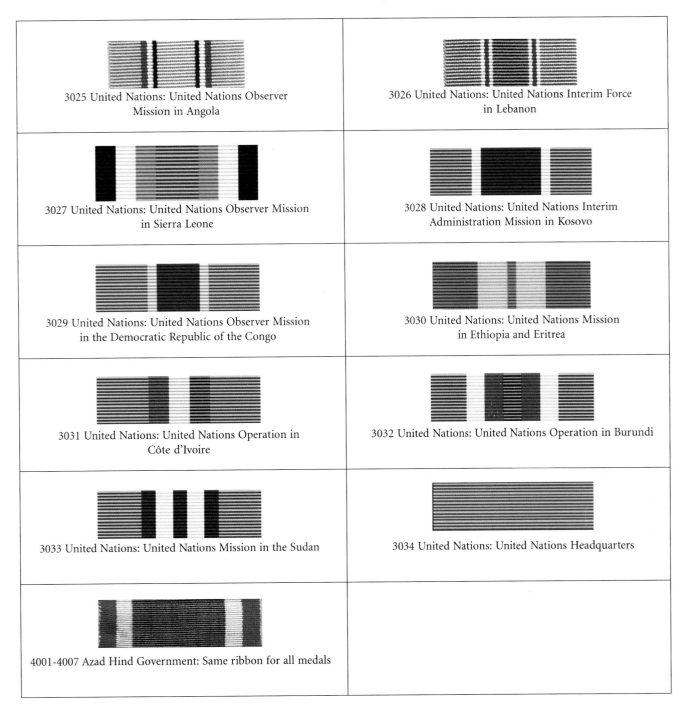

3025 United Nations: United Nations Observer
Mission in Angola

3026 United Nations: United Nations Interim Force
in Lebanon

3027 United Nations: United Nations Observer Mission
in Sierra Leone

3028 United Nations: United Nations Interim
Administration Mission in Kosovo

3029 United Nations: United Nations Observer Mission
in the Democratic Republic of the Congo

3030 United Nations: United Nations Mission
in Ethiopia and Eritrea

3031 United Nations: United Nations Operation in
Côte d'Ivoire

3032 United Nations: United Nations Operation in Burundi

3033 United Nations: United Nations Mission in the Sudan

3034 United Nations: United Nations Headquarters

4001-4007 Azad Hind Government: Same ribbon for all medals

Governors-General, Presidents, and Prime Ministers

GOVERNORS-GENERAL

1947-48	Louis Francis Mountbatten, Earl Mountbatten of Burma
1948-50	Chakravarthi Rajagopalachari

PRESIDENTS

1950-62	Rajendra Prasad
1962-67	Sarvapalli Radhakrishnan
1967-69	Zakir Husain
1969	Varahagiri Venkata Giri (acting)
1969	Muhammad Hidayat Ullah (acting)
1969-74	Varahagiri Venkata Giri
1974-77	Fakhruddin Ali Ahmed
1977	Basappa Danappa Jatti (acting)
1977-82	N. Sanjiva Reddy
1982-87	Zail Singh
1987-92	Ramaswamy Venkataraman
1992-97	Shankar Dayal Sharma
1997-2002	K.R. Narayanan
2002-07	A.P.J. Abdul Kalam

PRIME MINISTERS

1947-64	Jawaharlal Nehru
1964	Gulzarilal Nanda
1964-66	Lal Bahadur Shastri
1966	Gulzarilal Nanda
1966-77	Indira Gandhi
1977-79	Morarji Desai
1979-80	Charan Singh
1980-84	Indira Gandhi
1984-89	Rajiv Gandhi
1989-90	Vishwanath Pratap Singh
1990-91	Chandrashekhar
1991-96	P.V. Narasimha Rao
1996	Atal Behari Vajpayee
1996-97	H.D. Deve Gowda
1997-98	Inder Kumar Gujral
1998-2004	Atal Behari Vajpayee
2004-	Manmohan Singh

APPENDIX 2

Financial Rewards

The question of what financial reward the holder of a gallantry decoration should receive is a complex and at times controversial one. Whether such recipients should be additionally rewarded at all, or whether an existing reward is too high or too low are political questions that transcend the focus of this book. Nevertheless, it is valuable to survey briefly the practices that prevail with regard to the Indian honours system.[1]

NATIONAL

In addition to rewarding post-1947 gallantry recipients, the Republic of India inherited the need to continue the financial rewards of recipients of awards from the colonial period. As of 2001, the following scale of monthly financial reward was in place:

TABLE A1

	Award	For each bar
Indian Order of Merit First Class (1911-44)	Rs. 300	Rs. 300[2]
Indian Order of Merit Second Class (1911-44)	Rs. 250	Rs. 250[3]
Indian Order of Merit Single Class (1944-47)	Rs. 350	Rs. 350[4]
Distinguished Service Cross	Rs. 200	Rs. 200
Military Cross	Rs. 200	Rs. 200
Distinguished Flying Cross	Rs. 200	Rs. 200
Indian Distinguished Service Medal[5]	Rs. 70	Rs. 70
Conspicuous Gallantry Medal	Rs. 200	Rs. 200
Military Medal	Rs. 90	Rs. 90
Distinguished Flying Medal[6]	Rs. 50	Rs. 50

There are several interesting observations to be made from this table. The government has, helpfully, included financial benefits for several awards for which second-award bars were never awarded or were never earned by Indians (only bars to the Military Cross, Distinguished Flying Cross, Indian Distinguished Service Medal and the Military Medal were ever bestowed to Indians—and in any case some of the recipients of these medals went to Pakistan with partition), even while ignoring other gallantry awards that were earned (the Victoria Cross, George Cross, George Medal, and Distinguished Service Medal). Jangi Imams from both World Wars are still honoured at the rate of Rs. 100 per month, for two lives for WWI and for one life for WWII. Overall, the table reflects the ignorance prevalent in official circles about the functional dy-

[1] Throughout this section, most of our information has been drawn from: India, Ministry of Defence, Adjutant General, 'Entitlement of Cash Grants and Concession to Awardees, 2001'.
[2] There was no provision for a bar to this award.
[3] There was no provision for a bar to this award.
[4] No bars were ever awarded.
[5] Although the IDSM was awarded for a higher standard of gallantry than the Military Medal, recipients of the former paradoxically draw a lower monetary allowance than the latter medal. For the structure of Indian gallantry awards and allowances sanctioned during the Second World War, see Rana Chhina, *The Indian Distinguished Service Medal* (New Delhi, 2001), pp. 28-31.
[6] There were, however, no Indian recipients of the Distinguished Flying Medal.

namics of pre-Independence honours and awards.

In May 2004, Punjab added provincial pensions for pre-1947 gallantry medal winners: Victoria Cross, Rs. 10,000 per month, Indian Order of Merit First Class, Rs. 2,000 per month, Indian Order of Merit Second Class, Rs. 1,500 per month, Military Cross, Rs. 7,500 per month, Indian Distinguished Service Medal, Rs. 1,000; Conspicuous Gallantry Medal, Rs. 2,000 per month, and Military Medal, Rs. 3,500 per month. While there are some distinct oddities in this list, it is interesting to see at least one province with a sense of pre-1947 history.

For post-1947 awards, some details on financial aspects have been given in the individual entries for each award, and the reader is encouraged to consult these sections. The central government's monthly allowances for gallantry awards were revised in 2001 (see Table A2):

TABLE A2

Param Vir Chakra	Rs. 1,500
Ashoka Chakra	Rs. 1,400
Maha Vir Chakra	Rs. 1,200
Kirti Chakra	Rs. 1,050
Vir Chakra	Rs. 850
Shaurya Chakra	Rs. 750
Sena Medal/Nao Sena Medal/Vayu Sena Medal for Gallantry (only)	Rs. 250

In the eyes of many, these are still far too low. These allowances are exempt from income tax. Each bar—when such has been awarded—would carry an additional allowance equal to the allowance for the medal itself.

PROVINCIAL

Since late in World War II, a policy was developed by which individual provinces supplemented by cash, land grants, or other rewards, the financial compensation provided to gallantry award recipients by the central government. In general, the central government had shifted to the provinces the major burden in rewarding gallantry medal recipients. This general policy has changed and shifted over time and it is neither possible nor especially desirable to trace it in all its fluctuations and details. It is, however, valuable to survey the individual state and union territory rewards, by decoration, as they stood in July 2005. While some of these figures may have changed since that time, they still provide a useful picture of the patterns of provincial rewards (see Table A3).

TABLE A3

For the Param Vir Chakra

	Cash grant	Cash in lieu of land	Annuity
Andhra Pradesh	Rs. 22,500	Rs. 1,50,000	Rs. 1,000
Arunachal Pradesh	Rs. 22,500	Rs. 1,50,000	Rs. 1,000
Assam	Rs. 22,500	–	–

Bihar	Rs. 22,500	Rs. 1,50,000	Rs. 1,000
Chhattisgarh	Rs.22,500	Rs. 1,50,000	–
Goa	Rs. 22,500	Rs. 1,50,000	Rs. 1,200
Gujarat	Rs. 22,500	–	Rs. 500 for 30 years
Haryana	Rs. 22,500	Rs. 1,50,000	Rs. 3,000
Himachal Pradesh	Rs. 22,500	Rs. 1,50,000	Rs. 4,500 for 30 years
Jharkhand	Rs. 22,500	Rs. 1,50,000	Rs. 1,000
Jammu & Kashmir	Rs. 22,500	Rs. 1,50,000	Rs. 2,000
Karnataka	Rs. 22,500	Rs. 1,50,000	Rs. 1,000
Kerala	Rs. 28,125	Rs. 1,65,000	Rs. 1,100
Madhya Pradesh	Rs. 22,500	Rs. 1,50,000	–
Maharashtra	Rs. 22,500	Rs. 1,50,000	Rs. 1,000 if posthumous (after 20 November 1990)
Manipur	Rs. 22,500	–	–
Meghalaya	–	–	–
Mizoram	Rs. 22,500	–	–
Nagaland	Rs. 22,500	Rs. 1,50,000	Rs. 1,000
Orissa	Rs. 22,500	Rs. 1,50,000	–
Punjab	Rs. 25,00,000	–	Rs. 12,500/mo.
Rajasthan	Rs. 22,500	25 *bighas* of irrigated land or 50 *bighas* of unirrigated land	–
Sikkim	Rs. 22,500	Rs. 1,50,000	Rs. 1,000
Tamil Nadu	Rs. 22,500	–	–
Tripura	Rs. 22,500	–	–
Uttar Pradesh	Rs. 2,00,000	–	Rs. 1,000 for 30 years
Uttaranchal	Rs. 2,00,000	–	Rs. 1,000
West Bengal	Rs. 22,500	Rs. 1,50,000	Rs. 1,000
Andaman & Nicobar	Rs. 22,500	–	–
Chandigarh	Rs. 22,500	Rs. 1,50,000	–
Delhi	Rs. 22,500	Rs. 1,50,000	Rs. 1,000
Pondicherry	–	–	–

For the Ashoka Chakra

	Cash grant	Cash in lieu of land	Annuity
Andhra Pradesh	Rs. 20,000	Rs. 1,25,000	Rs. 600
Arunachal Pradesh	Rs. 20,000	Rs. 1,25,000	Rs. 800
Assam	Rs. 20,000	–	–
Bihar	Rs. 20,000	Rs. 1,25,000	Rs. 800
Chhattisgarh	Rs. 20,000	Rs. 1,25,000	–
Goa	Rs. 20,000	Rs. 1,25,000	–
Gujarat	Rs. 20,000	–	–
Haryana	–	–	–
Himachal Pradesh	Rs. 20,000	Rs. 1,25,000	Rs. 4,000 for 30 years
Jammu & Kashmir	Rs. 20,000	Rs. 1,25,000	Rs. 1,600
Jharkhand	Rs. 20,000	Rs. 1,25,000	Rs. 800
Karnataka	Rs. 20,000	Rs. 1,25,000	Rs. 800
Kerala	Rs. 25,000	Rs. 1,37,500	Rs. 880
Madhya Pradesh	Rs. 20,000	Rs. 1,25,000	–
Maharashtra	Rs. 20,000	Rs. 1,25,000	Rs. 1,000 if posthumous (after 20 November 1990)

	Cash grant	Cash in lieu of land	Annuity
Manipur	Rs. 20,000	–	–
Meghalaya	–	–	–
Mizoram	Rs. 20,000	–	Rs. 180/mo.
Nagaland	Rs. 20,000	Rs. 1,25,000	Rs. 800
Orissa	Rs. 20,000	Rs. 1,25,000	–
Punjab	Rs. 25,00,000	–	Rs. 7,500/mo.
Rajasthan	Rs. 20,000	25 *bighas* of irrigated land or 50 *bighas* of unirrigated land	–
Sikkim	Rs. 20,000	Rs. 1,25,000	Rs. 800
Tamil Nadu	Rs. 20,000	–	–
Tripura	Rs. 20,000	–	–
Uttar Pradesh	Rs. 40,000	–	Rs. 400 for 30 years
Uttaranchal	Rs. 40,000		Rs. 400
West Bengal	Rs. 20,000	Rs. 1,25,000	Rs. 800
Andaman & Nicobar	Rs. 20,000	–	–
Chandigarh	Rs. 20,000	Rs. 1,25,000	–
Delhi	Rs. 20,000	Rs. 1,25,000	Rs. 800
Pondicherry	–	–	–

For the Sarvottam Yuddh Seva Medal

	Cash grant	Cash in lieu of land	Annuity
Andhra Pradesh	Rs. 17,000	Rs. 1,00,000	Rs. 600
Arunachal Pradesh	Rs. 17,000	Rs. 1,00,000	Rs. 600
Assam	Rs. 17,000	–	–
Bihar	Rs. 17,000	Rs. 1,10,000	Rs. 600
Chhattisgarh	Rs. 17,000	Rs. 1,10,000	–
Goa	Rs. 17,000	Rs. 1,10,000	–
Gujarat	Rs. 17,000	–	–
Haryana	Rs. 17,000	Rs. 1,10,000	Rs. 2,300
Himachal Pradesh	Rs. 17,000	Rs. 1,10,000	Rs. 1,500 for 30 years
Jammu & Kashmir	Rs. 17,000	Rs. 1,10,000	Rs. 1,200
Jharkhand	Rs. 17,000	Rs. 1,10,000	Rs. 600
Karnataka	Rs. 17,000	Rs. 1,10,000	Rs. 600
Kerala	Rs. 21,250	Rs. 1,21,000	Rs. 660
Madhya Pradesh	Rs. 17,000	Rs. 1,10,000	–
Maharashtra	Rs. 17,000	Rs. 1,10,000	–
Manipur	Rs. 17,000	–	–
Meghalaya	–	–	–
Mizoram	Rs. 17,000	–	–
Nagaland	Rs. 17,000	Rs. 1,10,000	Rs. 600
Orissa	Rs. 17,000	Rs, 1,10,000	–
Punjab	Rs. 17,000	Rs. 1,10,000	Rs. 100/mo.
Rajasthan	Rs. 17,000	25 *bighas* of irrigated land or 50 *bighas* of unirrigated land	–
Sikkim	Rs. 17,000	Rs. 1,10,000	Rs. 600
Tamil Nadu	Rs. 17,000	–	–
Tripura	Rs. 17,000	–	–
Uttar Pradesh	Rs. 1,25,000	–	Rs. 150 for 30 years
Uttaranchal	Rs. 1,25,000	–	Rs. 150
West Bengal	Rs. 17,000	Rs. 1,10,000	Rs. 600
Andaman & Nicobar	Rs. 17,000	–	–

Chandigarh	Rs. 17,000	Rs. 1,10,000	–
Delhi	Rs. 17,000	Rs. 1,10,000	Rs. 600
Pondicherry	–	–	–

For the Param Vishisht Seva Medal

	Cash grant	Cash in lieu of land	Annuity
Andhra Pradesh	Rs. 15,000	Rs. 1,00,000	Rs. 400
Arunachal Pradesh	Rs. 15,000	Rs. 1,00,000	Rs. 400
Assam	Rs. 15,000	–	–
Bihar	Rs. 15,000	Rs. 1,00,000	Rs. 400
Chhattisgarh	–	–	–
Goa	Rs. 15,000	Rs. 1,00,000	–
Gujarat	Rs. 15,000	–	–
Haryana	–	–	–
Himachal Pradesh	Rs. 15,000	Rs. 1,00,000	Rs. 2,700 for 30 years
Jammu & Kashmir	Rs. 15,000	Rs. 1,00,000	Rs. 800
Jharkhand	Rs. 15,000	Rs. 1,00,000	Rs. 400
Karnataka	Rs. 15,000	Rs. 1,15,000	Rs. 400
Kerala	–	–	–
Madhya Pradesh	–	–	–
Maharashtra	Rs. 15,000	Rs. 1,00,000	–
Manipur	Rs. 15,000	–	–
Meghalaya	–	–	–
Mizoram	Rs. 15,000	–	Rs. 180/mo.
Nagaland	Rs. 15,000	Rs. 1,00,000	Rs. 400
Orissa	Rs. 15,000	–	–
Punjab	Rs. 15,000	Rs. 1,00,000	Rs. 200/mo.
Rajasthan	–	–	–
Sikkim	Rs. 15,000	Rs. 1,00,000	Rs. 400
Tamil Nadu	Rs. 15,000	–	–
Tripura	Rs. 15,000	–	–
Uttar Pradesh	Rs. 15,000	–	Rs. 400 for 30 years
Uttaranchal	Rs. 15,000	–	Rs. 400
West Bengal	Rs. 15,000	Rs. 1,00,000	Rs. 400
Andaman & Nicobar	Rs. 15,000	–	–
Chandigarh	Rs. 15,000 for 1971 awardees only	Rs. 1,00,000 for 1971 awardees only	–
Delhi	–	–	–
Pondicherry	–	–	–

For the Maha Vir Chakra

	Cash grant	Cash in lieu of land	Annuity
Andhra Pradesh	Rs. 15,000	Rs. 1,00,000	Rs. 400
Arunachal Pradesh	Rs. 15,000	Rs. 1,00,000	Rs. 400
Assam	Rs. 15,000	–	–
Bihar	Rs. 15,000	Rs. 1,00,000	Rs. 400
Chhattisgarh	Rs. 15,000	Rs. 1,00,000	–
Goa	Rs. 15,000	Rs. 1,00,000	–
Gujarat	Rs. 15,000	–	–
Haryana	Rs. 15,000	Rs. 1,00,000	Rs. 1,200
Himachal Pradesh	Rs. 15,000	Rs. 1,00,000	Rs. 3,600 for 30 years

Jammu & Kashmir	Rs. 15,000	Rs. 1,00,000	Rs. 800
Jharkhand	Rs. 15,000	Rs. 1,00,000	Rs. 400
Karnataka	Rs. 15,000	Rs. 1,00,000	Rs. 400
Kerala	Rs. 18,750	Rs. 1,10,000	Rs. 660
Madhya Pradesh	Rs. 15,000	Rs. 1,00,000	–
Maharashtra	Rs. 15,000	Rs. 1,00,000	Rs. 1,000 if posthumous (after 20 November 1990)
Manipur	Rs. 15,000	–	–
Meghalaya	–	–	–
Mizoram	Rs. 15,000	–	–
Nagaland	Rs. 15,000	Rs. 1,00,000	Rs. 400
Orissa	Rs. 15,000	Rs. 1,00,000	–
Punjab	Rs. 15,00,000	–	Rs. 7,500/mo.
Rajasthan	Rs. 15,000	25 *bighas* of irrigated land or 50 *bighas* of unirrigated land	–
Sikkim	Rs. 15,000	Rs. 1,00,000	Rs. 400
Tamil Nadu	Rs. 15,000	–	–
Tripura	Rs. 15,000	–	–
Uttar Pradesh	Rs. 1,25,000	–	Rs. 400 for 30 years
Uttaranchal	Rs. 1,25,000	–	Rs. 400
West Bengal	Rs. 15,000	Rs. 1,00,000	Rs. 400
Andaman & Nicobar	Rs. 15,000	–	–
Chandigarh	Rs. 15,000	Rs. 1,10,000	–
Delhi	Rs. 15,000	Rs. 1,00,000	Rs. 400
Pondicherry	–	–	–

For the Kirti Chakra

	Cash grant	Cash in lieu of land	Annuity
Andhra Pradesh	Rs. 12,000	Rs. 75,000	Rs. 350
Arunachal Pradesh	Rs. 12,000	Rs. 75,000	Rs. 350
Assam	Rs. 12,000	–	–
Bihar	Rs. 12,000	Rs. 75,000	Rs. 350
Chhattisgarh	Rs. 12,000	Rs. 75,000	–
Goa	Rs. 12,000	Rs. 75,000	–
Gujarat	Rs. 12,000	–	–
Haryana	–	–	–
Himachal Pradesh	Rs. 12,000	Rs. 75,000	Rs. 3,300 for 30 years
Jammu & Kashmir	Rs. 12,000	Rs. 75,000	Rs. 700
Jharkhand	Rs. 12,000	Rs. 75,000	Rs. 350
Karnataka	Rs. 12,000	Rs. 75,000	Rs. 350
Kerala	Rs. 15,000	Rs. 82,500	Rs. 385
Madhya Pradesh	Rs. 12,000	Rs. 75,000	–
Maharashtra	Rs. 12,000	Rs. 75,000	Rs. 1,000 if posthumous (after 20 November 1990)
Manipur	Rs. 12,000	–	–
Meghalaya	–	–	–
Mizoram	Rs. 12,000	–	Rs. 140/mo.
Nagaland	Rs. 12,000	Rs. 75,000	Rs. 350
Orissa	Rs. 12,000	Rs. 75,000	–

Punjab	Rs. 15,00,000	–	Rs. 7,500/mo.
Rajasthan	Rs. 12,000	25 *bighas* of irrigated land or 50 *bighas* of unirrigated land	–
Sikkim	Rs. 12,000	Rs. 75,000	Rs. 350
Tamil Nadu	Rs. 12,000	–	–
Tripura	Rs., 12,000	–	–
Uttar Pradesh	Rs. 25,000	–	Rs. 300 for 30 years
Uttaranchal	Rs. 25,000	–	Rs. 300
West Bengal	Rs. 12,000	Rs. 75,000	Rs. 350
Andaman & Nicobar	Rs. 12,000	–	–
Chandigarh	Rs. 12,000	Rs. 75,000	–
Delhi	Rs. 12,000	Rs. 75,000	Rs. 350
Pondicherry	–	–	–

For the Uttam Yuddh Seva Medal

	Cash grant	Cash in lieu of land	Annuity
Andhra Pradesh	Rs. 10,000	Rs. 65,000	Rs. 350
Arunachal Pradesh	Rs. 10,000	Rs. 65,000	Rs. 350
Assam	Rs. 10,000	–	–
Bihar	Rs. 10,000	Rs. 65,000	Rs. 350
Chhattisgarh	Rs. 10,000	Rs. 65,000	–
Goa	Rs. 10,000	Rs. 65,000	–
Gujarat	Rs. 10,000	–	–
Haryana	Rs. 10,000	Rs. 65,000	Rs. 2,100
Himachal Pradesh	Rs. 10,000	Rs. 65,000	Rs. 1,500 for 30 years
Jammu & Kashmir	Rs. 10,000	Rs. 65,000	Rs. 700
Jharkhand	Rs. 10,000	Rs. 65,000	Rs. 350
Karnataka	Rs. 10,000	Rs. 65,000	Rs. 350
Kerala	Rs. 12,500	Rs. 71,500	Rs. 385
Madhya Pradesh	Rs. 10,000	Rs. 65,000	–
Maharashtra	Rs. 10,000	Rs. 65,000	–
Manipur	Rs. 10,000	–	–
Meghalaya	–	–	–
Mizoram	Rs. 10,000	–	–
Nagaland	Rs. 10,000	Rs. 65,000	Rs. 350
Orissa	Rs. 10,000	Rs. 65,000	–
Punjab	Rs. 10,000	Rs. 65,000	Rs. 100/mo.
Rajasthan	Rs. 10,000	25 *bighas* of irrigated land or 50 *bighas* of unirrigated land	
Sikkim	Rs. 10,000	Rs. 65,000	Rs. 350
Tamil Nadu	Rs. 10,000	–	–
Tripura	Rs. 10,000	–	–
Uttar Pradesh	Rs. 75,000	–	Rs. 100 for 30 years
Uttaranchal	Rs. 75,000	–	Rs. 100
West Bengal	Rs. 10,000	Rs. 65,000	Rs. 350
Andaman & Nicobar	Rs. 10,000	–	–
Chandigarh	Rs. 10,000	Rs. 65,000	–
Delhi	Rs. 10,000	Rs. 65,000	Rs. 350
Pondicherry	–	–	–

For the Ati Vishisht Seva Medal

	Cash grant	Cash in lieu of land	Annuity
Andhra Pradesh	Rs. 7,000	Rs. 50,000	Rs. 300
Arunachal Pradesh	Rs. 7,000	Rs. 50,000	Rs. 300
Assam	Rs. 7,000	–	–
Bihar	Rs. 7,000	Rs. 50,000	Rs. 300
Chhattisgarh	–	–	–
Goa	Rs. 7,000	Rs. 50,000	–
Gujarat	Rs. 7,000	–	–
Haryana	–	–	–
Himachal Pradesh	Rs. 7,000	Rs. 50,000	Rs. 2,400 for 30 years
Jammu & Kashmir	Rs. 7,000	Rs. 50,000	Rs. 600
Jharkhand	Rs. 7,000	Rs. 50,000	Rs. 300
Karnataka	Rs. 7,000	Rs. 50,000	Rs. 300
Kerala	–	–	–
Madhya Pradesh	–	–	–
Maharashtra	Rs. 7,000	Rs. 50,000	–
Manipur	Rs. 7,000	–	–
Meghalaya	–	–	–
Mizoram	Rs. 7,000	–	Rs. 140/mo.
Nagaland	Rs. 7,000	Rs. 50,000	Rs. 300
Orissa	Rs. 7,000	–	–
Punjab	Rs. 7,000	Rs. 50,000	Rs. 175/mo.
Rajasthan	–	–	–
Sikkim	Rs. 7,000	Rs. 50,000	Rs. 300
Tamil Nadu	Rs. 7,000	–	–
Tripura	Rs. 7,000	–	–
Uttar Pradesh	Rs. 7,000	–	Rs. 300 for 30 years
Uttaranchal	Rs. 7,000	–	Rs. 300
West Bengal	Rs. 7,000	Rs. 50,000	Rs. 300
Andaman & Nicobar	Rs. 7,000	–	
Chandigarh	Rs. 7,000 for 1971 awards only	Rs. 50,000 for 1971 awards only	–
Delhi	–	–	–
Pondicherry	–	–	–

For the Vir Chakra

	Cash grant	Cash in lieu of land	Annuity
Andhra Pradesh	Rs. 7,000	Rs. 50,000	Rs. 300
Arunachal Pradesh	Rs. 7,000	Rs. 50,000	Rs. 300
Assam	Rs. 7,000	–	–
Bihar	Rs. 7,000	Rs. 50,000	Rs. 300
Chhattisgarh	Rs. 7,000	Rs. 50,000	–
Goa	Rs. 7,000	Rs. 50,000	–
Gujarat	Rs. 7,000	–	–
Haryana	Rs. 7,000	Rs. 50,000	Rs. 900
Himachal Pradesh	Rs. 7,000	Rs. 50,000	Rs. 2,700 for 30 years
Jammu & Kashmir	Rs. 7,000	Rs. 50,000	Rs. 600
Jharkhand	Rs. 7,000	Rs. 50,000	Rs. 300
Karnataka	Rs. 7,000	Rs. 50,000	Rs. 300
Kerala	Rs. 8,750	Rs. 55,000	Rs. 330
Madhya Pradesh	Rs. 7,000	Rs. 50,000	–

Maharashtra	Rs. 7,000	Rs. 50,000	Rs. 1,000 if posthumous (after 20 November 1990)
Manipur	Rs. 7,000	–	–
Meghalaya	–	–	–
Mizoram	Rs. 7,000	–	–
Nagaland	Rs. 7,000	Rs. 50,000	Rs. 300
Orissa	Rs. 7,000	Rs. 20,000	–
Punjab	Rs. 10,00,000	–	Rs. 3,500/mo.
Rajasthan	Rs. 7,000	25 *bighas* of irrigated land or 50 *bighas* of unirrigated land	–
Sikkim	Rs. 7,000	Rs. 50,000	Rs. 300
Tamil Nadu	Rs. 7,000	–	–
Tripura	Rs. 7,000	–	–
Uttar Pradesh	Rs. 57,000	–	Rs. 300 for 30 years
Uttaranchal	Rs. 50,000	–	Rs. 300
West Bengal	Rs. 7,000	Rs. 50,000	Rs. 300
Andaman & Nicobar	Rs. 7,000	–	–
Chandigarh	Rs. 7,000	Rs. 50,000	–
Delhi	Rs. 7,000	Rs. 50,000	Rs. 300
Pondicherry	–	–	–

For the Shaurya Chakra

	Cash grant	Cash in lieu of land	Annuity
Andhra Pradesh	Rs., 5,000	Rs. 40,000	Rs. 250
Arunachal Pradesh	Rs., 5,000	Rs. 40,000	Rs. 250
Assam	Rs., 5,000	–	–
Bihar	Rs., 5,000	Rs. 40,000	Rs. 250
Chhattisgarh	Rs. 5,000	Rs. 40,000	–
Goa	Rs. 5,000	Rs. 40,000	–
Gujarat	Rs. 5,000	–	–
Haryana	–	–	–
Himachal Pradesh	Rs. 5,000	Rs. 40,000	Rs. 2,400 for 30 years
Jammu & Kashmir	Rs., 5,000	Rs. 40,000	Rs. 500
Jharkhand	Rs. 5,000	Rs. 40,000	Rs. 250
Karnataka	Rs., 5,000	Rs. 40,000	Rs. 250
Kerala	Rs. 6,250	Rs. 55,000	Rs. 330
Madhya Pradesh	Rs. 5,000	Rs. 40,000	–
Maharashtra	Rs. 5,000	Rs. 40,000	Rs. 1,000 if posthumous (after 20 November 1990)
Manipur	Rs. 5,000	–	–
Meghalaya	–	–	–
Mizoram	Rs. 5,000	–	Rs. 100/mo.
Nagaland	Rs., 5,000	Rs. 40,000	Rs. 250
Orissa	Rs. 5,000	Rs. 40,000	–
Punjab	Rs. 10,00,000	–	Rs. 3.500/mo.
Rajasthan	Rs. 5,000	25 *bighas* of irrigated land or 50 *bighas* of unirrigated land	–
Sikkim	Rs., 5,000	Rs. 40,000	Rs. 250
Tamil Nadu	Rs. 5,000	–	–

Tripura	Rs. 5,000	–	–
Uttar Pradesh	Rs. 10,000	–	Rs. 200 for 30 years
Uttaranchal	Rs. 10,000	–	Rs. 200
West Bengal	Rs., 5,000	Rs. 40,000	Rs. 250
Andaman & Nicobar	Rs. 5,000	–	–
Chandigarh	Rs., 5,000	Rs. 40,000	–
Delhi	Rs., 5,000	Rs. 40,000	Rs. 250
Pondicherry	–	–	–

For the Yuddh Seva Medal

	Cash grant	Cash in lieu of land	Annuity
Andhra Pradesh	Rs. 4,000	Rs. 30,000	Rs. 250
Arunachal Pradesh	Rs. 4,000	Rs. 30,000	Rs. 250
Assam	Rs. 4,000	–	–
Bihar	Rs. 4,000	Rs. 30,000	Rs. 250
Chhattisgarh	Rs. 4,000	Rs. 30,000	–
Goa	Rs. 4,000	Rs. 30,000	–
Gujarat	Rs. 4,000	–	–
Haryana	Rs. 6,000	Rs. 30,000	Rs. 1,900
Himachal Pradesh	Rs. 4,000	Rs. 30,000	Rs. 1,500 for 30 years
Jammu & Kashmir	Rs. 4,000	Rs. 30,000	Rs. 500
Jharkhand	Rs. 4,000	Rs. 30,000	Rs. 250
Karnataka	Rs. 4,000	Rs. 30,000	Rs. 250
Kerala	Rs. 5,000	Rs. 33,000	Rs. 275
Madhya Pradesh	Rs. 4,000	Rs. 30,000	–
Maharashtra	Rs. 4,000	Rs. 30,000	–
Manipur	Rs. 4,000	–	–
Meghalaya	–	–	–
Mizoram	Rs. 4,000	–	–
Nagaland	Rs. 4,000	Rs. 30,000	Rs. 250
Orissa	Rs. 4,000	Rs. 30,000	–
Punjab	Rs. 4,000	Rs. 30,000	Rs. 100/mo.
Rajasthan	Rs. 4,000	25 *bighas* of irrigated land or 50 *bighas* of unirrigated land	–
Sikkim	Rs. 4,000	Rs. 30,000	Rs. 250
Tamil Nadu	Rs. 4,000	–	–
Tripura	Rs. 4,000	–	–
Uttar Pradesh	Rs. 35,000	–	Rs. 100 for 30 years
Uttaranchal	Rs. 35,000		Rs. 100
West Bengal	Rs. 4,000	Rs. 30,000	Rs. 250
Andaman & Nicobar	Rs. 4,000	–	–
Chandigarh	Rs. 4,000	Rs. 30,000	–
Delhi	Rs. 4,000	Rs. 30,000	Rs. 250
Pondicherry	–	–	–

For the Sena Medal, Nao Sena Medal, and Vayu Sena Medal

	Cash grant	Cash in lieu of land	Annuity
Andhra Pradesh	Rs. 3,000	Rs. 20,000	Rs. 250
Arunachal Pradesh	Rs. 3,000	Rs. 20,000	Rs. 250
Assam	Rs. 3,000	–	–
Bihar	Rs. 3,000	Rs. 20,000	Rs. 250
Chhattisgarh	Rs. 3,000	Rs. 20,000	–
Goa	Rs. 3,000	Rs. 20,000	–
Gujarat	Rs. 3,000	–	–
Haryana	Rs. 3,000	Rs. 20,000	–
Himachal Pradesh	Rs. 3,000	Rs. 20,000	Rs. 1,500 for 30 years
Jammu & Kashmir	Rs. 3,000	Rs. 20,000	Rs. 500
Jharkhand	Rs. 3,000	Rs. 20,000	Rs. 250
Karnataka	Rs. 3,000	Rs. 20,000	Rs. 250
Kerala	Rs. 3,750	Rs. 22,000	Rs. 275
Madhya Pradesh	Rs. 3,000	Rs. 20,000	–
Maharashtra	Rs. 3,000	Rs. 20,000	–
Manipur	Rs. 3,000	–	–
Meghalaya	–	–	–
Mizoram	Rs., 3,000	–	–
Nagaland	Rs. 3,000	Rs. 20,000	Rs. 250
Orissa	Rs. 3,000	Rs. 20,000	–
Punjab	Rs. 5,00,000	–	Rs. 2,000/mo. if for gallantry
Rajasthan	Rs. 3,000	Rs. 2000	–
Sikkim	Rs. 3,000	Rs. 20,000	Rs. 250
Tamil Nadu	Rs. 3,000	–	–
Tripura	Rs. 3,000	–	–
Uttar Pradesh	Rs. 3,000	–	Rs. 100
Uttaranchal	Rs. 3,000	–	Rs. 100
West Bengal	Rs. 3,000	Rs. 20,000	Rs. 250
Andaman & Nicobar	Rs. 3,000	–	–
Chandigarh	Rs. 3,000	Rs. 20,000	–
Delhi	Rs. 3,000	Rs. 20,000	Rs. 250
Pondicherry	–	–	–

For the Vishisht Seva Medal

	Cash grant	Cash in lieu of land	Annuity
Andhra Pradesh	Rs. 3,000	Rs. 20,000	Rs. 250
Arunachal Pradesh	Rs. 3,000	Rs. 20,000	Rs. 250
Assam	Rs. 3,000	–	–
Bihar	Rs. 3,000	Rs. 10,000	Rs. 250
Chhattisgarh	–	–	–
Goa	Rs. 3,000	Rs. 20,000	–
Gujarat	Rs. 3,000	–	–
Haryana	–	–	–
Himachal Pradesh	Rs. 3,000	Rs. 30,000	Rs. 2,100 for 30 years
Jammu & Kashmir	Rs. 3,000	Rs. 20,000	Rs. 400
Jharkhand	Rs. 3,000	Rs. 20,000	Rs. 250
Karnataka	Rs. 3,000	Rs. 20,000	Rs. 250
Kerala	–	–	–
Madhya Pradesh	–	–	–
Maharashtra	Rs. 3,000	Rs. 20,000	–
Manipur	Rs. 3,000	–	–

Meghalaya	–	–	–
Mizoram	Rs. 3,000		Rs. 100/mo.
Nagaland	Rs. 3,000	Rs. 20,000	Rs. 250
Orissa	Rs. 3,000	–	–
Punjab	Rs. 3,000	Rs. 20,000	Rs. 150/mo.
Rajasthan	–	–	–
Sikkim	Rs. 3,000	Rs. 20,000	Rs. 250
Tamil Nadu	Rs. 3,000	–	–
Tripura	Rs. 3,000	–	–
Uttar Pradesh	Rs. 3,000	–	Rs. 200 for 30 years
Uttaranchal	Rs. 3,000	–	Rs. 200
West Bengal	Rs. 3,000	Rs. 20,000	Rs. 250
Andaman & Nicobar	Rs. 3,000	–	–
Chandigarh	Rs. 3,000 for 1971 awards only	Rs. 20,000 for 1971 awards only	–
Delhi	–	–	–
Pondicherry	–	–	–

For Mention in Despatches

	Cash grant	Cash in lieu of land	Annuity
Andhra Pradesh	Rs. 2,000	Rs. 10,000	Rs. 150
Arunachal Pradesh	Rs. 2,000	Rs. 10,000	Rs. 150
Assam	Rs. 2,000	–	–
Bihar	Rs. 2,000	Rs. 10,000	Rs. 150
Chhattisgarh	Rs. 2,000	Rs. 10,000	–
Goa	Rs. 2,000	Rs. 10,000	–
Gujarat	Rs. 2,000	–	–
Haryana	Rs. 2,000	Rs. 10,000	–
Himachal Pradesh	Rs. 2,000	Rs. 10,000	Rs. 1,500 for 30 years
Jammu & Kashmir	Rs. 2,000	Rs. 10,000	Rs. 300
Jharkhand	Rs. 2,000	Rs. 10,000	Rs. 150
Karnataka	Rs. 2,000	Rs. 10,000	Rs. 150
Kerala	Rs. 2,500	Rs. 11,000	Rs. 165
Madhya Pradesh	Rs. 2,000	Rs. 10,000	–
Maharashtra	Rs. 2,000	Rs. 10,000	–
Manipur	Rs. 2,000	–	–
Meghalaya	–	–	–
Mizoram	Rs. 2,000	–	–
Nagaland	Rs. 2,000	Rs. 10,000	Rs. 150
Orissa	Rs. 2,000	Rs. 10,000	–
Punjab	Rs. 2,000	Rs. 10,000	Rs. 1,000/mo.
Rajasthan	–	–	–
Sikkim	Rs. 2,000	Rs. 10,000	Rs. 150
Tamil Nadu	Rs. 2,000	–	–
Tripura	Rs. 2,000	–	–
Uttar Pradesh	Rs. 2,000	–	Rs. 50 for 30 years
Uttaranchal	Rs. 2,000	–	Rs. 50
West Bengal	Rs. 2,000	Rs. 10,000	Rs. 150
Andaman & Nicobar	Rs. 2,000	–	–
Chandigarh	Rs. 2,000	Rs. 10,000	–
Delhi	Rs. 2,000	Rs. 10,000	Rs. 150
Pondicherry	–	–	–

FREE TRAVEL AWARDS

In many countries—in the erstwhile Soviet Union, for example—gallantry award winners have historically been granted additional benefits such as priority access to government housing, not having to queue for cinemas, or free travel. In 1996, the free travel benefit was extended to Indian gallantry award winners when Indian Railways allowed gallantry award winners (P.V.C., A.C., M.V.C., K.C., Vr.C., and S.C.) free travel in first class/AC two-tier accommodations; this concession was later extended to cover the widows of posthumous awardees and one companion for the award winner.

In 2001 Air India allowed concessional economy travel at 75 per cent discount to recipients of the highest gallantry awards (Param Vir Chakra, Ashoka Chakra, Victoria Cross, and George Cross) and at 50 per cent discount to second-level gallantry award winners (Maha Vir Chakra, Kirti Chakra, Distinguished Service Cross, Military Cross, Distinguished Flying Cross, and George Medal).

OTHER BENEFITS

Recipients of gallantry awards, war widows, and disabled soldiers have, since 2000, been allowed 50 per cent discount on normal rental charges for telephones (the same provision extended to freedom fighters). As has been mentioned earlier, the payments and stipends paid to gallantry award winners (P.V.C., A.C., M.V.C., K.C., Vr.C., S.C., and gallantry awards of the S.M./N.M./V.M.) were declared exempt from income tax in 2000.

Thoughts on the Honours System in Independent India

At no point in time in the writing of this book was it ever our intent to stray into the realms of the political or to address issues of honours policy as it has been crafted and implemented in the decades since India's Independence. Yet, as this project proceeded, one point became inescapably obvious: we were examining India's military and civilian honours in the sort of systematic and rigorous fashion that this honours system had never heretofore enjoyed. And so, though it might force us to stray into policies and politics, might lead us to offer cautionary criticisms, the very novelty of our enquiry might well have placed on us the responsibility of offering some informal thoughts on the strengths and weaknesses of independent India's system of honours. Such comments, though they may have lain implicit in the main text, did not belong there, but did deserve separate focused attention. This section constitutes that attention.

It is useful, perhaps, to begin with the simple observation that, when we speak of an 'honours system', we may be conjuring up a myth. To refer to a 'system' seems to imply, somehow, a centrally planned and coordinated rigorous set of assumptions and rules which are applied over time as part of the unchanging tradition of the State and of State iconography. It is difficult to argue that such a 'system' existed before 1947 and there is ample evidence that no such system has ever existed since Independence. Policies towards honours have always—even in tradition-bound States like the United Kingdom—been fluid and ever-evolving, undergoing shaping and reshaping as political and social norms and needs changed and as internal and external conceptualizations of important national institutions such as the military or the police altered over time.

Yet, once upon a time, there was an effort at central co-ordination of India's honours systems. Before 1947, there existed within the central administration the office of the Private Secretary to the Viceroy. Chief among the responsibilities of this individual was the coordination of all aspects of India's honours system: military, paramilitary, and civilian. All decisions, all recommendations flowed to and through a central office, one which attempted to maintain balanced standards and was even on guard against the inflation of honours and their attendant loss of significance and which blocked the introduction of new, frivolous awards. Even the climactic event of India's Independence in 1947 brought but limited change to the role of this office, as the Private Secretary to the Governor-General inherited many of the responsibilities of the Viceregal secretary, though there was little honours system to manage, as none appeared constitutionally possible.

With the promulgation of India's new Constitution in 1950, things appeared, on the surface, to have clarified. As Head of State, the President of India assumed the functions—and the residence—of the Viceroy and Governor-General. Honours now flowed from a 'fount of honour' on Raisina Hill and not one in London. At least they did so in theory. Early confusions regarding the relative role of the President and the Prime Minister clouded the lines of authority regarding honours and no 'Private Secretary to the President' emerged to coordinate honours policy, and even analogous offices never embraced honours work as a part of their job description. In general, the President formally controlled honours issues, but the Prime Minister took over most routine work in this regard. In reality, however, the ministries of government now functioned almost autonomously, with little central control, and minimal 'quality control' from above.

These structural deficiencies must, however, be understood in the context of the ideology of the day. Newly independent India had broken with a feudal imperial past, a past of slavish subservience to one's 'betters', and had emerged into a new world of equality, secular socialism, egalitarian progress, and *panchsheel*. All the feudal nonsense of CSIs and Rai Bahadurs was merely a relic of a past now gone and deservedly forgotten. Some systems of recognizing achievement might, over time, prove necessary, but they were seen—as they perhaps deserved to be seen—as low priorities, as issues to be postponed to another day. The military and police had emerged from beneath a cloud as the loyal servants and willing muscle-men of imperialism, to be seen as the defenders and protectors of the newly independent republic, but with diminished prominence and symbolic visibility as the new State anticipated it would have scant need for such projectors of public force. While there was an early awareness of the need for decorations for combat and non-combat gallantry, for campaign awards for the military, and for a limited set of awards for the police, there was no sense that any significant expansion was a pressing policy need or, indeed, even a desirable step in the longer term. Military and civilian ceremonials were seen as part of the obsolete toolbox of empire, and a spare, even spartan, military uniform, with perhaps two rows of ribbons for the most senior of officers, came to be viewed as an appropriately underplayed mani-festation of the state's modest honours requirements. Over time, this *swadeshi* ideal would evaporate, but it would have shaped the first generation of the Republic's honours policies.

Even as new awards came into the lists in the 1950s and 1960s, there was no abiding sense of a need for centralized co-ordination. These new awards were, however, seen as ideo-logically consistent with the values of the Republic. For example, a medal for peacekeeping and international responsibility (the Videsh Seva Medal, 1052) now stood beside a campaign medal for purely military actions. As acts of gallantry could be performed by any rank, so could the distinguished service recognized by the new Vishisht Seva Medal series (1007, 1013, and 1027).

Yet by 1971, the older values had begun to erode. Rather than the clasps to the general service medal which had represented India's conflicts in 1948 and 1962, the 1971 war was commemorated by two stars for combat service and a medal for general service in wartime (amplifying a trend begun in the 1965 war). Senior combat decorations (especially the Maha Vir Chakra, 1008) increasingly went to senior officers for able combat leadership (more of a revival or the pre-1947 Distinguished Service Order) than to *jawans* for combat gallantry (unless it was a posthumous award). Likewise, the medals for distinguished service (the Vishisht Seva series) came to be awarded more and more, and in large and larger numbers, to senior officers, and not to JCOs, NCOs, or enlisted personnel, essentially as ancillary badges of rank for lieutenant generals and major generals. Since then, the venerable tradition of a general service medal with clasps added to represent battles, conflicts, wars, or campaigns has been replaced by a proliferation of new medals, apparently serving largely to fill up empty spaces above uniform left breast pockets.

The civilian honours (Bharat Ratna and the 'Padma series', 1001, 1004, 1005, and 1010) have also come in for re-evaluation, and appropriate questions regarding their constitutionality have been raised, as have concerns regarding the 'transparency' of the awards process—though it is difficult to imagine how an inherently confidential process of reviewing objective merit can be 'transparent' or, for that matter, remain entirely free from infection from political cronyism or fawning personal loyalties. Recent cautions from the Home Ministry that these awards are just that, no more, and certainly not titles, and that you may not append 'Padma Bhushan' to either your name or calling card represent an effort, though perhaps belated, to regain control over the civilian awards and imbue them with some degree of respect. In India, as in the United Kingdom, public and media attention to the honours system may prove a good thing, at least in reminding people of the existence of such awards and in engendering the sort of periodic fine-tuning that seems necessary to keep any set of public honours alive, vibrant, and relevant.

As the responsibilities of the Indian police—and especially various paramilitary subsets of the police—have expanded, so have their awards and their pretensions. Even in the early days of Independence, the police enjoyed an odd and unique position: only they continued to receive awards held over from before 1947, only they continued to receive awards for gallantry bearing the image and obsolete titles of the King-Emperor (see 1017, 1028, and 1054). While it may have made sense at the time, especially in respect of the immense hardships endured by the police in the context of the traumas surrounding Partition, this decision set a number of precedents which, we must observe, now seem to have been unfortunate. First, it represented a continuation of the anachronistic authority of the King-Emperor through the award, in his name and with his image, of medals to police no longer under his command; this may be compared with the situation in the military where no gallantry awards were available until the proclamation of the Republic in 1950. Second, it maintained and further solidified the sense of the police as separate and special when it came to awards. Third, this decision is especially significant in that the pre-existence of a separate series of awards for the police led to them being excluded from the regular civilian and non-combatant military gallantry awards, the Ashoka Chakra series (see 1003, 1009 and 1015) when they were established in 1952. In retrospect, this exclusion of police from the Ashoka Chakra has led to not only a massive proliferation of duplicative police awards but also a considerable ambiguity regarding the police and prominence of the Ashoka Chakra series within India's honours system. From the police medals awarded by the non-existent King-Emperor, it seemed an easy step to medals established by the President of the Indian Republic. And, over the years, this simple evolutionary step has resulted in the proliferation of a bewildering range of police, fire services, home guards, and correctional service medals. This is especially a cause for concern as the police services have adopted more and more quasi-military trappings—collar tabs, star plates on their cars, flags on automobiles—and as paramilitary police forces have taken on many of the roles and accompanying medals of what might normally be considered an armed forces role. Similarly, there has been recent proliferation of awards for the para-military Coast Guard, up to and including a special medal commemorating the 25th anniversary of the Coast Guard (1072). This process has perhaps reached its logical (illogical?) conclusion in the Police (Special Duty) Medal (1050) where, even though the medal is an unnamed general service medal, the instituting notification, blindly copying the form of existing (Presidential) police awards, stipulates that the names of recipients be notified in the Gazette of India. The almost unbelievable size of the Jeevan Raksha Padak series of medals belies the belief that they could actually be designed for wear by recipients. Yet, their very size and design underscores the fact that non-military agencies have very little institutional understanding of the concept and underlying dynamics of the working of a national honours and awards system. Even the armed forces, long the guardians of hallowed honours systems are gradually losing their traditional clarity of vision in the face of growing *ad-hoc* responses and a changing cultural ethos.

While the honours system of a society is both the product and the mirror of the social and political aspirations of its constituents, the *de facto* dynamics of the Indian system acutely depict both the lack of coordinated vision and the dichotomy between its professed aims and its practised ends. Unless these issues are appropriately addressed by the State, awards will continue to proliferate, or be inappropriately awarded, and always poorly understood, with an attendant loss of national credibility and prestige in the long term.

Thematic Table of Indian Medals

National Achievement
1001 Bharat Ratna
1004 Padma Vibhushan
1005 Padma Bhushan
1010 Padma Shri

Combat Gallantry
1002 Param Vir Chakra
1008 Maha Vir Chakra
1014 Vir Chakra
1023 Sena Medal
1024 Nao Sena Medal
1025 Vayu Sena Medal
1084 Mention in Despatches
1085 Commendation Cards and Badges

Peacetime Gallantry and Lifesaving
1003 Ashoka Chakra
1009 Kirti Chakra
1011 Sarvottam Jeevan Raksha Padak
1015 Shaurya Chakra
1017 King's Police and Fire Services Medal for Gallantry
1018 President's Police and Fire Services Medal for Gallantry
1019 President's Police Medal for Gallantry
1020 President's Fire Services Medal for Gallantry
1021 President's Correctional Service Medal for Gallantry
1022 President's Home Guards and Civil Defence Medal for Gallantry
1026 President's Coast Guard Medal
1028 Indian Police Medal for Gallantry
1029 Police Medal for Gallantry
1030 Fire Services Medal for Gallantry
1031 Correctional Service Medal for Gallantry
1032 Home Guards and Civil Defence Medal for Gallantry
1033 Uttam Jeevan Raksha Padak
1053 Coast Guard Medal
1067 Jeevan Raksha Padak
1086 Prime Minister's Life Saving Medal

Distinguished and Meritorious Service

1006 Sarvottam Yuddh Seva Medal
1007 Param Vishisht Seva Medal
1012 Uttam Yuddh Seva Medal
1013 Ati Vishisht Seva Medal
1016 Yuddh Seva Medal
1023 Sena Medal
1024 Nao Sena Medal
1025 Vayu Sena Medal
1026 President's Coast Guard Medal
1027 Vishisht Seva Medal
1053 Coast Guard Medal
1054 King's Police and Fire Services Medal for Distinguished Service
1055 President's Police and Fire Services Medal for Distinguished Service
1056 President's Police Medal for Distinguished Service
1057 President's Fire Services Medal for Distinguished Service
1058 President's Correctional Service Medal for Distinguished Service
1059 President's Home Guards and Civil Defence Medal for Meritorious Service
1062 Indian Police Medal for Meritorious Service
1063 Police Medal for Meritorious Service
1064 Fire Services Medal for Meritorious Service
1065 Correctional Service Medal for Meritorious Service
1066 Home Guards and Civil Defence Medal for Meritorious Service
1085 Commendation Cards and Badges

Wounds

1034 Wound Medal/Parakram Padak

Police, Fire Services, and Allied Medals

1017 King's Police and Fire Services Medal for Gallantry
1018 President's Police and Fire Services Medal for Gallantry
1019 President's Police Medal for Gallantry
1020 President's Fire Services Medal for Gallantry
1021 President's Correctional Service Medal for Gallantry
1028 Indian Police Medal for Gallantry
1029 Police Medal for Gallantry
1030 Fire Services Medal for Gallantry
1031 Correctional Service Medal for Gallantry
1050 Police (Special Duty) Medal
1051 Police (Internal Security) Medal
1054 King's Police and Fire Services Medal for Distinguished Service
1055 President's Police and Fire Services Medal for Distinguished Service
1056 President's Police Medal for Distinguished Service
1057 President's Fire Services Medal for Distinguished Service

1058 President's Correctional Service Medal for
     Distinguished Service
1062 Indian Police Medal for Meritorious Service
1063 Police Medal for Meritorious Service
1064 Fire Services Medal for Meritorious Service
1065 Correctional Service Medal for Meritorious Service
1071 Independence Medal 1950
1086 Prime Minister's Life Saving Medal

Campaign Medals

1035 General Service Medal, 1947
1036 Samanya Seva Medal, 1965
1037 Special Service Medal
1038 Samar Seva Star, 1965
1039 Poorvi Star
1040 Paschimi Star
1041 Siachen Glacier Medal
1042 Garaj Star
1043 Op Vijay Star
1044 Raksha Medal, 1965
1045 Sangram Medal
1046 Op Vijay Medal
1047 Op Parakram Medal

Service Medals

1048 Sainya Seva Medal
1049 High Altitude Service Medal
1050 Police (Special Duty) Medal
1051 Police (Internal Security) Medal
1052 Videsh Seva Medal

Long Service Medals

1060 Meritorious Service Medal
1061 Long Service and Good Conduct Medal
1068 Territorial Army Decoration
1069 Territorial Army Medal
1075 30 Years Long Service Medal
1076 20 Years Long Service Medal
1077 9 Years Long Service Medal
1078 Unnat Raksha Suraksha Corps Medal
1079 Raksha Suraksha Corps Medal
1080 National Cadet Corps Twelve Years Long Service
     Medal
1081 National Cadet Corps Seven Years Long Service
     Medal
1082 20 Years Coast Guard Service Medal
1083 09 Years Coast Guard Service Medal

Commemorative Medals

1070 Indian Independence Medal, 1947
1071 Independence Medal, 1950
1072 25th Independence Anniversary Medal
1073 50th Anniversary of Independence Medal
1074 Coast Guard Silver Jubilee Medal

Other Medals

1087 Asiad Vishisht Jyoti
1088 Asiad Jyoti
1089 MacGregor Memorial Medal
1090 Mount Everest Expedition Medal, 1953

Bibliography

Abbott, P.E., and J.M.A. Tamplin, *British Gallantry Awards*, Enfield: Guiness Superlatives Ltd., 1971.

Banerji, L.K., 'Awards', *Now* 3, 21, 24 February 1967: 22.

Baranwal, S.P., *Heroic Deeds in Free India*, New Delhi: Army Educational Stores, 1965.

'Bharat Rakshak' web forum: http://www.bharat-rakshak.com/

Cardozo, Ian, ed., *The Indian Army: A Brief History*, New Delhi: Centre for Armed Forces Historical Research, United Service Institution of India, 2005.

Cardozo, Ian, *Param Vir: Our Heroes in Battle*, New Delhi: Roli Books, 2003.

Chakravorty, B., *The Congo Operation, 1960-63*, ed. S.N. Prasad, *Armed Forces of the Indian Union*, New Delhi: Historical Section, Ministry of Defence, Government of India, 1976.

————, *Stories of Heroism*, Part I, New Delhi: Historical Section, Ministry of Defence, Government of India, 1987.

————, *Stories of Heroism (PVC & MVC Winners)*, ed. U.P. Thapliyal, New Delhi: History Division, Ministry of Defence, Government of India, Allied Publishers, 1995.

————, *Stories of Heroism, Vol. II (Ashoka Chakra & Kirti Chakra Winners)*, ed. U.P. Thapliyal, New Delhi: History Division, Ministry of Defence, Government of India, 1997.

Chhina, Rana, *The Indian Distinguished Service Medal*, New Delhi: Invicta India, 2001.

Clarke, John D., *Gallantry Medals and Awards of the World*, Sparkford: Patrick Stephens Limited, 1993.

Das, Chand N., *Traditions and Customs of the Indian Armed Forces*, New Delhi: Vision Books, 1984.

Dhawan, S.K., *Bharat Ratnas (1954-1991)*, Delhi: Wave Publications, 1991.

Dorling, H. Taprell, *Ribbons & Medals: Naval, Military, Air Force and Civil*, London: George Philip & Son Ltd., 1963; rev. and ed., Alec A. Purves, Ontario: Fortress Publications, 1983.

Faulconbridge, B.G., 'Honours and Awards of the Republic of India since It's Independence', privately circulated manuscript, December 1984.

'Gallantry Awards' Money to Go Up', *The Hindustan Times* (online edition), 20 March 1999.

[Gandhi, S.S.], *India's Highest Gallantry Awards and the Men Who Won Them, 1947-1995*, New Delhi: The Defence Review, 1995.

————, *Encyclopedia of Soldiers with Highest Gallantry Awards*, New Delhi: The Defence Review, 1980.

Giani, Kesar Singh, *Indian Independence Movement in East Asia*, Lahore: Singh Brothers, 1947.

Gordon, L.L., *British Battles and Medals*, 4th edn., rev. Edward C. Joslin, London: Spink & Son Ltd., 1971.

Hamond, Robert, *History of the MacGregor Memorial Medals 1889-1989*, New Delhi: Lancer Paperbacks, 1994.

Haynes, Edward S., 'Decorations and Medals of the Republic of India', International Electronic Phaleristic Encyclopedia, http://haynese.winthrop.edu/india/medals/INDMED.html, 2 February 1999.

————, 'Medals and Decorations of the Republic of India', *The Medal Collector* 22, 8, August 1971: 1-50.

India, *Gazette of India*, 1947—

————, *State Decorations and Awards*, New Delhi: Publications Division, Ministry of Information and Broadcasting, 1958.

————, Constituent Assembly, *Constituent Assembly Debates* (on-line edition, at http://parliamentofindia.nic.in/ls/debates/debates.htm).

————, Lok Sabha, *Lok Sabha Debates*.

————, Ministry of Home Affairs, *A Compilation of the Recipients of Bharat Ratna and Padma Awards [1954-88]*, 3 vols., New Delhi: Ministry of Home Affairs, Government of India, 1988-90.

The Indian Army: United Nations Peacekeeping Operations, New Delhi: Lancer Publishers, 1997.

Johnson, M.C., 'The Medals of the Republic of India', *Journal of the Orders and Medals Research Society*, spring 1989: 38-45.

Joslin, E.C., A.R. Litherland and B.T. Simpkin, *British Battles & Medals*, London: Spink, 1988.

Kalidas, S., 'The Lotus Baiters of Democratic India', *India Today* web exclusive, 3 February 2000, http://www.india-today.com/webexclusive/kalidas/20000203.html.

Kaushala, R.S., *Gallantry Awards for Armed Forces of India*, Pathankot: Krishna Book Depot, 1961.

Khera, P.N., *Operation Vijay: The Liberation of Goa and Other Portugese Colonies in India (1961)*, ed. S.N. Prasad, *Armed Forces of the Indian Union*, New Delhi: Historical Section, Ministry of Defence, Government of India, 1974.

Kleitmann, K.G., 'Awards of the Provisional Government of "Azad Hind"', *The Medal Collector* 13, 2, February 1962: 1-5.

Laslo, Alexander J., *A Glossary of Terms used in Phaleristics—The Science, Study, and Collecting of the Insignia of Orders, Decorations, and Medals*, Albuquerque: Dorado Publishing, 1995.

Litherland, A.R. and B.T. Simpkin, *Spink's Standard Catalogue of British and Associated Orders Decorations & Medals with Valuations*, London: Spink, 1990.

Mackay, James and John W. Mussell, eds., *The Medal Yearbook, 1999*, Honiton: Token Publishing Limited, 1999.

———, *The Medal Yearbook 2001*, Honiton: Token Publishing Limited, 2000.

———, *Medal Yearbook 2002*, Honiton: Token Publishing Limited, 2001.

McClenaghan, Tony, *Indian Princely Medals: A Record of the Orders, Decorations and Medals of the Indian Princely States*, New Delhi: Lancer Publishers, 1996.

McDaniel, Paul and Paul J. Schmitt, *The Comprehensive Guide to Soviet Orders and Medals*, Arlington: Historical Research, 1997.

Military Year Book, New Delhi: Guide Publications, 1966-70.

O'Toole, E., 'The Indian National Army and the Indian Legion', *OMRS Notes*, n.d., pp. 91-4.

Palat, K.R., *My Adventures with the I.N.A.*, Lahore: Lion Press, 1946.

Peterson, James W., 'Medals of the United Nations', *The Medal Collector* 13, 1, January 1962: 2-7.

Poulson, N.W., *Catalogue of Campaign and Independence Medals Issued During the 20th Century to the British Army*, Newcastle, 1969.

Prakasa, Sri, 'Of Titles and Awards', *Indian & Foreign Review* 6, 18, 1 July 1969: 20-1.

Prasad, S.N., *History of Custodian Force (India) in Korea 1953-54*, ed. B. Chakravorty, *Armed Forces of the Indian Union*, New Delhi: Historical Section, Ministry of Defence, Government of India, 1976.

———, *Operation Polo: The Police Action against Hyderabad*, *Armed Forces of the Indian Union*, New Delhi: Historical Section, Ministry of Defence, Government of India, 1972.

Prasad, S.N. and Dharam Pal, *History of Operations in Jammu and Kashmir*, *Armed Forces of the Indian Union*, New Delhi: Historical Division, Ministry of Defence, Government of India, 1987.

Reddy, Kittu, *Bravest of the Brave: Heroes of the Indian Army*, New Delhi: Ocean Books Pvt. Ltd., 1997.

'Regierung Bose stiftet Auszeichnungen', *Deutsche Uniform Zeitung* 4 (1944): 2.

'SAGongs' web forum and Yahoo group: http://sagongs. ipbhost.com/ and http://groups.yahoo.com/group/ SAGongs/

St. Martin [K.G. Kleitmann], 'Auszeichnungen der Prov. Regierung "Azad Hind"', privately published, *c.* 1960.

Scandaluzzi, Franco, *Medal Ribbons of the World*, 6 vols., privately published by the author, 1984.

Shaw, Albert M., 'The MacGregor Memorial Medals of the United Service Institution of India', in *The Journal of the Orders and Medals Society of America: The Medal Collector* 42, 3, March 1991: 4-14.

Singh, Durlab, ed., *Formation and Growth of the Indian National Army (Azad Hind Fauj)*, Lahore: The Hero Publications, 1946.

Singh, Jaswant, ed., *Indian Armed Forces Year Book*, Bombay: Youth Publishers, 1960-68.

Sundaram. J., *Operation Shanti (Indian Army on Peace Mission in Egypt 1956-1967)*, ed. U.P. Thapliyal, *Armed Forces of the Indian Union*, New Delhi: Historical Section, Ministry of Defence, Government of India, 1990.

Tuson, Ashley R., '*Medals will be Worn*': *Wearing Medals Past and Present, 1844-1999*, Honiton: Token, 1999.

Venkateswaran, A.L., *Defence Organisation in India*, New Delhi: Publications Division, Ministry of Information and Broadcasting, Government of India, 1967.

'Wayward Awards', *Now* 3, 18, 3 February 1967: 51.

Werlich, Robert, *Orders and Decorations of All Nations: Ancient and Modern, Civil and Military*, Washington: Quaker Press, 1965.

Index